The *Angel of the Lord* is a masterful work of ⌐
theology, it is also a much-needed apologeti
Angel of the Lord" plagues believers and unb
to that question is much more than a healing balm for the doubting. To
understand the nature and identity of the Angel of the Lord is to understand God, himself. This book will bolster your understanding of trinitarian theology, your understanding and interpretation of Old Testament
narrative, and help you bridge the gap between deep, heady theology and
practical life application. Rare is the book that would fit well on the shelf
of both the professional scholar and the armchair theologian. *Angel of the
Lord* is precisely that kind of book.

~ *VODDIE BAUCHAM (D.Min., D.D.), Dean of the Seminary at African
Christian University*

Most works on Christ in the Old Testament focus on prophecy and typology but overlook the obvious: The Angel of Yahweh. Foreman and Van
Dorn aim to correct this oversight. They insightfully expound the many
texts that feature the Angel, and they convincingly argue that these visita-
tions are nothing less than close encounters of the messianic kind. If you
want to see Christ in all of Scripture, I enthusiastically recommend this
stimulating study!

~ *DR. ROBERT R. GONZALES JR., Dean Reformed Baptist Seminary*

Thought-provoking, thorough, biblical exploration of the most amazing
and mysterious figure in the Old Testament. I used to think you had to
find Jesus "hidden" in Old Testament symbols, allusions and messianic
prophecy. This book has helped me to see Him more "out in the open" as
the Angel of the Lord of the Old Testament, and it's transformed my reading of Scripture. Foreman and Van Dorn take some real hardcore biblical
theology and explain it in language that can be understood by laity, without
losing its depth. This isn't about mere "doctrine," this book helps you understand the person of Jesus Christ, with real spiritual impact.

~ *BRIAN GODAWA, American screenwriter and author of the best-selling
Chronicles of the Nephilim*

The identification of the Angel of the LORD as Jesus pre-incarnate has a
long pedigree. Despite its rejection by much of modern scholarship, a re-
newed appreciation is emerging—not as a simple return to a pre-modern
idea bypassing the insights of modern scholarship, but as a full-orbed

biblical-theological rediscovery of the exegetical, historical, and theological underpinnings of a broader concept known as the Divine Council. This book by Foreman and Van Dorn fits within this framework, serving as a helpful introduction to both historical and contemporary discussions. That is, through patient exegesis text after text, informed by early Jewish and Christian reflection, the authors highlight the ubiquitous presence of an embodied YHWH variously identified as the Angel, the Word, the Presence, the Glory, and the Name. As an OT theologian already familiar and on board with the thesis, I still learned a lot and was reaffirmed in my understanding. I hope this book gains a large readership. Not every point or argument is convincing, but one would be hard-pressed to dismiss the book's overall thrust and impulse. Detractors must at least engage the arguments and be willing to respond with same seriousness and depth.

~ *DR. KENNETH J. TURNER, Professor of Old Testament and Biblical Languages, Toccoa Falls College*

Matt Foreman and Doug Van Dorn have written a fascinating book on a topic that gets far too little attention in the Church today. *The Angel of the Lord* will be an entirely new framework for many readers and will answer questions they never knew they had. Christians will often read their Bible and make quick assumptions about what the text might be referring to when it references the Angel of the Lord or the Word of God without understanding the massive significance of these names. But when Christians are equipped with the tools and knowledge to spot the second person of the Trinity at work throughout the entire Old Testament, a new and exciting journey will begin, and the text will make more sense than it ever did before. The authors of this book did their homework and make a strong case for their claims, rooted in a rich theological history. Read *The Angel of the Lord* and change the way you read your Bible forever.

~ *NICHOLAS KENNICOTT, Ph.D. student, Faulkner University, pastor of Redeemer Baptist Church, President of the Institute of Pastoral and Theological Training (IPTT) in Egbe, Nigeria*

If reformation is retrieval, this is one of the most Reformed books of recent years. With sweeping grandeur, Foreman and Van Dorn take readers on a spiritual journey to the only place worth really going: to see Jesus. Christless preaching plagues our otherwise orthodox churches, and the saints suffer. Where did the wonder go? It's still here, in the living pages of the Old Testament, where the Son of God walks. The Israelites knew it. The Apostles knew it. The Fathers and the Reformers knew it. Are we the only generation of believers from the foundation of the world that knows it not? Read this book, and we won't be for long.

~ LUKE WALKER, *pastor of Redeeming Cross Community Church; author,*
He Gave Them Judges: Jesus in the Book of Judges

Doug Van Dorn and Matt Foreman have published a truly unique book. Their focus is Jesus in the Old Testament, not typologically, but physically. The angel who visits Abraham and pulls Lot out of Sodom, the Word who visits the prophets, the Man of war who appears to Joshua, these are all none other than the pre-incarnate Christ. While some may not agree with every conclusion, this book persuasively demonstrates that Jesus was there in the Old Testament. This is a must read for anyone interested in the Angel of the Lord or beholding Christ in an even more glorious way.
Soli Deo Gloria,

~ MICHAEL EMADI, *Lecturer of Biblical Languages, Reformed Baptist Seminary*
and Covenant Baptist Theological Seminary

It is always a challenge to ensconce theological questions in the proper historical and cultural contexts. In the case of the Angel of the Lord, this is abundantly clear, but this book accomplishes that aim. Matt Foreman and Doug Van Dorn have produced an engaging look at the identity of this Angel, demonstrating with sound reasoning and scholarship that it is the Christ. Read and you will think, you will be edified, and you will be amazed. I can recommend this book without reservation. It is a necessary addition to the library of any serious student of the Bible.

~ DR. JUDD H. BURTON, *Director and Senior Fellow of the Institute of Biblical*
Anthropology

Back in the 1940's, Geerhardus Vos, in his epic work Biblical Theology, called the Angel of the Lord, "The most important characteristic form of revelation in the patriarchal period." And now in 2020, Matt Foreman and Doug Van Dorn masterfully unfold the truth that Vos barely began to scratch the surface. They give amplified meaning to David Murray's profound slogan: "Jesus on Every Page." The book is a cannonball blast through the walls of your long settled and comfortable theological castle, exposing passageways and footprints of the Friend of Sinners who strangely first appeared not in Bethlehem, but in Eden, and beyond. The authors painstakingly show how they're saying nothing new, and just riding in the wake of titans like Athanasius, Luther, Calvin, John Owen, Thomas Watson, Matthew Henry, Jonathan Edwards,

Charles Spurgeon, Charles Hodge, J.I. Packer, Joel Beeke, Philip Ryken, and many more. For me, my Old Testament will never again be the same. Hallelujah, what a Savior!

~ *MARK CHANSKI, Pastor, Harvard Reformed Baptist Church, Coordinator elect of the Reformed Baptist Network*

Foreman and Van Dorn have provided a long overdue study of the Angel of the LORD. As they note, once one notices the central place this person plays in the Old Testament story, you get a much more integrated view of the Old and New Testaments and the Mediator they reveal. Though this is a theological study, it exhibits a warm devotional style as well. The book is clear and accessible. It will help readers better understand and trust the promise of Psalm 34:7, "The angel of the LORD encamps around those who fear him and delivers them."

~ *BRAD SWYGARD, Ph.D. student, Midwestern Baptist Theological Seminary*

Foreman and Van Dorn have achieved here a remarkable and long-needed treatment of the most mysterious and significant, yet sadly neglected Person of the entire Old Testament. As one who fifty years ago devoured Geerhardus Vos's *Biblical Theology* and has searched since then for a thorough study of the topic, I am delighted to recommend it. The authors' exhaustive research and compilation gives us here the most comprehensive Biblical study on the Angel of the Lord in the English language. They provide footnotes on this important subject that alone make the book invaluable. The authors faithfully live out biblical truth and love as they pastor churches and serve the Angel of the Lord—Jesus Christ. May He bless this work of their hands and hearts to the edification of thousands in Christ's Church.

~ *JAMES E. ADAMS. D.Min. Westminster Seminary California, author of War Psalms of the Prince of Peace, pastor Cornerstone Church in Mesa, Arizona, professor of theology at Reformed Baptist Seminary and in Latin America.*

THE ANGEL
OF THE LORD

THE ANGEL
OF THE LORD

A BIBLICAL, HISTORICAL, AND THEOLOGICAL
STUDY

Matt Foreman * Doug Van Dorn

Waters of Creation Publishing
Dacono, Colorado

Waters of Creation Publishing
2020

Unless otherwise noted, references are from the *English Standard Version* (ESV) of the Bible.

Cover Design by David Adams

ISBN-13: 978-1-7350038-0-1 (Waters of Creation Publishing)

Table of Contents

Dedicated to:

The Angel of the LORD ... Incarnate, the Word made flesh for us

MICHAEL S. HEISER

Over the years in various interviews, podcasts, and lectures I've mentioned how, over my seventeen-year academic journey through Bible college, seminary, and graduate school, I was exposed to one clock hour—a mere sixty minutes—of classroom instruction on the unseen world of the Bible. Not surprisingly, neglect of this magnitude gives students the impression that there is little to think about with respect to gods, angels, demons, Satan, principalities, etc., and that the meaning of the (presumably) scant data that appear in Scripture is self-evident. This is absolutely untrue.

The response to my own published research on these subjects has revealed the hunger of many Christians to know what the Bible teaches on these matters. Unfortunately, serious biblical theology on the unseen spiritual world, both in terms of God's loyal heavenly servants and the powers of darkness, is hard to find. Commentaries frequently do little more than repeat the obvious when discussing passages dealing with the heavenly host or God's supernatural enemies. And as this book illustrates, systematic theologies do even less. The "end user" of these materials, the pastor or the person charged with teaching "the whole counsel of God" to those under their care, is ill-served and poorly equipped for this portion of that task.

This book by Matt Foreman and Doug Van Dorn on the Angel of the Lord takes a significant step in addressing these shortcomings. It is to date the most thorough work on the subject. The authors provide detailed consideration of the biblical data. That much is expected in a book of this length. But they also demonstrate that important aspects of this figure, such as his identity as the pre-incarnate Son of the Godhead, is not an idiosyncratic understanding. Rather, they have successfully excavated the works of important thinkers and theologians to demonstrate how their conclusions in regard to certain aspects of what Scripture teaches about the Angel of the Lord align with historic Christianity and inform points of Christian theology.

This importance of this last point must not be missed. Foreman and Van Dorn have done the believing Church a great service by demonstrating that the Old Testament data about the Angel of the Lord, understood in their original ancient contexts, is no threat to historic Christian teaching. The language, literary strategies, cultural influences, idiomatic expressions, and modes of thought of the writers of the Old Testament are often obscure and unfamiliar to Christian thinkers of any post-biblical context. This can cause consternation and even distrust. Sometimes, it has led theologians to miss what the text was originally saying or misinterpret it. However, due to the blessings of Providence, we now live at a time when we have tens of thousands of ancient texts from the rabbis and Israel's neighboring cultures available to us in our own languages. These texts enable us to think like the biblical writers and to comprehend what they were trying to communicate to people of their own day. Their original meaning and mindset becomes more clear. Even the Church Fathers understood this. So this should not disturb readers—it should excite them.

This book reflects serious attention to understanding the Old Testament figure of the Angel of the Lord in ancient Israelite and Jewish contexts. Foreman and Van Dorn capably demonstrate that, while the way scholars might talk about this or that passage in the Old Testament due to the enterprise of reading it through the lens of distant contexts and worldviews may sound new, it's actually very old and the theology that historic Christianity handed down to us remains intact and is strengthened. While a work of this depth will no doubt contain something with which any given reader might disagree, it should be mined for insights and inspiration. My hope is that many will give this book careful attention and utilize it in their preaching, teaching, and personal study.

Michael S. Heiser
Jacksonville, FL 2020

MATT'S PREFACE

A FEW YEARS AGO, WHILE PREACHING through the book of Exodus, I became more and more intrigued by the concept and prominence of the Angel of the Lord throughout the Old Testament. I came from a theological background that emphasized preaching Christ from the Old Testament, reading the Old Testament in light of the New as Christian Scripture. I believed that God is and always has been a Trinitarian God. I knew that the Son of God was revealed and anticipated in the Old Testament in types and shadows and in prophesy. I even knew that God sometimes revealed himself in theophanies that were "likely" pre-incarnate revelations of the Son of God. But I *also* believed that the Trinity wasn't *really* revealed until the New Testament, that the Son was withheld until the New Testament, and that the Old Testament really emphasized a monistic approach to the knowledge and worship of God.

But while studying through Exodus 23:20-33 (and related passages), I began to notice things I'd never seen before - that the Old Testament speaks of the Angel of the Lord as both Yahweh and distinct from Yahweh, sent from Yahweh, yet bearing the name Yahweh and speaking as God himself. I began to see this in numerous other texts.

My friend, Doug, happened to be preaching through Genesis in his church during the same time. He and I began comparing notes and discussing some of the intriguing passages together. Doug introduced me to scholarly articles he had come across on the subject of Jewish Binatarianism, or "Two Powers" theology—the idea among parts of the Jewish tradition that there were actually two Yahwehs in the Old Testament—a Yahweh sent from Yahweh, manifested in the created realm, revealing himself sometimes even visibly to his people; and a Yahweh in heaven, who generally remains invisible. Some Jewish rabbis spoke of the Angel of the Lord and also the Word of the Lord as a hypostatic manifestation of the invisible God. Jewish "Two Powers" Theology, according to the Jewish scholar Alan Segal, was a significant strand of theological discussion prior to the first century AD.[1] Only after the emergence of Christianity did it eventually become heresy and anathema among the Jews, for obvious reasons.

What if the Trinity is more prominent in the Old Testament than people realize? What if the Son of God is more actively and personally present in the Old Testament than people think?

About that time, I went to the library at my alma mater, Westminster Theological Seminary, to find everything I could on the Angel of the Lord. I had found the Angel discussed often in conservative volumes of theology as a manifestation of the Son. But the only full-length books on the subject that I found were written by liberal scholars. Some of these treatments were fascinating and insightful in places, but were incredibly undermined by a humanistic hermeneutic, an evolutionary theory of religion, and a rejection of the authoritative inspiration of Scripture by God. As far as I could find, there had been no focused treatment on the subject of the Angel of the Lord in the Evangelical tradition in the last 100 years!

As Doug and I discussed these things, it became our burden that a book needed to be written. While Doug has written several books and I've always wanted to write, I'd never found something that compelled me to write. This was the first time I'd felt such a compulsion. If nobody else was writing on these things, we needed to.

We're concerned that a lot of Christians have lost how to read the Old Testament and have failed to see their Savior Jesus as active in the Old Testament. Modern-day Christians, even some Christian theologians, unfortunately read the Old Testament as if it is about a monistic, flatly monotheistic (think Islam or modern Judaism) God. Popular treatments of the Trinity often fail to mention a single Old Testament

---

[1] See Alan F. Segal, *Two Powers In Heaven: early Rabbinic reports about Christianity and Gnosticism* (Waco, TX: Baylor University Press 2012).

reference to the Trinity,[2] or, at least, seem hesitant to definitively identify the Persons of the Trinity in the Old Testament. This is very different than the practice of the early Church Fathers, who thought it was very important to identify the Trinity in the Old Testament and were constantly discussing the identity and activity of the Person of the Son in the Old Testament.

So, we believe something has been lost. Our understanding of Trinitarian revelation has been diminished. We believe that the role of the Angel of the Lord is more prominent and pronounced than many have realized. We think an understanding of the role of the Angel of the Lord is crucial for understanding the Old Testament *and* the trajectory of God's revelation in the *whole* Bible. We want people to love Jesus more. And when you learn to see Jesus as the Old Testament Angel of the Lord—what he was doing for his people then, what he was promising to do, what he finally accomplished in the New Testament—we believe your love and appreciation and faith in him will only increase.

---

[2] Michael Reeves book, *Delighting In the Trinity* (Downer's Grove, IL: IVP Academic, 2012) is an excellent popular introduction to the doctrine of the Trinity. Nevertheless, when speaking about the Persons of the Trinity, and specifically, the Person of Christ, he fails to mention a single Old Testament passage.

DOUG'S PREFACE

I CAN REMEMBER THE FIRST TIME it hit me that the Second Person of the Godhead was present in the Old Testament. I mean really there, as in an actual character in the story. It was like a cannonball blasting through the ramparts of my otherwise secure theological fortress. You see, when you grow up as so many Christians do—as I did—with the view that Jesus[3] is basically only there in prophecy, this discovery is almost too overwhelming.

When the cannonball hit, I didn't mind. It was a near miss. I wasn't hurt, merely shaken, but in a good way. For, I quickly discovered that the hole it blew open gave me views of the Scripture outside of my predefined walls that I always dreamed were there but was never able to see. My previous view was at most like paintings on the interior wall of what someone else said it was like outside. I couldn't go look for myself. The windows were obscured by heady theological words seemingly

---

[3] Some might feel it inappropriate to call the Second Person in the OT "Jesus," since this is the name he was given at the incarnation. Nevertheless, his half-brother Jude calls him Jesus back then (Jude 5) in a textual variant that is almost certainly the original. See Bruce Manning Metzger, United Bible Societies, *A Textual Commentary on the Greek New Testament*, Second Edition a Companion Volume to the United Bible Societies' Greek New Testament (4th Rev. Ed.) (London; New York: United Bible Societies, 1994), 657; and more recently Kurt Aland et al., *Novum Testamentum Graece*, 28th Edition. (Stuttgart: Deutsche Bibelgesellschaft, 2012), Jud 5. He is also called Christ (Messiah) by Paul (1Co 10:4, 9), even though he had not yet come in his human capacity as Messiah. On a similar variant to Jude 5 found in 1Co 10:9, see p. 494.

meant to keep me from seeing. The stairs to the top of the rampart were guarded by my extra-biblical traditions, the origins of which were not steeped in the Church Fathers. My lack of information and proper categories became a closed and secured castle gate. So, I was left staring at someone else's tapestries, what they pictured for me. Their conceptions were of a very shadowy Christ in the OT at best.

I'm certainly not against looking at those more shrouded portraits. In fact, the *incarnated* Christ is *only* there in type and shadow. But what of the Second Person, the *pre*incarnate Christ, Jesus prior to becoming a man? He is there all over the place. What a finding this was.

I'm not alone in feeling the thrill of this discovery. When others begin to see it, many are blown away. I can't tell you how many times I've had people say to me when I teach on this topic, "How come no one has ever told me this before?" These are hardly uneducated, newborn Christians. Once you see it, it seems so obvious and ubiquitous. Recently someone wrote to me and said, "I've known about Jacob wrestling the Son of God and a few others through the OT, but I had no idea that Christ shows up so frequently. I've believed for a while that the OT points to Christ and is about Christ, but it wasn't until recently that I realized that Christ was physically in the OT."

My friend and co-author Matt's experience is similar to mine, and he—like myself—is a seminary graduate. After wondering how such a thing could be so absent from so much of our training (or at least how we received that training) and time in churches of various stripes, we began to talk about how we could get this information out there to a wider audience. We concluded that a good way to do it might be a study on the Angel of the LORD, for it is our firm conviction that he is the preincarnate Christ, and he is there much more often than most people can even begin to fathom. As such a study as this simply does not exist in this kind of format, this became the catalyst that began to move us to writing.

We hope that you enjoy the information presented here and that it will do wonders for how you read your Bible. We know it has done that for us. So, may God bless you as you enter a world that was new to us, but that is as ancient as the very first book of the Bible.

THE ANGEL OF THE COVENANT

T HE OLD 1950'S TELEVISION SHOW, *The Adventures of Superman*, began with this famous line: "Look! Up in the sky! It's a bird ... It's a plane. No ... It's Superman!" Perhaps, Christians have sometimes had this reaction when reading the Old Testament. We are taught that Jesus was prophesied about in the Old Testament; he was foreshadowed and symbolized. But was Jesus ever actively working and actively revealed? You read about theophanies of God and wonder, "Could this really be Jesus?"

Christians believe two unique things: that God is a Trinity and that Jesus Christ is central to salvation and to history. Christians teach that there is one God, who eternally exists in three Persons, that these Persons are distinct from one another, that they are each God, the same in substance, equal in power and glory—yet one God, both three and one in a divine mystery. Christians believe that Jesus is the eternal Son of God who came to accomplish salvation in his death and resurrection for all who believe in him. The New Testament teaches that these things are essential for understanding God and receiving comfort and salvation from God.

But how does this accord with the Old Testament? How was the Son of God revealed in the Old Testament? Was the Trinity a New Testament break from the Old—a new revelation never conceived before? If it was not revealed in the Old Testament, and Jewish religion was fervently monistic, how did Jesus convince so many Jews to worship him as God? Why doesn't the New Testament spend more time explaining the Trinity? Doesn't it seem strange that the NT almost seems to *assume* the Trinity? It never seems to spend that much direct time on it and doesn't seem to treat it as surprising. While it takes the disciples some time to realize that Jesus is the eternal, pre-existent Son of God, they seem to receive it fairly easily and seem to say that they should have seen Jesus' identity from the OT in the first place.

But where would they have seen it? One of the places the church has historically identified Christ in the Old Testament is in the figure of the Angel of the LORD. In the early books of the Old Testament, a mysterious figure repeatedly appears—visibly, audibly, even physically—to the Patriarchs, to Moses, to the Prophets. He is variously called "the Angel of the LORD," "the Angel of God," "the Angel of his presence," even just "a man"—a man who wrestles with Jacob or who commands the armies of the LORD. Yet this Angel receives worship, speaks with the authority and voice of God himself, and bears God's own name. On one hand, he is an Angel "sent" from God. On another hand, he seems to be God himself.

Who is this Angel? If he is simply God himself, why is he called "an angel?" If he is simply a lesser spiritual being, why are such divine characteristics attributed to him? Why do people worship him? Given such language and actions, are Christians justified in asking, "Could this really be Jesus? Is this evidence for the Son in the Old Testament?" It is our contention in this book that it *must* be Jesus; he is the only explanation that makes sense. "It's not a bird, it's not a plane; it is Superman!" In fact, we think the "Angel of the LORD" is the most important and central figure in the Old Testament, the most frequent way God is revealed, and appears way more often than most people realize. The storyline of the Bible from the Old Testament to the New is about him.

To start to demonstrate this point, we need to begin with three foundational passages that show the sweeping storyline of the "Angel of the LORD" through the Old Testament.

Exodus 23 and the Promised Angel of the Covenant

In Exodus 23:20-33, right after God gives the Ten Commandments and explains the Law, he gives his people a special promise to motivate their obedience and faithfulness. He says,

Behold, I send an angel before you to guard you on the way and to bring you to the place that I have prepared. Pay careful attention to him and obey his voice; do not rebel against him, for he will not pardon your transgression, for my name is in him. But if you carefully obey his voice and do all that I say, then I will be an enemy to your enemies and an adversary to your adversaries. When my angel goes before you and brings you to the Amorites and the Hittites and the Perizzites and the Canaanites, the Hivites and the Jebusites, and I blot them out, you shall not bow down to their gods nor serve them, nor do as they do, but you shall utterly overthrow them and break their pillars in pieces. You shall serve the LORD your God, and he will bless your bread and your water, and I will take sickness away from among you. None shall miscarry or be barren in your land; I will fulfill the number of your days. I will send my terror before you and will throw into confusion all the people against whom you shall come, and I will make all your enemies turn their backs to you. And I will send hornets before you, which shall drive out the Hivites, the Canaanites, and the Hittites from before you. I will not drive them out from before you in one year, lest the land become desolate and the wild beasts multiply against you. Little by little I will drive them out from before you, until you have increased and possess the land. And I will set your border from the Red Sea to the Sea of the Philistines, and from the wilderness to the Euphrates, for I will give the inhabitants of the land into your hand, and you shall drive them out before you. You shall make no covenant with them and their gods. They shall not dwell in your land, lest they make you sin against me; for if you serve their gods, it will surely be a snare to you.

At the center of God's covenant promises to his people was his promise to send with them a special guardian angel to guide them and guard them and to drive out their enemies. God speaks of this angel in remarkable terms.

Of course, the word "angel" (the Hebrew word מלאך – *mal'ak*) originally just meant "messenger."[4] In the Old Testament, it was

---

[4] The consonants *l'k* mean to "send" in several Semitic languages, specifically with a commission or a message. The *ma-* prefix turns the verb into a noun, and as such identify the vehicle through which the action of sending takes place. Hence, the word means "a messenger." See S. A. Meier, "Angel I," ed. Karel van der Toorn, Bob Becking, and Pieter W. van der Horst, Dictionary of Deities and Demons in

sometimes used for human messengers, and only later became most often used for spiritual beings, as we think of angels today. So, some commentators have suggested that, when God promises to send his "angel," maybe he is just talking about a human leader they need to follow and obey—like Moses or Joshua.[5] Or perhaps, he is just promising to send a supernatural angel, one of the heavenly court to be with them. Yet the way God speaks of this angel is extraordinary and unique—not just a human representative, and not even a lesser supernatural being.

This angel is described in terms intimately connected with Yahweh himself. In vs. 21, God tells the people, "Pay careful attention to him and obey his voice; do not rebel against him, for he will not pardon your transgression." The people are to obey the voice of the angel (this will become important later when we come to our second passage in Judges 2) because, amazingly, God says that this angel holds the prerogative over forgiveness, has authority to "pardon" or "not pardon" their sins - an authority that usually belongs to God alone (see Mark 2:7, "Who can forgive sins but God alone?")! It should not surprise us that Christians[6] have made the argument that the Angel is divine (because

---

the Bible (Leiden; Boston; Köln; Grand Rapids, MI; Cambridge: Brill; Eerdmans, 1999), 45.

[5] Tertullian and Augustine took the Joshua interpretation. However, both also interpreted that it was the Person of Jesus himself speaking to Moses. Tertullian wrote, "For He who ever spoke to Moses was the Son of God Himself; who, too, was always seen. For God the Father none ever saw, and lived. And accordingly it is agreed that the Son of God Himself spoke to Moses, and said to the people, Behold, I send mine angel before thy—that is, the people's—face" (Tertullian, *An Answer to the Jews* 9; in *Latin Christianity: Its Founder*, Tertullian, ed. Alexander Roberts, James Donaldson, and A. Cleveland Coxe, trans. S. Thelwall, vol. 3, The Ante-Nicene Fathers [Buffalo, NY: Christian Literature Company, 1885], 163). Augustine, "Then, again, it is the Word of God Himself who speaks when He promises to provide this successor to Moses, speaking of him [Joshua] as an angel..." (Augustine, Reply to Faustus 19; in *St. Augustin: The Writings against the Manichaeans and against the Donatists*, ed. Philip Schaff, trans. Richard Stothert, vol. 4, A Select Library of the Nicene and Post-Nicene Fathers of the Christian Church, First Series [Buffalo, NY: Christian Literature Company, 1887], 226).

[6] J. M. Wilson writes, "While the angel and Yahweh are at times distinguished from each other, they are with equal frequency, and in the same passages, merged into each other. How is this to be explained? It is obvious that these apparitions cannot be the Almighty Himself, whom no man has seen, or can see... In Ex. 23:20ff. God promises to send an angel before His people to lead them to the Promised Land; they are commanded to obey him and not to provoke him, 'for he will not pardon your transgression; for my name is in him.' Thus the angel can

he is Jesus). But it might come as a shock that some Jews[7] were also making a similar argument, albeit without believing in Jesus Christ.

The angel has this amazing authority, God says, because "my name is in him." This is a remarkable statement! As we will see later in this book, God's name is crucially important in the Exodus and throughout the Old Testament. God's name is a powerful expression of his being and character. When God first appeared to Moses in the burning bush, God had revealed his special name. Throughout the Old Testament, God's name becomes a representation of God himself, almost a personification of God himself. God's name was an expression of his Person.[8]

Then, in vs. 22, it says, "But if you carefully obey his voice and do all that I say, then I will be an enemy to your enemies and an adversary to your adversaries." There is a unified connection between the voice of the angel and what God says. As the text continues, God continues "to move back and forth between what he will do and what the angel will do," as

---

forgive sin, which only God can do, because God's name, i.e., His character and thus His authority, are in the angel." J. M. Wilson, "Angel," ed. Geoffrey W. Bromiley, *The International Standard Bible Encyclopedia*, Revised (Wm. B. Eerdmans, 1979–1988), 125.

[7] For example, Sanhedrin 38b: "R. Nahman said: 'He who is as skilled in refuting the Minim as is R. Idith [MS. M: R. Idi] let him do so; but not otherwise. Once a Min said to R. Idi: 'It is written, And unto Moses He said: Come up to the Lord (Ex. 24:1). But surely it should have stated, Come up to me!'—'It was Metatron,' he replied, whose name is similar to that of his Master, for it is written, For My name is in Him. (Ex. 23:21). 'But if so, we should worship him!' 'The same passage however,' replied R. Idi, 'says: Be not rebellious against Him [i.e., exchange Me not for him.'] 'But if so, why is it stated: He will not pardon your transgression?' (Ex. 23:21). He answered: 'By our troth [lit: we hold the belief] we would not accept him even as a messenger, for it is written, And he said unto him, If Thy presence go not etc.' (Ex. 33:15).'" Segal comments on the meaning, "The passage is ascribed to R. Nahman, a Babylonian who lived in the late third century. He, in turn, praises the rhetorical skills of R. Idi (or Idith), who apparently lived in Palestine in the generation previous to R. Nahman. R. Nahman warns that it is dangerous business to get into arguments with the heretics. One should refrain unless one has the skill of R. Idi." Alan Segal, *Two Powers in Heaven* (Boston: Brill, 2002), 68.

[8] Isaiah 30:27, "Behold the name of the Lord comes from far, burning with his anger, and in thick rising smoke." Psalm 20:1, 7, "May the Lord answer you in the day of trouble! May the name of the God of Jacob protect you... Some trust in chariots and others in horses, but we trust in the name of Yahweh, our God." When Jesus says in John 17:6, "I have manifested your name to the people you gave me out of the world" - Jesus' disciples knew exactly what he was saying.

Ryken explains.[9] It goes on in vs. 23, "When my angel goes before you and brings you to the Amorites and the Hittites and the Perizzites and the Canaanites, the Hivites and the Jebusites, and I blot them out..."

Vs. 25 is most remarkable, "You shall serve the LORD your God, and he will bless your bread and your water, and I will take sickness away from among you." Notice the change of subjects! Amazingly, the angel is now apparently called "Yahweh your God"![10] In other words, there is a blurring here of identity. The way the angel is described becomes virtually inseparable from Yahweh himself. The people were to give him the obedience and respect owed to God himself. (The same kind of language appears earlier in Exodus 16:26 - "If you will diligently listen to the voice of the LORD your God, and do that which is right in his eyes, and give ear to his commandments and keep all his statues, I will put none of the diseases on you that I put on the Egyptians, for I am the LORD, your healer.")[11][12]

Even vs. 27, which says, "I will send my terror before you..." is probably also a reference to the Angel of God being a terror. Notice the

---

[9] Ryken, Philip, *Exodus: Saved for God's Glory* (Wheaton, IL: Crossway, 2005) p.767

[10] When the word "LORD" in all caps is used in most English translations of the Old Testament, it is translating the underlying Hebrew tetragrammaton YHWH, the divine covenant name of God - see Exodus 3:14-15. To honor this divine name, Hebrew readers would not actually say the name, but would substitute the Hebrew word *Adonai*, which means "Lord." In fact, the Masoretic Hebrew text would place the vowel markers for *Adonai* under the letters YHWH, leading to the unlikely word "Jehovah," which later confused most English translators. What is important is to know that the capitalized "LORD" signifies the divine name 'Yahweh'.

[11] A.W. Pink writes, "Observe how such language is used there by one Person about another Person as precludes our identifying Him as a single Person; yet both are certainly Divine. Thus, we must not exclude Jehovah the Father wholly from these communications to the Old Testament saints and attribute all the messages unto the Son immediately. We are to admit the presence of the first Person per se (by Himself), as well as the second: two Persons with Divine attributes, employing the name of Jehovah in common, the one the Sender, the other the Sent—the latter communicating directly with men." Pink, *Gleanings in Joshua* (Chicago: Moody Press, 1964), 142.

[12] Also noteworthy is the change from the 1st person to the 3rd person in the 3rd commandment. After using "I" and "me," God switches to the third person and says, "You shall not take the name of the LORD your God in vain, for the LORD will not hold him guiltless who takes his name in vain" (Exodus 20:7). Considering the connection with this Angel who bears the "name" in ch. 23, the change is eye-opening.

difference between Psalm 34:7 which says, "The *angel of the LORD* encamps around those who fear him, and delivers them," and Psalm 35:5 which says of God's enemies, "Let them be like chaff before the wind, with the *angel of the LORD* driving them away! Let their way be dark and slippery, with the *angel of the LORD* pursuing them!" The Angel of Yahweh is the promised protector and deliverer of God's people. *And he is the one who strikes terror into their enemies and drives them away.*

To reiterate, as part of his covenant blessing, God gives his people a special promise—to "send" with them a special "angel" who mediates the very presence of Yahweh.[13] If they listen to him and obey his voice, he will guide them and guard them and fight for them against their enemies. They are to follow and obey him and him only. They must not worship the gods of the nations nor enter into a covenant with them, for God says they "will surely be a snare to you" (vs. 33).

This language of promise and warning is very important in light of the next passage we need to consider.

Judges 2 and the Angel's Judgment

Judges 2 occurs after the time of Joshua, after Israel has entered the Promised Land and had begun to drive out the nations of the land, but had ultimately failed to drive them out. We are told:

> Now the angel of the LORD went up from Gilgal to Bochim. And he said, "I brought you up from Egypt and brought you into the land that I swore to give to your fathers. I said, 'I will never break my covenant with you, and you shall make no covenant with the inhabitants of this land; you shall break down their altars.' But you have not obeyed my voice. What is this you have done? So now I say, I will not drive them out before you, but they shall become thorns in your sides, and their gods shall be a snare to you." As soon as the

---

[13] In fact, as we will see in later chapters, this "angel" had been with them all along in the Exodus as the one "sent" to rescue them from Egypt. Moses says in Numbers 20:16, "When we cried to the LORD, he heard our voice and sent an angel and brought us out of Egypt."

angel of the LORD spoke these words to all the people of Israel, the people lifted up their voices and wept. And they called the name of that place Bochim. And they sacrificed there to the LORD.

(Judges 2:1-5)

Like so many Old Testament passages, the "angel of the LORD" here is presented without comment or special introduction. Apparently, a manifestation of the angel "moved" from Gilgal to Bochim.

Gilgal had been the location of Israel's first encampment after crossing the Jordan River into the Promised Land and from where they launched their military campaign against the nations of the land. It was the location of the 12 stones they had taken from the middle of the Jordan and had set up as a memorial place of sacrifice (see Josh 4:20). It was where the new generation of Israel had been circumcised, had taken the Passover, and had been set apart in covenant to the LORD (Josh 5:1-12). And it was also where Joshua first met the "angel of the LORD" before the battle of Jericho and worshiped him (Josh 5:13-15). In other words, Gilgal was the first place of cultic worship and covenant in the land, where they met with God and were sent out to do battle and obey his will.[14]

When "the Angel of the LORD went up from Gilgal to Bochim," he was symbolically showing his displeasure and the removal of his presence from the camp of the people.[15]

But what is of special note are his words to the people. In language directly reminiscent of Exodus 23, the Angel speaks as Yahweh himself and the Angel of the covenant. He says, "*I* brought you up from Egypt and brought you into the land *I* swore to give to your fathers." He claims to be the promise-making God of the patriarchs and their direct liberator from Egypt. Further, notice the parallels between the two passages...

---

[14] See W. H. Brownlee, "Gilgal," ed. Geoffrey W Bromiley, *The International Standard Bible Encyclopedia*, Revised (Wm. B. Eerdmans, 1979–1988), 470.

[15] He may also have been showing the need for a new location and recommitment for worship. The Greek translation of Judges 2:1 identifies Bochim with Bethel, which becomes the next location for the tabernacle. (This Greek translation, known as the Septuagint (LXX), was the text most often used during the time of the New Testament.)

Judges 2:1-5	Exodus 23:20-33
[1] I brought you up from Egypt and brought you into the land I swore to give to your fathers.	[20] I send an angel before you to guard you on the way and to bring you to the place I have prepared.
[2] You have not obeyed my voice.	[21] Pay careful attention to him and obey his voice.
[3] You shall make no covenant with the inhabitants of the land.	[22] You shall make no covenant with them and their gods.
[2] You shall break down their altars.	[24] You shall utterly overthrow them and break their pillars in pieces.
[2] I will not drive them out before you.	[22, 27-28] If you carefully obey his voice...I will be an enemy to your enemies...I will make all your enemies turn their backs to you...drive out the Hivites, the Canaanites, and the Hittites from before you.
[3] They shall become thorns in your sides, and their gods shall be a snare to you.	[33] If you serve their gods, it will surely be a snare to you.

In other words, the "Angel of the LORD" is speaking as both the God of Israel and the Angel of the Covenant, and explicitly referencing the covenant promise and warning of Exodus 23:20-33. The warning is coming to pass, and the promise of the Angel's assured presence given them success is being withdrawn. No wonder the people "lifted up their voices and wept" and named the place Bochim, which means "weeping."

More Than an Angel

Obviously, this "angel" was not Moses or Joshua, nor was he a mere human messenger. Neither was he simply a lesser spiritual being. There are other occasions of "angelic messengers" coming to God's people (Dan 8:15-17, 9:21-22, Matt 1:20-21, Luke 1:19, 26-38). At no time do they speak about God in the first person. Nor do they accept or receive worship as this angel does. In fact, when the Apostle John prostrated himself to worship before an angel in Revelation 22:8-9, the angel says, "You must not do that! I am a fellow servant with you… Worship God!"

Some scholars argue that a royal representative spoke with the king's authority and could expect his words to be received as the words of the king. Therefore, an "angel" could be identified as Yahweh and not be Yahweh.[16] However, speaking with the king's authority does not give the right to be "identified" as the king.[17] The angel's adamant refusal in Rev 22:9 shows that such an identification would be idolatrous and treasonous. Given the clear and just jealousy of God in the Scriptures not to "share his glory with another" (Isa 42:8), this "authoritative messenger" argument becomes very suspect.

In contrast, the angel of the LORD receives worship (Josh 5:13-15), speaks as Yahweh himself (Ex 3:6, 14), is identified as the appearing of God himself (Jdg 6:22, Jdg 13:21-22), bears God's special name (Ex 23:21, Jdg 13:18), and has Yahweh's authority to redeem and judge. He appears in crucial passages as the central figure in the redemptive promises of God. As Phil Ryken says, this angel was "distinguished from God,

---

[16] This is called the doctrine of the shaluah ("one who is sent"). See Israel Herbert Levinthal, "The Jewish Law of Agency," *Jewish Quarterly Review* 13:2 (Oct 1922), esp. 124-125. Some Unitarians and even Christians argue that the *shaluah* always and only speaks for God, and therefore the Angel cannot be God, because he is a *shaluah*. For a Christian example see René A. López, "Identifying the 'Angel of the Lord' in the Book of Judges: A Model for Reconsidering the Referent in Other Old Testament Loci," *BBR* 20 (2010): 1–18 (López does not use the term shaluah but the idea is there). We believe this kind of argument commits both the fallacy of begging the question and the false dichotomy. For if the Angel is God and a *shaluah* simultaneously, the argument falls apart. Only exegesis can answer this question. Thanks to Aleksandar for the email correspondence alerting us to the *shaluah*.

[17] See Von Heijne, "According to Samuel A. Meier, the puzzling narratives about 'the angel of the Lord' are the only texts in biblical and ancient Near Eastern literature where no distinction is made between sender and messenger. Although the messengers sometimes speak in the first person as if they were the senders of the message, they normally report who sent them ... Meier writes, 'It must be underscored that the angel of YHWH in these perplexing biblical narratives does not behave like any other messenger known in the divine or human realm. Although the tern 'messenger' is present, the narrative itself omits the indispensable features of messenger activity and presents instead the activities which one associates with Yahweh and other gods of the ancient Near East ... From these passages it is evident that the *ma'lak* YHWH is closely associated with Yahweh in name, authority and message, and that he represents Yahweh in the human realm, whereas Yahweh's own immediacy is actualized in realms outside human perception.'" Camilla Helena von Heijne, *The Messenger of the Lord in Early Jewish Interpretations of Genesis* (New York: de Gruyter, 2010), 49.

yet at the same time had uniquely divine attributes."[18] As we will see, this happens repeatedly throughout the Old Testament.

How could the Old Testament present us with a being who was both distinguished from Yahweh and yet also was Yahweh? Could this really be an Old Testament revelation of a multiplicity of Persons in the Godhead, a Trinity in the Old Testament?

Yes! In fact, why would Christians think any differently? What's interesting is how often Christians, even Christian theologians, read the Old Testament, as if the Old Testament is about a monistic God. They admit that God has always been a Trinitarian God (one God existing in three Persons), but they act like it wasn't revealed until the New Testament and seem hesitant to see the Trinity in the Old Testament at all—there at best only in prophetic or typological form. Our commentaries skip right over these kinds of things, failing to mention them or point out their significance. In short, we have become functional Old Testament Unitarians, afraid of reading into the Old Testament things that are not there. But what if they are there?

In contrast, as we will see, the early Christians definitely located and defended the doctrine of the Trinity from the Old Testament. Even more, as we will also see in later chapters, even some Jewish teachers were writing about a multiplicity to Yahweh in the Old Testament.

For now, it is enough to say that the Old Testament reveals a divine figure, at times synonymous with God himself, at other times "sent" from Yahweh, who is the divine redeemer and primary promise of God's presence in the Old Testament. He is the angel of the covenant, whose presence and blessing is withdrawn because of Israel's disobedience to the covenant stipulations.

He's not just a bird ... he's not just a plane...! But is there any explicit reason to see this angel as Jesus?

In fact, at the end of the Old Testament, God makes a promise about the angel that is explicitly connected to the New Testament. This last passage connects the dots and brings the story of the "angel" to its penultimate conclusion.

---

[18] See Phil Ryken, *Exodus: Saved for God's Glory* (Wheaton, IL: Crossway 2005) p.767.

Malachi 3 and the Angel's Return

The book of Malachi was written after the exile, when the people of Israel had returned from Babylon. The Temple had been rebuilt, the walls of Jerusalem had been restored. But the people were still repressed by foreign rulers and hostile neighbors. The Messiah had not come. The promised glory had not arrived. The Old Testament was ending with a whimper, with spiritual decline, disappointment, and cynicism about God's promises. The people were complaining that God was either favoring the wicked or simply ignoring his people and his promises (Mal 2:17).

But in Malachi 3, God responds to their complaints with a prophecy. He gives them a promise of grace yet warns them that this promise won't be what they are expecting. God says,

> Behold, I send my messenger, and he will prepare the way before me. And the Lord whom you seek will suddenly come to his temple; even the messenger of the covenant in whom you delight, behold, he is coming, says the LORD of hosts. But who can endure the day of his coming, and who can stand when he appears? For he is like a refiner's fire and like fullers' soap. He will sit as a refiner and purifier of silver, and he will purify the sons of Levi and refine them like gold and silver, and they will bring offerings in righteousness to the LORD. Then the offering of Judah and Jerusalem will be pleasing to the LORD as in the days of old and as in former years.
>
> (Malachi 3:1–4)

Notice that in vs. 1, God promises to send two "messengers." In both cases, the word in Hebrew is *malak*, which we usually translate as "angel." As we have seen, an angel is a "messenger," and can be either a human or a spiritual being depending on the context.

In this case, the first messenger is a herald who will "prepare the way" for God's coming. God has a work to do and it comes in stages, and it comes with preparation. The people of Israel have heard before about this messenger who "prepares the way." Isaiah 40 prophesied about a "voice in the wilderness" crying "prepare the way of the LORD; make straight in the desert a highway for our God," a "herald of good news" who would say to the cities of Judah, "Behold your God!" (Isaiah 40:3, 9). So now, many years later, God confirms this promise through

Malachi of the messenger who will come to prepare the way. When a king would make a royal visit to a city, a royal messenger would come to prepare the city for the king's coming—to smooth out the roads and to make for a glorious welcome. Of course, for God's coming, the preparations are not so much physical as they are spiritual—to prepare people's hearts. Malachi actually identifies this "messenger" in 4:5-6, "Behold, I will send you Elijah the prophet before the great and awesome day of the LORD comes. And he will turn the hearts of fathers to their children and the hearts of children to their fathers, lest I come and strike the land with a decree of utter destruction."

Those familiar with the Bible will know that the New Testament explicitly identifies the first messenger of Malachi 3:1 with John the Baptist (Matt 11:10, Mark 1:2-3, Luke 7:27, etc.).

But notice what Malachi records next, "And the Lord (ha-adon) whom you seek will suddenly come to his temple; even the messenger (or "angel") of the covenant in whom you delight, behold, he is coming, says the LORD of hosts." The first "Lord" here is not the Hebrew divine name YHWH (as in the end of the verse), but the simpler Adonai for "Lord." Yet the word also has a definite article "ha" attached to the front of it. In the Old Testament, the word adonai with the definite article is a term usually also reserved for God himself.

Notice the progression of thought! The first messenger, God says, comes to prepare the way "before me." But then a second figure is promised, whose appearing will be unexpected; he will come "suddenly." He is called "the Adonai whom you seek" who comes to what can be called "his temple." In other words, a figure comes in God's place, whose coming is also God's coming. And then God calls him "the angel of the covenant in whom you delight."

It should be clear by now who Malachi is describing. God promises a figure to come, whose coming is God's coming, who comes to "his" temple, who is the "angel of the covenant." What "angel of the covenant" is he talking about? Obviously, it is the angel of Exodus 23!—the special angel who was the crowning glory of God's covenant promises, the angel of God's presence, the angel who reveals God and is God.[19]

---

[19] Joseph Packard, commenting on Malachi 3, writes, "From a very early period we find mention of an extraordinary Messenger, or Angel, who is sometimes called the Angel of God, at others, the Angel of Jehovah. He is represented as the

John Mackay writes, "Here it is the Lord Almighty (the Father) who is speaking of his coming, and yet refers to one who is distinct from him and one with him (the Son). This is none other than the Messiah, who is both God and man... The Angel of the covenant is the one who is the mediator of the new covenant, whose role is that of the Angel of God's presence to save his people."[20]

In Malachi's time, the people had rebuilt Jerusalem and rebuilt the Temple. But God had not descended in fire and cloud as with Moses' tabernacle, as with Solomon's Temple. There was no clear sign that God had fully restored his presence to his people. The "angel of the covenant," who had walked with their fathers, who had rescued the people out of Egypt, who had given them the covenant promises, who had dwelt in the Temple—had not appeared. But God ends the Old Testament with a promise that he will come! He will come and do a work, but it would not be what they expected. It would not be a work of military triumph and national prosperity. Instead, it would be a time of spiritual refinement and purification for true worship.

As this figure finally descends, it is now clear who he is! "It's not a bird ... it's not a plane..."

As Jude says, "Now I want to remind you, although you once fully knew it, that Jesus, who saved a people out of the land of Egypt, afterward destroyed those who did not believe" (Jude 5). As John says, "In the beginning was the Word, and the Word was with God and the Word was God. He was with God in the beginning... And the Word became flesh and tabernacled among us, and we have seen his glory, glory as of

---

Mediator between the invisible God and men in all God's communications and dealings with men. To this Angel divine names, attributes, purposes, and acts are ascribed. He occasionally assumed a human form... He is called the face of God, because though no man can see his face and live, yet the Angel of his face is the brightness of his glory, and the express image of his person. In him Jehovah's presence is manifested, and his glory reflected, for the glory of God shines in the face of Jesus Christ. There is thus a gradual development in the Old Testament of the doctrine of the incarnation, of the distinction of persons in the Godhead, not brought to light fully, lest it should interfere with the doctrine of the unity of God." John Peter Lange, Philip Schaff, and Joseph Packard, *A Commentary on the Holy Scriptures: Malachi* (Bellingham, WA: Logos Bible Software, 2008), 19.

[20] John L. Mackay, *Haggai, Zechariah, Malachi: God's Restored People*, Focus on the Bible Commentary (Ross-shire, Scotland: Christian Focus Publications, 2003), 319.

the only Son from the Father, full of grace and truth... No one has ever seen God; the only God, who is at the Father's side, he has made him known" (John 1:1, 14, 18).

Later, when Jesus was Transfigured with divine, even angelic, glory and a voice came from heaven, saying, "This is my Son, whom I have chosen; listen to Him" (Luke 9:35)—the language echoes Exodus 23:21, "Pay careful attention to him and obey his voice."

And you understand, when Jesus says at the end of Matthew, "All authority in heaven and on earth has been given to me. Go therefore and make disciples of all nations, baptizing them in the name (singular) of the Father and of the Son and of the Holy Spirit, teaching them to obey all that I have commanded you. And behold, I am with you always, even to the end of the age" (Matt 28:20). Jesus was re-instituting the promise of Exodus 23, now on the basis of a new and better covenant through his own blood - that he would be with us and would never leave us or forsake us.

I've found a friend, O such a friend,
All power to Him is given,
To guard me on my onward course,
And lead me safe to heaven.
James G. Small, 1866

Phil Ryken writes,

Like the Israelites, we have received salvation. We have crossed from death to life through the crucifixion and resurrection of Jesus Christ. But we have not yet reached the Promised Land, and the way is long and hard. We must endure many trials and suffer many painful sorrows in the journey of our faith. But God has given us a Guardian Savior who will lead us where we need to go. Jesus will protect us from danger along the way. If we listen to his Word, he will tell us everything we need to know. And in the end he will lead us home to God.[21]

This is the great story of the Bible and, from beginning to end, it has been about Jesus.

---

[21] Ryken, p.768.

The Reason for This Book

Obviously, many have made these connections before us. Even in recent years, there have been many books discussing the Angel. But we have come to the conclusion that many of the popular studies haven't gone deep enough biblically or historically. And, as far as we have found, there has actually been no full-length book treatment devoted specifically to an exhaustive study of the Angel of the Lord in the Evangelical tradition in the last 100 years!

That isn't to say that there aren't good resources that touch on the subject. Graham Cole has recently written an important book on the incarnation. He looks at theophanies and draws similar conclusions to us about an "embodied God" in the OT. However, his focus is on these "preparing for" the incarnation and not on the significance of the Second Person in the OT per se.[22] Vern Poythress has an excellent introduction to theophanies, particularly Christ-appearances in the OT. However, his focus is not on the person of these appearances so much as on the nature of the traditionally accepted appearances.[23] Ron Rhodes has a classic popular level book that deals with Christ in the OT, but its focus is not so much on a systematic treatment of him as a person, but topical treatment. It is great for what it is, but we believe more is needed.[24] James Borland has a fine work that deals with Christ appearances in the OT systematically. But he does not take into consideration the other names of the Angel which, when understood, dramatically increase the number of appearances in the OT.[25] In fact, there are few modern works that do that,[26] even though all of these affirm that Christ is in the OT!

---

[22] Graham A. Cole, *The God Who Became Human: A Biblical Theology of Incarnation*, ed. D. A. Carson, vol. 30, New Studies in Biblical Theology (England; Downers Grove, IL: Apollos; InterVarsity Press, 2013).

[23] Vern Poythress, *Theophany: A Biblical Theology of God's Appearing* (Wheaton, IL: Crossway, 2018).

[24] Ron Rhodes, *Christ Before the Manger: The Life and Times of the Preincarnate Christ* (Eugene, OR: Wipf and Stock, 2002). Excellent primer on many aspects of Christ in the OT. Includes a chapter devoted to the Angel and one to the Shepherd.

[25] James Borland, *Christ in the Old Testament: A Comprehensive Study of Old Testament Appearances of Christ in Human Form* (Chicago: Moody Press, 1978).

[26] Other books that deal with the Angel in one way or another include Michael Barrett, *Beginning at Moses: A Guide to Finding Christ in the Old Testament* (Greenville, SC: Ambassador International, 2010); Edmund Clowney, *the Unfolding Mystery: Discovering Christ in the Old Testament* (Phillipsburg, NJ: P&R,

We have come to realize that, in recent centuries, we have lost some things that were known and valued to earlier theologians and teachers of the Church and that need to be recovered. In fact, we believe that to study the Angel of the Lord is to unlock some of the most glorious truths of the Bible. So, in this book, we are going to make some unique claims.

1) We are going to show that the Angel of the LORD appears far more often than most people realize. In fact, the Angel of the LORD appears in the OT sometimes under different titles. Some of these titles include: the Word of the Lord, the Name of the Lord, the Glory of the Lord, the Face of the Lord, the Arm/Hand of the Lord, the Prince/Commander, even the "Son". We will show that sometimes these titles clearly suggest a second Divine figure. And we will show that Jesus is identified in the NT with all of these titles associated with the Angel of the LORD.

2) We will show that this view of the Angel in the OT was not just a Christian thing. Among the ancient Jews, there was a lot of speculation and discussion about the Angel of the LORD. In fact, scholars have recently shown that, prior to Christianity, there existed a significant minority Jewish tradition that recognized two Yahwehs in the Old Testament. Many of the titles (like Glory, Word, Name, etc.) were seen as mediated revelations of God. Certain OT passages were debated by the rabbis and seen as (in their own words) "Two Powers" texts. Many of these same tests are used by the NT and by Jesus himself as references and identifiers of Jesus. The scribes of Jesus day are shown to be familiar with this tradition and these texts and to know what Jesus was claiming - that he was claiming to be the OT Divine Angel.

3) We will show that this interpretation of the Divine Angel, and even the Jewish interpretations of the Angel, were known and used by the Church Fathers, and even up to the time of the Reformation. This wholistic understanding of the Angel is the

---

2013); Clowney, *Preaching Christ in All of Scripture* (Wheaton, IL: Crossway, 2003); Bradley J. Cummins, *YHWH Preincarnate Jesus: Lost in Translation* (Enumclaw, WA: WinePress Publishing, 2010); Jonathan Stephen, *Theophany: Close Encounters with the Son of God* (Epsom, England: Day One Publications, 1998); Charles Drew, *The Ancient Love Song: Finding Christ in the Old Testament* (Phillipsburg, NJ: P&R, 2000); David Murray, *Jesus on Every Page: 10 Simple Ways to Seek and Find Christ in the Old Testament* (Nashville: Thomas Nelson, 2013).

majority and original Christian interpretive tradition. The church has historically seen Trinitarian theology as exegetically grounded in the OT.

The Structure of the Book

To accomplish these things, *Part 1* of our book will be an exegetical study of the Angel throughout the Bible. We will look at the Angel of the LORD throughout the Old Testament identified under different names and titles. Then we will explore how Jesus is identified in the New Testament with all these same titles associated with the Angel of the Lord.

In Part 2, we will explore some of the history of interpretation surrounding the Angel of the Lord among the ancient Jews, in the early church, and up to the Reformation and the modern day. We will show that this view of the Angel of the Lord is the original Christian interpretive tradition.

Part 3 will explore how the Angel of the LORD might influence and affect various aspects of systematic theology and then offer some practical applications for how this doctrine can affect our spiritual lives today.

The book will conclude with *Part IV* and a series of Appendices on various related subjects to the Angel.

A Note on Method

What we are claiming in this book is nothing new. We argue it is the majority view of Christian history. But in the last 300 years, it seems to have become more controversial, disputed, and held in some skepticism. There are multiple reasons for this. In some circles, it is because of an anti-supernatural bias that affects even conservative scholarship. Sometimes there has been an overreaction to the supposed "allegorical" method of the early church. Certain rules of exegesis have been taught that create very wooden readings of texts. Sometimes, people today are not as familiar with how ancient peoples—especially the ancient Jews—read texts. Christians don't want to be guilty of eisegesis and worry about being accused of reading too much back into the Old Testament. This is a legitimate concern but must be held in tension with the interpretive key that the New Testament is meant to give us into Old Testament understanding.

In the first part of the book particularly, we will follow a biblical-theological and redemptive-historical method to develop an understanding of the Angel's role in Biblical history. One of the core axioms of biblical interpretation is "the analogy of faith," which means that Scripture interprets itself—that less clear passages are to be interpreted by clearer ones. The meaning of one passage may give some insight, but its meaning may be unclear. By comparing related texts whose meanings are clearer, the less clear passage becomes much more understandable. This is one of the fundamental building blocks for systematic theology. But it has often been criticized. Some people reject systematic theology entirely as imposing philosophical speculations on the text or importing meanings into texts (and certainly, importing meanings is a danger). On the other hand, Christians believe that there is an inspired unity to biblical truth. We can't impose a system on the Bible, but we do believe that the Bible itself teaches a "system".

In this book, we will sometimes deal with passages that may not immediately appear to be related to the Angel of the Lord. Their meanings may seem obscure and open to multiple interpretations. If you were to take some of these passages by themselves, without reference to other texts, the interpretations we will give could at first appear to be speculative "stretching" or unwarranted "extrapolation." But to properly see and understand the Angel of the Lord, it will require an approach of comparing Scripture with Scripture. We will try to show that the "clearer" passages bring into focus what is happening in the "less clear" passages and that the "less clear" passages are working in the same ways.[27] Looking at just a few texts may not be convincing. But when all the evidence is taken into account, we believe our conclusions are compelling.

---

[27] For an example of what we mean, see our discussion of "The Angel of his Presence.'

THE ANGEL AND BIBLICAL THEOLOGY

Chapters 1-15

Biblical Theology: *That branch of Exegetical Theology which deals with the process of the self-revelation of God deposited in the Bible.* ~ Geerhardus Vos

In Part I we will look at the Angel of the LORD as he is unfolded in the Holy Scripture from Genesis to Revelation. We will work our way through the books of Moses, on into the latter history books, the psalms and prophets, and finally into the New Testament itself.

1

THE ANGEL IS GOD

The Angel and a Woman

Did He Really Hear God?

ONE OF MY DAUGHTERS RECENTLY ASKED ME, "Dad, Moses was talking to God, right?"

"Yes."

"And he heard him, like, in his ears?"

"Yes."

"But how? That doesn't make any sense. And he saw God too?"

"Yep."

"But no one can see God. I don't understand any of this."

"All of that is correct. But..." I told her, "You have to understand that God talked to people in the OT through the Angel of the LORD. They weren't talking to the sky, and they weren't merely hearing things in their head. This was not their wild imaginations running away with fancy ideas. The Angel appeared to them in various ways. This is the God they saw and with whom they spoke. In the New Testament, we know him as Jesus."

It is our contention that until we understand this basic concept, all the stories where God speaks to people in the OT will be misunderstood from the outset, beginning in the Garden and going right on through to the very last prophet. As we begin to unfold these Angel texts, we are going to look at one main idea in each chapter. The basic point we want to explain in this chapter is how the Angel of the LORD *is* the LORD. This is the necessary first step to understanding all subsequent revelation about him. Most miss this altogether. Many have never seen it. But we will see it *many* times in the future. Amazingly, while this idea is both virtually absent in modern Christian thinking, it is crystal clear in the very first explicit occurrence of the phrase "the Angel of the LORD" in the Bible.

Hagar and the Angel: Genesis 16

Setting Up His Identity

Geerhardus Vos calls the Angel of the LORD, "The most important and characteristic form of revelation in the patriarchal period."[28] This is not hyperbole. Though, as we will progressively unfold in this book, Vos barely began to scratch the surface. The phrase "The Angel of the LORD" first appears in the Bible in—of all places—the story of Hagar, Sarah's handmaid. While we do not believe this is even close to his first appearance in the Scripture, it is the first time he is described with this phrase. Thus, it seems quite natural to begin our study here.

However, before moving into the story, this fact in and of itself is worth pondering for a moment. How astounding that the first formal appearance of "the Angel of the LORD" is to a servant-concubine, Gentile-Egyptian, cast-out slave woman who won't share in the covenant blessings of Abraham! Who does this? Who makes a first undisputed appearance in this way? Yet it is exactly like the God described in the Bible to do such a thing—always surprising, always doing things on his terms. The phrase occurs four times in five verses:

> *The angel of the LORD* found her by a spring of water in the wilderness, the spring on the way to Shur. And he said, "Hagar, servant of Sarai, where have you come from and where are you going?" She said, "I am fleeing from my mistress Sarai." *The angel of the LORD* said to her, "Return to your mistress and submit to her." *The angel*

---

[28] Geerhardus Vos, *Biblical Theology: Old and New Testaments* (Eugene, OR: Wipf & Stock Publishers, 2003), 72.

of the LORD also said to her, "I will surely multiply your offspring so that they cannot be numbered for multitude." And *the angel of the LORD* said to her, "Behold, you are pregnant and shall bear a son. You shall call his name Ishmael, because the LORD has listened to your affliction."

(Genesis 16:7-11)

So who is this angel? Here are some facts from the story. First, let's look at the phrase itself. He is called "the Angel of the LORD." "The" in English is the definite article, and it designates a specific individual. While the equivalent (*ha-*) does not appear in the Hebrew, the grammar of that language also does not allow for it. So it may or may not be definite in Hebrew.[29] Therefore, we will not place too much emphasis on it here as we try to identify this angel.

"LORD" (all caps) is the word "YHWH," from which we get Yahweh or Jehovah (same thing).[30] It is a proper name for God. He later reveals it to us as his covenant name. As the Angel *of* the LORD, this is Yahweh's Angel.

It is our contention that there is only one supernatural entity in the entire Bible that ever gets such a close designation to Yahweh himself. This is fueled by facts that come to us through many of the stories of the Angel. All other angels are simply called angels. Yes, there are

---

[29] It is called a construct state. Nouns in a construct relationship cannot take a definite article even though it is definite because it is a proper name, and as we will see, this name is a demonstration that this Angel is not a created being, but a manifestation of God himself. For a short discussion on the grammar see René A. López, "Identifying the 'Angel of the Lord' in the Book of Judges: A Model for Reconsidering the Referent in Other Old Testament Loci," *BBR* 20 (2010): 2-3 [1–18]. A longer discussion is S. A. Meier, "Angel of Yahweh," ed. Karel van der Toorn, Bob Becking, and Pieter W. van der Horst, *Dictionary of Deities and Demons in the Bible* (Leiden; Boston; Köln; Grand Rapids, MI; Cambridge: Brill; Eerdmans, 1999), 54-59.

[30] LORD (in all caps) is the word English Bibles use to translate the OT name Yahweh. An interesting side-note here. Yahweh becomes "Jehovah" in the Latin. The origin of this word is curious. Hebrew was written in all consonants. Because the time came in the life of Israel where the Jews would no longer say the divine name, people forgot what its vowels were. The actual pronunciation was lost. To avoid saying the name inadvertently, yet still being able to translate the word, a merging of the consonants YHVH (Where Y = J if you remember your Indiana Jones and also V = W, as our preferred spelling is YHWH) with the vowels of a word for "Lord" (Adonai), the result was Jehovah (Jehovah = Jahovah).

angels "from" God. But this is the only "Angel of the LORD," sometimes simply called "The Angel."[31] "Of" is specific. It is possessive. Thus,
the title is itself cryptically descriptive of something very important as
it regards this person. As we already saw in the *Introduction*, somehow
the Name (Yahweh/LORD) is in him.

The second thing to notice is his question. "Where have you come
from, and where are you going?" This follows on the heels of the Angel
"finding" Hagar by a spring. The scene is eerily reminiscent to Adam
and Eve in the Garden when the LORD comes to them in the cool of
the day and cries out, "Where are you?" (Gen 3:9). Neither question is
said out of ignorance, but rather is a kind of spiritual probing. He seeks
out the rejected, the sinner, the outcast. But he does so in an intimate,
personal way as he goes into the heart of sin and brokenness and judgment and shows grace.

The third thing to point out is that he commands Hagar to do
something. "Return to Sarai and submit to her." Other angels do similar
things in the Bible. Yet, when combined with a few more facts, his
"commanding" takes on much deeper significance. This is especially
true in light of the next observation.

Fourth, this Angel promises to multiply her offspring. "I will
surely multiply your offspring." Like other birth announcements, this
demonstrates God's great interest in the birth of children as a fulfillment of his promises and purposes. But here it shows something even
more wonderful. God is displaying to her compassion, protection, and
care for her present and her future, and this even though she will not
be part of the Abrahamic covenant or of God's special people Israel!
Such is the grace and kindness of God in the most unexpected of places.

The key to understanding is the little pronoun. This is said in the
first person: I. The *Angel* will do it. Yet, multiplying someone's descend-
ants is what *God* does in Genesis. "The LORD" will multiply Eve's pain
in childbearing (Gen 3:16). "The LORD" makes a covenant with

---

[31] There is one instance in the New Testament of "the angel of the Lord" (Matt
1:24). While some may suggest that this is the same Angel we find throughout the
OT, he is not called simply "the Lord" as the Angel in the OT is. This and the
numerous reasons we give for the Angel's identity in this book convince us that
this NT instance is probably someone like Gabriel, a created angel who an-
nounces the coming of the Messiah.

Abraham and promises to multiply him greatly (Gen 17:2). "God" says I have blessed Ishmael and will make him multiply (17:20). In Genesis 22, the Angel of the LORD will multiply Abraham's offspring (22:15-17). This vital connection reveals much about who this Angel is.

Fifth, he tells her that Yahweh has listened to her affliction. We will see something like this again when the Angel returns to Hagar in Genesis 21. The response here occurs in the immediate context of the multiplying of seed. In fact, he tells her that she is pregnant, and this is the sign that the LORD has listened to her.

What is Hagar's response to all of this? It says, "So she called the name of the LORD who spoke to her, 'You are a God of seeing,' for she said, 'Truly here I have seen him who looks after me'" (16:13). Notice here "the name of the LORD." It seems almost separate from the actual name she gives him. As if we could capitalize it: the Name. This is something we will return to in later chapters, but it has murky roots here in the story of Hagar.

Then there is the phrase, "…who looks after me." The Hebrew here is difficult (רָאִיתִי אַחֲרֵי רֹאִי, *ra'iti 'ahare ro'i*). However, it bears a striking resemblance to what the LORD told Moses when he said "You shall see my back (וְרָאִיתָ אֶת־אֲחֹרָי, *wara'ita 'et-'ahoray*), but my face shall not be seen" (Ex 33:23). So here is an Egyptian slave woman, not part of the promise of Israel, yet who is given opportunity to "see" God in a way that reminds us of Moses himself. Granted, in her case the LORD sees her. Nevertheless, she still sees him.

One more point about this while we are here. Israel was the chosen people of God. Sarah was their first mother. The thing that led Hagar into the desert in the first place was Sarah's treatment of her Egyptian handmaiden after she "dealt harshly" (Gen 16:6) with her. Ironically, this is the same treatment Israel would later receive from the Egyptians in slavery. Thus, in the story of Hagar and the Angel, Israel is being reminded that they are not so different from their enemies. They "practice the very same things" (Rom 2:1), but their God is a God of compassion.

The Angel is Yahweh

Perhaps the most frequently missed part of Hagar's response, and one worth thinking long and hard over, is how the text identifies the

God who spoke to her simply as "Yahweh." Did you see it? The Angel of the LORD is speaking to her, so she calls *Yahweh who spoke to her* something. The text calls the Angel Yahweh. She gave him a name, perhaps meaning that he had not revealed himself to her as Yahweh. Nevertheless, the Angel of the LORD is shortened to simply "the LORD," for he is the one speaking to her. This is why someone like Charles Hodge is able to say, "The angel, who appeared to Hagar, to Abraham, to Moses, to Joshua, to Gideon, and to Manoah, who was called Jehovah and worshipped" [underline mine].[32] This vital piece of information becomes normative throughout the rest of Scripture, even as we will argue it was before it.

For example, Adam and Eve (with whom we have just seen a literary connection to Hagar) talk to "the LORD." Everything about that story feels physical. Adam talks. The LORD brings animals to Adam. Satan, Eve, and Adam all hear the LORD pronounce a curse upon them. The LORD even kills some animal and clothes our first parents with its skin. How are they not having an encounter with an embodied Person? Why would it be anyone other than the LORD that Hagar is talking to?

The same would be true of Noah in the covenant God makes with him prior to building the ark. He hears from "the LORD." He receives very specific directions about the ark. He is given prophecies about a Flood, and so on. Everything about this seems embodied in some way, perhaps through a vision or perhaps not. What we are seeing here with Hagar is that from the very first story where we read about "the Angel of the LORD," the Scripture sets the table for the way all subsequent revelations of him will speak. So why not also those that have come before it? After all, even the story with Hagar presupposes that she and others know about this Angel. This is clearly not his first appearance in the world of men.

This point is worth lingering on, because we will see this done so often that it is our contention that most times we find God or the LORD speaking to someone or appearing to them, it is the Angel of the LORD who is in mind. Not that "Yahweh" *only* describes the Angel. It most certainly doesn't. It also describes the Father and perhaps sometimes

---

[32] Charles Hodge, *Systematic Theology*, vol. 1 (Oak Harbor, WA: Logos Research Systems, Inc., 1997), 490.

even the Spirit. But when there is some kind of sensory manifestation, especially when God is speaking to someone, the Angel should be our default view unless there is reason to expect, from the passage, that it is one of the other Persons.

God does not come to people in his bare essence. He comes through the Persons of the Holy Trinity, and they in different ways from one another. It is difficult (though not impossible) to think of places where Father is seen or heard directly by people. The same is *not* true of the Son. While we will be able to see this much better by the end of the book, we can see even here that the Bible is setting this up for us very early. The language is clear. It expects us to "get it."

Adding to this, next we see that she calls the Angel, "The God who sees." The text speaks of "the Name of Yahweh who spoke to her." This is "The God who sees." "God who sees" is the compound word *El-roi*. Its root is a word that is very common for God: *El*. Hence, she calls the Angel "God." The Angel of the LORD is called the God who sees. At the very least, she believes he is *a* god. We believe that he is *The* God— the Second Person of the Godhead.

The Angel is Christ

This story is an anticipation of the Gospel—of God's blessing on all nations through Abraham; of God's revelation of himself to all flesh; that we are all sinners, but God has sought us out in amazing grace; that God cares for the needy and afflicted of all the earth and does so through Jesus Christ. During his ministry, the incarnated Jesus (incarnated meaning that he took on human flesh) did things like "see" Nathanael under the tree or come to a Samaritan woman by a well and offer her living water. Such things harken back to the Angel's meeting with Hagar.

As for the story of Hagar, we learn that this Angel has a name that hints at a fundamental union to the LORD, but with a fundamental distinction from the LORD; that he speaks for God, but also does things that only God does; and that he is called Angel, but also Yahweh and God. But are we alone in our understanding of this Angel as God himself? Based upon these observations from the text itself, there is a long history of interpreting this Angel as God, and more specifically as Christ.

Hilary of Poitiers (c. 315–367) said, "The Angel of God speaks to

Hagar; and this same Angel is God" (Hilary, *On the Trinity* 5.11). He got this from even older Christians, who more specifically said that this is Christ himself.[33] Puritans followed suit. Henry Ainsworth (1571–1622) (and through a quotation of him, Benjamin Keach [1640-1704]) writes at this very point in his commentary on Genesis 16, "Sometimes this name Angel is given to Christ himself, who is the Angel of the covenant, Mal 3:1. And of God's face (Isa 63:9), in whom God's name is, Ex 23:20. And this angel which here found Hagar, speaks as God."[34] Andrew Willet (1562 - 1621) is a little more guarded, but is at least willing to entertain the idea. "This was not some prophet … but an Angel. The Angel speaks in the person and authority of God, by whom he was sent, as it is usual in scripture for the messenger to use the name of the sender : and it may well be, that Christ was the chief in all such imbassages [delegations]."[35] John Richardson even noticed what we observed earlier that "Christ the Angel of the Covenant, Mal 3:1" is "called here Jehovah."[36] If this is

---

[33] For example, "Scripture sets forth this angel as both Lord and God—for He would not have promised the blessing of seed unless the angel had also been God. Let them ask what the heretics can make of this present passage. Was that the Father that was seen by Hagar or not? For He is declared to be God. But far be it from us to call God the Father an angel, lest He should be subordinate to another whose angel He would be. But they will say that it was an angel. How then shall He be God if He was an angel? … We ought to understand it to have been God the Son, who, because He is of God, is rightly called God, because He is the Son of God. But, because He is subjected to the Father, and the Announcer of the Father's will, He is declared to be the Angel of Great Counsel [Isa 9:6 LXX]. Therefore … this passage … is suited to … the person of Christ that He should be both God because He is the Son of God, and should be an angel because He is the Announcer of the Father's mind" (Novatian of Rome [d. 258 AD], *On the Trinity* 18).

[34] Henry Ainsworth, *Annotations Upon the First Book of Moses, called Genesis* (s.l.: s.n., 1616), Gen 16:7. [Spelling and punctuation modernized]. Benjamin Keach who, quoting Ainsworth to some extent says, "Sometimes the name Angel is given to Christ himself, who is the Angel of the covenant, and the Angel of God's face or presence, Isa 63:1. 'In whom God's name is,' Ex 23:21. Thus Ainsworth. And in another place he says, 'That one of the two Angels that appeared to Abraham was Jesus Christ, whom Abraham called the Judge of all the earth, Gen 28:2, 25, who is called Jehovah.'" Benjamin Keach, *GTropologia: A Key to Open Scripture Metaphors* (London: William Hill, 1858), 642. [Spelling and punctuation modernized].

[35] Andrew Willet, *Hexapla in Genesin* (Cambridge, 1605; second ed., enlarged, 1608), 182-83. [Spelling and punctuation modernized]."

[36] John Richardson, *Choice Observations and Explanations upon the Old Testament* (London: s.n., 1657), comments on Genesis 16:7.

correct, then how much greater of a marvel is it that that Jesus would come to that woman at the well? For here in the OT, he offers a foretaste of grace to a lost and lonely woman by a spring of water.

Before leaving this story, we must note that, sadly, many have not seen Christ here at all. They do not want to see things that are not there, and rightly so. But they become too guarded here, as they do things like fail to notice the shortening of the Angel to Jehovah or how she calls him "God." They are not taking proper account of other details of the story. It is not good to be more guarded than the text itself. When we are, our Christology, indeed our Theology Proper suffers greatly for it. But are there other reasons to be more guarded? Let's look at the second appearance of the Angel to Hagar next.

Hagar and the Angel: Genesis 21

Hagar will encounter the Angel one more time. In this account, he is not called "The Angel of the LORD," but rather the "Angel of God" (Gen 21:17). "God" is the very common word "Elohim." The word is plural in form (*-im* is the plural ending of Hebrew words), but can be either singular or plural in translation, depending on the context. Think of it like "sheep" or "deer." You don't know if you have one sheep or many sheep until you get the context. "Look! A deer is in the backyard." "Look, deer are in the backyard." We know from the verbs that the first sentence has one deer in mind, while the second has two. Elohim very often refers to God (singular), such as the first verse of the Bible, "In the beginning, God (*elohim*) created (singular verb) the heavens and the earth" (Gen 1:1). But it also means "gods" (plural) as in the First Commandment, "You shall have no other gods (*elohim*) before me" (Ex 20:3). In this story, it is very clearly singular. This is God's Angel.

This change from "LORD" to "God" is interesting, but the truly curious thing about the verse is the rest of the language. First, the Angel speaks in a strange manner: "Fear not, for God has heard the voice of the boy [Ishmael] where he is" (Gen 21:17). This is similar to what we saw earlier where Yahweh had heard Hagar's affliction. Is the Angel speaking on behalf of God? We would answer, "Yes." And yet, the next thing he says is, "Up! Lift up the boy, and hold him fast with your hand, for I will make him into a great nation" (18). The Angel will make him into a great nation? Isn't this the kind of thing that God does in Genesis? Next it says, "And God opened her eyes..." (19). Did God do it or did the Angel do it? It says that God did, but does this really answer our question?

We are raising these thoughts based on what we have already learned about the Angel from the first story. Now we want to add to the strangeness by pointing out how the Angel is introduced here. It says, "And God heard the voice of the boy, and the Angel of God called to Hagar from heaven and said..." (Gen 21:17). It seems as if there is a distinction being made here between "God" and "the Angel of God." In fact, there is. But because there is, and because of the other questions we have just raised, this has caused not a few people to stumble over their interpretation of the Angel here as well. Why? Because we Christians believe in only one God. But if God and the Angel of God are two distinct beings, then this must prove that the Angel is not God. Right? He is simply an angel "from" God. Not entirely.

While rooted in good intentions (and to some degree even good theology), this idea fails to come to terms with the language of the OT and how it expresses a very real theology of the Trinity. Yes, Christians worship one God and believe that there is only one uncreated all-powerful being. But as we have already pointed out, Christians are Trinitarians, not Unitarians.

This verse bears a striking resemblance to a verse that appears just two chapters earlier in Genesis 19. "Then the LORD rained on Sodom and Gomorrah sulfur and fire from the LORD out of heaven" (Gen 19:24).

Genesis 21:17	Genesis 19:24
"And God heard the voice of the boy [Ishmael], and the Angel of God called to Hagar from heaven..."	"Then the LORD rained on Sodom and Gomorrah sulfur and fire from the LORD out of heaven."

Genesis 19:24 was a common text used by early Christians to show the distinction between the Father and the Son. In fact, it was one of the most common, being used by almost every major Church Father of the early church (see the Appendix at the end of the book). For example, Justin Martyr—one of the earliest of the Fathers—wrote in his defense of Christianity to the Jew Trypho:

> Therefore neither Abraham, nor Isaac, nor Jacob, nor any other man, saw the Father and ineffable Lord of all, and also of Christ, but [saw] Him who was according to His will His Son, being God, and the Angel because He ministered to His will; whom also it pleased Him to be born man by the Virgin; who also was fire when He conversed with Moses from the bush. Since, unless we thus comprehend the Scriptures, it must follow that the Father and Lord of all had not been in heaven when what Moses wrote took place: *"And the Lord rained upon Sodom fire and brimstone from the Lord out of heaven."*
>
> (Justin, *Dialogue with Trypho* 127)

Earlier he had said,

> I shall attempt to persuade you, since you have understood the Scriptures, [of the truth] of what I say, that there is, and that there is said to be, another God and Lord subject to the Maker of all things; who is also called an Angel, because He announces to men whatsoever the Maker of all things—above whom there is no other God—wishes to announce to them ... If I could not have proved to you from the Scriptures that one of those three [men who met Abram at the Oaks of Mamre in Gen 18] is God, and is called Angel, because, as I already said, He brings messages to those to whom God the Maker of all things wishes [messages to be brought].
>
> (*Dialogue 56*)

The importance of this needs to be apprehended. Justin is using a verse where he sees two Yahwehs, saying that one of them is the Second Person of the Trinity. This is not a NT proof-text but goes back to the very first book of the Bible, which is what you would expect when trying to prove the deity of Christ to a Jew. It also follows perfectly with what we saw the passage do as it shortened "The Angel of the LORD" to simply "The LORD."

If the Fathers are correct, then the author of Genesis knew a Second Yahweh. He knew different Persons to be the LORD. Moses was a Monotheist, but not a Unitarian. Neither were the Patriarchs. For as Vos said, the Angel is the most important form of revelation in their days. They interact with the Angel on a regular basis. But what could their stories add that will help us understand this figure of the Angel of the LORD even better?

2

THE ANGEL AS "THE WORD"

The Angel and Abraham

In the Beginning...

I N THE BEGINNING WAS THE WORD, and the Word was with God, and the Word was God" (John 1:1). This famous opening line of the Gospel of John is a treasure to Christians, a bane to heretics, and a mess when it comes to understanding its roots. Why would John begin his Gospel in such a strange way? Where did he get this idea that Jesus is "the Word"? Was he combating some kind of early form of Gnosticism that denied the real humanity of Jesus? Was he using Greek philosophy to counter it? These are a couple of the answers you will sometimes hear when discussing this verse.

John was a Jew. His Gospel is about the Lord Jesus Christ who was also a Jew. While it is true that later on, the Gnostics perverted certain essential teachings about Jesus, we can't forget the Jewishness of the Gospel. It makes little sense that John would use pagan philosophy to begin his Gospel of a Jewish carpenter. But it makes a lot of sense if he is getting this idea from his own Scripture—our Old Testament, especially if he wants to prove how something from the OT finds its NT expression in Jesus Christ. We want to unfold the origin of this idea that Jesus is "The Word" as we look at the Angel of the LORD in the life of Abraham. (Later, we will return to it in a chapter on the prophets, where we will see how truly prevalent it is in the Scripture.)

Abraham and the Angel: Genesis 22

The second place "the Angel of the LORD" is explicitly mentioned by name in Scripture is in the story of Abraham. It is the famous account of Abraham about to sacrifice his son Isaac. "Angel of the LORD" appears twice in this story. The saga begins by telling us that "God" tested Abraham saying, "Abraham!" And Abraham said, "Here I am" (Gen 22:1).

"God" (Elohim) tells Abraham to take his only son Isaac, whom he loves, and sacrifice him as a burnt offering on a special mountain in the land of Moriah (Gen 22:2). Abraham sets out, and after three days (4), when they come to the place God told him, he builds an altar and lays Isaac on top to be sacrificed (9-10). Suddenly, "The Angel of the LORD called to him from heaven and said, 'Abraham, Abraham!' And he said, 'Here I am" (11). It is worth noting here that this language parallels the first verse in the story:

Genesis 22:1	Genesis 22:11
"After these things *God* tested Abraham and said to him, 'Abraham!' And he said, 'Here I am.'"	"*The Angel of the LORD* called to him from heaven and said, 'Abraham, Abraham!' And he said, 'Here I am.'"

In other words, this is a verbal clue that "the Angel of the LORD" is the "God" who told him to go in the first place.

From here, the language becomes rather strange. The Angel said, "Do not lay your hand on the boy or do anything to him, for now I know that you fear God, seeing you have not withheld your son, your only son, from me" (11). Who is "God" here? Is it the Angel? Is it someone else? We've raised these kinds of questions in the previous chapter. Abraham believed he was going to offer the boy as a sacrifice *to God*; and yet we discover that the Angel says the boy has not been withheld from *him*. In other words, the Angel is the God to whom Abraham was offering Isaac.

At just that moment, when the Angel spoke, Abraham spotted a ram caught in a thicket (13). After offering the ram instead of his son, Abraham called the place *Yahweh-Yir´eh* (sometimes you will see *Jehovah-Jireh*). This is often translated as "The LORD will Provide" (14). "Provide" comes from a word meaning "to see" (*ra´ah*). While not the same word Hagar uses, it isn't difficult to see the relationship to her calling the Angel, "The God who Sees." In fact, later translations (both

Jewish and Christian) of the earlier phrase, "land of Moriah," translate it as "the land of seeing from / the mountain of vision." So when Abraham later calls it "Jehovah-Jireh," there was a word play happening.

But this is surely more than a word play. It is a foreshadowing of coming divine grace, for it is upon this very mountain that Solomon built the temple (2Ch 3:1). And this is the same place upon which the Lord Jesus would be offered up as a sacrifice. Even the "three days" it took to get to the mountain (Gen 22:1) looks ahead to the three days of Jesus in the tomb. Truly, God's "seeing" from this mountain casts a gaze beyond that which we could see, to places and times that only he could. Yet, the story gives us a glimpse of such grace even back in the days of Abraham.

After this, "the Angel of the LORD called to Abraham a second time from heaven and said, 'By myself I have sworn, declares the LORD, because you have done this and have not withheld your son, your only son, I will surely bless you, and I will surely multiply your offspring as the stars of heaven and as the sand that is on the seashore. And your offspring shall possess the gate of his enemies, and in your offspring shall all the nations of the earth be blessed, because you have obeyed my voice" (15-18).

In the story, the Angel is certainly speaking for the LORD (whom we would call the Father). That is what angels do after all; they speak for others. But it could also be read that he is speaking for himself. Such is the strange way we will discover that the Angel often talks. Vos summarizes the problem by calling it, "The peculiarity ... that, on the one hand, the Angel distinguishes himself from Jehovah, speaking of Him in the third person, and that, on the other hand, in the same utterance he speaks of God in the first person."[37] We brought this up in the *Introduction* and in the first chapter because it is important to understand.

Something we want to point out now is that when we come to the NT, this is very similar to the strange way that Jesus often speaks about himself, especially in the Gospel of John. Here he tells them over and over that he is distinct from the Father (cf. John 5:17; 6:32, 8:16; etc.). Yet he also says that to see him is to see the Father (John 14:9) and that he and the Father are One (John 10:30). That kind of language is not new. It comes virtually every time the Angel of the LORD shows up.

Again, Christians have seen this person in the Abraham and Isaac

---

[37] Vos, *Biblical Theology*, 72.

story as God. One of the more interesting we found comes from Calvin's protégé Theodore Beza who wrote a play about this story. At one point he has the following dialogue:

<table>
<tr><td></td><td>Angel</td></tr>
</table>

"Abraham, Abraham."

                                                    Abraham

"My God here I am."

                                                    Angel

Into the sheath put up your knife,
And see you do not take his life,
Nor hurt the child in any way.
For now I see before my eyes,
What love you bear to the Lord,
And honor unto him afford,
In that you do so willingly
Your son thus offer even to die.

                                                    Abraham

O God.

                                                    Isaac

O God.

                                                    Angel

O Abraham

                                                    Abraham

Lord Here I am.

                                                    Angel

Thus says the Lord, I promise you
By my eternal majesty
And by my Godhead : Since you
Have showed yourself so willing now,
To obey me, as to forebear
Your only Isaac's life : I swear,
That mawgre [displeasure] Satan to his face,
I will bless you and all your race.[38]

Beza clearly sees the Angel as God here. It is part of our great inherited tradition. Genesis 22 is the only time that the specific terminology is used that Abraham spoke with "the Angel of the LORD." However, it would be a huge mistake to think that this was the only time it happened.

---

[38] Theodore Beza, *A Tragedie of Abrahams Sacrifice*, trans. Arthur Golding (Toronto: University of Toronto Library, 1906), 59-61. [Spelling and language modernized].

Abraham and the LORD: Genesis 11-19

God "Appearing" in Genesis 11 and 17

A way to get at this is through the language of "appearance." Angels are often "seen" in the Bible. Certainly, Hagar and Abraham saw the Angel. It just so happens that Abraham has seen the LORD on many occasions prior to this. For example, Genesis 17 begins, "The LORD appeared to Abram and said to him, 'I am God Almighty [El Shaddai]; walk before me, and be blameless'" (Gen 17:1). El-Shaddai introduces a new word for God to our study. It has the same root (El) as "the God who sees" from Hagar's declaration. El Shaddai probably means "God of the mountain."[39] God comes on many mountains in the OT: Ararat, Sinai, Moriah, and in Jesus Christ—Zion or Calvary. These names are introducing different aspects of who God is.

The more important feature of this verse for now is that, apparently, Abram saw God. He saw Yahweh. He saw El Shaddai. Even though, "No one has ever seen God" (John 1:18), for no one may see God and live (Ex 33:20; cf. Jdg 6:22; 13:33; Isa 6:5).[40]

This was not the first time the LORD had appeared to this man.

---

[39] A good discussion is Nahum M. Sarna, *Exodus*, The JPS Torah Commentary (Philadelphia: Jewish Publication Society, 1991), 269. Also E. A. Knauf, "Shadday," ed. Karel van der Toorn, Bob Becking, and Pieter W. van der Horst, Dictionary of Deities and Demons in the Bible (Leiden; Boston; Köln; Grand Rapids, MI; Cambridge: Brill; Eerdmans, 1999), 749-50.

[40] One of the burdens of this book is to demonstrate that what John repeatedly says is true of Jesus Christ in the flesh in the NT, is true only of the Angel in the OT. We are not suggesting that the Son is the only Person of the Godhead to appear in the OT. The Spirit appears very often, and we even have appearance of the Father. A key verse summarizing this is, "No one has ever seen God; the only God who is at the Father's side, he has made him known" (John 1:18). This verse has two "Gods" in it—one is the Father, the other is the Son. There is a textual variant here. On the reading that the second "God" (Theos) is original see Roger L. Omanson and Bruce Manning Metzger, *A Textual Guide to the Greek New Testament: An Adaptation of Bruce M. Metzger's Textual Commentary for the Needs of Translators* (Stuttgart: Deutsche Bibelgesellschaft, 2006), 165.

An opposite approach to ours is taken by Andrew S. Malone, "The Invisibility of God: A Survey of a Misunderstood Phenomenon," *EQ* 79.4 (2007): 311-329. Malone starts with the assumption that there appears to be contradictory evidence in the OT and NT as to whether God can be seen. He proposes a different understanding of "invisibility" and rejects any purposeful identification of the Angel as the Second Person. For a critique of Malone's views, see Appendix III.

The first appearance is explained by Stephen in the book of Acts, "Brothers and fathers, hear me. The God of glory appeared to our father Abraham when he was in Mesopotamia, before he lived in Haran, and said to him, 'Go out from your land and from your kindred and go into the land that I will show you'" (Acts 7:2-3). "Glory" is a word often associated with the appearing of God, and also Jesus (cf. John 1:14; 12:41).

We might be tempted to think that this refers to Genesis 12:1, "Now the LORD said to Abram, 'Go from your country and your kindred and your father's house to the land that I will show you.'" But Abram is in Haran in this verse. Stephen is thinking of the situation just a couple of verses earlier. "Terah took Abram his son and Lot the son of Haran, his grandson, and Sarai his daughter-in-law, his son Abram's wife, and they went forth together from Ur of the Chaldeans to go into the land of Canaan, but when they came to Haran, they settled there" (Gen 11:31).

Again, what is important for our purposes is that Stephen calls this an "appearance." The word he uses is *horao*. It means "to see; see; become visible; appear; look at." This is similar to the Hebrew word *ra'ah*, which means "to see." Simply put, this is the language of eyes.

God "Appearing" as the Word in Genesis 15

Abram sees God again in Genesis 15:1. The language is truly remarkable. "After these things the Word of the LORD came to Abram in a vision: 'Fear not, Abram, I am your shield; your reward shall be very great.'" This is strange because "words" do not come in "visions." Again, we Christians are familiar with Jesus as the Word of God, but this is due almost entirely to John's Gospel. "In the beginning was the Word (*logos*), and the Word was with God, and the Word was God. He was in the beginning with God ... And the Word became flesh and dwelt among us, and we have seen his glory, glory as of the only Son from the Father" (John 1:1-2, 14). Again, notice how the "glory" is seen, this time in the person of Jesus Christ.

But why do we think of the Word as being a NT-only phenomenon? Perhaps you don't, but too many people do. Maybe we do not stop to think that if John was just making this up (even if he heard it from God himself) that it would have little to no apologetic value. Perhaps we have come to rely upon the NT to the exclusion of the OT. Maybe we just don't know the OT well enough to know any better. Whatever the case, it is the Holy Scripture that our Faith is rooted in, and for someone like John, this meant what we call the Old Testament.

The fact of the matter is, Genesis 15:1 is a foundational verse in the OT for John's subsequent theology of the *logos*. Scholars have recently shown that John is not combating Gnosticism in his Prologue so much as he is talking to Jews who knew their OT.[41] We should also point out that this becomes the stock language of prophetic visions and authority throughout the OT.[42]

Let's look a little more closely at this. First, the phrase "word of the LORD"[43] has "word" as the subject, not "LORD." In its most basic form, eliminating the prepositional phrase, you get "the word came to Abram." Second, notice that it is "word" *singular*, not "words" plural. Third, the "word" actually begins to speak.

As we look at the rest of the passage in more detail, we see some wonderful sights. In response to the Word appearing, Abram replies, "O Lord GOD (Adonai Yahweh) ..." (Gen 21:2). So the Word comes, and Abram calls it "Lord GOD." After a short discussion, it says, "And he brought him outside and said, 'Look toward heaven, and number the stars ... so shall your offspring be'" (5). Who is the "he" here? He is

---

[41] Cf. Daniel Boyarin, "The Gospel of the Memra: Jewish Binitarianism and the Prologue to John," *Harvard Theological Review* 94:3 (2001): 243-84; John L. Ronning, "The Targum of Isaiah and the Johannine Literature," *Westminster Theological Journal* 69:2 (2007): 247-78; John Ronning, *The Jewish Targums and John's Logos Theology* (Grand Rapids, MI: Baker Academic, 2010). We should point out that part of Boyarin's argument is that Gnosticism actually comes, at least in part, from Jewish paganism like the Kabballah, rather than from Greek philosophy, so in a roundabout way, it ends up combating Gnosticism later on.

[42] "The word of the LORD that came" or "The word of the LORD came to": Abram (Gen 15:1); Samuel (1Sa 15:10); Nathan (2Sa 7:4); Gad (2Sa 24:11); *David* (1Ch 22:8); Solomon (1Kg 6:11); *Jehu* (1Kg 16:1); *Shemaiah* (2Ch 11:2); *Elijah* (1Kg 17:1); *Isaiah* (Isa 38:4; 2Kg 20:4); *Jeremiah* (Jer 1:11); *Ezekiel* (Ezek 1:3); *Hosea* (Hos 1:1); *Joel* (Joel 1:1); *Jonah* (Jonah 1:1); *Micah* (Mic 1:1); *Zephaniah* (Zeph 1:1); *Haggai* (Hag 1:1); *Zechariah* (Zech 1:1); *Malachi* (Mal 1:1). Amos (Amos 1:1); Obadiah (Oba 1:1); Nahum (Nah 1:1); Habakkuk "saw" an oracle of the LORD in a vision (Hab 1:1). Note: *italics* = "word" = *logos* in LXX, but not in plural form (i.e. "words").

[43] The Hebrew is a construct relationship, meaning that it is considered a single unit that shows possession, like our word "of." The same is true of "The Angel of the LORD."

the Word—the Lord GOD. The Word appears in such a way that he can bring Abraham outside. This "it" is therefore a "him."

Importantly for the Christian Faith, Abram "believed the LORD, and he counted it to him as righteousness" (Gen 15:6). This verse, cited several times in the NT, shows the object of Abram's faith. In the verse, the object of that faith is "the LORD." But we have seen how "LORD" can sometimes be a shortened form of "the Angel of the LORD." As it is a visible person called the Word who is bringing Abram outside and talking to him face to face, we suggest that this is the Angel even though it is calling him the LORD (this by no means implies that we think only the Second Person is the LORD in the OT, only that because this is a visible manifestation of a person talking to Abram, that it fits the Angel motif and should be considered the Angel here). This is "the LORD who brought you out from Ur of the Chaldeans to give you this land to possess" (7). Abram's faith was not in some monad "god," some "unmoved mover," not in some brute essence, but in the Second Person of the Holy Trinity. It is explicit in the text, and this is the very point the NT makes in citing the verse as a reason to believe in *Christ Jesus*. The Apostle's point is not merely that Abram believed in God and therefore you should too. It is that Abraham believed in Jesus, and you should too.

As if this weren't enough, a covenant ceremony is enacted so that the LORD might swear by nothing greater than himself. He tells Abram to "bring me a heifer three years old" as well as other animals (9). Where is he supposed to bring them, if the LORD isn't actually physically present? Then, when this great Patriarch had brought them, he cut them in half and laid each half over against the other (10), and when the sun had gone down and Abram was in a deep sleep (12), the LORD walked between the pieces (17). True, it says "a smoking fire pot and a flaming torch passed between these pieces," but this is not a Disney cartoon with walking, singing spoons and cups.

It uses this language symbolically (the Triune God was there—especially Son and Spirit who were the guarantors of the covenant for the Father). It uses it because there was a "dreadful and great darkness" (12). And, the picture foreshadows the mighty Exodus event to come where God would come "hidden" in fire and judgment upon Egypt after 400 years of captivity (13-14; cf. Ex 14:18-22). In other words, Abram was not allowed to see the person holding the pot and torch, for this was a very sacred moment. But someone was in fact carrying them. This same person then covenants with Abram, swearing to him that he will fulfill his promises, lest the same fate that befell those animals happen to him. We can now see the beginnings of John's *logos* theology. The Word appeared to Abram in a vision!

God "Appearing" in Genesis 18-19

One more story in the life of Abraham is worth examining. It is the prelude to our Genesis 19:24 two-Yahwehs verse. In fact, it explains this verse contextually. The story begins with "the LORD" "appearing" again to Abraham (Gen 18:1). How did he appear this time? We read that Abraham was camping near the oaks of Mamre one day, and as he sat at the door of his tent (vs.1), he lifted up his eyes, "And behold, three men (*'ish*) were standing in front of him" (2). As the story unfolds, two of these men are called "angels" (19:1, 15). Who could the other one be?

Abraham immediately recognizes that these are no ordinary visitors, either because they simply appeared out of nowhere and/or because their appearance was instantly recognizable to him.[44] Whatever the case, before they said a word he immediately ran and bowed himself to the earth (2). He addresses one of them as "Lord" (small caps = *Adonai*), a title which in this case refers to Abraham's being a servant. Suddenly, he begs for a blessing (3), and then shows them hospitality by bringing water to wash their feet (4). Note: These men have feet and they can be washed!

While they are washing, Abraham calls for a huge banquet to be prepared immediately (5-7). This is not a request. His wife and servants must do it ... pronto. Once prepared, Abraham stands by them under the tree while they eat (8). This is no apparition. These are not ghosts or phantoms. He is not merely seeing a vision. This is corporeal, physical.

After dinner, "They said to him, 'Where is Sarah your wife?'" (9). The verse reads like they are all speaking. But suddenly, "The LORD said, 'I will surely return to you about this time next year, and Sarah your wife shall have a son'" (10). A change in speakers from many to One takes place. One of the three starts talking himself. He is called "the

---

[44] On their possible fascinating appearance, see the corresponding section "Angels vs. Men" in the chapter dealing with questions of systematic theology.

LORD" (Yahweh). Importantly, this is the same promise that "God" had made in the previous chapter.

In the previous chapter where the LORD also "appears" to him, it says, "God (*elohim*) said to Abraham, 'As for Sarai your wife, you shall not call her name Sarai, but Sarah shall be her name. I will bless her, and moreover, I will give you a son by her'" (Gen 17:15-16). Who is speaking there? Again, the text calls him "Yahweh," as it said, "The LORD appeared to Abram and said to him, 'I am God Almighty (El Shaddai); walk before me, and be blameless'" (17:1).

As readers of chapter 18, we are expected to know that this is exactly what happened, since it was less than one chapter earlier that this promise was made. Now, the promise comes again, this time from a man who is talking to Abraham and is overheard by Sarah, for she "was listening at the tent door behind him" (Gen 18:10) and suddenly began to laugh out loud (12). This was no voice in Abraham's head; Sarah heard it too. In fact, "The LORD" starts speaking to both of them (13), and Sarah becomes afraid because she was denying that she laughed when she was questioned by God himself!

At this point, the story changes scenes. "The men set out from there, and they looked down toward Sodom. And Abraham went with them to set them on their way" (16). Two of them go on ahead into the wicked city where they are now called "angels" (Gen 19:1). But Yahweh stays behind (18:22), and a drawn-out conversation with Abraham about the fate of those towns by the Dead Sea ensues. "The LORD said, 'Shall I hide from Abraham what I'm about to do … Because the outcry against Sodom and Gomorrah is great and their sin is very grave, I will go down to see whether they have done altogether according to the outcry that has come to me. And if not, I will know'" (21).

Abraham and the LORD then enter into a famous plea-bargain debate, where he first asks the LORD if he will destroy the city if there are fifty righteous people in it (23-24). Then the number goes to forty-five (28), then forty (29), and so on down to ten (32). When the conversation is over, "The LORD went his way" (33), following after the other two sometime later. Something to take note of here is the language of *going down to see*. This is the same language we find in the Tower of Babel story. "And the LORD came down to see the city and the tower, which the children of man had built" (Gen 11:5). Is this a clue that we have the same kind of physical coming by the same Person in both stories?

The other thing of interest is to follow the trail of the LORD after he went his way. Let's see how this plays out in the rest of the story. As the horrible night in the city is winding down and the unspeakable things that were attempted by the men of Sodom come to a crashing halt, the two angels tell Lot, "We are about to destroy this place, because the outcry against its people has become great before the LORD, and the LORD has sent us to destroy it" (Gen 19:13). Obviously, they are emissaries of Yahweh and "angels" is a good term for them. They are not human.

As they are fleeing the city, Lot asks if he may go to a place less far away. Suddenly, the "they" turns into a "he" again (see 18:9-10). "He said to him, 'Behold, I grant you this favor'" (21). It appears that Yahweh has "caught up" with them. This is itself incredible. Abraham was in Mamre. The traditional location of Mamre is a monastery that still houses what is thought to be the remnant of a 5,000-year-old oak tree. From this point to the "Sodom cave" (which is probably not far from the location of Sodom and Gomorrah at the southwestern side of the Dead Sea) on Google Earth, it is 35.37 miles as the crow flies, through mountainous and hot desert terrain. Both he and the other two angels appear to have gotten to Sodom almost instantaneously.

At any rate, when they are finally far enough away, the destruction comes. It is explained to us in that very strange verse where Jews and Christians alike have seen two Yahwehs, "Then the LORD rained on Sodom and Gomorrah sulfur and fire from the LORD out of heaven" (Gen 19:24). It concludes, "And he overthrew those cities" (25). Who is the "he" here? Clearly, it is the LORD.

These Abraham stories add to our view of the Angel. Not only is he called simply "the LORD," but he is also called the Word. The Glory is associated with him. Visible manifestations that are corporeal in terms of eating and washing come into play with a man who is clearly more than a mere human being. We meet this man again later in Genesis, where he shows up in a very well-known passage with Abraham's son, Jacob.

3

THE ANGEL AS "MAN"

The Angel and Jacob

Let's Get Ready to Rumble

PHYSICALITY IS SOMETHING WE PRIZE AS HUMANS. With it, we experience all the pleasures God gave us to enjoy in his material creation. We know that beasts share this with us, but it is not something we normally associate with angels. After all, angels are spirits, so how could they also be physical? It is also not something we really want to associate with Christ in the OT. In fact, the idea that he could be there physically—all the more as a "man"—feels extremely dangerous. The incarnation of Jesus in the womb of the virgin Mary is the very pillar of our Faith, the unique event of its kind in history. To even imply something like it would be heresy.

Indeed, there is nothing like the incarnation in all of history. And in the OT, Jesus is not a human being. Nevertheless, he is called in our Bibles a "man," but this is not akin to being a hu-*man*. This needs to be understood properly. It is a vital piece to being able to recognize the Angel of the LORD when he isn't called as such by the Holy text. Michael Barrett is helpful here:

> Before considering some of the great issues taught by the Christophanies, we must emphasize that these several appearances of the Son

of God were pre-incarnate. Incarnation means "in flesh" and refers to the eternal Son of God's being conceived by the virgin through the operation of the Holy Spirit and being born in the barn at Bethlehem. Pre-incarnate, then, designates the time before the eternal Son took to Himself human flesh. Christophanies, therefore, were occasions when the Second Person of the Holy Trinity appeared as a man but was not a man. He took the form of man but not the nature of man.[45]

We would simply say that because angels are called "men," that Jesus took the form of an angel-man, whatever that looked like we have no idea. But to assume that it necessarily means he looked fully human is pure speculation, much less that he was a human, which is simply unacceptable. Indeed, it is heretical.

Jacob and the Angel of Bethel: Genesis 31

The exact phrase "the Angel of the LORD" appears in Genesis only with Hagar and Abraham. However, the phrase "the Angel of God" occurs explicitly one more time (after Hagar)—in a story with Jacob in Genesis 31. We read that Jacob is fleeing his uncle Laban who no longer regards him with favor (Gen 31:1-2). Vs. 3 says,

> *Yahweh* said to Jacob, "*Return to the land of your fathers* ... and I will be with you."

But then in vv. 11-13, Jacob reports to his wives,

> *The angel of God said* to me in the dream, "Jacob," and I said, "Here I am!" And he said ... "I am the God of Bethel, where you anointed a pillar and made a vow to me. Now arise, go out from this land and *return to the land of your kindred.*"

Thus, he is given the identical message to return home to the Promised Land by "God" and by "the Angel." The language implies that

---

[45] Michael P. V. Barrett, *Beginning at Moses: A Guide to Finding Christ in the Old Testament* (Greenville, SC: Ambassador International, 2010), Apple Books.

Yahweh who spoke to him in vs. 3 becomes the Angel of God in vs. 11—
the Angel who called to him in a dream, "'Jacob,' and I said, 'Here I
am!'" (This is the same language we saw with Abraham in Genesis 22:
"Here I am."). A curious translation in the Septuagint (LXX)[46] adds support to this. Vs. 13 reads, "I am the God that appeared to you in the
place of God." This translation is attested at least as early as Philo (25
BC – 50 AD) in a section where he identifies this first "God" as the "angel," as the "angel-word," and "his image," yet without changing God's
own "real nature."[47]

The Angel then says, "I am the God of Bethel, where you anointed
a pillar and made a vow to me."[48] Calling himself "God," the Angel is
referring back to Genesis 28:10-22 and the famous "Jacob's Ladder"
story. Interestingly, in Genesis 28, the "Angel" is never mentioned in so
many words. Instead we read,

> And behold, the LORD stood above [it or him] and said, "I am the
> LORD, the God of Abraham your father and the God of Isaac. The
> land on which you lie I will give to you and to your offspring …
> Behold, I am with you and will keep you wherever you go, and will
> bring you back to this land. For I will not leave you until I have done
> what I have promised you." Then Jacob awoke from his sleep and
> said, "Surely the Lord is in this place, and I did not know it." And
> he was afraid and said, "How awesome is this place! This is none
> other than the house of God, and this is the gate of heaven." So early
> in the morning Jacob took the stone that he had put under his head
> and set it up for a pillar and poured oil on the top of it. He called
> the name of that place "Bethel."
>
> (Genesis 28:13,15-19)

---

[46] We have not talked much about the LXX yet. This is the Greek translation of
the OT. It was done about 200 years before Christ by Jews living in Egypt. The
LXX became the most often quoted Bible by NT authors and the Church Fathers
used it regularly.

[47] Philo, *On Dreams* 1.41.238-39 in Charles Duke Yonge with Philo of Alexandria,
The Works of Philo: Complete and Unabridged (Peabody, MA: Hendrickson, 1995),
386. Philo, as a good Jew, makes it plain in other places that even though there is
what he calls a "second God" who appears in some passages, there is only One
God (on this see *Dreams* 1.228-230).

[48] "Angel of God" is shortened simply to "God." So "the Angel of the LORD" can
become just "LORD;" so also "the Angel of God" can become just "God."

Much later, in Genesis 35, Jacob is eventually told to return and live in Bethel,

> God said to Jacob, "Arise, go up to Bethel and dwell there. Make an altar there to the God who appeared to you when you fled from your brother Esau." So Jacob said to his household and to all who were with him … "Let us arise and go up to Bethel, so that I may make there an altar to the God who answers me in the day of my distress and has been with me wherever I have gone." … God appeared to Jacob again, when he came from Paddan-aram, and blessed him.
>
> (Genesis 35:1-3, 9)

Notice again the verbal distinction: God says to Jacob, "Make an altar there to the God who appeared to you." In other words, we are meant to understand each of these "appearances" at Bethel as the Angel of the LORD who appeared, who spoke, and who guided and directed Jacob's life. And this Angel who appeared was God appearing. God, when he appears, appears in the Person of His Angel, who speaks and acts as God Himself. When we meet him, it's as if we are ushered into the very house of God.

He had appeared to Jacob at the beginning of his journey, before Jacob really knew who God was, a time when Jacob was a young liar and cheat and deceiver, when he was running from Esau and running from the consequences of his own deceptions. Over the course of Jacob's life, he had brought Jacob through many trials and hardships and lessons, had shaped and transformed and blessed his life. And he brings Jacob back as a changed man to worship again at the place where God had first sought Jacob out and made himself known. As Jacob says, he was "the God who answers me in the day of my distress and has been with me wherever I have gone."[49] In many ways, this story presents us

---

[49] In fact, this same Angel probably had a hand even further back in Jacob's history. Jacob may have first heard of this Angel from his father Isaac, who heard from his grandfather Abraham. When Abraham had sent his servant to find a wife for Isaac, Abraham had told him, "The LORD, the God of heaven…will send his angel before you, and you shall take a wife for my son from there" (Gen 24:7; cf. 40, 42). It is difficult from Abraham's language to figure out if this is "an" angel or "the" Angel. But given the role "the" Angel often plays, being "sent" by the Father to guard and guide his people, to "prosper" their way (see Gen 24:40, 42), it is reasonable to see this as the divine Angel who is also God. He went before

with the *Gospel* in the Old Testament—God coming to an unworthy people, claiming them as his own, intervening in their lives, purposing to be their God, to give them a home and a future and a purpose to one day bless the whole earth.

So what we have seen is that, when Yahweh appears to his people and works to direct their lives, he does so through the divine Angel of his presence. When God appeared to Jacob repeatedly at Bethel, it was the Angel of God appearing and speaking to Jacob, and that Angel was himself Yahweh.[50]

Jacob Wrestles the Man: Genesis 32

There is another passage where Jacob has a mysterious divine encounter. In Genesis 32, Jacob has returned to the Promised Land and is about to face his brother Esau again after many years, with major anxieties about the meeting. As at Bethel, when he had left the Promised Land and God had given him a vision of angels ascending and descending on the stairway, on returning, Jacob is met with another vision of angels - "Jacob went on his way, and the angels of God met him. And when Jacob saw them he said, 'This is God's camp!'" (Gen 32:1–2).[51] That night, Jacob finds himself in the camp alone. Suddenly, a "man"

Isaac, found his wife Rebekah, and this is how he proved himself to be Isaac's God. Thus, where Abraham says the Angel will prosper his son; the servant says it is Yahweh (cf. 41-43). Yahweh sent his Angel, something he will do later in the days of Moses (Ex 23:20). This in turn will become the very language that Jesus will use in the NT of being "sent" by his Father (John 5:23, etc.).

[50] In John 1:51, Jesus references Jacob's encounter at Bethel. Jesus speaks to Nathanael and claims to have known him before they even met. Nathanael responds with amazement and worship. And Jesus says, "Because I said to you, 'I saw you under the fig tree,' do you believe? You will see greater things than these." Then he said to him, "Truly, truly, I say to you, you will see heaven opened, and the angels of God ascending and descending on the Son of Man" (John 1:50–51). Jesus is saying—like God revealed himself to Jacob at Bethel, I've come down to be revealed again. I am the true gate of heaven and true "house of God" (see John 2:21). Jesus is the greater ladder, the greater mountain (ziggurats, which is what Jacob seems to have seen, were man-made mountain-temples), the greater Rock, the greater Bethel, the greater Anointed.

[51] Like with Elisha and his servant in 2 Kings 6, God graciously meets with Jacob and gives him a vision of his presence and protection - that there is another camp, that he is not alone, that God will protect him.

appears before him:

> And a man wrestled with him until the breaking of the day. When the man saw that he did not prevail against Jacob, he touched his hip socket, and Jacob's hip was put out of joint as he wrestled with him. Then he said, "Let me go, for the day has broken." But Jacob said, "I will not let you go unless you bless me." And he said to him, "What is your name?" And he said, "Jacob." Then he said, "Your name shall no longer be called Jacob, but Israel, for you have striven with God and with men, and have prevailed." Then Jacob asked him, "Please tell me your name." But he said, "Why is it that you ask my name?" And there he blessed him. So Jacob called the name of the place Peniel, saying, "For I have seen God face to face, and yet my life has been delivered." The sun rose upon him as he passed Penuel, limping because of his hip.
>
> (Genesis 32:24–31)

The scene quickly becomes the first WrestleMania in history. The match begins at midnight. A mysterious man, but unmasked, enters the ring. Jacob gets the early upper hand. That's when "the man" pulls a Rick Flair and cheats; "He touched his hip socket, and Jacob's hip was put out of joint as he wrestled with him" (25). Hey, there are no rules in a cage match.

Nevertheless, Hulk Hogan is not to be denied. Jacob still has the man in a headlock. The man demands, "Let me go, for the day has broken" (26).[52] This is where things start to get very interesting. Jacob said, "I will not let you go unless you bless me." What a strange thing to say *… unless you know who it is you are wrestling.* Having this man bless him is exactly what his grandfather Abraham asked from this same man many years earlier (Gen 18:3). This is no ordinary man. Rick Flair and the Hulk don't hold a candle to this man.

The man asks him his name and he says, "Jacob" (Gen 32:27). Then he said, "Your name shall no longer be called Jacob, but Israel, for you have striven with God (*elohim*) and with men (*'ish*), and have prevailed" (28). Jacob had been wrestling with God and man? Furthermore, this man claims to know the story of Jacob's life and to have authority to give him a new name (see Genesis 17:5), a name ("Israel"), which at least

---

[52] Apparently, the man wants to leave because he does not want to be fully seen. If you were an Israelite later, you would remember God's words to Moses, "You cannot see my face and live" (Exodus 33:20).

one ancient tradition says means "The One Who Sees God."[53]

Jacob returns the favor. There were no introductions in this wrestling match, no "Let's get ready to rumbleeeeeee." "Please tell me your name" (Gen 32:29). But he said, "Why is it that you ask my name?" (29). "And there he blessed him. So Jacob called the name of the place Peniel, saying, 'For I have seen God face to face, and yet my life has been delivered'" (30). There is a lot here that we will return to in subsequent chapters, including this idea of "face to face" and the significance of his asking about the name.

Who is this "man"? We saw previously in Genesis 18 that three "men" (´ish) came to visit Abraham. Later in that story, two of them are called "angels," and it is clear from what they do that these are not ordinary human messengers. They are supernatural beings. The third supernatural being with them was simply called "Yahweh" even though he was also called a "man" (´ish).

Let's take a moment to consider this Hebrew word for "man." 'Ish is the term used, as it was with the men who came to Abraham. But 'ish is also a word used to describe Adam in the Garden (Gen 2:23). So the semantic domain (as scholars call it) has the word being able to describe both men and angels.[54] Alternatively, there is another word in Hebrew that describes human beings. It is the well-known word 'adam. This is

---

[53] Jerome H. Neyrey, *The Gospel of John in Cultural and Rhetorical Perspective* (Grand Rapids, MI: Eerdmans, 2009), 94. This tradition, which has its skeptics, originates in Egypt with people like Philo or the Jewish Prayer of Joseph (Fragment A) where Israel means "A man seeing God." The idea is that the Hebrew word *ra'ah* ("to see" found in the Hagar story in Genesis 16:13 and the Abraham story of Genesis 22:14) is part of the root of Israel, which may be a play on the words *'ish* (man), *ra'ah* (to see) and *el* (God), hence, "a man seeing God." See Camilla Hélena von Heijne, *The Messenger of the Lord in Early Jewish Interpretations of Genesis* (New York: De Gruyter, 2010), 66, 82-83, 182, etc. A further curiosity is that the word Jershurun, sometimes used as a synonym for "Jacob" (Isa 44:2) and "Israel" (Deut 33:5) also comes from a root word (shur) meaning "to see." See M. J. Mulder, "Yeshurun," *TDOT*, ed. G. Johannes Botterweck and Helmer Ringgren (Grand Rapids, MI: Eerdmans, 1990), 6:474, n. 16 (472-77).

[54] In at least one place it also describes animals. "Take with you seven pairs of all clean animals, the male (´ish) and his mate, and a pair of the animals that are not clean, the male (´ish) and his mate" (Gen 7:2). In this case, however, it does not seem to be describing the ontology of the animal (i.e. it is an *'ish* creature). Rather, it is describing its function as a mate to a female *'ishshah*. Therefore, the word can describe maleness or a relationship in conjunction with a female counterpart.

a word that *never* describes angels.[55] It only describes human beings, that is their human nature as opposed to merely their form or appearance.[56] M'Causland concludes, "The words 'Adam' and 'ish' are clearly different in meaning; and to use them indiscriminately, as having the same signification, tends obviously to obscure the true import and

---

[55] There are two exceptions we have found to this in the Bible; neither destroys this thesis. Both are in apocalyptic contexts, meaning that the imagery is full of symbolism. Apocalyptic is an ancient Jewish genre of literature that is not to be read like one would read sober history such as Chronicles or Samuel.

The first is Ezekiel 1, an apocalyptic vision of "living creatures" who have the "appearance" of man (*'adam*) (Ezek 1:5). "Appearance" does not mean they "are" *'adam*, only that they appeared like this. Further, these living creatures are symbolic of the cosmos using what scholars call "Astral mythology" (cf. David E. Aune, *Revelation 1–5*, vol. 52A, Word Biblical Commentary [Dallas: Word Incorporated, 1998], 291). The same kind of astral mythology was at play in the way the tribes of Israel encircled tabernacle as they wandered through the desert (A. R. Fausset, "The Revelation of St. John the Divine," in Robert Jamieson, A. R. Fausset, and David Brown, *A Commentary, Critical and Explanatory, on the Old and New Testaments* ([Oak Harbor, WA: Logos Research Systems, Inc., 1997, 1877], Rev. 4:8 and Doug's sermon "A Boot to the Head" on Genesis 49:1-28, http://www.rbcnc.com/Genesis%2049.1-28%20A%20Boot%20to%20the%20Head.pdf). While many commentaries point out this astronomical connection to the living creatures, the point is, the four living creatures are not to be taken literal-physically as if they are actual human beings.

The second is found in Daniel 8 and 10. Here we have Daniel hearing "a man's (*'adam*) voice" (Dan 8:16). While the voice is clearly angelic, it is interesting to note that Jerome tells us, "The Jews assert that this man who directed Gabriel to make Daniel understand the vision was Michael" (Jerome, *Commentary on Daniel* cited in John Joseph Collins and Adela Yarbro Collins, *Daniel: A Commentary on the Book of Daniel*, ed. Frank Moore Cross, Hermeneia—a Critical and Historical Commentary on the Bible [Minneapolis, MN: Fortress Press, 1993], 336). It is Doug's opinion that it is also Michael who is described as an *'adam* in Dan 10:16 and 18. What's interesting about this is that many have seen Michael as a proper name for the Angel of the LORD, the very same person who we believe is prophetically described as one like a "son of man (*enash*)" in Daniel 7:13. In other words, this appears to be the only angelic figure described with the human term *'adam*, not because he has come as an *'adam* yet, but rather the apocalyptic genre seems almost to be cryptically typological or prophetic of his future human coming, the way Daniel 7 is, even while he is still only called "the likeness" of a human being (Dan 10:16), meaning it is still only a metaphor.

[56] James A. Borland, *Christ in the Old Testament: Old Testament Appearances of Christ in Human Form*, 2nd ed., revised and expanded (Fearn, Rossshire: Christian Focus Publications, 1999), 20ff.

significance of the Scripture text."[57]

Thus, angels and man are both *'ish*-men, but only humans are *'adam*-men. This hints that when Jesus comes in the NT, something is very, very different. As we are arguing, the Son of God "appears" in the Old Testament, often as a "man" (*'ish*). But he never *appears* as *'adam*, except in Daniel 8 and 10, which we will deal with at the appropriate time. His *becoming* a human being (*'adam*) is reserved for the incarnation in the New Testament. As Girdlestone explains of this and the Ezekiel parallels, *"Like* an Adam, and yet not an Adam, because not yet incarnate … represented in human form but clothed with Divine attributes—not yet 'a son of Adam,' but 'One *like* a son of Adam.'"[58]

We believe that one of the reasons people miss the Angel in the OT is because sometimes he is simply called a man rather than an Angel. An explicit place to see this is Zechariah 1:8-11. In the vision, the prophet sees "A man (*'ish*)… standing among the myrtle trees" (Zech 1:8). The same is repeated again. He sees "The man who was standing

---

[57] Dominick M'Causland, *Adam and the Adamite; or The Harmony of Scripture and Ethnology*, 2nd ed. (London: Richard Bentley, 1868), 171. It was quite popular in the 19th century, especially in England, to distinguish between the two words. We believe the general points of distinction still hold, and some scholars agree. For example, Fischer explains it in a kind of taxonomy that all men (*'adam*) are sons of men (*'ish*), but not all men (*'ish*) are sons of Adam. Richard James Fischer, *Historical Genesis: From Adam to Abraham* (Lanham, MD: University Press of America, 2008), 54-57.

At that time, this distinction seems to have been driven by an agenda—to help scholars harmonize Scripture and science. Whether that is a legitimate endeavor or not, this seems to have been a tributary of the "pre-Adamite" theory of humans that supposedly existed prior to Adam. This theory coincided with the so-called "Gap theory" of Genesis 1. A serious problem began to show itself, however, quite apart from whether there was or wasn't such a thing as pre-Adamite humans. In some of these writings, there are fairly suggestive racist overtones, as the typical (both prior and after) understanding of *'adam* as being "lowly" men and *'ish* as being "exalted" men was flipped on its head, as the Adamite race was often thought to be "white," with the other nations not being privileged to his image-bearing. We do not subscribe to these wranglings of the words, as they are speculative at best and bigoted at worst. A positive example which doesn't fall into this is Robert Baker Girdlestone, *Synonyms of the Old Testament: Their Bearing on Christian Doctrine*. (Oak Harbor, WA: Logos Research Systems, Inc., 1998).

[58] Robert Baker Girdlestone, *Synonyms of the Old Testament: Their Bearing on Christian Doctrine*. (Oak Harbor, WA: Logos Research Systems, Inc., 1998), 46-47.

among the myrtle trees" (10). But in the next verses it becomes, "The Angel of the LORD was who was standing among the myrtle trees" (11). Calvin says here, "If we regard this angel to be Christ, the idea is consistent with the common usage of Scripture."[59]

This idea can be offensive—again, even sounding heretical—when it is not understood properly against the uniqueness of the incarnation. And indeed, when misunderstood, heretics have seized upon it to teach things that are contrary to the biblical understanding of the full deity of this Angel-Man. But as we have seen, the Angel is sometimes just called "the Word," or "the LORD," or "God," and yet, he is the Angel. Why isn't he called "the Angel" every time? Wouldn't that make it easier for us? Perhaps. But remember that the Bible is also good literature, and repeating the same idea every single time gets boring. Besides, there are other ways of describing him that are equally important and revealing. Each of these terms identifies something unique about the Angel of the LORD that we need to explore.

For Jacob, what becomes clear is that the "man" Jacob wrestled was God. Jacob begins the match attacked by this man; he ends the match refusing to let the man go because he *knows* who the man is! Paraphrasing Waltke, Jacob starts out wrestling with God and ends clinging to him.[60] In many ways, that was the point. All of Jacob's life, he had been wrestling: wrestling with Esau, wrestling with Laban, wrestling with his family. In reality, all his life he had been wrestling with God. And *he finally wins when he loses!*

In Hosea it says, "In the womb [Jacob] took his brother by the heel, and in his manhood he strove with God. He strove with the angel and prevailed; he wept and sought his favor. He met God at Bethel, and there God spoke with us-- the LORD, the God of hosts, the LORD is his memorial name" (Hos 12:3-5). His "striving with God" was "striving with the angel"[61] (in fact, the Hebrew can literally read, "He strove with El-Angel," where *el* is a name for God, hence, "the God-angel")[62] —the

---

[59] Comments on Zech 1:7-11. In John Calvin and John Owen, *Commentaries on the Twelve Minor Prophets*, vol. 5 (Bellingham, WA: Logos Bible Software, 2010), 33.
[60] Bruce K. Waltke, *Genesis* (Grand Rapids: Zondervan, 2001), 448.
[61] Hosea has changed *'ish* to "angel," a perfectly natural thing to do when you understand how the term is used.
[62] On "el" being a word for God see Hans Walter Wolff, *Hosea: A Commentary on the Book of the Prophet Hosea*, Hermeneia—a Critical and Historical Commentary

Angel who had met him at Bethel and had been with him his whole life. Jacob "prevailed" when he finally "wept and sought his favor." Derek Kidner wrote, "Jacob emerged broken [but] named and blessed... It was against [God]... that he had been pitting his strength, as he now discovered; yet the initiative had been God's as it was this night, to chasten his pride and challenge his tenacity."[63]

The Fourth Man in the Furnace: Daniel 3

While there are other places after the wrestling story where the Angel is specifically called a man, and we will deal with some of these at a later time under a different aspect of the Angel also mentioned in those passages, we do want to look at one more specific story later on in the prophet Daniel here as a kind of foreshadowing. This is the famous story of the three Jewish boys being thrown into the fiery hot furnace because they refused to bow down and worship the king of Babylon.

After being thrown into a fire heated seven times hotter than normal (Daniel 3:19-21), not one but two astonishing sights were seen. First, the furnace that was so hot that it incinerated those who threw Shadrach, Meshach, and Abednego into it, even though they were still outside (22), yet it did not kill the Jewish lads who were walking around inside the furnace.

The second sight was, if possible, even stranger. King Nebuchadnezzar, who was watching it all in a fury of narcissistic self-importance at the unmitigated gall of these Hebrew boys who would not bow their knee, looked inside and declared, "Did we not cast three men bound into the fire?" (3:24). "True, O king," came the reply. "But I see four men unbound, walking in the midst of the fire ... and the appearance of the fourth is like a son of the gods."

Two things are relevant at this point to our discussion of the Angel as a man. First, Nebuchadnezzar uses a fairly common word for a human

on the Bible (Philadelphia: Fortress Press, 1974), 212; Francis I. Andersen and David Noel Freedman, Hosea: *A New Translation with Introduction and Commentary* , vol. 24, Anchor Yale Bible (New Haven; London: Yale University Press, 2008), 608.

[63] Derek Kidner, Genesis: An Introduction and Commentary, vol. 1, Tyndale Old Testament Commentaries (Downers Grove, IL: InterVarsity Press, 1967), 180.

(the Aramaic *gebar*, the cousin of the Hebrew *geber*). It is clear that there is some kind of similarity between this fourth "man" and the other three. And yet there is also a difference. He wasn't *exactly* the same.

The Masoretic text calls him someone who looks like *"a son of the gods."* The TNK Jewish translation renders it *"… like a divine being."* Here is where things get interesting (and we won't even raise the question at this point of the "sons of God" as we will save that for a more appropriate time). While the later Greek Theodotion reads *"a son of God"* or possibly *"the Son of God"* (thus similar to the Hebrew), the LXX has *"an angel of God."* Thus, this passage has in it exactly what we are discussing with Jacob.

The Christian tradition has always seen this as Christ.[64] The Church Father Hippolytus is representative when he asks:

> Who was this angel who was revealed in the furnace and who preserved the boys as his own children under his enfolding arms … Let me not deceive, he was not any other person, but the very one who judged the Egyptians with the water … This was he who received the authority of judgment from the Father. He who also showered fire and divine retribution upon the Sodomites, and destroyed them on account of their lawlessness and wicked impiety. And Ezekiel agrees with this [Ezek 10:2, 6-7] … Concerning this Isaiah says, "And his name shall be called Angel of Great Counsel" (Isa 9:6 LXX). For Scripture also likens this one to be an angel of God. For it was he himself who reported to us the mysteries of the Father … [Nebuchadnezzar] called the names of the three, but he found he was not able to declare the fourth. For Jesus had not yet been born of the virgin.
>
> (Hippolytus, *Commentary on Daniel* 2.32–34)

---

[64] See Bogdan G. Bucur, "Christophanic Exegesis and the Problem of Symbolization: Daniel 3 (the Fiery Furnace) as a Test Case," *Journal of Theological Interpretation* 10.2 (Fall 2016): 227-244. Martine Dulaey, "Les trois hébreux dans la fournaise (Dn 3) dans l'interprétationsymbolique de l'église ancienne," *Revue des Sciences Religieuses* 71 (1997):42-46.

The Angel-God, My God: Genesis 48

Returning to Jacob, at the end of his life, the last great patriarch of Israel makes one final mention of this Angel who had been with him and guided his whole life. What he says is crystal clear yet so often missed. On his deathbed, as he is blessing his sons, Jacob turns to Joseph. It says:

> And he blessed Joseph and said,
> *"The God* before whom my fathers Abraham and Isaac walked,
> *the God* who has been my shepherd all my life long to this day,
> *the angel* who has redeemed me from all evil, bless the boys…"
> (Gen 48:15-16)

This passage is so important that we have a second, shorter supplemental book dedicated to it.[65] For now, what we will notice is simply that in this short recap of his life to his favorite son, Jacob explains that his God is the Angel, just like Hosea told us earlier. "God," "God," and "angel" are parallel and thus interpret one another. The redeemer of his life is the Angel who is God.[66]

A Closing Statement

Jacob's confession is a devastating blow to those who think that the Angel of the LORD is not in fact God. Jacob couldn't speak any clearer. Commenting on Genesis 48:16 John Calvin writes,

> He so joins the Angel to God as to make him his equal. Truly he offers him divine worship, and asks the same things from him as from God. If this be understood indifferently of any angel whatever, the sentence is absurd. … It is necessary that Christ should be here meant, who does not bear in vain the title of Angel, because he had become the perpetual Mediator. … He had not yet indeed been sent by the Father, to approach more nearly to us by taking our flesh, but

---

[65] See John Owen, Peter Allix, and Gerard De Gols, *The Angel of Yahweh in Jewish and Reformation History*, Christ in All Scripture Series Book 4, ed. Douglas Van Dorn (Erie, CO: Waters of Creation Publishing, 2018).
[66] The word 'redeemer' (*go´el*) is commonly used as a title for Yahweh (see Isa 41:14; 43:1; 47:4; 54:5).

because he was always the bond of connection between God and man ... there was always so wide a distance between God and men, that, without a mediator, there could be no communication ... and because God formally manifested himself in no other way than through him, he is properly called the Angel."[67]

Martin Luther says something similar,

This Angel is that Lord or Son of God whom Jacob saw and who was to be sent by God into the world to announce to us deliverance from death, the forgiveness of sins, and the kingdom of heaven ... Therefore one must note carefully that Jacob is speaking about Christ, the Son, who alone is the Angel or Ambassador, born a man in time from the Virgin Mary—not the Father, not the Holy Spirit. For he makes a clear distinction among the three Persons. Yet he adds: "May He bless these lads."[68]

This kind of thinking has been around since the early church. Athanasius says,

None of created and natural Angels did [Jacob] join to God their Creator, nor rejecting God that fed him, did he from any Angel ask the blessing on his grandsons; but in saying, 'Who delivered me from all evil,' he showed that it was no created Angel, but the Word of God, whom he joined to the Father in his prayer, through whom, whomsoever He will, God does deliver. For knowing that He is also called the Father's 'Angel of great Counsel' (Isa 9:6 LXX), he said that none other than He was the Giver of blessing, and Deliverer from evil."[69]

We want to bring this discussion to an end by making an observation about this statement from Jacob and using it as an example of a troubling phenomenon we have already raised several times in this

---

[67] John Calvin and John King, *Commentary on the First Book of Moses Called Genesis*, vol. 2 (Bellingham, WA: Logos Bible Software, 2010), 428-29.

[68] Martin Luther, *Luther's Works, Vol. 8: Lectures on Genesis: Chapters 45-50*, ed. Jaroslav Jan Pelikan, Hilton C. Oswald, and Helmut T. Lehmann, vol. 8 (Saint Louis: Concordia Publishing House, 1999), 164.

[69] Athanasius of Alexandria, "Four Discourses against the Arians" 3.12, in *St. Athanasius: Select Works and Letters*, ed. Philip Schaff and Henry Wace, trans. John Henry Newman and Archibald T. Robertson, vol. 4, A Select Library of the Nicene and Post-Nicene Fathers of the Christian Church, Second Series (New York: Christian Literature Company, 1892), 400.

book. Incredibly, in the early church, as far as our research has been able to uncover, Athanasius stands alone in his comments on Christ in this passage. Very few even mention this text. Fewer still see the devastating argument that Jacob is making that this Angel *is* God. The *Ancient Christian Commentary Series* has nothing. Logos Software searches of two different complete sets of Church Fathers garner nothing.

This bewildering blindness moves right on into modern commentators who, though exegeting the text, nevertheless do not make the associations we have seen with these three towering figures from church history, even though one would think that this is a very significant observation for our understanding of God in the OT. For example, Wenham makes the fascinating observation, "'May the God, … may the God … may the angel.' This blessing foreshadows the later priestly blessing in its tripartite structure, 'May the Lord, … may the Lord, … may the Lord,' and, like the priestly blessing, Jacob's has also been used in Jewish liturgy."[70] Yet he fails to connect the dots in any kind of explicit way between the Angel and God. Same goes for Walton, "The grammatical parallel indicates that the angel need not be a title for deity … In other words, Jacob is blessing Ephraim and Manasseh by putting them under the care of God, who shepherds, under his angel, who delivers."[71] Nothing about our connection. Currid sees a foreshadowing of Christ, but not Christ himself: "His statement here highlights the work of redemption of God through the Angel of Yahweh: certainly this is a foreshadowing of the work of the Messiah, Jesus Christ!"[72] Hamilton doesn't mention Christ.[73] Matthews is utterly baffled, "What precisely Jacob refers to or whether he is speaking only generally cannot be confidently determined."[74]

---

[70] Gordon J. Wenham, *Genesis 16–50*, vol. 2, Word Biblical Commentary (Dallas: Word, Incorporated, 1998), 465.

[71] John H. Walton, *Genesis*, The NIV Application Commentary (Grand Rapids, MI: Zondervan, 2001), 712.

[72] John D. Currid, *A Study Commentary on Genesis: Genesis 25:19–50:26*, vol. 2, EP Study Commentary (Darlington, England; Carlisle, PA: Evangelical Press, 2003), 367.

[73] Victor P. Hamilton, *The Book of Genesis, Chapters 18–50*, The New International Commentary on the Old Testament (Grand Rapids, MI: Wm. B. Eerdmans Publishing Co., 1995), 637-38.

[74] K. A. Mathews, *Genesis 11:27–50:26*, vol. 1B, The New American Commentary (Nashville: Broadman & Holman Publishers, 2005), 879.

Sarna comes close then it passes him by. "Verses 15-16 strongly suggest that 'angel' is here an epithet of God ... Admittedly, 'Angel' as an epithet for God is extraordinary, but since angels are often simply extensions of the divine personality, the distinction between God and angel in the biblical texts is frequently blurred [cf. Gen 31:3, 11, 13; Ex 3:2, 4]. Nevertheless, this verse may reflect some tradition associated with Bethel, not preserved in Genesis, concerning an angelic guardian of Jacob."[75] He seems hesitant to make the connection because of an interesting observation. "No one in the Bible ever invokes an angel in prayer, nor in Jacob's several encounters with angels is there any mention of one who delivers him from harm. When the patriarch feels himself to be in mortal danger, he prays directly to God, as in 32:10-13, and it is He who again and again is Jacob's guardian and protector (28:15, 20; 31:3; 35:3)." Even though he probably comes the closest to making the connection in this list, Sarna is the only non-Christian in these examples. As a modern Jew, he did not make Trinitarian distinctions. Jesus, of course, taught us to pray to the Father. And in the NT, he is seen as the mediator, and thus we commonly pray through or in Christ's name. But because he is also God, we have NT examples of praying to Jesus (Acts 8:22-24; 1Co 1:2; Eph 5:19; etc.). If we allow that these distinctions between various persons are present in the OT as well, then any time someone prays to the LORD, he is almost certainly praying to the Son.

We choose these commentaries because they are the best that we have available to us in modern times. But they all display the same weakness. They aren't connecting the Angel-God dots. Why a Christian would be so hesitant to see Christ here is beyond us. The fact that it doesn't even enter most of our minds is quite concerning, especially since the NT from beginning to end is basically a commentary on Christ in the OT. Put another way, this is how our NT reads the OT on virtually every page. We hope that this study of the Angel of the LORD in Genesis with Hagar, Abraham, and Jacob has merely whetted your appetite for more so that you can begin to see the glories wrapped up in this person called the Angel of the LORD.

---

[75] Nahum M. Sarna, *Genesis*, The JPS Torah Commentary (Philadelphia: Jewish Publication Society, 1989), 328.

4

THE ANGEL AS "THE NAME"

The Angel and Moses: Part I

The Angel in the Flames: Exodus 3 and 14

B Y THE TIME WE GET TO THE EXODUS, we have already seen the "Angel of the LORD" appear repeatedly. He speaks as God himself, and he works with divine purpose to guide and guard his people. At the beginning of Exodus, the Angel appears again dramatically in what may be his most famous appearance of all:

> Now Moses was keeping the flock of his father-in-law, Jethro, the priest of Midian, and he led his flock to the west side of the wilderness and came to Horeb, the mountain of God. And the angel of the LORD appeared to him in a flame of fire out of the midst of a bush. He looked, and behold, the bush was burning, yet it was not consumed. And Moses said, "I will turn aside to see this great sight, why the bush is not burned." When the LORD saw that he turned aside to see, God called to him out of the bush, "Moses, Moses!" And he said, "Here I am." Then he said, "Do not come near; take your sandals off your feet, for the place on which you are standing is holy ground." And he said, "I am the God of your father, the God of Abraham, the God of Isaac, and the God of Jacob." And Moses hid his face, for he was afraid to look at God.

Then the LORD said, "I have surely seen the affliction of my people who are in Egypt and have heard their cry because of their taskmasters. I know their sufferings, and I have come down to deliver...

Then Moses said to God, "If I come to the people of Israel and say to them, 'The God of your fathers has sent me to you,' and they ask me, 'What is his name?' what shall I say to them?" God said to Moses, "I AM WHO I AM." And he said, "Say this to the people of Israel: 'I AM has sent me to you.'" God also said to Moses, "Say this to the people of Israel: 'The LORD, the God of your fathers, the God of Abraham, the God of Isaac, and the God of Jacob, has sent me to you.' This is my name forever, and thus I am to be remembered throughout all generations."

(Exodus 3:1-7, 13-15)

The story of Moses is very familiar. He had been adopted as a baby by the daughter of Pharaoh and had grown up as a Prince of Egypt. But when he discovered his true identity, he tried to help his people—the Hebrews. He murdered a man and then had to run away into the wilderness, where he had lived for many years. At this point in his life, Moses had never met God. He was in the wilderness, watching over sheep, disengaged from the plan and people of God, not even looking for Him. But as happens so often in the Bible, God came down looking for a man, and he turned Moses' life upside down.

As in Genesis, it is the "Angel of the LORD" who appears to Moses. Interestingly, here he appears "in a flame of fire out of the midst of a bush." In the Old Testament, a "flame of fire" becomes an often-used visible symbol of God's presence. God had appeared as a flaming fire pot to Abram (Gen 15:17). Later in Exodus, God is going to appear in a pillar of fire and cloud, leading the people in the wilderness (Ex 13:21, 14:24). When the tabernacle and Temple are built, God appears again as a flame of fire (Ex 40:34-38, cf. 1Kg 8:10-11). Moses later came to say, "The LORD your God is a consuming fire" (Dt 4:24).

In this case, the Angel was *in* the flame of fire" in the *"midst* of the bush." The "fire" was *not* the Angel, but the Angel was *in* the fire. The same thing is described in Exodus 13:21-22,

And the Lord went before them by day in a pillar of cloud to lead them along the way, and by night *in* a pillar of fire to give them light, that they might travel by day and by night. The pillar of cloud by day and the pillar of fire by night did not depart from before the people.

Notice also Exodus 14:19 and 24,

The *angel of God* who was going before the host of Israel moved and went behind them, and the pillar of cloud moved from before them and stood behind them... And in the morning watch the LORD in the pillar of fire and of cloud looked down on the Egyptian forces and threw the Egyptian forces into a panic.

Again the "angel of God" is also just called "Yahweh." They are used interchangeably. Yahweh's presence with his people becomes manifest in the cloud and fire. Because the Holy Spirit is pictured in fiery ways (cf. Acts 2:3-4) and manifested with more symbolic than human characteristics, many believe that possibly two of the divine Persons are actually present and manifested here—the fire and cloud is the Spirit who envelops the Angel in the fire.[76]

Whatever the case, Moses is amazed by the sight of the bush on fire that isn't being consumed. What did this mean? Most obviously, the bush was not the thing *fueling* the fire. Moses is seeing—not a bush fueling the fire, but *the fire that fuels the bush*. He is being shown a sign of the brightness of the glory of God who sustains the universe. In other words, something of God's holiness and glory was being manifested to Moses. When God later says, "Do not come near; take your sandals off your feet, for the place you are standing is holy ground" (Ex 3:5),[77] the whole experience is telling him that great care must be taken when coming into the presence of God. Fire is something that warms you and fire is something you need, but fire is something you don't want to touch. Fire can destroy you and is something with which you have to be very careful. This fire is attractive, and this fire is dangerous.

But in grace, when Moses turns aside to see the bush, God calls to Moses out of the bush, "'Moses, Moses!' And he said, 'Here I am'" (4). As we have seen before, this is the same pattern of naming and response seen with the Angel and Abraham (Gen 22:11) and the Angel and Jacob

---

[76] For example, Meredith G. Kline, *Images of the Spirit* (Eugene, OR: Wipf & Stock, 1980), 71.

[77] Stephen tells us that "God" and "the Lord" spoke these words to Moses (Acts 7:32-33).

(Gen 31:11). Then the Angel says, "I am the God of your father, the God of Abraham, the God of Isaac, and the God of Jacob" (Ex 3:6).

In other words, once again, God was the one who sought out Moses and who already knows Moses' name. Phil Ryken says, "Moses didn't need to tell God who he was. God already knew who Moses was."[78] In C. S. Lewis' *The Horse and His Boy*, the lion Aslan comes to the boy Shasta, who thinks he had been chased by many lions in his life. Aslan says,

> There was only one lion ... I was the lion who forced you to join with Aravis. I was the cat who comforted you among the houses of the dead. I was the lion who drove the jackals from you while you slept. I was the lion who gave the horses the new strength of fear for the last mile so that you should reach King Lune in time. And I was the lion you do not remember who pushed the boat in which you lay, a child near death, so that it came to shore where a man sat, wakeful at midnight, to receive you.[79]

So here, God comes to Moses and says, "I am the God who has been leading you by the hand all through your life. I was the God who was there at your birth and guided your basket through the waters to the princess, and I was the one who drew you out and brought you out of Egypt and brought you to me. I am the God of Abraham, Isaac, and Jacob—the God of your Fathers. I still remember my covenant. I have seen the affliction of my people and I am 'coming down' again to deliver them."

Remember that it is "the angel of the LORD" saying all these things. The Angel may be only mentioned in vs. 3, but we have already established a pattern that the designation can be used interchangeably with Yahweh and God, and yet still be the Angel. As Moses says later, "When we cried to the LORD, he heard our voice and sent an angel and brought us out of Egypt" (Num 20:16). Once again, the text repeatedly demands that we see a distinction *as well as* a fundamental unity of identity between the Angel and Yahweh.

---

[78] Philip Graham Ryken, 84.
[79] C. S. Lewis, *The Horse and His Boy*, Chronicles of Narnia vol. 5 (Hong Kong, Enrich Spot Ltd., 2016), 121-22.

I AM Who I AM

Now, in Exodus 3:13 when Moses, like Jacob before him (Gen 32:29), asks for the Angel-God's name, it is significant how he finally responds. He wouldn't give Jacob a name. He does give Moses one. And what a name it is! "'I AM WHO I AM.'[80] … Say this to the people of Israel: 'I AM has sent me to you.' … 'This is my name forever, and thus I am to be remembered throughout all generations'" (14-15).

As we have been reminded several times briefly, in the Old Testament, names are very important. Names were an expression of being and character. They told you not only how to identify someone, but what he was like, what marked him out, what made him special (cf. 1Sa 25:25). To know someone's name was to know the person (cf. Ps 9:10). God's name becomes a representation of God himself, almost a personification of himself. God's name was an expression of his Person. So, to know and call upon God's name was to know and call upon God.[81]

Now it is clear that the patriarchs knew something of God's name *Yahweh*.[82] The name occurs 160 times in the book of Genesis, and Abraham himself calls him *Yahweh-yireh* ("Yahweh will provide," Gen 22:14). But sometimes "knowing" someone's name means knowing the Person more deeply—*really* knowing him. In Exodus 16:11, God says, "At twilight you shall eat meat, and in the morning you shall be filled with bread. *Then* you shall *know* that I am the LORD your God"

---

[80] John Ronning believes that "I AM WHO I AM" is rather meaningless and instead argues for "I WILL BE WHO I HAVE BEEN," meaning that he is the same God now as he was in his dealings with the fathers, he is "the same yesterday, today, forever." In private correspondence he makes the astute observation that this means, "Jesus in the flesh is the same as before the incarnation, doing the same kinds of things, except with eternal effect, not just earthly redemption." See John Ronning, *The Jewish Targums and John's Logos Theology* (Grand Rapids, MI: Baker Academic, 2010); Ch. 3.

[81] Joel 2:32, "Everyone who calls on the name of the Lord shall be saved." Genesis 12:8, "There he built an altar to the Lord and called upon the name of the LORD." 1Kg 18:24, "You call upon the name of your god, and I will call upon the name of the Lord, and the God who answers by fire, he is God." See R. J. Way, "God, Names of," in *The International Standard Bible Encyclopedia, Revised*, ed. G. W. Bromiley (Grand Rapids, MI: Eerdmans, 1982): 2:504-05 [504-09].

[82] Exodus 6:2 says, "…by my name the LORD I did not make myself known to them." But see our discussion as the explanation to this often misunderstood verse.

(see also Ex 6:7; 29:46). God was about to do something wonderful! The patriarchs "knew" Yahweh as their God, but they may not have known what the divine name really meant and may not have known him as he was going to make himself known throughout the Exodus, as the Most High [*Elyon*] over all gods, the true Creator-God capable of doing anything.

God says here (in slightly different verbal form), "My name is: I AM WHO I AM." What does this mean? Many answers have been given.[83] The phrase can mean both "I am who I am" and "I will be who I will be." Plainly, God is saying: I am the God who is; I am the God of existence, the God of being. Moses may have been asking, "What proof can I give the people of who you are, of your authority to do what you have said?" God answers, "The proof I give you is Myself. I am the Self-Sufficient, Self-Existent, Self-Evident God. There is nothing outside of myself, nothing higher than myself that can be used to explain me, to describe me, to justify me. I just am. The God who is on your side is the self-existent God of the universe." Ryken writes, "Who is God? God is who he is, and that's all there is to it."[84] Alexander MacLaren writes,

> All other being is derived, and therefore limited and changeful; this being is underived, absolute, self-dependent, and therefore unalterable forevermore. Because we live, we die. In living, the process is going on of which death is the end. But God lives forevermore, a flame that does not burn out; therefore his resources are inexhaustible, his power unwearied... He gives and is none the poorer. He works and is never weary. He operates unspent; he loves and he loves forever. And through the ages, the fire burns on, unconsumed and undecayed.[85]

The name is also recognized as a name that describes a personal relationship with a people in covenant. It is his covenant name. Exodus 6:2-4 says, "I am the LORD ... I also established my covenant with them [the Patriarchs]." In Exodus 19:3-6 we read, "The LORD called to [Moses] out of the mountain saying, '... If you will indeed obey my voice

---

[83] Ibid., 506-507.
[84] Ryken, 97.
[85] Alexander Maclaren, *Expositions of Holy Scripture*, 11 vols. (Grand Rapids: Wm. B. Eerdmans, 1952–59), 1:23–24.

and keep my covenant, you shall be my treasured possession among all peoples, for all the earth is mine.'" Who makes the covenant with Israel? In many places, the Angel is specifically identified as the covenant-maker (Gen 15:18; 17:1-4; Jdg 2:1; Mal 3:1; etc.).

In this light, we again remember that it is Angel of the LORD who reveals this divine name to Moses. He who is identifying himself as Yahweh is also the Angel. This may give us a hint about a phenomenon that begins to occur repeatedly in the Old Testament—where the "name" begins to be used as a personification for God himself. For instance, Isaiah 30:27 says, "Behold the *name* of the LORD comes from far, burning with *his* anger, and in thick rising smoke." Psalm 20:1, 7 says, "May the LORD answer you in the day of trouble! May the *name* of the God of Jacob protect you… Some trust in chariots and others in horses, but we trust in the *name* of Yahweh, our God." Psalm 54:1 says, "O God, save me by your name." More passages could be cited.

Most commentators have considered these uses as just Hebraisms, where the "name" is sometimes treated even separately from Yahweh. However, if, as we have seen, the Angel is a latent Trinitarian revelation in the Old Testament, and the Angel also bears the "name" of Yahweh, these passages begin to take on a clearer and more powerful meaning. Further, they bring clarity to Jesus' own declarations in the New Testament—John 17:6, "I have manifested your *name* to the people you gave me out of the world." Jesus' disciples, who were more familiar with their Old Testaments and Old Testament theology, knew very clearly what he was saying.

Here in the Old Testament, the divine-angel "sent" from the Father (Num 20:17) manifests the covenant name of Israel's God. As in Genesis, he is the redeemer of his people, who comes to rescue them, to call them out to worship, and promises to be with them wherever they go. He is the God of Israel who has claimed them as his special inheritance (Dt 32:8-9).

5

THE ANGEL AS "FACE" OR "PRESENCE"

The Angel and Moses: Part II

Face to Face

L IVING IN AN AGE OF MEDIA AND CELEBRITY, it is easy to fool yourself into thinking you know someone simply because you've seen
his or her face. It must be a strange thing to have everyone on the
street gawk at you even though you've never met them. This is the power of
a face posted across the magazines, movies, and other forms of media.

But we really don't know someone until we are actually in their presence. Not in their presence with 75,000 screaming fans, but in their presence personally—face-to-face. It is the presence of a person that communicates true knowledge of what otherwise might just be another pretty face.
This is why disembodied communication just isn't the same, why people
so easily become "trolls" on the internet, and why every fiber of our being
longs for True Presence, be it with other humans or God himself.

The Angel and Sinai: Exodus 33

Skipping over some important material that properly belongs under a different heading that we will tackle in the next chapter, we come
now to well-known story that takes place immediately after the

infamous golden calf incident at Mt. Sinai.

A Different Angel?

Perhaps one of the biggest *challenges* to the argument that the "Angel of the Covenant" (Exodus 23:20, Mal.3:1) is both God and "sent" from God—a Second Divine Person—is found in Exodus 33. After the people broke God's Covenant Law by sinning with the golden calf, God comes to Moses with devastating words:

> The LORD said to Moses, "Depart; go up from here, you and the people whom you have brought up out of the land of Egypt, to the land of which I swore to Abraham, Isaac, and Jacob, saying, 'To your offspring I will give it.' *I will send an angel* before you, and I will drive out the Canaanites, the Amorites, the Hittites, the Perizzites, the Hivites, and the Jebusites. Go up to a land flowing with milk and honey; *but I will not go up among you*, lest I consume you on the way, for you are a stiff-necked people."
>
> (Exodus 33:1-3)

Notice God's words—"*you* and the people whom *you* have brought up out of the land of Egypt." Because of their sin, God no longer identifies them as *his* people. He tells them to leave Sinai, to go to the Promised Land. He even promises "an *angel*" to drive out their enemies. "But," he says, "*I* will not go up among you."

The language sounds very similar to Exodus 23:20, "Behold, I send an angel before you..." But unlike before, where the angel was identified with God himself and bore the divine name, this angel is no longer identified with Yahweh. God still promises "an angel," but the angel is obviously not God, so perhaps the first angel was not really God either?

The early Jewish rabbis in the 2nd or 3rd century A.D. used this very fact as an argument against the early Christians who were claiming that Jesus was the "angel of the covenant" who was God. A passage in the Babylonian Talmud shows an argument between the rabbis and the *Minim* ("heretics"). The heretics (likely Christian) were using Exodus 23:20-21 to argue that they should worship the "angel" as God. Rabbi Idith responded, "By our troth [lit. we hold the belief], we would not accept him even as a messenger, for it is written: 'And he said unto him,

If Thy presence go not etc.' (Ex 33:15)."[86] In other words, the rabbis sought to clarify Exodus 23:20 with Moses' words in 33:15, that only God himself is acceptable as Israel's guide. An angel, then, is clearly not enough and can't be God.

The rabbis seem to make a water-tight argument: "The angel was never God himself, but simply a representative. God is one. Period!" But in fact, as we are going to see, the argument is not as cut-and-dried as it may initially look. Exodus 33 is a lot more complicated than the rabbis were letting on. It actually will become clear that the "angel" God mentions in Ex 33:2 is not the same "angel" that was promised before and who represents God's *"presence"* with his people.

Having God's "Presence"

The key word of the chapter is, in fact, the word "presence." In Hebrew, it's the word *paneh*, and it can be translated as either "face" or "presence." The word occurs six crucial times in the chapter. We have already encountered the word before (see p. 61)—in Genesis 32:30, when after wrestling with the angel of God, Jacob named the place "Peniel, saying, 'For I have seen God face to face (*paneh* to *paneh*), and yet my life has been delivered.'"

Exodus 33 begins with God withdrawing the promise of his ongoing "presence" with the people because of their idolatry with the golden calf (ch. 32). It was a crisis moment in the nation. The entire future of Israel, their entire relationship with God was in question. God says, "Under these circumstances of sin, I cannot go with you, lest I consume you in my holiness." They could have the Promised Land, but without God himself. In response to this "disastrous word" (vs. 4), the people mourn and repent (vs. 4-6), and Moses goes into the tent of meeting to meet with God and to plead for the people (vs. 7-13).

We're told, seemingly as an editorial comment, "When Moses entered the tent, the pillar of cloud would descend and stand at the entrance of the tent, and the LORD would speak with Moses ... Thus the LORD used to speak to Moses *face to face* (*paneh* to *paneh*), as a man speaks to his friend" (33:9, 11). (Notice the parallel with Gen 32:30!)[87]

---

[86] See the Babylonian Talmud: Sanhedrin 38b.
[87] In both Ex 33:11 and Gen 32:30, the words are in a plural idiom - *panim* to *panim*.

As we've seen before, the "pillar of cloud and fire" was another visible manifestation of God's presence and it was the Angel of the LORD, we saw, who was *in* and *obscured* by the cloud.[88] Nevertheless, there was such an intimacy and directness to God's communication to Moses in the cloud that God was said to meet with Moses *"face to face*, as a man speaks to his friend."

Moses then, in the tent of meeting, says to God, "See, you say to me, 'Bring up this people,' but you have not let me know whom you will send with me..." (Ex 33:12). Moses wants to know *'who this angel is'* that God is going to send with them (vs. 2), since it's not going to be God. Moses is saying, "You're telling me to take the people to the Promised Land, but you're not telling me *who* is going to go with us. You're telling me that my job remains the same, but *you* are not going to go. You're going to send *some* angel, but *which* angel? We don't want just any old angel." To Moses, it seems like he's being demoted. He has the same job, but he's losing access to the CEO; he's only going to have access to some secretary![89]

So Moses pleads, "If I have found favor in your sight, please show me now *your* ways, that I may know *you* in order to find favor in your sight. Consider too that this nation is *your* people" (33:13). Moses says, "I want to know YOU! I want YOU to lead us in the way!" Further, he says, "I want *you* to identify again with *your* people! They're not just *my* people! Don't speak that way, God. They are *your* people."

In response to Moses' pleading, God shows mercy and relents.

---

[88] See Ch. 5; especially Ex 14:19, 24; also Ex 3:2; 13:21.

[89] This interpretation can also be seen in the Aramaic Targum of Song of Songs 3:1-3: When the people of the House of Israel saw that the cloud of glory had been withdrawn from over them and that the crown of holiness which had been given them at Sinai was removed from them, they were left in darkness like the night. And they sought the crown of holiness which had been lifted from them but they did not find it. The Children of Israel said to one another, "Let us rise and go and surround the Tent of Meeting which Moses spread outside the camp, and let us request instruction from Yahweh and the *Shekinah* which has been removed from us." Then they went around in the towns, streets, and squares, but they did not find it. The Assembly of Israel said, "Moses and Aaron and the Levites, who keep watch over the Word of Yahweh of the Tent of Meeting and who go around it, found me, and I asked them about the *Shekinah* of Yahweh which had been removed from me. Moses, the great Scribe of Israel, answered and this is what he said, 'I will ascend to heaven on high and pray before Yahweh. Perhaps He will forgive your guilt and make His *Shekinah* dwell among you as before.'"

And he says, "My presence (*paneh*) will go with you, and I will give you rest" (vs. 14). Moses affirms, "If your presence (*paneh*) will not go with me, do not bring us up from here" (vs. 15). What God promises and Moses asks is for a continuation of the relationship they have had. Moses doesn't want to lose access to God's "face" (his *paneh*-presence) that he's had with the pillar of cloud and fire and meeting with God in the tent of meeting. Because of Moses' intercession, God promises again his "presence-face" to go with the people—not just "any old angel," but God himself will go.[90]

At this point, Moses seems to go "all-in." In response to God's mercy, Moses famously asks, "Please show me your glory" (vs. 18). It's a very interesting request. What does it even mean? We've just been told that Moses meets with God "face to face" (vs. 11). Even more, the book of Exodus records that Yahweh had repeatedly "appeared" to Moses in visible manifestations. In Exodus 16:10, "the *glory* of the LORD *appeared* in the cloud." In 24:16-17, "The *glory* of the Lord dwelt on Mount Sinai, and the cloud covered it six days... Now the *appearance* of the *glory* of the Lord was like a devouring fire on the top of the mountain." Earlier in 24:9-11, at the completion of the covenant ceremony, we are told,

> Then Moses and Aaron, Nadab, and Abihu, and seventy of the elders of Israel went up, and they *saw* the God of Israel. There was under his feet as it were a pavement of sapphire stone, like the very heaven for clearness. And he did not lay his hand on the chief men of the people of Israel; they *beheld* God, and ate and drank.

Moses had repeatedly "seen" God. So, what is Moses asking for here?

---

[90] Jonathan Edwards agrees with this interpretation and gives citations from other Jewish scholars as evidence, "As Aben Ezra observes [*see Gill* in loc.] that this was not the angel promised before (Ex 23) but an inferior one, which the Lord threatened to send with them instead of the former; though afterwards he relented and promised his own presence, which seems to be the same as intended in Isaiah by the 'angel of his presence'. So Rabbi Menachem saith, 'This angel is not the angel of the covenant, of whom he spake in the time of favorable acceptance, *My presence shall go*: for now the holy blessed God had taken away his divine preference from among them, and would have led them by the hand of another angel' [Ainf. in Ex 32:34]." See Jonathan Edwards, *History of the Work of Redemption (with notes)* (London: T. Pitcher, 1793] 202.

Seeing God's "Face"

God's response to Moses is very interesting:

"I will make all my goodness pass before you and will proclaim before you my name 'The LORD' ... But," he said, "you cannot *see* my *face*, for man shall not *see* me and live." And the Lord said, "Behold, there is a place by me where you shall stand on the rock, and while my glory passes by I will put you in a cleft of the rock, and I will cover you with my hand until I have passed by. Then I will take away my hand, and you shall see my back, but my *face* shall not be *seen*.

(Exodus 33:19-23)

The word here for "face" is again the word *paneh*. It's the same word translated as "presence" in vs. 14 when God says, "My *presence* (*paneh*) will go with you." So we have seen the following:

33:11   "Thus the Lord used to speak to Moses panim to panim..."

33:14   "My paneh will go with you..."

33:15   "If your paneh will not go with me, do not bring us up from here..."

33:20   "You cannot see my paneh, for man shall not see me and live..."

33:23   "You shall see my back, but my paneh shall not be seen."

Clearly, something strange is going on with the word *paneh* in this chapter; the text is telling us there was a subtle mystery in how God was interacting with Moses; Moses was seeing something of the "glory" of God, he was speaking personally and intimately in some way with a visible manifestation of God himself, yet Moses also knows there is more to be seen. God is being seen and yet not being seen.

In one way, there is a lesson in that! That's exactly how God would be. God *can* be seen and yet *cannot* be seen. God can be known and yet not known. God reveals himself in ways we can understand, but also reveals that we will never fully understand him—because he is God and we are not.

God gives Moses a *yes and no answer*. He promises to reveal something of himself, not just verbally but visibly.

But he also warns that Moses can't fully "see" his face, that a full perception of God would be deadly. So, God promises protection from deadly exposure and a passing glimpse at the "after-effects of the Lord's presence" (Mackay).[91] And after God's glory passes by, God promises to remove his "hand" for an instant to let Moses see the "back" of God's passing glory.

Now most commentators interpret all this as figurative anthropomorphism—that God is speaking figuratively about his face, his back, his hand. Ryken writes, "He was expressing the invisible majesty of his eternal being in *terms* of human body parts … God's face refers in some way to the direct revelation of the essence of his divine majesty. To see God's back is to have some lesser experience of his glory…"[92] God doesn't really have a "hand," a "face," a "back," right?

But we must be careful here. This is not figurative poetry. It is recorded history. *Something* was "speaking" and "appearing" to Moses! In Numbers 12:6-8, God says,

> Hear my words: If there is a prophet among you, I the LORD make myself known to him in a vision; I speak with him in a dream. Not so with my servant Moses. He is faithful in all my house. With him I speak mouth to mouth, clearly, and not in riddles, and *he beholds the form of the LORD*.

What in the world does that mean? The last statement of Numbers 12:8 is very significant. The word "form" (Hebrew - *tamunah*) is the same word translated "likeness" in many of the Law's prohibitions against idolatry. For example, "You shall not make for yourself a carved image, or any *likeness* of anything" (Ex 20:4). Much later, speaking about the events at Sinai, Moses says to the people, "The LORD spoke to you out of the midst of the fire. You heard the sound of words, but saw no *form* (*tamunah*); there was only a voice" (Dt 4:12). Yet, Numbers 12:8 tells us that Moses saw *more*! He saw "the *form* of the LORD."[93]

This is probably referring to what happens next in Exodus 34:

---

[91] John L. Mackay, *Exodus*, Mentor Commentaries (Fearn, Ross-shire, Great Britain: Mentor, 2001), 559.

[92] Ryken, 1036.

[93] See also Psalm 17:15 - "As for me, I shall behold your face (*paneh*) in righteousness; when I awake, I shall be satisfied with your likeness (*tamunah*)."

> The LORD descended in the cloud and stood with him there, and proclaimed the name of the LORD. The LORD passed before him and proclaimed, "The LORD, the LORD, a God merciful and gracious, slow to anger, and abounding in steadfast love and faithfulness" … And Moses quickly bowed his head toward the earth and worshiped. And he said, "If now I have found favor in your sight, O Lord, please let the Lord go in the midst of us, for it is a stiff-necked people, and pardon our iniquity and our sin, and take us for your inheritance."
>
> (Exodus 34:5–9)

Pay careful attention to the wording here. Some visible manifestation of Yahweh "descended in the cloud" and "stood" with Moses and "proclaimed the name of Yahweh." Then some visible manifestation of Yahweh "passed before him" (not in the cloud?). Remember, God had said, "While my glory passes by I will put you in a cleft of the rock, and I will cover you with my hand until I have passed by. Then I will take away my hand, and you shall see my back, but my *face* shall not be *seen*" (Ex 33:22-23). So something of Yahweh (described as "my hand") would actually "cover" Moses *from* Yahweh *while* Yahweh 'passes' by. Ryken writes, "Moses was protected *by* God *from* God."[94] *Then* Yahweh would take away his "hand," and Moses would be able to see Yahweh's "back" (or as Num 12:8 says, a "form / likeness").

These verses, and others like them, gave rise to early Jewish discussion that there were actually two manifestations of Yahweh being described in the text—there is a Yahweh covering him with his hand *and* there is a Yahweh passing by.[95] Even the repetition of "The LORD, the LORD" drove some of the rabbis crazy—especially in the complexities of the text—that two Yahwehs were being proclaimed.

Notice also Moses' request: "O Lord (*adonai*), please let the Lord (*adonai*) go in the midst of us" (vs. 9)—the kind of "third person" language we have seen before. While this idiom may seem obscure, we have seen repeated use of this kind of "strange" grammar to describe Yahweh's appearances and interactions with his people. The language becomes highly intriguing!

---

[94] Ryken, Ibid.
[95] We will deal with this more thoroughly in a later chapter.

The Angel of the "Paneh"

So what do we do with all this? Whatever is going on, this is clearly not simple anthropomorphism. This is visible and special theophany. Something truly covered Moses from the passing glory. Something truly passed by with form and shape and face. And Moses saw "glory" from the back—not just some "thing," but *someone*! This *someone* is called God's *paneh*—his "face / presence." It was God's *paneh* then who met with Moses in the tent of meeting, obscured by the pillar of cloud (Ex 33:11). It was God's *paneh* that Moses wanted to go with them, and not just another angel (33:12-15). It was the back of God's *paneh* that Moses saw in the cleft of the rock as the "form of Yahweh" (33:20, 23; Num 12:8).

This leads inextricably to the conclusion that God's *paneh*-presence is a hypostatization, a hypostasis of God. "Hypostasis" is technical jargon that was used in the early church to describe one of the three persons of the Trinity. For our purposes, we can think of it as a synonym for "person." In other words, the *paneh*-presence is a Person of the Godhead. It is not an abstraction or an anthropomorphism. It is a person.

This is what we saw with God's "Name" becoming a personification of God. Now it is God's "presence" as a Personalized representation of God. Both are depicting the same Person of the Trinity. Deuteronomy 4:37 says, "[God] loved your fathers and chose their offspring after them and brought you out of Egypt with his own *presence* (*paneh*)." David said, "From your presence (*paneh*) let my vindication come... As for me, I shall behold your face (*paneh*) in righteousness" (Psalm 17:2, 15).[96] Similarly, Psalm 27:8, "You have said, 'Seek my face (*paneh*).' My heart says to you, 'Your face (*paneh*), Lord, do I seek'."

For our purposes, the most important and revealing text of all is Isaiah's description of the Exodus in Isaiah 63:9, "In all their affliction he was afflicted, and *the angel of his presence* (*paneh*) saved them; in his love and in his pity he redeemed them; he lifted them up and carried them all the days of old."

In the introduction, we explained "the analogy of faith," that Scripture interprets Scripture, and that clear passages help explain less clear passages. Isaiah 63:9 is a perfect example. The phrase "angel of his

---

[96] From a New Testament perspective, it is intriguing that the Temple show-bread is also called "the bread of the Presence (*panim*)" (see Ex 25:30 *et al*).

presence" is not found anywhere else in the inspired OT. But its use in the context of Isaiah 63 is highly provocative. Where did this idea come from? It suggests an interpretive tradition linking the Angel and the *paneh*—a tradition that is now being affirmed in the inspired record. The verse then legitimately becomes an interpretive key to other passages where the Angel and the *paneh* are involved. It brings greater light and clarity to the connection between the two. The manifestations of God's *paneh* are the Divine Angel and vice-versa. When this larger use is then confirmed in Jewish interpretive tradition, even very early Jewish tradition, it becomes clear that the Jews and early Christians saw it the same way. It becomes part of the Two Powers view that God's revelation was consistently being mediated by the Divine Angel who appears under many names.

The conclusion is indisputable. The *paneh* is God's *special* angel—the Divine Angel. Though ch. 33 doesn't mention "the Angel of the LORD" as a formal title, the gathered witness of the Old Testament shows it was the Angel of the LORD that Moses spoke to and saw on Mount Sinai. He is the Angel of God's *paneh*, who manifests Yahweh's "presence" with his people.[97] When Moses asks, "Who are you going to send with me?" (Ex 33:12), God agrees to send his *paneh*, the "angel of his presence" with them, despite their sin.[98]

---

[97] An obscure, but interesting parallel occurs in Ecclesiastes 5:6, which says, "Let not your mouth lead you into sin, and do not say before *the messenger* (or "angel") that it was a mistake. Why should God be angry at your voice and destroy the work of your hands?" The Septuagint translates the same verse, "Do not set your mouth to make your flesh sin, and do not say *before God's face*, 'It is ignorance,' lest God become angry at your voice and destroy the works your hands." In other words, the "angel" is again identified as "God's face."

[98] Notice again Joseph Packard on Malachi 3 - "He is called the *face of God*, because though no man can see his face and live, yet the Angel of his face is the brightness of his glory, and the express image of his person. In him Jehovah's presence is manifested, and his glory reflected, for the glory of God shines in the face of Jesus Christ. There is thus a gradual development in the Old Testament of the doctrine of the incarnation, of the distinction of persons in the Godhead, not brought to light fully, lest it should interfere with the doctrine of the unity of God." Lange, J. P., Schaff, P., & Packard, J. (2008). *A commentary on the Holy Scriptures: Malachi* (p. 19). Bellingham, WA: Logos Bible Software.

Charles Gieschen writes, "Thus, Isa 63:9 interpreted the Divine Name Angel who went *before* Israel to be God's Presence *with* Israel." *Angelomorphic Christology: Antecedents and Early Evidence* (London: Brill Academic, 1998), 117-18.

The Old Testament is trying to describe how people can "see" and "know" God. Moses is "seeing" the unseen God. The God of the universe, who cannot be seen, is showing his presence to his people by sending a mediated form who is the presence of God. If we are Christians, we have to understand this in a *Christian* way. Nothing short of a Christian reading will do. The glorious explanation is that this is the Son of God manifest as the Angel of the LORD in the Old Testament, albeit in a deliberately mysterious way.

The Angel and Sinai, Ex 33: Jesus as the God of Sinai

If the OT is obscure and confusing on this point, one of the great burdens of the NT is to make it clear. It is most definitely *not* mysterious on the point! Consider John 1:14-18 again,

> And the Word became flesh and dwelt among us, and we have *seen his glory*, glory as of the only Son from the Father, full of grace and truth. (John bore witness about him, and cried out, "This was he of whom I said, 'He who comes after me ranks before me, because he was before me.'") For from his fullness we have all received, grace upon grace. For the law was given through Moses; grace and truth came through Jesus Christ. *No one has ever seen God; the only God, who is at the Father's side, he has made him known.*

This is all Exodus language—the Word "dwelling" among us, "seeing" his "glory." With an echo of Exodus 33, John says, "No one has ever seen God; the only God, who is at the Father's side, he has made him known." This refers, not just to the New Testament, but to the Old Testament. Jesus himself says,

> The Father who sent me has himself borne witness about me. His voice you have never heard, his *form* you have never seen, and you do not have his word abiding in you, *for* you do not believe the one whom he has sent. You search the Scriptures because you think that in them you have eternal life; and it is they that bear witness about me, but you refuse to come to me that you may have life … I have come in my Father's *name*, and you do not receive me. If another comes in his own name, you will receive him. How can you believe, when you receive glory from one another and do not seek the *glory*

that comes from the only God? Do not think that I will accuse you to the Father. There is one who accuses you: Moses, on whom you have set your hope. For if you believed Moses, you would believe me; for he wrote of me. But if you do not believe his writings, how will you believe my words?

(John 5:37-40, 43-47)

Why did the Jewish leaders want to kill Jesus? Because they understood all too well what he was saying. He was "making himself equal to God" (John 5:18). Jesus was claiming that he was the one "sent" from the Father who reveals the "form" of the Father, who reveals the Father's "name," who is the "glory that comes from the only God," that Moses "wrote" about him.

As another example, the Apostle Paul's words are unmistakable: "We all, with unveiled face, beholding the glory of the Lord, are being transformed into the same image" (2Co 3:18). How can we today behold the "glory" of the Lord? Paul makes it clear, "[God] has shone in our hearts to give the light of the knowledge of the glory of God *in the face of Jesus Christ*" (2Co 4:6). Paul was a scholar of the Old Testament. He knew exactly what he was saying when he says "the *face* of Jesus Christ" reveals "the glory of God."

And once more we can't help but think about Jude, the half-brother of the Lord himself! Where Moses said the "presence" saved the people out of Egypt (Dt 4:37), Jude says, "Jesus saved" them (Jude 5). Why? How? Because Jesus is the *paneh* of God.

In the Old Testament, you couldn't see God's face and live. Moses got as close as you could. He saw a manifestation of God's face from the backside. The reason Moses could not see God's full glory, in part, was because of his finiteness and sin, and because of the ultimate transcendence of God. But from a historical perspective, it was because the world was not ready. It was because God's covenantal purpose in redemptive history was not complete yet. Moses couldn't go as far as he would because God's angel was not ready to be fully unveiled.

But *we* can see God's face! The angel of his face is no longer obscured. Instead, he has become flesh, clothed in our frailty to protect us, come physically that all could see him and that we may know him fully.

Now we understand even more the meaning of the old priestly blessing:

Thus you shall bless the people of Israel: you shall say to them,
The LORD bless you and keep you;
the LORD make his face (*paneh*) to shine upon you and be gracious
to you;
the LORD lift up his countenance (*paneh*) upon you and give you
peace.
So shall they put my name upon the people of Israel, and I will bless
them.

(Numbers 6:23-27)

God's *paneh* has finally shone out through "the face of Jesus Christ!"

Historical Testimony

Finally, notice how many of the early Christians used these very arguments to prove the divinity and appearing of Christ in the Old Testament:

Cyril of Jerusalem (313-386 AD):

> For our object is to prove that the Lord Jesus Christ was with the
> Father. The Lord then says to Moses, *I will pass by before thee with My
> glory, and will proclaim the name of the Lord before thee*. Being Himself
> the Lord, what Lord doth He proclaim? Thou seest how He was covertly teaching the godly doctrine of the Father and the Son.[99]

Ambrose of Milan (340-397 AD):

> Scripture makes clear that that which is the Father's Name, the same
> is also that of the Son, for the Lord said in Exodus: "I will go before
> thee in My Name, and will call by My Name the Lord before thee."
> So, then, the Lord said that He would call the Lord by His Name.
> The Lord, then, is the Name of the Father and of the Son.[100]

---

[99] Cyril of Jerusalem. (1894). The Catechetical Lectures of S. Cyril, Archbishop of Jerusalem. In P. Schaff & H. Wace (Eds.), R. W. Church & E. H. Gifford (Trans.), *S. Cyril of Jerusalem, S. Gregory Nazianzen* (Vol. 7, p. 59). New York: Christian Literature Company.
[100] Ambrose of Milan. (1896). Three Books of St. Ambrose on the Holy Spirit. In P. Schaff & H. Wace (Eds.), H. de Romestin, E. de Romestin, & H. T. F.

Novatian (200-258 AD),

> In another passage, we note that Moses says that "God appeared unto
> Abraham." Yet the same Moses hears from God that "No man can see
> God and live." If God cannot be seen, how did he appear? Or if he
> appeared, how is it that he cannot be seen? John too says, "No man
> hath seen God at any time," and the Apostle Paul, "Whom no man
> hath seen or can see." Assuredly Holy Scripture does not lie; God re-
> ally was seen. We are led to understand that it was not the Father, Who
> never has been seen, that was here seen, but the Son, Who repeatedly
> descended to this earth and so was seen. For he is "the image of the
> invisible God"; being so in order that weak and frail human nature
> might in time become accustomed to see, in Him, Who is the Image
> of God, that is, in the Son of God, God the Father... The only intelli-
> gible explanation is that He is both angel and God.[101]

Tertullian (155-240 AD):

> We declare, however, that the Son also, considered in Himself (as the
> Son), is invisible, in that He is God, and the Word and Spirit of God;
> but that He was visible before *the days of* His flesh, in the way that He
> says to Aaron and Miriam, "And if there shall be a prophet amongst you,
> I will make myself known to him in a vision, and will speak to him in a
> dream; not as with Moses, with whom I shall speak mouth to mouth,
> even *apparently*, that is to say, in truth, and not *enigmatically*" that is to
> say, in image; as the apostle also expresses it, "Now we see through a
> glass, darkly (or enigmatically), but then face to face." Since, therefore,
> He reserves to some future time His presence and speech face to face
> with Moses—a promise which was afterwards fulfilled in the retirement
> of the mount (of transfiguration), when as we read in the Gospel, "Mo-
> ses appeared talking with Jesus"—it is evident that in early times it was
> always in a glass, (as it were,) and an enigma, in vision and dream, that
> God, I mean the Son of God, appeared—to the prophets and the patri-
> archs, as also to Moses indeed himself.[102]

Duckworth (Trans.), *St. Ambrose: Select Works and Letters* (Vol. 10, p. 111). New
York: Christian Literature Company.
[101] Novatian. *A Treatise of Novatian concerning the Trinity*. In Translations of
Christian Literature, Series II, Latin Texts. (MacMillan Company: New York
1919) 80-81.
[102] Tertullian. (1885). Against Praxeas. In A. Roberts, J. Donaldson, & A. C. Coxe
(Eds.), P. Holmes (Trans.), *Latin Christianity: Its Founder, Tertullian* (Vol. 3, p.
609). Buffalo, NY: Christian Literature Company.

More recent writers make the same arguments:

Geerhardus Vos:

> [God appears in] human/visible form. Behind this visible form is the impression that God is altogether invisible ... behind the Angel speaking as God, and who embodied in Himself all the condescension of God to meet the frailty and limitations of man, there existed at the same time another aspect of God, in which he could not be seen and materially received after such a fashion, the very God of whom the Angel spoke in the third person ... The Angel-conception points back to an inner distinction within the Godhead, so as to make the Angel a prefiguration of the incarnate Christ, then plainly the Person appearing in the revelation was uncreated, because God.[103]

Hermann Bavinck:

> The spiritual and eternal clothed itself in the form of the natural and temporal. God himself, Elohim, Creator of heaven and earth, as Yahweh, the God of the covenant, came down to the level of the creature, entered into history, assumed human language, emotions, and forms, in order to communicate himself with all his spiritual blessings to humans and SO TO PREPARE FOR HIS INCARNATION, his permanent and eternal indwelling in humanity. We would not even have at our disposal words with which to name the spiritual had not the spiritual first revealed itself in the form of the natural. Sensory creatures that we are, we can only express spiritual things analogically. If the eternal had not come within our reach in time, if God had not become a human, then neither could his thought have been conveyed to us in our language in Holy Scripture. God WOULD HAVE REMAINED PERPETUALLY UNKNOWABLE to us, and we would always have had to remain silent about him.[104]

---

[103] Geerhardus Vos, *Biblical Theology*, 74-75.
[104] Hermann Bavinck., *Reformed Dogmatics, vol.3.* (Grand Rapids, MI: Baker Academic, 2006), 221.

6

THE ANGEL AS "RIGHT-HAND MAN OF WAR"

The Angel and Joshua

Lord Sabaoth

ROWING UP IN CHURCH, WE REGULARLY SANG Martin Luther's famous hymn, "A Mighty Fortress." There is a line that goes, "Lord
Sabaoth his name. From age to age the same." Sabaoth is a
word few people ever use, and most have no idea what it meant. Was it a
misspelling of Sabbath? That didn't make much sense. But Luther provides
the very context needed to understand this magnificent song about Christ.
"And he must win the battle." Sabaoth, then, is a word that means "host of
heaven" (from the Hebrew *saba* meaning the same). Somehow, the meek,
mild Jesus that so many only think of because of how he came to us in the
New Testament is supposed to fit with him being the Lord of Hosts, that is
the Lord of the armies of heaven, who fights and wins wars for his people.

In what follows, we want to take a more detailed look at this aspect
of the Angel of the LORD. As the chief text to us seems to come in
Joshua, we have saved this discussion until now, even though it is clearly
revealed earlier to Moses who sings about it in the book of Exodus.

Joshua 5:13-15 is actually a crucially important text for identifying
the Angel of the Lord throughout the Old Testament and revealing the
explicit connections with Jesus in the New Testament. The study of this
passage will lead us to see connections with several other passages that

will dramatically expand the scope of the Angel's influence and identity throughout the Bible.

Month after month, year after year, through four decades of wandering in the wilderness, Moses would go inside the tent of meeting to talk with the *panim*—the face of the LORD. We have seen how "The LORD used to speak to Moses *face to face*, as a man speaks to his friend." What we have not seen is how his protégé, Joshua, would guard the tent in his absence (Ex 33:11). It says that he would not depart "from" (ESV) or "out of" (KJV) the tent. It isn't necessarily that Joshua was inside the tent with Moses, but at the very least he was near it, and often. He must have heard the discussions taking place within. He must have known the voice speaking to Moses.

Near the end of his time on earth, the LORD told Moses to commission Joshua as his successor, who would lead the people into the Promised Land. We are told,

> And Moses and Joshua went and presented themselves in the tent of meeting. And the LORD appeared in the tent in a pillar of cloud. And the pillar of cloud stood over the entrance of the tent ... And the LORD commissioned Joshua the son of Nun and said, "Be strong and courageous, for you shall bring the people of Israel into the land that I swore to give them. I will be with you."
>
> (Dt 31:14, 15, 23)

Just as the Angel of the LORD had appeared to Moses in the cloud, he appeared and spoke to Joshua. After Moses' death, the LORD continued speaking, saying, "No man shall be able to stand before you all the days of your life. Just as I was with Moses, so I will be with you. I will not leave you or forsake you" (Joshua 1:5).

The phrase "Angel of the LORD" is never actually mentioned in the book of Joshua. But as we have seen, the Angel of the LORD is the typical way God revealed himself in the Old Testament. Even when "the Angel" isn't explicitly mentioned, it becomes clear that he was the actor, mysteriously mediating the presence of God. Sometimes he is just called Yahweh, sometimes the Word, sometimes a Man, sometimes the Name, sometimes the Presence. Similarly, in the book of Joshua, he was the one who appeared and spoke to Joshua in the cloud. But as we will see, he also appeared to Joshua in different and instructive ways.

Commander of the Armies of the LORD: Joshua 5

Early in the book of Joshua, there is a strange and startling confrontation between Joshua and a mysterious warrior. The nation of Israel had finally crossed the Jordan into the Promised Land and were preparing for battle, facing the impenetrable fortress of Jericho—a city built to outlast any siege. The task before Israel was impossible, humanly speaking. Joshua, as the military leader now of the people, faced a daunting task.

While Joshua was scouting out the city, he "lifted up his eyes" (Josh 5:13; this is the same language used when the Angel and two other angels came to Abraham; Gen 18:2) and saw someone he did not expect to see: "Behold, a man (*'ish*) was standing before him with his drawn sword in his hand."[105]

The man was standing in battle posture, ready for attack. There was obviously something impressive about him. But Joshua did not immediately recognize him, at least not at first. So, as a man of courage, Joshua went up to the man and challenged him, "Are you for us or for our adversaries?" (13). Joshua boldly wanted to know, "Do you fight for us or fight against us? There's no other option in this battle. You're either with us or against us."

In one of the classic responses in the Bible, the man simply says "No." "No? No, what? That was an either/or question, not a yes or no! Who does this guy think he is?"

"No; but I am the commander of the army of the LORD. Now I have come" (14). What a way to introduce yourself! Some translations say "neither." The man seems to say, "False dichotomy, Joshua. Wrong question. It's not about whether I'm on your side or their side. The real question is: Are you on *my* side? I am the commander of the army of the Lord. Now I have come."

What happens next is vital. When the man said this, "Joshua fell on his face to the earth and worshiped and said to him, 'What does my

---

[105] There are several parallels between Joshua's encounter here and Jacob's encounter wrestling the Angel in Genesis 32:1-2, 22-32. Both occur as part of journeys to the Promised Land, facing fearful circumstances. Both occur after crossing water. In both, the 'man' suddenly appears, leading to a divine encounter.

Lord say to his servant?'" (Joshua 5:14). Apparently, as soon as the man spoke, Joshua recognized who he really was. While Joshua had been with Moses in the tent of meeting and had seen the Angel in the cloud, the revelation had always been veiled. But as soon as Joshua heard the Commander speak, he knew exactly who he was, because he had been standing outside that tent all those years hearing the very same voice. He recognized this voice. Therefore, he worshiped.

What takes place next seems to put the matter to rest. Not only does this "man" accept Joshua's worship (something godly men in the Bible never do), he identifies himself to Joshua with the same language the Angel of the LORD gave to Moses: "And the commander of the LORD's army said to Joshua, 'Take off your sandals from your feet, for the place where you are standing is holy'" (15). Notice the parallels with Exodus 3:5:

Joshua 5:15	Exodus 3:5
Take your sandals off your feet, for the place on which you are standing is holy ground.	Take off your sandals from your feet, for the place where you are standing is holy.

The language is almost exactly the same. In fact, they are the only two times in the entire Old Testament such a command of worship is given. This is the first of several verbal clues that give us the identity of this "man." He is the Angel of the LORD.

But why does he call himself "the commander of the army of the LORD"? Why is he here before the battle of Jericho? And why does he have a drawn sword in his hand? The answers to these questions actually give us some crucial insights into the identity and role of the Divine Angel, with compelling connections to the Person of Jesus.

The "Commander" of the Lord's Army

Consider first the title "commander of the army of the LORD." The Hebrew word for "commander" is *sar*. It is elsewhere translated as "prince." One might think that this proves that he is perfectly human. But not so fast. Sometimes this word is used for heavenly princes. Daniel

10:13 refers, for example, to the "prince of Persia" and a few verses later (20) it talks about the "prince of Greece." These are clearly angelic principalities in mind, as is shown when it calls the great archangel Michael "your prince" (21). Curiously, the LXX translates the word here in Joshua as *archistrategos*. In Jewish Literature, *archistrategos* is synonymous with the word for archangel.

More intriguingly, in Daniel 8, the prophet has a dream of a heavenly rebellion against God—a little horn that grew exceedingly great, even to the host of heaven. And it says, "And some of the host and some of the stars it threw down to the ground and trampled on them. It became great, even as great as the Prince of the host (*sar hatzavah*). And the regular burnt offering was taken away from him, and the place of his sanctuary was overthrown" (Dan 8:10-11). One commentary explains, "In view of the mention of the daily offering and 'his sanctuary,' there can be no doubt that the reference is to God."[106] It is difficult to refute this logic, but it fits perfectly with the thesis of our book. The phrase, "Prince of the host" in Daniel 8:11 is the same wording as Joshua 5:14.

That this is a title for deity is further demonstrated in the parallels to Daniel 8:11 found in 8:25 and 11:36, where the "Prince of the host" becomes the "prince of princes" and then the "God of gods."[107]

Daniel 8:11, 25	Daniel 11:36
It [the little horn] became great, even as great as *the Prince of the host*. And the regular burnt offering was taken away from him, and the place of his sanctuary was overthrown … And he shall	And the king shall do as he wills. He shall exalt himself and magnify himself above

---

[106] John Joseph Collins and Adela Yarbro Collins, *Daniel: A Commentary on the Book of Daniel*, ed. Frank Moore Cross, Hermeneia—a Critical and Historical Commentary on the Bible (Minneapolis, MN: Fortress Press, 1993), 333. The same comment continues by explaining that some have identified this prince with Michael (see Dan 10:13, 21; 12:1; cf. Rev 12). Beale notes the close relationship between Daniel's horns and stars thrown to the ground and the great war between Michael and Satan in Revelation 12:3-9. (G. K. Beale, *The Book of Revelation: A Commentary on the Greek Text*, New International Greek Testament Commentary [Grand Rapids, MI; Carlisle, Cumbria: W.B. Eerdmans; Paternoster Press, 1999], 697). While Beale does not make the Michael-Christ connection (and the authors of this present book disagree on the matter), others have, even in Revelation.

[107] Collins, ibid.

even rise up against *the Prince of princes*, and he shall be broken—but by no human hand.	every god, and shall speak astonishing things against *the God of gods*.

Who is this "prince" who leads the armies of heaven and bears divine titles? Compellingly, in the New Testament, it is Jesus who describes himself as the head of the angelic armies of heaven. In the Gospel of Matthew, he says, "The Son of Man will send *his angels*, and they will gather out of his kingdom all causes of sin and all law-breakers" (Matt 13:41); "For the Son of Man is going to come with *his angels* in the glory of his Father, and then he will repay each person according to what he has done" (16:27); "All the tribes of the earth will mourn, and they will see the Son of Man coming on the clouds of heaven with power and great glory. And he will send out *his angels* with a loud trumpet call" (24:30-31). In Revelation 19:11-16, Jesus is described as coming on a white horse, with the armies of heaven following him on white horses. In fact, 19:16 says, "On his robe and on his thigh, he has a name written, King of kings and Lord of lords"—the same kind of language as found in Daniel![108]

So this figure in Joshua accepts worship as God himself, yet identifies himself as the "Prince of the armies of heaven." Joshua knows who he is and knows why he has come.

Yahweh as a Man of War: Exodus 15

In fact, the identification of the Divine Angel as a Divine warrior had already been made by Joshua's predecessor, Moses. In Moses' famed "Song of the Sea" (Exodus 15:1-19), he refers to "God" as a "man of war." He presents the God who had rescued them from Egypt, who went before them in the cloud and who defended them against the Egyptians, as a Divine Warrior.

> Then Moses and the people of Israel sang this song to the LORD, saying, "I will sing to the LORD, for he has triumphed gloriously; the horse and his rider he has thrown into the sea. The LORD is my

---

[108] See also Rev 17:14; 1Ti 6:15.

strength and my song, and he has become my salvation; this is my God, and I will praise him, my father's God, and I will exalt him. The LORD is a *man of war*; the LORD is his *name*."

(Exodus 15:1-3)

The song celebrates the promise of Exodus 14:14: "The LORD will fight for you. And you have only to be silent." God is depicted in the song as a victor who hurtled the Egyptians into the depths of the Red Sea. Later in the song, we are told that his victory came at his own right hand: "Your *right hand*, O LORD, glorious in power, your *right hand*, O LORD, shatters the enemy" (Ex 15:6).

This phrase "right hand" is extremely important and pregnant with meaning! It's easy to think of the "right hand" (or the parallel, God's "arm") as a literary anthropomorphism (attributing a human attribute to God) representing the disembodied idea of God's "power" (as in, "God's right hand is a symbol of his power"). But what if God's "right hand" is more than a disembodied idea? What if there is more to the "anthropomorphism" than meets the eye? In fact, as we have seen with God's Name and God's Presence, in the Old Testament, the phrases "God's right hand" or "God's arm" become a hypostasis of God, a very Person!

Consider how Isaiah describes the Exodus event, this time with the Arm in mind. "Where is he who put in the midst of them his Holy Spirit, who caused *his glorious arm* to go at *the right hand* of Moses, who divided the waters before them to make for himself an everlasting name" (Isa 63:11-12). "He" refers to God the Father. He put the Holy Spirit and the Arm there to fight the battle as Moses' right hand. We see the same kind of thing happening in several places.[109]

---

[109] With reference to the "arm," see also Isa 63:5, "I looked, but there was no one to help; I was appalled, but there was no one to uphold; so *my own arm* brought me salvation;" 59:16, "He saw that there was no man, and wondered that there was no one to intercede; then *his own arm* brought him salvation, and his righteousness upheld him." With reference to the Exodus, see also Isa 51:9-10, "Awake, awake, put on strength, O *arm of the LORD*; awake, as in days of old, the generations of long ago. Was it not you who cut Rahab in pieces, who pierced the dragon? Was it not you who dried up the sea, the waters of the great deep, who made the depths of the sea a way for the redeemed to pass over?" Most famously, see Isaiah 53:1, "Who has believed what he has heard from us? And to whom has *the arm of the LORD* been revealed?" Or Ex 9:3, "Behold, *the hand of the LORD* will

The "right hand" and "arm" is actually a way of talking about a military *commander* of a leader or king.[110] It's not an anthropomorphic *idea*, but an anthropomorphic *title* of a *Person*. In Isaiah's song, he is both the Father's "glorious arm" and Moses' "right hand." Who is this Commander? In fact, the Isaiah passage (which we also looked at in the last chapter) has already told us a few verses earlier. The one who was "sent" to be with Israel is explicitly called "the Angel of his presence (*panim*, face)" (Isa 63:9).

Similarly, this same phenomenon is also famously seen in Psalm 110—the psalm most quoted in the New Testament to refer to Jesus. "The LORD says to my Lord: "Sit at my *right hand*, until I make your enemies your footstool ... The Lord is at your *right hand*; he will shatter kings on the day of his wrath. He will execute judgment among the nations" (Ps 110:1, 5-6).[111] As the New Testament also identifies, there is an Adonai at the "right hand" of Yahweh, who is Yahweh's man of war to execute judgment on the earth.[112]

So when Moses sang that "the LORD is a man (*'ish*) of war; the LORD is his name" (Ex 15:3),[113] when he said, "your *right hand*, O

---

fall with a very severe plague upon your livestock that are in the field." There are many more. See also Ex16:3; Dt 2:15; Josh 4:24, 22:31; Jdg 2:15; 1Sa 5:6, 5:9, 7:13; 12:15; 2Sa 24:14; 1Chr 21:13; Job 12:9; Ps 118:14-16; Isa 25:10, 41:20, 51:17, 66:14; Ezek 33:22, 37:1, 40:1; etc.

[110] "God's arm stands for military power e.g. at Ex 15:16; Dt 4:34; Isa 30:30. This imagery is in most cases related to the liberation out of Egypt. God's arm stands for creative power in texts like Isa 51:9 and Ps 89:11, 14, where the imagery is linked to the battle with the monstrous →Rahab. God's arm is related to the depiction of →Yhwh as a judge at Isa 51:5; 59:16 and Ezek 20:33, 34 ... 'Arm' is used as a hypostasis in Isa 63:12. Here the *zerôa'* stands for an independent power going side by side with →Moses and stressing the function of Yhwh as →Shepherd and leader of his people" (B. Becking, "Arm," ed. Karel van der Toorn and Pieter W. van der Horst, *Dictionary of Deities and Demons in the Bible* [Leiden; Boston; Köln; Grand Rapids, MI; Cambridge: Brill; Eerdmans, 1999], 90).

[111] Cited in Matt 22:44; Mark 12:36; Luke 20:42-43, Acts 2:34-35.

[112] The martyr Stephen makes this connection in Acts 7:55-57, "But he, full of the Holy Spirit, gazed into heaven and saw the glory of God, and Jesus standing at the right hand of God. And he said, "Behold, I see the heavens opened, and the Son of Man standing at the right hand of God." But they cried out with a loud voice and stopped their ears and rushed together at him." The Hellenistic Jews opposing Stephen were very familiar with the language Stephen was using and what he was claiming, and that's why they wanted to kill him.

[113] We will return to the cryptic naming of this man as "wonderful" (Ex 15:11) in the next chapter.

LORD, shatters the enemy" (Ex 15:6), Moses was actually describing the Angel of the LORD as the divine warrior "sent" to fight for the people.

Unfortunately, again, many miss this connection and fail to consider that this could be something other than purely poetic language for God in his bare essence. But Isaiah's "angel," David's "Adonai," and Moses' "man" and "the name" are wed to the Angel who is in Exodus 14:19, guarding them from the Egyptians - "Then the angel of God who was going before the host of Israel moved and went behind them, and the pillar of cloud moved from before them and stood behind them" (with the cloud being an image of Isaiah's Holy Spirit). Thomas Watson says of this,

> This is a great ground of comfort to the church of God in the midst of all the combinations of the enemy, "Christ is king;" and he can not only bound the enemies' power, but break it. The church hath more with her than against her, she hath Emmanuel on her side, even that great King to whom all knees must bend. Christ is called "a man of war," Ex 15:3.[114]

[Excursus]

Exodus 15 was considered a "dangerous" passage by later rabbis, because of how many Jews at the time of Christ were interpreting it. In fact, some saw Yahweh appearing as a "man of war" as a different Yahweh from his appearing as an older man at Sinai. Some of the Rabbis saw the need to correct this "dangerous" misunderstanding. For example,

> R. Levi (290-320 C.E.) said: God faced them in many guises. To one He appeared standing, and to one seated; (See Gen 28:13 and Isa 6:1) to one as a young man, and to one as an old man. How so? At the

---

[114] Thomas Watson, *The Select Works of the Rev. Thomas Watson, Comprising His Celebrated Body of Divinity, in a Series of Lectures on the Shorter Catechism, and Various Sermons and Treatises* (New York: Robert Carter & Brothers, 1855), 128. Citing Wisdom 18:15-18, Isaac Watts adds the logos to this equation. "Thy almighty word leaped down from heaven, out of thy royal throne, as a fierce man of war, into the midst of a land of destruction, and brought thy unfeigned commandment as a sharp sword, and standing up filled up all things with death; and it touched the heaven, but it stood upon the earth." Isaac Watts, *The Works of the Rev. Isaac Watts*, vol. 6 (Leeds; London: Edward Baines; William Baynes; Thomas Williams and Son; Thomas Hamilton; Josiah Conder, 1813), 283

time the Holy One, blessed be He, appeared on the Red Sea to wage war for His children and to requite the Egyptians, He faced them as a young man, since war is waged best by a young man, as is said The Lord is a man of war, the Lord is His name (Ex. 15:3)."[115]

Rabbi Levi was attempting to "correct" this two-Yahweh's view.[116] Writing of this man of war, the *New Treasury of Scripture Knowledge* explains how, *"One appears to Joshua, calling himself 'The Captain of the Lord's host,' in form of a man of war; Joshua worships him; the place of his presence holy ground,"* but goes on, "Many persons have been puzzled to know what was intended by this extraordinary appearance of the angel to Joshua, because they supposed that the whole business ends with the chapter..."[117]

Early Christians, especially those writing the NT, were not puzzled. All the Scripture follows right in line with this, except that they gave this "man" a name. Think about the verse that begins the most famous Servant Song passage (Isaiah 53), a chapter entirely devoted to the coming Messiah. "Who has believed what he has heard from us? And to whom has *the arm of the LORD* been revealed?" (Isa 53:1).

In large part because so many Jews had become Christians, the rabbis after the fall of Jerusalem (70 A.D.) began systematically declaring any interpretation like this official heresy,[118] which meant banishment to anyone who held to it. Fossum writes,

> The earliest denials of the heresy—found in different versions of the Mekiltoth [parts of the Mishna, no earlier than the turn of the third century A. D.]—are aiming to show that the God who appeared as a "man of war" at the Red Sea (Ex 15:3) is the same as the God who appeared "like an old man full of mercy" on Mt. Sinai (see *Mekilta de R. Simeon ben Yohai, Bashalah* ch. xv; *Mekilta de R. Ishmael,*

---

[115] PR Piska 21 100b 1, cited in Segal, 34.

[116] For more on the Jewish "Two Yahweh's doctrine, see ch. 16.

[117] Jerome H. Smith, The New Treasury of Scripture Knowledge: The Most Complete Listing of Cross References Available Anywhere—Every Verse, Every Theme, Every Important Word (Nashville, TN: Thomas Nelson, 1992), 242-43.

[118] The rabbis called it the "Two Powers in Heaven" heresy because they "maintained that such conceptions implied an independent will for one of God's creatures, hence compromised monotheism" (Segal, 64). We will deal with this later in the book.

Baḥodesh ch. v; *Shirta* ch. iv). While the tradition in the Mekilta of R. Simeon says that the name YHWH is repeated twice in Ex 15:3 ("YHWH is a man of war; YHWH is His name") in order to make clear that it is the same God, even YHWH, who is appearing in both places, the Mekilta of R. Ishmael defines the dangerous doctrine as the idea that YHWH the man of war and the Elohim of Ex 24:10 ("And they saw the Elohim of Israel") were two different divine manifestations, one just and one merciful.[119]

The Angel of the LORD with a Drawn Sword: Numbers 22 and 1 Chronicles 21

All this is to say, when the man in Joshua 5:14 identifies himself as "the commander of the army of the LORD," Joshua immediately knows that this is God's "Hand" or "Arm," the Promised Angel sent to fight on their behalf, who deserves worship as God himself. But there is another important clue to his identity. The drawn sword in the man's hand is also very significant. This phrase ("drawn sword" or *weharbo shelupha*) appears only two other times. In both, it is the Angel of the LORD who has the drawn sword.[120]

In Numbers 22:22-23, when the pagan prophet Balaam was going to prophesy against Israel, we are told,

> God's anger was kindled because he went, and the angel of the LORD took his stand in the way as his adversary. Now he was riding on the donkey, and his two servants were with him. And the donkey saw the angel of the LORD standing in the road, with a drawn sword (*weharbo shelupha*) in his hand.

Many commentators will point out that the angel here is *seemingly* distinguished from God (in both 22:22 and 22:31), and so they conclude that this angel is a lesser spiritual messenger. If he is distinguished, this of course would be exactly what we would expect to see *sometimes* if the

---

[119] Jarl E. Fossum, *The Name of God and the Angel of the LORD: Samaritan and Jewish Concepts of Intermediation and the Origin of Gnosticism* (Tubingen: J. C. B. Mohr, 1985), 227.

[120] Michael S. Heiser, *The Unseen Realm: Recovering the Supernatural Worldview of the Bible*, First Edition. (Bellingham, WA: Lexham Press, 2015), 146.

Angel is in fact the Second Person of the Godhead. For he is both God and yet distinguished from the Father. Thus, this kind of language is quite in line with our own view of the Angel.

But in the same breath that he is distinguished, we also find him one with Yahweh. Notice the angel's words to Balaam, "Behold, I have come out to oppose you because your way is perverse *before me*" (22:32). Then the angel of the Lord said to Balaam, "Go with the men, but speak only the word that *I tell you*" (22:35). The Angel speaks here with the authority and prerogative of God himself. Thus, in the same text he is both distinguished and not distinguished from God. But the larger point for our study now is that the Angel is identified by his *drawn sword as a man of war opposing Israel's enemies.*

The second appearance of the "drawn sword" is in 1 Chronicles 21:16. Because of David's sin in calling for an unbiblical census (see 1Chr 21:1, also Exodus 30:11), the LORD determined to punish Israel. God gives David three options for Israel's punishment:

> So Gad came to David and said to him, "Thus says the LORD, 'Choose what you will: either three years of famine, or three months of devastation by your foes while the sword of your enemies over-takes you, or else three days of the sword of the Lord, pestilence on the land, with the *angel of the LORD* destroying throughout all the territory of Israel.' Now decide what answer I shall return to him who sent me." Then David said to Gad, "I am in great distress. Let me fall into *the hand of the LORD*, for his mercy is very great, but do not let me fall into the hand of man."
>
> (1Chr 21:11-13)

Notice what we've already seen: "the hand of the LORD" is not just a figure of speech but is a title for "the angel of the LORD" as the military representative of God himself. David asks for the punishment to come from the "angel" who is "the hand of the LORD," Yahweh's man of war, "for his mercy is very great." The text goes on:

> So the LORD sent a pestilence on Israel, and 70,000 men of Israel fell. And God sent the angel to Jerusalem to destroy it, but as he was about to destroy it, the LORD saw, and he relented from the calam-ity. And he said to the angel who was working destruction, "It is enough; now stay your *hand*." And the angel of the LORD was

standing by the threshing floor of Ornan the Jebusite. And David lifted his eyes and saw the angel of the LORD standing between earth and heaven, and in *his hand* a drawn sword (*weharbo shelupha*) stretched out over Jerusalem. Then David and the elders, clothed in sackcloth, fell upon their faces.

(1Chr 21:14–16)

As in Numbers 22, many commentators hesitate to identify the angel here with the Divine Angel. Again, the text appears to clearly distinguish the angel from God who "sent" him. However, he is called "the hand of the LORD," the Divine Warrior who represents God. Several other clues should lead us to identify the "angel working destruction" with the Divine Angel himself.[121]

Remember, the Angel of the LORD is not only the protector of God's people (Psalm 34:7), but also the Angel who carries out God's judgment: "Let [the wicked] be like chaff before the wind, with the angel of the Lord driving them away ... with the angel of the Lord pursuing them!" (Psalm 35:5-6).[122]

This Angel of destruction is often synonymous with God himself. During the final plague of the Exodus, in Exodus 12:23, we are told, "The LORD will pass through to strike the Egyptians, and when he sees the blood on the two doorposts, the LORD will pass over the door and will not allow the *destroyer* to enter your houses to strike you." It is the LORD himself passing through, and it's also "the destroyer."[123]

However, there is a more significant clue that the angel with the sword stretched out over Jerusalem is the Divine Angel himself. 1 Chronicles 21:15 tells us, "The angel of the LORD was standing by the threshing floor of Ornan the Jebusite." This is not extraneous information. The threshing floor of Ornan the Jebusite becomes the future location for the Jerusalem Temple. In 2 Samuel 24:18-19, the prophet Gad tells David at Yahweh's command to erect an altar on the threshing

---

[121] For even more than we were able to fit into this chapter, see the Appendix at the end of the book on the Angel and the *satan*.

[122] See the description of Jesus himself in 2Th 1:7-8, "... when the Lord Jesus is revealed from heaven with his mighty angels in flaming fire, inflicting vengeance on those who do not know God and on those who do not obey the gospel of our Lord Jesus."

[123] See also Isa 37:36, 2Kg 19:35.

floor. But in 1 Chronicles 21:18-19, we are told, "Now the angel of the LORD had commanded Gad to say to David that David should go up and raise an altar to the LORD on the threshing floor of Ornan the Jebusite. So David went up at Gad's word, which he had spoken in the name of the LORD." In 2 Samuel 24, it is Yahweh who commissions the altar; in 1 Chronicles 21, it is the "Angel of the LORD" who commissions the altar. His words are Yahweh's words.

Then 2 Chronicles 3:1 records, "Then Solomon began to build the house of the LORD in Jerusalem on Mount Moriah, where the LORD had *appeared* to David his father, at the place that David had appointed, on the threshing floor of Ornan the Jebusite." What LORD "appeared" to David at the threshing floor? In fact, it was the Angel of the LORD who appeared to David over the threshing floor, and the Bible identifies his appearing as the appearing of Yahweh! Yet the text also distinguishes the Angel and Yahweh!

The threshing floor happened to be on the top of a hill—a hill later known as Mt. Zion, but earlier known as Mt. Moriah! It was the same Mt. Moriah where the same Angel of the LORD had called to Abraham and stopped him from sacrificing Isaac (Gen 22:11). It is also the same hill where he promised to "put my name there" (Dt 12:5).

Do you see what's happening? Here's the Angel of the LORD, on the top of the same mountain, with a sword of judgment stretched over Jerusalem, and he *stops*. And where he stops, he tells David to build an altar—where one day the Temple is going to be built to make atonement for the people through sacrifice. After David builds the altar, in 1 Chronicles 21:26-27, "The LORD answered him with fire from heaven upon the altar of burnt offering. Then the LORD commanded the angel, and he put his sword back into its sheath." In other words, the judgment stops by the plan of God because of David's sacrifice, which foreshadows God's plan to build a Temple where he would dwell with the people, make atonement for their sin, and establish peace. The Angel of the LORD is there overseeing the whole process, and it's there, at the Mount of Jerusalem where the Angel puts away the sword![124]

---

[124] In fact, David seems to understand that God would no longer accept sacrifices anywhere else. At the end of 1Chr 21, we are told that the tabernacle and altar of burnt offering were "at that time in the high place at Gibeon, but David could

To make this even more interesting, as part of a prophecy of salvation, Zechariah 13:7 records these famous words, "'Awake, O sword, against my shepherd, against the man who stands next to me,' declares the LORD of hosts."[125] Who is the "man who stands next to" Yahweh? We already know his identity as "the right hand" of the LORD. He is the Angel who put away the sword at Jerusalem. One day, the "sword" the Angel "put away" would be turned "against" the Angel himself. The Angel who carried the sword, who stands next to God, puts away the sword at the very place where one day the sword would be turned against himself. So Zechariah 12:10 says, "When they look on me, on him whom they have pierced, they shall mourn for him, as one mourns for an only child, and weep bitterly over him, as one weeps over a firstborn." He "puts away the sword" by taking the punishment himself and putting to death the enmity.

In all of these cases, the "drawn sword" identifies the Angel of the LORD as the Commander of the Army of the LORD, the "right hand of the LORD" who is Yahweh's "man of war" and is Yahweh himself. This begins to explain why the rest of the book of Joshua simply shortens "Commander of the armies of the LORD" to "LORD" whenever he speaks to Joshua about an upcoming battle. This begins just a couple of verses later, "And the LORD said to Joshua, 'See, I have given Jericho into your hand, with its king and mighty men of valor" (Josh 6:2). It continues throughout the book such as when, "The LORD said to Joshua, 'Do not be afraid of them, for tomorrow at this time I will give over all of them, slain, to Israel" (Josh 11:5).

Do You Recognize Him?

So, returning to Joshua, why does this man of war appear to Joshua with a drawn sword who is called the commander of the army of the LORD? The answer was clear to Joshua. This was another appearing of

---

not go before it to inquire of God, for he was afraid of the sword of the angel of the LORD" (1Chr 21:29-30).

[125] See Matthew 26:31, "Jesus said to them, "You will all fall away because of me this night. For it is written, 'I will strike the shepherd, and the sheep of the flock will be scattered.'"

the promised and ever-present Angel of the LORD who would go with them into the Promised Land and would fight on their behalf.[126] A.W. Pink writes,

> Observe well how God suits the revelation of Himself unto His saints according to their circumstances and needs: to Abraham in his tent He appeared as a Traveler (Gen 18:1, 2, 13), to Moses at the backside of the desert in a bush (Ex 3:1, 2), to Joshua at the beginning of his campaign as 'a Man of war' (cf. Ex 15:3). In the celebrating of the Passover Christ had been prefigured as the Lamb, slain (vs. 11); here in verse 13, with drawn sword in hand, He appeared as 'the Lion of the tribe of Judah' (Rev 5:5)."[127]

John Calvin wrote,

> We have said that in the books of Moses the name of Jehovah is often attributed to the presiding Angel, who was undoubtedly the only-begotten Son of God. He is indeed very God, and yet in the person of Mediator by dispensation, he is inferior to God. I willingly receive what ancient writers teach on this subject—that when Christ anciently appeared in human form, it was a prelude to the mystery which was afterwards exhibited when God was manifested in the flesh … [God was] offering his assistance in the combats which were about to be waged, and promising by his arrival that the war would have a happy issue. It cannot be inferred with certainty from the worship which he offered, whether Joshua paid divine honor to Christ distinctly recognized as such; but by asking, What command does my Lord give to his servant? he attributes to him a power and authority which belong to God alone.[128]

---

[126] Justin Martyr wrote, "So my friends…I shall show from Scripture that God has begotten of Himself a certain rational power as a beginning before all other creatures. The Holy Spirit indicates this power by various titles, sometimes the Glory of the Lord, at other times, Son or Wisdom or Angel or God or Lord or Word. He even called himself commander-in-chief when he appeared in human guise to Joshua, the son of Nun" (*Dialogue* 61).

[127] A. W. Pink, Gleanings in Joshua, 202 - http://www.grace-ebooks.com/library/Arthur W. Pink/Gleanings in Joshua - Arthur W. Pink.pdf.

[128] Calvin, *Commentary on the Book of Joshua* (Bellingham, WA: Logos Bible Software), 87.

Jonathan Edwards amazingly summarizes this biblical-theological understanding of the Divine Angel as Christ, when he explains,

> As soon as man fell, Christ entered on his mediatorial work. Then it was that he began to execute the work and office of a mediator. He had undertaken it before the world was made. He stood engaged with the Father to appear as man's mediator, and to take on that office when there should be occasion, from all eternity. But now the time was come. Christ the eternal Son of God clothed himself with the mediatorial character, and therein presented himself before the Father. He immediately stepped in between a holy, infinite, offended Majesty, and offending mankind. He was accepted in his interposition; and so wrath was prevented from going forth in the full execution of that amazing curse that man had brought on himself. It is manifest that Christ began to exercise the office of mediator between God and man as soon as ever man fell, because mercy began to be exercised towards man immediately... When Satan, the grand enemy, had conquered and overthrown man, the business of resisting and conquering him was committed to Christ. He thenceforward undertook to manage that subtle powerful adversary. He was then appointed *the Captain of the Lord's hosts*, the Captain of their salvation. Henceforward this lower world, with all its concerns, devolved upon the Son of God: for when man had sinned, God the Father would have no more to do immediately with this world of mankind, that had apostatized from and rebelled against him. He would henceforward act only through a mediator, either in teaching men, or in governing, or bestowing any benefits on them. And therefore, when we read in sacred history what God did, from time to time, towards his church and people, and how he revealed himself to them, we are to understand it especially of the second person of the Trinity. When we read of God *appearing* after the fall, in some visible form or outward symbol of his presence, we are ordinarily, if not universally, to understand it of the second person of the Trinity.[129]

For this reason, the Angel of the Lord appeared as a man of war both to challenge and teach Joshua. Seeing the Angel as a Man of War was not a warm and fuzzy experience to Joshua. It was a reminder that

---

[129] Jonathan Edwards, *History of the Work of Redemption (with notes)* (London: T. Pitcher, 1793] 64.

God is holy. It was a reminder that you can't "presume" on God's help. He is not your servant. You must become his servant—be on his side. The only proper response is to fall on your face, take off your shoes, and let him command your life.

At one point, Jesus told his disciples, "Do not think that I have come to bring peace to the earth. I have not come to bring peace, but a *sword*... Whoever does not take his cross and follow me is not worthy of me" (Matt 10:34, 38).

The book of Revelation tells us that one day Jesus will come again as this mighty man of war and commander of the army of the LORD:

> Then I saw heaven opened, and behold, a white horse! The one sitting on it is called Faithful and True, and in righteousness he judges and makes war. His eyes are like a flame of fire, and on his head are many diadems, and he has a name written that no one knows but himself. He is clothed in a robe dipped in blood, and the name by which he is called is The Word of God. And the armies of heaven, arrayed in fine linen, white and pure, were following him on white horses. From his mouth comes a sharp sword with which to strike down the nations, and he will rule them with a rod of iron. He will tread the winepress of the fury of the wrath of God the Almighty. On his robe and on his thigh he has a name written, King of kings and Lord of lords.
>
> (Rev 19:11–16)

Behold, he has come! Are we ready to follow at his command?

7

THE ANGEL AS "WONDERFUL"

The Angel and Judges

How Wonderful!

I F YOU HAD TO PICK A BOOK OF THE BIBLE that mentioned "the Angel of the LORD" more times than any other, you might not think of Judges first. Many people have never even read Judges. It is a strange book that comes between the conquest and the monarchy, and its theme is, "Everyone did what was right in his own eyes" (Jdg 21:25). Why, then, might the author of this book have chosen to mention "the Angel of the LORD" almost twice as many times as any other Old Testament book? Perhaps it is because in the darkest hours of the nation, the people were in greater need of glimpsing their God and their Hope—the Angel of the LORD who is wonderful!

The Angel of the Covenant: Judges 2

The first story that references the Angel of the LORD is found in Judges 2:1-5—a text we already discussed in the *Introduction* (and to which we refer you back for more detailed exegesis than we will provide here). The Angel visibly left the original encampment of Israel in the land at Gilgal and moved to Bochim (which the LXX identifies with

Bethel). After the death of Joshua, the people had failed to obey the Angel's command, had failed to drive out the inhabitants of the land, and had made covenants with their enemies (Judges 2:2). As a result, the Angel says, "So now I say, I will not drive them out before you, but they shall become thorns in your sides, and their gods shall be a snare to you" (2:3). As we saw in Ch. 1, the warning of Exodus 23 was coming to pass, and the Angel of the Covenant was withdrawing his promise of full blessing to drive out their enemies. Though the people wept at Bochim and sacrificed to the LORD, their repentance did not last. Nevertheless, as we will see, the Angel doesn't totally abandon his people.

He certainly disciplines them for their sin by handing them over to their enemies. We are told, "Whenever they marched out, the *hand of the LORD* was against them for harm, as the LORD had warned, and as the LORD had sworn to them" (2:15). It is important to see the connection between this verse and the one previously mentioned, for here we have yet another example of "the Angel of the LORD" being shorted simply to "Yahweh." For it was no one other than the Angel who had sworn to do this earlier in the chapter.

But we can say this another way as well. The Angel, God's "right hand" (as we saw in the previous chapter) was no longer fighting for them, but against them. When the tribes failed to support and fight for one another, he judged them, as is described in the Song of Deborah - "'Curse Meroz,' says *the angel of the LORD*, 'curse its inhabitants thoroughly, because they did not come to the help of the LORD, to the help of the LORD against the mighty'" (5:23).

But despite these disciplines for sin, in mercy the Angel will also reveal himself to them and seek to remind them of his goodness and power to work wonders on their behalf. At crucial moments, he would once again appear and challenge them to see him as their "shield and exceeding great reward" (Gen 15:1).

The Angel and Gideon: Judges 6 & the Prince of Peace

The second visible appearance of the Angel of the LORD in Judges is in the story of Gideon. Once again, the people had fallen into sin and God had given them over to their enemies (Jdg 6:1-6). The people then cried to the LORD, and he sent a prophet to rebuke them (6:7-10). But after rebuking them, we are told,

> Now the *angel of the LORD* came and sat under the terebinth at Ophrah, which belonged to Joash the Abiezrite, while his son Gideon was beating out wheat in the winepress to hide it from the Midianites. And the *angel of the LORD* appeared to him and said to him, "The LORD is with you, O mighty man of valor."
>
> (Judges 6:11-12)

Just like with Abraham, Jacob, and Joshua, the Angel comes to Gideon in the appearance of a "man." In fact, the mention of the terebinth is a reminder of God's appearing to Abraham "by the terebinths at Mamre" (Genesis 18:1).[130] Gideon, however, does not immediately recognize the man's identity. Gideon is hiding his harvest in a winepress, fearful of the Midianites. So, the Angel's first words are somewhat

---

[130] The association with trees and God (or in paganism, the gods) and making contact with the spirit realm by them is ubiquitous in the ancient world. In the OT we think of Abraham: Gen 12:6-7 and 18:1; Jacob: Gen 35:4; Joshua: Josh 24:25-27; Deborah: Jdg 4:4-5; Gideon: Jdg 9:5-6; David: 2Sa 5:24-25; Pagan Trees: Dt 16:21; 1Kg 14:23; 2Kg 17:10; Jer 17:2. See Michael S. Heiser, "Sacred Trees in Israelite Religion," in *Faithlife Study Bible* (Bellingham, WA: Lexham Press, 2012, 2016).

Some words for trees and God(s) have the same basic root (*el*; see chart below). Often, the gods (Ex 15:27; Dt 4:28; Ezek 31:9) or God, including Christ himself, are linked to trees (think burning bush in Ex 3:2 or Dt 33:16 or marching in the trees in 2Sa 5:24 or terms linked more directly like "righteous branch" in Isa 4:2, or "stump of Jesse" in Isa 11:1, or "the vine" in John 15:5.

Ancient Word		Reference	Contextual Meaning
El		Gen 33:20	El, the God of Israel *
elohim		Gen 1:1 etc.	The God of Israel
elohim		Gn 6:2, 4; Jb 1:6, 2:1; 38:7	sons of God
elim		Exodus 15:11	gods
elim	('eylim)	Exodus 15:27	location of 70 palm trees in desert
elohim		Deuteronomy 32:17	demons
elohim		Dt 32:43 (LXX, DSS)	Angels (aggelos)
elohim		1 Samuel 28:13	spirit of Samuel
elim		Ps 29:1; 89:6	sons of God
elyon		Ps 82:6	sons of God
el	('eyl, form of ayil)	Ezekiel 31:11	mighty leader, god, or tree
eleyhem		Ezekiel 31:14	trees of Eden (terebinth tree), haughty(?)
elon **	('eylan, Aramaic)	Daniel 4	tree-king Nebuchadnezzar

* *El* probably derives from "mighty" or "first in rank."
** *Elon* (often meaning 'sacred tree') might be a back-formation of the plural *'elonim* (gods). See *William Foxwell Albright, Yahweh and the Gods of Canaan: A Historical Analysis of Two Contrasting Faiths* (Winona Lake, IN: Eisenbrauns, 1968), 165-166.

mocking and challenging: "The LORD is with you, O mighty man of valor." As happens so often in the Bible, God comes to an unworthy, weak, and even foolish people, and he reimagines and transforms their lives. Gideon will become a mighty man of valor, but he first needs a change of perspective.

In fact, Gideon thinks the LORD has abandoned them. He says, "Please, my Lord, if the LORD is with us, why then has all this happened to us? And where are all his wonderful deeds that our fathers recounted to us, saying, 'Did not the LORD bring us up from Egypt? But now the LORD has forsaken us and given us into the hand of Midian'" (Jdg 6:13). The "wonderful deeds" Gideon mentions is the word *niphlaotai* (from the word *pala'*)—which refers to the "wonders" God performed in Egypt to rescue his people. Gideon does not realize that he is speaking to the very One who "worked the wonders." God had not abandoned them, but even now was working his greater purpose to refine and purify them.

We are then told, "The LORD turned to him and said, 'Go in this might of yours and save Israel from the hand of Midian; do not I send you?'" (6:14). The text is very clear: The Angel who appeared to him was Yahweh appearing to him.[131] Vs.16 goes on, "And the LORD said to him, 'But I will be with you, and you shall strike the Midianites as one man.'"

Now, Gideon has begun to suspect who this man is, but he isn't entirely sure yet. So he asks, "If now I have found favor in your eyes, then show me a sign that it is you who speak with me. Please do not depart from here until I come to you and bring out my present and set it before you" (6:17-18). Gideon then goes into his house and prepares a young goat and "unleavened cakes from an ephah of flour" (6:19).

Now we need to understand what he's doing. Gideon is, in fact, self-consciously reenacting Abraham's actions in Genesis 18. As Abraham brought meat and bread and served it to Yahweh and the two angels "under the tree" (Gen 18:8), so Gideon brings it to the Angel "under the terebinth." In fact, the *quantity* of the food is an astounding amount,

---

[131] The LXX changes both vs. 14 and 16 to "the angel of the LORD." As Alan Segal has argued, even as early as the Septuagint, the Jewish rabbis felt the need to clarify the Hebrew in order to correct "2 Powers Theology" and preserve strict monotheism. They were worried about the obvious implications of the text that recognized a multiplicity in the Godhead. See Segal, *Two Powers in Heaven*.

and deliberately parallel to the Abraham story! Gideon's "ephah of flour" equaled around 22 liters (more than 5 gallons of flour)! Similarly, Abraham's "three seahs of flour" (Gen 18:6) also equaled 22 liters. Gideon is catching the vision and preparing a kingly feast for God. Rather than eating the food this time, however, we are told,

> Then the angel of God said to him, "Take the meat and the unleavened cakes, and put them on this rock, and pour the broth over them." And he did so. Then the angel of the LORD reached out the tip of the staff that was in his hand and touched the meat and the unleavened cakes. And fire sprang up from the rock and consumed the meat and the unleavened cakes. And the angel of the LORD vanished from his sight.
>
> (Judges 6:20-21)

Instead of eating, the Angel accepts the food as a sacrifice of worship. He visibly reaches out the staff in his hand (probably a reminder of Moses' "staff of God" at the Exodus; Ex 4:20). He touches the food and fire springs up to consume it (the fire also being a reminder of God's fiery presence). Then we are told,

> And the angel of the LORD vanished from his sight. Then Gideon perceived that he was the angel of the LORD. And Gideon said, "Alas, O Lord GOD! For now I have seen the angel of the LORD face to face." But the LORD said to him, "Peace be to you. Do not fear; you shall not die." Then Gideon built an altar there to the LORD and called it, *The LORD Is Peace*. To this day it still stands at Ophrah, which belongs to the Abiezrites.
>
> (Judges 6:21-24)

Several strange and remarkable things happen in these verses. Gideon has confirmed that he was talking to the angel of the LORD. He knows the Angel is the "face of Yahweh" (see ch. 6) and that a man cannot see Yahweh's "face" and live (Ex 33:20). He knows these things apply to the Angel of the LORD and so he assumes his death is imminent. But then Yahweh speaks to him—which is weird because the angel has already "vanished from his sight" (Jdg 6:21).

Notice the sequence in this chapter. It is quite revealing. In vs. 11, the Angel of Yahweh comes to Gideon. In vs. 12, the Angel speaks about

Yahweh in the third person—"Yahweh is with you." In vs. 14 and 16, the Angel's appearing and speaking is *Yahweh* appearing and speaking. The Angel accepts the sacrifice of worship and disappears (vs. 20-21). Gideon then cries to his Lord GOD about having seen the Angel (vs. 22). Then Yahweh again speaks to him (vs. 23), but apparently not via the Angel! Not only is there a blurring between the Angel and Yahweh, but it is as if two different Yahwehs have speaking roles. Michael Heiser writes, "The tactic is now familiar - putting both figures on par to blur the distinction. But in the case of Judges 6, the writer also makes them clearly separate ... [having them] both in the same scene."[132]

The mystery of the chapter is replete. Despite having seen Yahweh's "face," Yahweh says to Gideon, "Peace be to you. Do not fear; you shall not die" (6:23). Likely, Gideon did *not* see Yahweh's face in *full* display (as Moses was only able to see him from the back). He saw the Angel of the LORD in a veiled man-like form similar to the way Joshua saw him (Joshua 5:13-15), or Jacob (Gen 32:30) before him. We're not told *how* Gideon actually saw him. But Gideon *understood* that he had been shown wondrous mercy. Despite his sin and fear and weakness, the Lord had appeared to him and promised to be with him as a Prince of Peace. Gideon was convicted, laid low, and then comforted all at the same time. He came to know God as his Peace and, "Gideon built an altar there to the Lord and called it, The LORD Is Peace" (Jdg 6:24).

Many years later, the same Prince of Peace would rise from the ashes of his sacrificial death, suddenly "appear" to his disciples in a locked room, and say to them, "Peace be to you" (Luke 24:36, John 21:21).

The Angel and Manoah: Jdg 13 and A Wonderful Name

The final appearance of "the Angel of the LORD" (at least by the proper title) in Judges is in the strange birth narrative of Samson. As becomes typical in the book, the Israelites again did evil in the sight of the LORD and he gave them over to the Philistines for forty years (Jdg 13:1). With Israel in need of a deliverer, "The Angel of the LORD appeared" to an unnamed woman from the tribe of Dan. Her husband was named Manoah, and she was barren and childless (13:2-3). He promises her that

---

[132] See Heiser, *Unseen Realm*, 147-148.

she will conceive and bear a son and that he would *"begin* to save Israel from the hand of the Philistines" (13:5). The whole thing reminds us quite strongly of the time when the Angel came to Sarah and promised the same thing amidst the same kinds of circumstances (cf. Gen 18:10ff).

Later, when her husband comes home, she tells him, "A man of God came to me, and his appearance was like the appearance of the Angel of God, very awesome.[133] I did not ask him where he was from, and he did not tell me his name" (Jdg 13:6). She adds that he did promise her that she would have a son (7). We have seen with Moses and the bush how the name Yahweh is identified with the Angel, and how the Angel becomes an embodiment of the Name throughout the Old Testament. But this story picks up on something we have not yet discussed regarding the name.

It unfolds as Manoah prays to the LORD (8). "And God listened to the voice of Manoah, and the Angel of God came again to the woman as she sat in the field. But Manoah her husband was not with her" (9). After running to get her husband, they both return to the man. Manoah asks, "Are you the man who spoke to this woman?" He said, "I am" (11)—a very curious response, given the meaning of the name revealed in Exodus 3![134]

After talking about the future child, Manoah said "to the Angel of the LORD" (although he did not yet know it was the Angel), "Please let us detain you and prepare a young goat for you" (15). Instead of food, the Angel tells him to prepare a burnt offering, "'… then offer it to the LORD.' (For Manoah did not know that he was the Angel of the LORD)" (16). The LORD?

Suddenly, Manoah said to the Angel of the LORD, "What is your name, so that, when your words come true, we may honor you?" (17). The Angel's response is classic. "Why do you ask my name, seeing it is *wonderful (peli'y)*" (18). What is the significance of this?

First, the meaning of the word. It indicates something like "beyond understanding" or "extraordinary."[135] Speaking of the Trinity, but having the Son strongly in mind, Gregory of Nyssa wrote to a heretic

---

[133] On his possible appearance, see the section "Angels vs. Men" in the chapter dealing with questions of systematic theology.

[134] The words are different in Hebrew (*'ani* vs. *'anoki* in Ex 3:6 or *hyeh* in 3:14). But the LXX translates them all the same way (*ego eimi*), the same phrase Jesus uses in John 8:58 as he hearkens back to this identification of God to Moses.

[135] Daniel Isaac Block, *Judges, Ruth*, vol. 6, The New American Commentary (Nashville: Broadman & Holman Publishers, 1999), 413.

named Eunomius that this was the name given, "… so that by this we learn that there is one name significant of the Divine Nature—the wonder, namely, that arises unspeakably in our hearts concerning it."[136] Truly, the name is given as a means by which we would first and foremost worship Christ, even as Manoah did.[137]

We can see this more clearly with a conjunction of our Manoah story with the Jacob wrestling match, the burning bush, and Moses' Song of the Sea. When Manoah says, "What is your name?" this is the same question Jacob asked the man with whom he wrestled (Gen 32:29). Along with Sarah and Abraham, this gives our passage another tie-in to Genesis and the Angel. Also, remember that Moses asked the Angel the same question (Ex 3:13). With Jacob, he simply said, "Why is it that you ask my name?" With Moses he told him "I AM WHO I AM," and this may have been hinted at in the Angel's earlier response (see note above).

What about the song of Moses? Again, we looked at this song previously where Moses calls the LORD "a man of war" (Ex 15:3) and "the right hand" (6). In the same song, Moses uses the word "Wonderful" to describe this "man." He sings, "Who is like you, O LORD, among the gods? Who is like you, majestic in holiness, awesome in glorious deeds, doing wonders? (pele')."

In Judges 13, commentators tell us, the name *Wonderful* "May have been chosen here because of its connections with the Exodus."[138] Webb explains, "The cognate noun, *pele'* (wonder), is used thirteen times in the Old Testament as a whole (in the singular or plural), *always in connection with God*, especially his acts of salvation and judgment in history, his laws, his final acts of apocalyptic judgment, and (in one case) his Messiah." [Emphasis ours][139]

---

[136] Gregory of Nyssa, *Against Eunomius* 8.1, in *Gregory of Nyssa: Dogmatic Treatises, Etc.*, ed. Philip Schaff and Henry Wace, trans. William Moore et al., vol. 5, A Select Library of the Nicene and Post-Nicene Fathers of the Christian Church, Second Series (New York: Christian Literature Company, 1893), 201.

[137] Consider the connection in Revelation 19:12, "… and he has a name written that no one knows but himself."

[138] Block, ibid.

[139] Barry G. Webb, *The Book of Judges*, ed. R. K. Harrison and Robert L. Hubbard Jr., The New International Commentary on the Old Testament (Grand Rapids, MI; Cambridge, UK: William B. Eerdmans Publishing Company, 2012), 356. He lists the references: Ex 15:11; Ps 77:11, 14; 78:12; 88:10, 12; 89:5; 119:129; Isa 25:1; 29:14; Lam 1:9; Dan 12:6. The messianic reference is in Isa 9:6. See also E. J. Young

This noun (*pele'*) also has a verbal parallel (*pala'*). At the very moment that God promises a son to Abraham through Sarah, the barren woman whom Samson's mother parallels, it says, "Is anything too hard [lit. *too wonderful*] for the LORD? At the appointed time I will return to you, about this time next year, and Sarah shall have a son" (Gen 18:14). Here the word is directly tied to Yahweh himself, whom we have also seen is the Angel.

Centuries later, Isaiah will pick up on this word in one of the most famous verses in the entire OT. A prediction of Messiah foresees, "For to us a child is born, to us a son is given; and the government shall be upon his shoulder, and his name shall be called *Wonderful* Counselor, Mighty God, Everlasting Father, Prince of Peace" (Isa 9:6). (Some translations render it, "wonderful, counselor" with a comma; YLT). In this way the name Wonderful is now directly linked to Jesus Christ.

But it gets even more interesting. The LXX renders this verse in a very strange way. Quoted in this ancient Greek translation by the church fathers literally hundreds of times, it says, "For a child is born to us, and a son is given to us, whose government is upon his shoulder: and his name is called *the Angel of great counsel*" (Isa 9:6 LXX). In his dissertation on the divine council, Michael Heiser explains,

> Although many scholars would render the phrase "angel of great counsel," I would suggest the alternative is to be preferred. The reference to the divine council (בְּסוֹד־קְדֹשִׁים) in Ps 89:8 (Hebrew; LXX = 88:8) is rendered ἐν βουλῇ ἁγίων ("in the council of the holy ones"). As J. Trigg noted in his study of the LXX of Isa 9:6, "βουλῇ can mean 'council' as well as 'counsel', so that, for readers of the LXX [megales boules aggelos] would suggest the angelic council of 1 Kings 22.[140]

We have not discussed the divine council much in this book. There is too much here to delve into it properly, so we will save it for its own

---

on Isaiah 9:6, "In the Bible the word *pele'* is employed of what God, never of what man, has done." —*The Book of Isaiah*, vol.1 (Grand Rapids, MI: William B. Eerdmans Publishing Company, 1965), 333.

[140] Michael S. Heiser, "The Divine Council in Late Canonical and Non-Canonical Second Temple Jewish Literature," A Dissertation at the University of Wisconsin-Madison, 2004, 219 (in the PDF).

chapter. Until then, it is enough to note that the LXX's "Angel of the Great Council" is a direct tie-in to the Angel of the LORD via the word "wonderful." Whenever the Church Fathers spoke of Christ as an angel in the OT, this verse was never far behind.

People have asked me (Doug) how I think such a dramatic change came about from the Hebrew to the Greek. Without knowing if the original Hebrew was changed or not, my suspicion is that the LXX is making a theological interpretation of words "wonderful counselor." It knows these connections with the Angel and the term "wonderful." It therefore uses this interpretation to help people see more clearly that Messiah is going to be linked to the Angel of the LORD in ways that most people have forgotten or never knew in the first place. If that is true, then the Jewish translator of this verse may very well have considered the Angel a manifestation of God himself. Whatever happened to get such differences, it is without question that both the Hebrew "Wonderful, counselor" and the Greek "Angel of the Great Council" are orbiting the same theological ideas, ideas that circulate around our figure: The Angel of the LORD, the one who both is and is not Yahweh.

As we finish the story, it is important to see how Samson's parents respond to all of this. After offering the grain offering "on the rock to the LORD, to the one who works wonders (p'lih)," we learn that Manoah and his wife just stood there "watching" (Jdg 13:19). Then something wonderful happened. "When the flame went up toward heaven from the altar, the angel of the LORD went up in the flame of the altar" (20). Instantly, the soon-to-be parents "fell on their faces to the ground" (20). Worship is the common theme we have seen towards the Angel from everyone we have studied.

"The angel of the LORD appeared no more to Manoah and to his wife. Then Manoah knew that he was the Angel of the LORD" (21). While this verse may not tell us exactly what we want to know about his identity (though it does reveal that the man finally figures out that this was extraordinary), the next verse puts the whole thing to rest, at least in their understanding. "And Manoah said to his wife, 'We shall surely die, for we have seen God'" (22).

The statement was true, yet not true. True, they had seen God. Not true—they had not seen God *in his essence*. That would be impossible. Instead, they had seen him in a veiled appearing of the Second Person, who was giving them a foretaste of the kind of salvation they really needed.

In this remarkable story, the Angel of the Lord was foreshadowing a salvation to come. God would send a Savior to a people who were lost in the darkness of sin. He would send a supernatural baby born of a virgin, who would bring the salvation of God and reveal God and atone for sins by becoming a sacrifice for us. He would send someone who would not just *"begin"* to save his people (13:5), but would *finish* God's deliverance for the world. This coming man would not only accept the sacrifice, but would go up himself in the smoke of the sacrifice, becoming the sacrifice, showing the glory of God. As Isaiah would later say, "For to us a child is born, to us a son is given..." (Isa 9:6).

The woman's faith comes to the forefront: "If the LORD had meant to kill us, he would not have accepted a burnt offering and a grain offering at our hands, or shown us all these things, or now announced to us such things as these" (Jdg 13:23). Then she gave birth to a deliverer and called him Samson, meaning "A Little Sun." Soon he would deliver the people. But later, "The Sun of Righteousness" would rise with healing in its wings upon this world of men, and they would call his name Jesus.[141]

---

[141] In an appendix we will deal with some of the skepticism out there regarding the identity of the Angel with the Second Person in the journals. Our focus there will be on one man who has written voluminously on the subject. But there are others, including some who have taken the time to write about how the Angel is not Christ in Judges. See René A. López, "Identifying the 'Angel of the Lord' in the Book of Judges: A Model for Reconsidering the Referent in Other Old Testament Loci," *BBR* 20 (2010): 1–18.

8

MORE OF THE ANGEL AS "WORD"

The Angel and the Prophets

Hearing the Word of the LORD

O NE OF THE MAIN MARKS OF A TRUE PROPHET OF GOD is that they have and speak forth God's word. This is so important to emphasize that nearly every prophetic book begins with this thought in one way or another. The formulas, "The word of the LORD that came" or "The word of the LORD came" occur with reference to Samuel (1Sa 15:10); Nathan (2Sa 7:4); Gad (2Sa 24:11); David (1Ch 22:8); Solomon (1Kg 6:11); Jehu (1Kg 16:1); Shemaiah (2Ch 11:2); Elijah (1Kg 17:1); Isaiah (Isa 38:4; 2 Kgs 20:4); Jeremiah (Jer 1:11); Ezekiel (Ezek 1:3); Hosea (Hos 1:1); Joel (Joel 1:1); Jonah (Jonah 1:1); Micah (Mic 1:1); Zephaniah (Zeph 1:1); Haggai (Hag 1:1); Zechariah (Zech 1:1); Malachi (Mal 1:1). Most of these are either in the first verse of a prophetic book or introduce a prophet to us in a history book. It is also interesting to note (given John 1:1) that the LXX translates the Hebrew "word" as *"logos"* with Gad, David, Jehu, Shemaiah, Elijah, Isaiah, Jeremiah, Ezekiel, Hosea, Joel, Jonah, Micah, Zephaniah, Haggai, Zechariah, and Malachi. Finally, Amos (Amos 1:1), Obadiah (Oba 1:1), Nahum (Nahum 1:1), and Habakkuk (Hab 1:1) all "saw" an oracle of the LORD in a vision.

The Angel as the Word with Samuel: 1 Samuel 3

When you consider the idolatry and sin of the nation of Israel, God's patience and mercy are astounding. Throughout the early chapters of the Old Testament, God has repeatedly sent his special Angel to an unworthy and wandering people. What they needed most was to know this Angel's presence, to know his attributes, to trust his promises and power, to hear and obey his voice, and to worship him only because he was their God; he was the Angel of the Presence, the Angel of the Covenant, who bore God's Name and manifested God's Word and was the strength of God's arm to fight on their behalf. They needed faith *in Him*! Nevertheless, at the end of the period of the Judges and approaching the period of the Monarchy, the people were in decline and spiritual twilight. At the beginning of the book of Samuel, even the priesthood, through the family of Eli, was in idolatry and rebellion against God. Yet God still heard the tearful prayers of a humble and barren woman and gave her a baby who would become a priest and prophet to a spiritually barren people. As so often before, starting with Samuel, the Angel of the LORD continued revealing himself and working through the prophets to reveal his Word.

The specific phrase "the Angel of the LORD" does not appear in the story of Samuel. But, as we've seen, the Angel can appear under different names and guises. To Samuel, like Abraham before him, he appears as the "word of the LORD." 1 Samuel 3 begins,

> Now the boy Samuel was ministering to the LORD in the presence of Eli. And *the word of the LORD* was rare in those days; there was no frequent *vision*. At that time Eli, whose eyesight had begun to grow dim so that he could not see, was lying down in his own place. The lamp of God had not yet gone out, and Samuel was lying down in the temple of the Lord, where the ark of God was.
>
> (1 Samuel 3:1-3)

As in Genesis 15, the "word of the LORD" was not just an audible ringing in the ears; it was a *visual* revelation of God.[142] After the time of Moses and Joshua, God's visible manifestation to his people through his

---

[142] See ch. 2.

appointed prophets and judges became rarer and rarer. Their sin was creating a spiritual distance between themselves and God. The Angel's visible appearing to Gideon and Manoah, we saw, had rightly necessitated sacrifice.[143] Here, Eli's physical blindness (vs. 3) was actually symptomatic of his spiritual blindness and God's judgment on him as priest for the failure and rebellion of his sons (see 1Sam 2:12, 17, 27-36).

Nevertheless, we are told that he could barely see and also that "the lamp of God had not yet gone out" (vs. 3). Something visible is about to happen. Will the old man with a fragment of eyesight left see it? The lamp of the tabernacle was a symbol of God's spiritual presence and light. It was a reminder of the pillar of fire by which God had led his people at the Exodus. So the text is telling us there was still hope for God's presence to be mediated to his people.

In fact, there was a young boy Samuel who was there as an acolyte of the tabernacle "ministering to the LORD." However, we are told, "Now Samuel did not yet know the LORD, and *the word of the LORD* had not yet been revealed to him" (3:7). Of course, Samuel knew who Yahweh *was*, but Yahweh had never *appeared* to him and *spoken* to him in the Person of his Word.

So the LORD began calling Samuel by name (vs. 4, 6, 8, 10), much as he had called Abraham (Gen 22:11), Jacob (Gen 46:2), and Moses (Ex 3:4) by name. As the story continues, Samuel assumed Eli was calling him. Only after the third time did Eli realize that Samuel was hearing from the LORD (vs. 1Sa 3:8-9).

But it's important to point out that Samuel was not just "hearing" a *disembodied* voice! Vs. 10 makes this very clear, "And the LORD came and *stood*, calling *as at other times*, 'Samuel! Samuel!' And Samuel said, 'Speak, for your servant hears.'" We get the impression that the figure was shadowy, and could be easily mistaken. But, some manifestation of the LORD was *standing* there—like with Moses on the mountain: "The LORD descended in the cloud and stood with him there..." (Ex 34:5). Clearly, God was manifesting his "presence" to Samuel in a *visible* way. In fact, we're told, "Samuel was afraid to tell the vision to Eli" (1Sa 3:15).

After declaring judgment on Eli's household (and after Eli fails to repent - see 3:18), we are told,

---

[143] See the discussion of Judges 6 and 13 from ch. 7.

> And Samuel grew, and the LORD was with him and let none of his words fall to the ground. And all Israel from Dan to Beersheba knew that Samuel was established as a prophet of the LORD. And the LORD *appeared* again at Shiloh, for the LORD *revealed himself* to Samuel at Shiloh *by the word of the LORD.*
>
> (1Sa 3:19-21)

Notice carefully that the LORD's "appearing" was "by the word of the LORD." This could be taken in two ways. It could mean the LORD appeared to Samuel *according to plan, according to his declared intent.* But that would be a weird way of saying it and seemingly unnecessary as well! The Septuagint translators seem to have been so bothered by it that they dropped it out entirely and wrote, "And the Lord continued to appear at Shiloh because the Lord had revealed himself to Samuel"— which seems ridiculously redundant. But since, the "word of the LORD," as we have seen, is sometimes a title and hypostasis, it makes much more sense to say that the LORD's appearing was *by the Person of the Word, the Angel of the Lord.* Through the Word of the LORD, God appeared again at Shiloh!

The Angel as the Word with Jeremiah: Jeremiah 1

The same phenomena—a visible appearing of the Word of the LORD—can also be seen in the call of Jeremiah, who was young like Samuel.

> Now the *word of the LORD* came to me, saying, "Before I formed you in the womb I knew you, and before you were born I consecrated you; I appointed you a prophet to the nations." Then I said, "Ah, Lord GOD! Behold, I do not know how to speak, for I am only a youth." But the LORD said to me, "Do not say, 'I am only a youth'; for to all to whom I send you, you shall go, and whatever I command you, you shall speak. Do not be afraid of them, for I am with you to deliver you, declares the LORD." Then the LORD *put out his hand and touched my mouth.* And the LORD said to me, "Behold, I have put my words in your mouth…"
>
> (Jeremiah 1:4-9)

In other words, the "word of the LORD" coming to a prophet was the language of prophetic *vision*. The word of the LORD here was a visible coming of Yahweh to Jeremiah. A visible manifestation "put out his hand and touched [his] mouth." This is no anthropomorphism. It is the Angel of the LORD—the Word of God—reaching out with his hand to touch Jeremiah's mouth to fill him with his words. When the Word of the LORD came and spoke (vs. Jer 1:4, 11, 13), notice the change: Jeremiah responds to the voice, "Ah, Lord GOD (*Ahah Adon Yahweh*)!" (vs. 6).[144] Then it was Yahweh who spoke: "But the LORD said to me" (vs. 7, 12, 14). "Word of God" becomes "Lord GOD" and "Yahweh." This is the typical pattern that we have uncovered throughout our book.

This then is the kind of prophetic vision that occurs with the "coming of the Word of the LORD" to his prophets. *More often than realized, "the Word of the LORD" may actually have signified a visual appearing of the Angel of the LORD to the prophet.* Now it would go too far to say that every use of the "word of the LORD" entailed a visual manifestation (either in a vision, a dream, or into our physical world). But when visual language is used in a passage, clearly it is "Angel of the LORD" language that is being used.

The Angel as the Word with Elijah: 1 Kings 19

The language for "the Angel" and "the Word" appear together in a story of the prophet Elijah. Elijah had just humiliated and defeated the prophets of Baal on Mount Carmel (1 Kings 18). Nevertheless, King Ahab and his wicked pagan wife Jezebel did not repent, but remained in power and sought to kill Elijah. Elijah fled for his life into the wilderness full of depression and despair. And he "lay down and slept under a broom tree" (1 Kings 19:5). We are then told,

> Behold, *an angel* touched him and said to him, "Arise and eat."
> And he looked, and behold, there was at his head a cake baked on
> hot stones and a jar of water. And he ate and drank and lay down
> again. And *the angel of the LORD* came again a second time and
> touched him and said, "Arise and eat, for the journey is too great for

---

[144] The same phrase and title are used by Gideon in Judges 6:22. See also Gen 15:8.

you." And he arose and ate and drank, and went in the strength of that food forty days and forty nights to Horeb, the mount of God.

(1 Kings 19:5-8)

While the "angel" could have been a lesser spiritual messenger, it is more consistent to recognize that this was indeed the divine Angel. Why? Elijah was a prophet of the LORD. The "word of the LORD" had repeatedly come to him (1Kg 17:2, 8, 18:1).[145] Elijah had prophetic access to the council of God (Job 15:8), a topic we will discuss in a few chapters.

Furthermore, Elijah's journey was reenacting the Exodus journey of God's people to Mount Horeb (Sinai). Like Moses, Elijah seems to have (mistakenly) believed that he was the only faithful man left (1Kg 19:10) and that God needed to "start over" with him. Elijah apparently believed that by going to Sinai, he was the faithful Israelite coming out of slavery again to worship God, to have a new encounter with God, and for God to reveal his glory again.

So just as "the Angel of the LORD" provided manna and water to the people for their forty-year journey in the wilderness (see Ex 17:13, 18:6), the Angel was coming to Elijah in the wilderness and providing food and drink for his forty-day journey. As at the Exodus, God was slowly teaching Elijah to trust him day by day, providing what Elijah *needed*, not always what he *wanted*. Then we are told,

> There he came to a cave and lodged in it. And behold, *the word of the LORD* came to him, and he said to him, "What are you doing here, Elijah?" He said, "I have been very jealous for the LORD, the God of hosts. For the people of Israel have forsaken your covenant, thrown down your altars, and killed your prophets with the sword, and I, even I only, am left, and they seek my life, to take it away."
>
> (1Kg 19:9-10)

Elijah had gone all the way to Horeb, to Mount Sinai, probably to the same place where Moses met God, maybe even the same cleft in the rock. Why? He was desperate to understand what God was doing. He came to the place where God made a covenant with the people and

---

[145] See also 2 Kings 1:3, 15, 17 where "the Angel of the LORD" repeatedly speaks to Elijah and his words are later called "the word of the LORD."

essentially asked, "What has become of your promises?" He knew the people had "forsaken" the covenant. He thinks he is the only one left. Who
knows? He may even have thought that God might *start over* with him.

In this place, we are told "the word of the LORD came to him"
and began to question him. Let's again not miss the strangeness of the
language: The word said? The word spoke? If the Word is not itself something distinct from what it says, this language is completely redundant.
In fact, it is unintelligible. But as we have seen, the word of the LORD
was often another title for the divine Angel. The word of the LORD
"coming" was not just a *message* from God, but an *interaction* with God.

Here, he puts up with Elijah's complaint, but begins to give Elijah
an encounter that changes his perspective. So the word of the LORD
said to Elijah, "Go out and stand on the mount before the LORD"
(19:11). Mysteriously, the word of the LORD again speaks about "the
LORD" in the third person. Afterward, we are told,

> And behold, the LORD passed by, and a great and strong wind tore
> the mountains and broke in pieces the rocks before the LORD, but
> the LORD was not in the wind. And after the wind an earthquake,
> but the LORD was not in the earthquake. And after the earthquake
> a fire, but the LORD was not in the fire. And after the fire the sound
> of a low whisper. And when Elijah heard it, he wrapped his face in
> his cloak and went out and stood at the entrance of the cave. And
> behold, there came a voice to him and said, "What are you doing
> here, Elijah?"
>
> (1Kg 19:11-13)

The passage is highly unusual. After the Word spoke *about* the
LORD, *then* the LORD passed by. When the LORD's passing by had
declined to the "voice" (*kol*) of a whisper, then a "voice" (*kol*) spoke
again. Along with so many of these divine appearances, the language is
highly and deliberately obscure.

Unfortunately, it doesn't appear in our English translation, but in
fact, another title appears here that we have already explored. When Elijah is told to stand on the mount "before the LORD" and when it says
the rocks were broken in pieces "before the LORD," the phrase in Hebrew is literally, "before the face of the LORD" (*li-panay Yahweh*).
Though the phrase is a Hebrew idiom and can mean simply "before the

LORD"—given the importance of the *paneh* we discussed in Exodus 33-34 (see ch. 5), the connection to the Exodus is lost without the more literal translation of the "face." In fact, we are being told, Elijah was going to be allowed to see something of the "face of the LORD," like Moses before him.

Commentators over the centuries have often speculated about the meaning of the storm and the earthquake and the fire ... and the still small voice. Why was the Lord not "in the wind ... in the earthquake ... in the fire?" Perhaps, Elijah was being reminded of his personal need for the mercy of God. Elijah had wanted God to come in judgment, and he's reminded that such judgment would consume even him. Even after the fire and destruction on Mount Carmel, God perhaps reminds Elijah that the real need of the people was for mercy. And so, when Elijah hears the "still, small voice," he sees his own need for mercy and then goes out (vs. 13).[146]

Putting aside speculation, however, Elijah was self-consciously following Moses before him. He knew he wasn't able to see the full glory of Yahweh's "face" (Ex 33:20). The storm and earthquake and fire were manifestations of the "glory" of God passing by. And so, Elijah waited for the "still, small voice" as the after-effects of God's "glory." Only then, he "wrapped his face in his cloak," further protecting himself from seeing God, and "went out" to speak again with God.

After he lodges his same complaint (1Kg 19:14), the LORD explains to Elijah that God's plan was not limited to Elijah's expectations, that Elijah was only one part of a larger plan that God was working out, and that there were actually 7,000 in Israel who had not bowed to Baal (19:15-18). Certainly, Elijah had needed to be humbled before the Lord. He needed to be reminded that God's power was not limited, that God's judgment would come at the appropriate time. But still what God's people needed most was the merciful revelation of God. Elijah was shown that the covenant Angel of Israel was still providing for his people, the

---

[146] Irenaeus says, "For by such means was the prophet—very indignant, because of the transgression of the people and the slaughter of the prophets—both taught to act in a more gentle manner; and the Lord's advent as a man was pointed out, that it should be subsequent to that law which was given by Moses, mild and tranquil, in which He would neither break the bruised reed, nor quench the smoking flax..." (*Against Heresies* 4.20.10).

Word of the Lord was still revealing Yahweh, the Face of the Lord was still willing to reveal himself and to work through his prophet to accomplish his will.

Though Elijah was not allowed to see God's "glory" in his lifetime, we know that many years later, he was allowed to see and speak with the "glory of the LORD"—when the Lord Jesus was transfigured on the mountain and Moses and Elijah met with him (Luke 9:28-36)![147]

The church father Irenaeus of Lyons wrote:

> Two facts are thus signified: that it is impossible for man to see God; and that, through the wisdom of God, man shall see Him in the last times, in the depth of a rock, that is, in His coming as a man. And for this reason did He [the Lord] confer with [Moses] face to face on the top of a mountain, Elijah being also present, as the Gospel relates, He thus making good in the end the ancient promise ... The prophets, therefore, did not openly behold the actual face of God, but [they saw] the dispensations and the mysteries through which man should afterwards see God ... If, then, neither Moses, nor Elijah, nor Ezekiel, who had all many celestial visions, did see God; but if what they did see were similitudes of the splendour of the Lord, and prophecies of things to come; it is manifest that the Father is indeed invisible, of whom also the Lord said, "No man hath seen God at any time." But His Word, as He Himself willed it, and for the benefit of those who beheld, did show the Father's brightness, and explained His purposes (as also the Lord said: "The only-begotten God, which is in the bosom of the Father, He hath declared [Him];" and He does Himself also interpret the Word of the Father as being rich and great); not in one figure, nor in one character, did He appear to those seeing Him, but according to the reasons and effects aimed at in His dispensations ... Thus does the Word of God always preserve the outlines, as it were, of things to come, and points

---

[147] Cyril of Jerusalem wrote, "But though it has been proved possible for [Christ] to be made Man, yet if the Jews still disbelieve, let us hold this forth to them: What strange thing do we announce in saying that God was made Man, when yourselves say that Abraham received the Lord as a guest? What strange thing do we announce, when Jacob says, For I have seen God face to face, and my life is preserved? ... Nay more, we produce two witnesses, those who stood before Lord on Mount Sinai: Moses was in a cleft of the rock, and Elias was once in a cleft of the rock: they being present with Him at His Transfiguration on Mount Tabor, spoke to the Disciples of His decease which fire should accomplish at Jerusalem." (*Catechetical Lectures* 12.16).

out to men the various forms (*species*), as it were, of the dispensations of the Father, teaching us the things pertaining to God."[148]

So how are we to understand the *appearing* of "the Word of the LORD" to the Old Testament prophets? God's revelation consistently suggests the same themes we have already begun to explore. The "Word of the LORD" was a Person sent from God who reveals God and who is God. God's people's greatest need is spiritually to see him, know him, and trust him. And God had an amazing plan to answer that need.

---

[148] Irenaeus of Lyons. (1885). Irenæus, *Against Heresies*. In A. Roberts, J. Donaldson, & A. C. Coxe (Eds.), *The Apostolic Fathers with Justin Martyr and Irenaeus* (Vol. 1, p. 492-492). Buffalo, NY: Christian Literature Company.

9
THE ANGEL AS INTERCESSOR

The Angel in Job and Zechariah

Angelic Intercession in Job

THE BOOK OF JOB IS ONE OF THE MOST PROFOUND and difficult books in the Old Testament, exploring the themes of human suffering and divine providence and sovereignty. The book begins with a glimpse into the heavenly courtroom of God (similar to 1 Kings 22:19-23). Because of Satan's accusations (and for God's own eternal purposes), God allows Job to be struck with terrible suffering. The rest of the book follows the discussion between Job and his friends as Job wrestles with what has happened to him.[149]

There is an often-overlooked theme that arises in the course of the discussion. Job is very aware of the distance between himself and God, his own insignificance, and his unworthiness to question God. Because of this distance, Job wonders whether there is any justice at all, any way for him to appeal to God. A repeated theme arises: that Job is in need of a *mediator*.[150] In Job 9:32-33, he says, "For [God] is not a man, as I am,

---

[149] Job may not even have been a Hebrew, but is described as a man of the East and a God-fearer likely living during the time of the patriarchs; see Job 1:1-3.

[150] William Barrick writes, "Perhaps the mediator is the most significant contribution made by the Book of Job to Old Testament thought." Barrick, "Messianic Implications In Elihu's Mediator Speech: Job 33:23-28," ETS National

that I might answer him, that we should come to trial together. There is no arbiter between us, who might lay his hand on us both."

Job is full of contradictions. He knows the truth that a man can't be in the right before God (9:1), but he doesn't know what he's done wrong. He doesn't think he deserves what he has suffered. He wants to appeal to God, but knows that man has no ground to question Him. An alternate translation of vs. 33 says, "Would that there were an arbiter between us!"[151]

It is a theme that is repeated through the book. In Job 4:17-18, Eliphaz says, "Can a mortal man be in the right before God? Can a man be pure before his Maker? Even in his servants he puts no trust, and his angels he charges with error."[152] Then Eliphaz says, "Call now; is there anyone who will answer you? To which of the holy ones (*qadosh*; קְדֹשִׁים) will you turn?" (5:1). The "holy ones" is a term for "angels."[153] Eliphaz implies that angels are possible mediators between God and men,[154] but since neither men nor angels are pure before God, even an angel is not going to heed Job's complaint. (Eliphaz and Job are unaware that Job's suffering arose from interactions in the heavenly court to begin with - see 1:6). The point is that Job is looking for a mediator.

Job makes the point again, "Even now, behold, my witness is in heaven, and he who testifies for me is on high. My friends scorn me; my eye pours out tears to God, that he would argue the case of a man with God, as a son of man does with his neighbor ... Lay down a pledge (*erabon*, עֶרָבֵנִי) for me with yourself; who is there who will put up

---

Meetings (Nov 15, 2016). At: https://drbarrick.org/files/papers/other/job33.pdf, last accessed July 14, 2017.

[151] The Hebrew word is a *mochiah* (מוֹכִיחַ) and means a "judge" or "arbitrator." The LXX uses the term *mesitēs* (μεσίτης), or "mediator"; see 1Ti 2:5, "For there is one God, and there is one mediator between God and men, the man Christ Jesus."
[152] Eliphaz repeats the same argument in Job 15:14-16. See Ch. 11.
[153] The LXX translates the verse, "Inquire whether anyone will listen to you or whether any of the holy angels will take heed." See also Psalm 89:6-7, "For who in the skies can be compared to the LORD? Who among the heavenly beings is like the LORD, a God greatly to be feared in the council of the holy ones, and awesome above all who are around him?"; Zech 14:5, "Then the LORD my God will come, and all the holy ones with him"; Dan 8:13, "Then I heard a holy one speaking, and another holy one said to the one who spoke, 'For how long is the vision...?'"
[154] Consider the Apocryphal 1 Enoch 9:3, "And now to you, the holy ones of heaven, the souls of men make their suit, saying, 'Bring our cause before the Most High.'"

security (*taqa*, עָקַתְ) for me?" (Job 16:19-21; 17:3). Job is saying that only in heaven do they know the truth of the matter. He pleads with God for a mediator to "argue" his case "with God," to represent him and "put up security" for him.

Toward the end of the book, a fourth friend of Job speaks: Elihu the son of Barachel the Buzite. Elihu believes that both Job and his other friends are in the wrong. The friends were wrong in thinking they could deduce that the harsh providences were a direct result of specific sins in Job's life. But Job was wrong in justifying himself, in beginning to doubt God's justice and goodness, and in not recognizing that God's ways and purposes are higher than ours. As Michael Horton writes, "He chides Job for saying that although he is in the right, God will not hear his case. It belongs to all of us to suffer as part of our common curse, he tells Job."[155]

Elihu says that God is always working out his purpose, though man does not always "perceive it" (33:14). God uses providence to warn people from trusting themselves, to humble their pride, in order to "keep back his soul from the pit, his life from perishing by the sword" (33:18). Through suffering, God reminds man of his own mortality so that his "soul draws near to the pit" (33:22). (God's purpose, as Elihu says later, is to deliver "the afflicted by their affliction and open their ear by adversity" - 36:15).[156] Then Elihu says something very interesting,

> If there be for him an angel, a mediator, one of the thousand, to declare to man what is right for him, and he is merciful to him, and says, "Deliver (*pada*, פְּדָעֵהוּ) him from going down into the pit; I have found a ransom (*kopher*, כֹּפֶר); let his flesh become fresh with youth; let him return to the days of his youthful vigor"; then man prays to God, and he accepts him; he sees his face with a shout of joy, and he restores to man his righteousness. He sings before men and says: 'I sinned and perverted what was right, and it was not repaid to me.

---

[155] Michael Horton, *Too Good To Be True* (Grand Rapids, MI: Zondervan, 2006), 121.

[156] Later, Elihu argues that nothing unfair has happened to Job. When even "righteous" people suffer, they are still sinners and should be humble for their remaining sins and turn to God (Job 36:7-12). It's the godless who "cherish anger" and "do not cry for help" (36:13). But for the godly, God "delivers the afflicted by their affliction and opens their ear by adversity" (36:15).

He has redeemed my soul from going down into the pit, and my life shall look upon the light.'

(Job 33:23-28)

Commentators have struggled with how to interpret these verses.[157] Some have suggested that the "angel" here is a human messenger, like a preacher, who comes and speaks to the man caught in sin and encourages him to repent. The word for "mediator" here (*lits*, מֵלִיץ) means an "interpreter" or "intermediary."[158] However, it is unlikely that a human messenger is intended, because this intermediary not only declares "to man what is right," but also appears to represent him in the heavenly court, saying, "Deliver him from going down into the pit; I have found a ransom."[159] The phrase "one of the thousand" (or "one from among the thousand") likely refers to the "thousands" of angels in the heavenly court.[160]

Since a "divine council perspective" has governed the whole book[161] and was part of the discussion between Job and his friends, Elihu seems to be talking about something that happens in the court of heaven that impacts the man on the earth. Remember, Elihu is talking about God's purposes: "For God speaks in one way, and in two, though man does not perceive it ... Behold, God does all these things, twice, three times, with a man, to bring back his soul from the pit, that he may be lighted with the light of life" (Job 33:14, 29-30). Elihu seems to be saying that, unbeknownst to man, God himself allows an angelic mediator to come forward[162]—the best among the thousands of angels, not

---

[157] In fact, the LXX changes the meaning of vs. 23 entirely. As Barrick records, the LXX translator of Job omitted up to 35% of Elihu's speech in chs. 32-37. This may be why Job 33 is never discussed among the early church fathers, who were otherwise very interested in the Old Testament angel passages: their Greek Bibles completely changed the verse.

[158] See Isa 43:26-27, 2Ch 32:31.

[159] Psalm 49:7-8 says, "Truly no man can ransom another, or give to God the price of his life, for the ransom of their life is costly and can never suffice."

[160] See Dan 7:10, Ps 68:17.

[161] Delitzsch writes, "The Elihu section has a strong angelological coloring in common with the book of Job." Keil and Delitzsch, *Commentary on the Old Testament: Vol. 4 – Job* (Grand Rapids, MK: Eerdmans, 1980), 228. We will discuss this important topic of the divine council and how it relates to the Angel in a later chapter.

[162] By contrast, compare 1 Kings 22:19-23.

just any one of the "holy ones" as Eliphaz had suggested (5:1).[163] This mediator pleads the case of the man, and when he does so, a change happens in the man: his countenance changes and he begins to hope and pray to God and repent! It's like he becomes *reborn*: "His flesh becomes fresh with youth" (33:25). God then "accepts him; he sees his face[164] with a shout of joy, and he restores to man his righteousness" (33:26). And the man gives God all the glory (33:27-28).[165]

Elihu is describing how God works in man's life. As Michael Horton writes,

> This is why we need to turn from trusting in our own righteousness to the mediator who announces to the court that he has found a ransom to deliver us from final destruction … Job had struggled toward this in his previous confession of faith in a living Redeemer who will raise him from the dead, but Elihu presses him toward the place where he will stop justifying himself and accept his place with the rest of us sinners who have no plea but Christ."[166]

Elihu's point is that Job should not lose hope in God's promise of a supernatural mediator to ransom sinners. Elihu seems to be encouraging faith in an angelic messiah![167]

Many commentators have expressed the same interpretation. Franz Delitzch writes,

---

[163] Barrick writes, "A more adequate interpretation of Elihu's phraseology, however, is in the sense of 'unique.' It is a hyperbole referring to something (or someone) rare or difficult to find. As Hartley explains, 'This angel is one in a thousand, i.e., 'one of a kind,' meaning that there is only one such angel. Elihu recognizes that no earthly person can fulfill that role. It must be a heavenly messenger" (Barrick, 12).

[164] Notice the *paneh* again!

[165] Elihu seems to be describing effectual calling through divine intercession. Before the prayer is heard and God accepts him, there is a mediation that must take place. The hearing of the prayer does not result in the pardon; it results from the pardon. Our hope that God will hear and answer comes from the Mediator of mercy and grace alone.

[166] Horton, 122.

[167] The pseudepigraphical Testament of Dan says, "And now fear the Lord, my children, be on guard against Satan and his spirits. Draw near to God and to the Angel who intercedes for you, because He is the Mediator between God and men for the peace of Israel" (TDan 6:1-2).

In the extra-Israelitish world a far more developed doctrine of angels and demons is everywhere found than in Israel ... Within the patriarchal history after Gen 16, that *malak elohim* appears, who is instrumental in effecting the progress of the history of redemption, and has so much the appearance of the God of revelation, that He even calls himself God, and is called God ... Taking up this perception, Elihu demands for the deliverance of man from the death which he has incurred by his sins, a superhuman angelic mediator. The "Angel of Jehovah" of primeval history is the oldest prefigurement in the history of redemption of the future incarnation ... and the angelic form is accordingly the oldest form which the hope of a deliverer assumes.[168]

Again, he says,

If we connect the mediating angel, like the angel of Jehovah of the primeval history, with God Himself, as then the logos of this mediating angel to man can be God's own logos communicated by him, and he therefore as מֵלִיץ, God's speaker (if we consider Elihu's disclosure in the light of the New Testament), can be the divine Logos himself, we shall here readily recognize a presage of the mystery which is unveiled in the New Testament: "God was in Christ, and reconciled the world unto Himself" ... At any rate, Elihu expresses it as a postulate, that the deliverance of man can only be effected by a superhuman being, as it is in reality accomplished by the man who is at the same time God, and from all eternity the Lord of the angels of light.[169]

Similarly, the *Anglican Study Bible* of 1873:

---

[168] Delitzsch, 229.
[169] Ibid, 232.
Delitzsch also wrote, in his book Messianic Prophecies, "Here we see in the Book of Job, which is elsewhere remarkable for its angelology, that the redemption of man can only be mediated by means of a superhuman being. The *angelus internuntius* is a preformation of the Redeemer going forth from the range of the Godhead. The angelic form is the oldest, which the hope of a mediator of salvation gives (Gen. xlviii. 16). It is taken up again ... in Mal. iii. 1 (cf. also the remarkable translation of the Septuagint of Isa. ix. 5). The מַלְאַךְ הַבְּרִית of prophecy is the reality of the מַלְאָךְ מֵלִיץ postulated by the Chokma." Franz Delitzsch, Messianic Prophecies in Historical Succession, trans. by Samuel Ives Curtiss (reprinted; Eugene, OR: Wipf and Stock Publishers, 1997), 105.

One angel, however, stands apart from all others in the Old Testament; His office, rank, and apparently His nature, are represented as peculiar, He bears the holy name; and whether Elihu or other Patriarchs felt the full significance of their own words or not, they use no expressions which are unsuitable to the true and only Mediator. The objection that the expression is misplaced in the mouth of Elihu, an Aramean, has no weight. The angel of the Lord was known to the patriarchs.[170]

William Barrick is unwilling to say unequivocally who this angel is; nevertheless, he writes,

> The revelation contained in both OT and NT restricts our understanding of the individual who properly fits the description in Job 33:23-24. The Hebrew Bible itself proclaims emphatically that no human being can fulfill the assignment. Although there is no equivalent elimination of angelic beings from consideration, no passage of either testament attributes to an angel any such capabilities. In all of divine revelation there is only one who can fulfill the offices and actions Elihu describes: the Messiah, Jesus Christ. Elihu may not have understood that at all, but he did accurately define what is involved in the identification of Job's true mediator. The OT title for the pre-incarnate Son of God is *malak* Yahweh."[171]

Charles Spurgeon, in his sermon "Footsteps of Mercy" wrote,

> I prefer to believe with many expositors, that the full meaning of these words will never be found in ministers of mortal race; we must rather refer it to the Great messenger of the covenant, the Great interpreter between God and man whose presence to the sin-sick soul is a sure prophecy of mercy! Where God the Father sends His beloved Son to a man—where Christ comes to the man's conscience, and talks with him, showing the credentials of a Savior, and

---

[170] *The Holy Bible According to the Authorized Version (A.D. 1611) With An Explanatory and Critical Commentary and A Revision of the Translation*, ed. F. C. Cook (London: John Murray, 1873), 4:118.
https://books.google.com/books?id=PIUXAAAAYAAJ&pg=PA118&lpg=PA118&dq=#v=onepage&q&f=false.
[171] Barrick, 15.

compelling the faith of the sinner—there it is that salvation is obviously intended by the Lord, and will be effectually perfected in that
man unto everlasting life! With this view I proceed, regarding our
Lord Jesus Christ as the herald of mercy. Mark well the titles, a messenger, an interpreter, one among a thousand. Is there any other
than Jesus to whom they so fitly belong? Let us contemplate Him as
a messenger; that is just what Jesus Christ is. Now, a messenger
comes not in his own name; he must be sent, and it is a great comfort
to know that Jesus Christ did not come to save men merely on His
own account, but He came commissioned by the Father! He was sent
of God; God has appointed Christ to be the Savior; those who accept
Christ, and trust in Him, accept the very person God, Himself, has
ordained. Christ is no amateur Savior, who comes without a commission; in His hands He bears the royal stamp of the divine authority. O trembling sinner! Trust Him whom God has trusted! Lay hold
of Him whom God has appointed![172]

Whatever Elihu actually understood, he correctly describes the
biblical doctrine of redemption. 1 Timothy 2:5 says, "For there is one
God, and there is one mediator between God and men, the man Christ
Jesus." In Isaiah 59:16, the prophet says that God saw "that there was no
man, and wondered that there was no one to intercede; then his own
arm brought him salvation, and his righteousness upheld him."[173] In the
book of Revelation, John weeps "because no one was found worthy to
open the scroll" until he is told, "Weep no more; behold, the Lion of
the tribe of Judah, the Root of David, has conquered, so that he can
open the scroll and its seven seals" (Rev 5:4-5). There is One among the
myriads of the heavenly host who fulfills everything Elihu described—
the Angel, who is God himself.

In other words, Elihu is anticipating the Gospel. Our hope in this
vain life is not in this fallen and difficult world. Our hope must come
from something eternal ... breaking into this world. Our one hope is
that there be for us "an angel, a mediator, the fairest of ten thousand."
As the hymn-writer says,

---

[172] Charles   Spurgeon,   "Footsteps   of   Mercy,"   MTP   905   -
http://www.spurgeongems.org/vols13-15/chs905.pdf.
[173] As we have seen, "the arm" is a title for the Angel of the LORD; see ch. 7.

Majestic sweetness sits enthroned
upon the Savior's brow
His head with radiant glories crowned,
His lips with grace o'erflow.
No mortal can with Him compare
among the sons of men;
Fairer is He than all the fair
that fill the heav'nly train.

Angelic Intercession in Zechariah

If Job 33 proposes the need for a unique angelic mediator and inter-cessor between God and man, the book of Zechariah shows such an an-gelic mediator in action.[174] In Zechariah 3, the prophet is shown a vision,

> Then he showed me Joshua the high priest standing before the
> angel of the LORD, and Satan standing at his right hand to accuse
> him. And the LORD said to Satan, "The LORD rebuke you, O Satan!
> The LORD who has chosen Jerusalem rebuke you! Is not this a brand
> plucked from the fire?" Now Joshua was standing before the angel,
> clothed with filthy garments. And the angel said to those who were
> standing before him, "Remove the filthy garments from him." And
> to him he said, "Behold, I have taken your iniquity away from you,
> and I will clothe you with pure vestments." And I said, "Let them
> put a clean turban on his head." So they put a clean turban on his
> head and clothed him with garments. And the angel of the LORD
> was standing by.
>
> (Zechariah 3:1-5)

Zechariah is given a shocking vision. The High Priest was the ap-pointed representative of the people before God. Once a year, on the
Day of Atonement, the priest would go into the Holy of holies and stand
before the mercy seat and make atonement for the sins of the people.
The preparations began weeks before—with rituals, washings and sacri-fices, making sure that the priest himself was clean, ready and accepta-ble to represent the people. Yet Zechariah has a vision of the higher

---

[174] Angels, the angel of the LORD, and the word of the LORD figure prominently
and occur repeatedly in the book of Zechariah. Furthermore, Zechariah is among
the most quoted books in the New Testament.

spiritual reality of the high priest's intercession. He is given a glimpse into the courtroom of heaven. And shockingly, Joshua the high priest is standing before the court in filthy rags![175] In other words, despite all the preparations, the high priest himself was still unclean before God. And if the high priest was unclean, what hope did the people have? It was a vision of spiritual disaster. Even the best and appointed representative of the people fell short of God's righteousness. Making matters worse, Satan, the accuser, is standing at Joshua's right hand to accuse him, in much the same way as the beginning of Job.

Now, in Job, "the sons of God came to present themselves before the LORD, and Satan also came among them...to present himself before the LORD" (Job 1:6, 2:1). And in the Job courtroom scene, it is the LORD who speaks to Satan about Job. But in the Zechariah scene, Joshua the high priest and Satan are standing "before the angel of the LORD"— meaning, even in the court of heaven, *Yahweh the LORD* who sits at the head of the court is *the angel of the LORD* sitting at the head of the court. Vs. 2 confirms this: "The LORD said to Satan..." In other words, the angel of the LORD before whom they are standing *is the LORD*.

Here is the marvel of the vision: despite Joshua's filthy rags and the accusations of Satan, we are told, "The LORD said to Satan, 'The LORD rebuke you, O Satan.' The LORD who has chosen Jerusalem rebuke you! Is not this a brand plucked from the fire?'" (3:2). Notice the language: Yahweh invokes Yahweh to rebuke Satan! The angel of the covenant who is the angel of God's presence invokes the God of the covenant who elected Jerusalem for the place of his name and mercy to rebuke their accuser. Then the angel says, "Remove the filthy garments from him ... Behold, I have taken away your iniquity from you, and I will clothe you with pure vestments" (3:4).

Here is the intercessor for which Job had prayed, pouring out "tears to God, that he would argue the case of a man with God" (Job 16:20-21). As Elihu had suggested, here is the highest of the heavenly court being merciful to Joshua (and through him the covenant people) and saying, "Deliver him from going down into the pit; I have found a ransom" (Job 33:24). As Isaiah says, The LORD himself "saw that there was no man and

---

[175] See Isaiah 64:6, "We have all become like one who is unclean, and all our righteous deeds are like a polluted garment. We all fade like a leaf, and our iniquities, like the wind, take us away."

wondered that there was no one to intercede; then his own arm brought him salvation, and his righteousness upheld him. He put on righteousness as a breastplate, and a helmet of salvation on his head... And a Redeemer will come to Zion..." (Isaiah 59:16-17, 20). The angel of the LORD, who is the "arm" of the LORD, and who is Yahweh himself at the head of the divine council, intercedes himself for his sinful people.

Then, at the angel's command, Joshua's filthy garments are removed, and Joshua is clothed with pure garments (Zech 3:4). This is one of the Bible's clearest pictures of the biblical doctrines of justification and imputation. Though we are sinners and unclean and unrighteous before God, God promises to take off our uncleanness, to wash us, and to clothe us in his righteousness.[176] Our guilt and sin is removed and paid for and we are given a righteous covering. As Isaiah again says:

> I will rejoice in the Lord; my soul will exult in my God, for he has clothed me with the garments of salvation; he has covered me with the robe of righteousness, as a bridegroom decks himself like a priest with a beautiful headdress, and as a bride adorns herself with jewels. For as the earth brings forth its sprouts, and as a garden causes what is sown in it to sprout up, so the Lord God will cause righteousness and praise to sprout up before all the nations.
>
> (Isaiah 61:10-11)[177]

Knowing the Mediator

Job, living at the time of the patriarchs apart from the covenant people of God, did not know that there was a mediator between God

---

[176] See also Eph 6:13-14, which references the LORD putting on righteousness as a breastplate in Isa 59:17, and says, "Take up the whole armor of God...having put on the breastplate of righteousness."

[177] See also Romans 3:21-26 - "But now the righteousness of God has been manifested apart from the law, although the Law and the Prophets bear witness to it—the righteousness of God through faith in Jesus Christ for all who believe. For there is no distinction: for fall have sinned and fall short of the glory of God, and are justified by his grace as a gift, through the redemption that is in Christ Jesus, whom God put forward as a propitiation by his blood, to be received by faith. This was to show God's righteousness, because in his divine forbearance he had passed over former sins. It was to show his righteousness at the present time, so that he might be just and the justifier of the one who has faith in Jesus."

and man *until* he met him in Job 38 and God himself spoke to him. Then Job repented and God restored to him his righteousness and blessing. The people of Israel knew that God himself had undertaken through the angel of his presence to be their representative in the court of heaven and their guardian upon the earth. But the ultimate display of his intercession and ransom was not complete until his incarnation—the Redeemer finally and fully coming to his people. Now, we know even more that "there is one God, and there is one *mediator* between God and men, the man Christ Jesus, who gave himself as a ransom for all" (1Ti 2:5-6). Now, "we have an *advocate* with the Father, Jesus Christ the righteous. He is the propitiation for our sins, and not for ours only, but also for the sins of the whole world" (1Jn 2:1-2).

10

THE ANGEL AS "GLORY"

The Angel in Ezekiel and Isaiah

Glory Be

T HE ANCIENT LITURGICAL HYMN KNOWN AS *The Lesser Doxology* or more familiarly *The Gloria Patri* proclaims:

> *Glory be to the Father*
> *And to the Son*
> *And to the Holy Ghost*

Basil the Great (329–379 A.D.) said that its roots could be traced to the early baptismal formulas of the Apostles. *The Book of Common Prayer* argues that we find traces of it in the Apostolic Fathers in *The Epistle of the Church of Smyrna*, the writings of Clement, and that Polycarp may have had a strong hand in bringing about what the Synod of Vasio (529 A.D.) would later help us know was the universal liturgical practice of singing this doxology in the West, East, and Africa, even as it then directs the churches in Gaul (Modern France) to follow suit.[178]

Perhaps the main reason the song was sung in the churches was as a test of orthodoxy. "The Arians," one dictionary explains, "took advantage ... and wrested some of the [words] so as to appear to favor their

---

[178] See Thomas Church Brownell, *Book of Common Prayer* (New York: Sidney's Press, 1823), 19; Adrian Fortescue, "Doxology," in *Catholic Encyclopedia* (New York: 1909).

own views."[179] One of their doxologies said:

> Glory be to the Father
> *By* the Son
> *In* the Holy Ghost

You can immediately see the problem. The only one worthy of glory to the Arians is the Father. But Christian orthodoxy maintains that the Father, Son, and Holy Spirit are all worthy of and full of Glory. In fact, it is more even than this, for the Scriptures teach us that all three are the very Glory of God. Here we are only going to look at how this applies to the Son, and more specifically to the Angel of the LORD.[180]

The Glory in Ezekiel

We begin in Ezekiel 1. The famous opening scene is full of wild and bizarre images: storms, clouds, fire (all reminding us of God's coming to Mt. Sinai), gleaming metal, living creatures with four faces, multiple wings, and eyes all around. They appeared like burning coals of fire, like torches moving about, like lightning flashes as they darted to and fro. There are wheels with rims beside the living creatures, one wheel for each creature. They appear as gleaming beryl.

Over the heads of the creatures was a vast expanse that shined like crystal. "And above the expanse over their heads there was the likeness of a throne, in appearance like sapphire; and seated above the likeness of a throne was *a likeness with a human appearance*" (Ezek 1:26). We are going to look more at this "human-like" appearance in a later chapter. What we want to call attention to here is his description. He is called *"the likeness of the glory of the LORD"* (28).

Through the parallelism of "likeness," "glory" becomes what some scholars have called a hypostasis—a word we have seen before,

---

[179] Walter Farquhar Hook, *A Church Dictionary*, seventh edition (London: John Murray, 1854), 352.
[180] That the Father is the Glory of God should be unquestioned by all. On the Spirit as the Glory see Meredith G. Kline, *Images of the Spirit* (Eugene, OR: Wipf and Stock, 1980).

especially with the Name and the Word in previous chapters.[181] The idea of the Glory as having a human form can be traced back to at least Moses at Mt. Sinai. In Exodus 16:10, "The glory of the LORD appeared in the cloud." The glory is not the cloud, but is *in* the cloud. Earlier we read that simply the LORD was in the cloud (Ex 13:21; 14:24), but also that the Angel of the LORD is fighting in the cloud (14:19).

The glory is personified at Mt. Sinai. "The glory of the LORD dwelt on Mount Sinai..." (24:16; cf. 19:9). Let's stop for a moment. The word "dwelt" here is important. It is the verb *shakan*. It is from this that the famous "Shekinah" derives. Shekinah is basically a word for "glory." Shekinah is not a biblical word; it is found throughout the Targums (like "Memra" for "Word"). In the Targums, one Bible dictionary says, "The *Shekinah* becomes a separate entity ... an intermediary between God and man."[182] The same dictionary says, "In the Targums '*shekinah*,' 'glory of God,' and 'word of God' are used synonymously. Thus, Jacob awoke from his sleep and said, 'Surely *the LORD is in this place*, and I did not know it.'" (Gen 28:16) becomes, "The *Glory* of the *Lord's Shekinah dwells* in this place, and I knew it not. (Gen 28:16 PJE). Moses hid his face, for he was afraid to look at *God* (Ex 3:6) becomes, 'He was afraid to look upon the height of the *glory* of the *Shekinah* of the Lord' (Ex 3:6 JPE)." This last one is interesting for us, because as we saw previously, it is the Angel of the LORD Moses is afraid to look at.

Continuing on with Exodus 24:16, "... and the *cloud* covered it for six days; and on the seventh day He called to Moses *from the midst of the cloud.*" "He?" This pronoun here refers to the Glory. The Glory is called "he." Later, in a passage we have looked at especially as it pertains to "the face," Moses asked God to show him his "glory." God covers Moses with a "hand" and allows him to see his "back" (Ex 33:18-23).

While many see this language as purely anthropomorphic and not to be taken literally in any sense, we have seen that it is much better to see Yahweh here in the form of the Angel of the LORD—an angel with

---

[181] On the Glory as a Hypostasis see Charles A. Gieschen, *Angelomorphic Christology: Antecedents & Early Evidence* (Boston: Brill, 1998), 78-88. Gieschen defines hypostasis as "an aspect of the deity that is depicted with independent personhood of varying degrees" and "shares the nature, authority, and will of the deity since it remains an aspect of deity" (45).

[182] Walter A. Elwell and Barry J. Beitzel, *Baker Encyclopedia of the Bible* (Grand Rapids, MI: Baker Book House, 1988), 1943.

an actual body. As Segal says, "Yahweh himself, the angel of God, and his Glory are peculiarly melded together, suggesting a deep secret about the ways God manifested himself to humanity."[183] In the same way, "Ezekiel seems likewise to have merged ideas about the LORD's glory with ideas about the LORD's angel ... Ezekiel does not look directly on God's face, or even directly on the face of the glory—rather, he sees the 'likeness of the glory.'"[184] We find it again in Zechariah where "the angel who talked with me" started talking to "another angel" (Zech 2:3) who said of Jerusalem, "I will be the glory in her midst" (5). Thus, he becomes what Kline calls the "Glory-Angel."[185]

It is remarkable that Ezekiel could say this about the glory because "Glory is preeminently a divine quality; ultimately considered, only God has glory."[186] Several centuries prior to Ezekiel, Isaiah heard the LORD say, "I am the LORD; that is my name; my glory I give to no other" (Isa 42:8). Therefore, when Ezekiel sees the likeness of the glory of the LORD, we must believe that this explains his opening statement in the book, "I saw visions *of God*" (Ezek 1:1).

Do not let the term "likeness" fool you, as if he isn't really seeing the Glory, but only something that looks like the Glory. Rather, "likeness" is an idea that the NT uses for Christ himself. He is the "radiance of the glory of God" and "the exact imprint of his nature" (Heb 1:3), but also the "likeness of men" (where the Greek term for "likeness," *homoioma*, is identical to the LXX's rendering of "likeness" in Ezek 1:26 and 28), which we know means that he was a real human being.

Thus, church history has identified the person Ezekiel saw as the Second Person of the Trinity. We see this as early as the NT itself. For example, Revelation depicts Jesus as one like a son of man (Rev 1:13), having a voice like the roar of many waters (15), feet like gleaming metal (15), and an appearance like the sun shining in full strength (16). These

---

[183] Alan Segal, *Paul the Convert*, 42.

[184] Susan R. Garrett, *No Ordinary Angel: Celestial Spirits and Christian Claims about Jesus*, The Anchor Yale Bible Reference Library (New Haven, CT: Yale University Press, 2008), 54.

[185] Meredith G. Kline, *Glory In Our Midst: A Biblical-Theological Reading of Zechariah's Night Visions* (Eugene, OR: Wipf & Stock, 2001), 27ff.

[186] Richard B. Gaffin Jr., "The Glory of God in Paul's Epistles," in *The Glory of God*, Theology in Community Series, ed. Christopher W. Morgan and Robert A. Peterson (Wheaton, IL: Crossway, 2010), 130 [127-52].

are all images taken from Ezekiel 1:24-28. Thus, while the Fathers did not use this text very often, the Reformers were keen on explaining that Ezekiel was seeing the preincarnate Christ.[187] In this respect, it is worth concluding with the observation that in Ezekiel himself, the Glory is later identified as the LORD. "Now the glory of the God of Israel had gone up from the cherub on which it rested to the threshold of the house. And he called to the man clothed in linen, who had the writing case at his waist. And the LORD said to him…" (Ezek 9:3-4). Who is speaking? The Glory. The Lord. The Angel.

The Glory in Isaiah

The second passage we want to look at is the famous Isaiah 6. We need only go as far as the first verse. "In the year that King Uzziah died I saw the Lord (Adonai) sitting upon a throne, high and lifted up; and the train of his robe filled the temple" (Isa 6:1). Isaiah has a vision of God in heaven. Yet no one can see God and live. Yet Isaiah saw "the Lord." So whom did he see?

The NT is quite clear here. John says, "Isaiah said these things because he saw his glory and spoke of him" (John 12:41). Who is the "he" and the "him" in this verse? In the context, it is Jesus (36). But John uses this language of "glory" to capture this. Yet Isaiah 6:1 does not use the word "glory."[188]

---

[187] Cf. Calvin, Commentary on Ezekiel 1; William Greenhill (1591–1671), *An Exposition of Ezekiel*; John Mayer (1583-1664), *Commentary Upon All the Prophets*; Matthew Meade (1629-1699), *The Vision of the Wheels*. These have all been compiled in Carl L. Beckwith, Timothy George, and Scott M. Manetsch, eds., *Ezekiel, Daniel: Old Testament*, vol. 12, Reformation Commentary on Scripture (Downers Grove, IL: IVP Academic, 2012), 16-19.

[188] Jerome (Es. 3.4 [VL.AGLB 23:13]) sums up the tradition when he says, "It was impious of a certain person [i.e., Origen] to understand the two seraphim to be the Son and the Holy Spirit. By contrast, we, in accordance with John, the evangelist (John 12:39-41), and with Paul, the apostle (Acts 28:25-27), teach that it is the son who is seen in the glory of his rule and the Holy Spirit who has spoken." Alfons Fürst, "Jerome Keeping Silent: Origen and his Exegesis of Isaiah," cited in *Jerome of Stridon: His Life, Writings and Legacy*, ed. Andrew Cain and Josef Lössl (University of Colorado: Routledge, 2016), 147. Someone else adds, "Its generally accepted reading in the Middle Ages was that of Jerome, who saw it as signifying Christ the Son." Conrad Rudolph, *The Mystic Ark: Hugh of Saint Victor,*

Here it may be important to remember the previous discussion on the Targums and the Shekinah. The Targum reads, "In the year that King Uzziah *was struck with it, the prophet* said, *I* saw *the glory* of the LORD resting upon a throne, high and lifted up *in the heavens of the height*; and the temple was filled by *the brilliance of his glory* ... For my eyes have seen *the glory of the Shekinah of the eternal king*, the LORD of hosts!" [Isa 6:1, 5. Italics are the Targum's additions to the Hebrew text]. We should also note that the LXX concludes the verse, "... and the house was full of his glory." John could be taking his cue from either source.

The larger picture is that John does this kind of thing regularly, collecting ideas of "the glory," "the word," and other things throughout his Gospel so that we may know that Jesus is those come in human form.[189] He writes, "And the Word became flesh and dwelt among us, and we have seen his glory, glory as of the only Son from the Father, full of grace and truth" (John 1:14). John equates the *logos*, the glory, and the Son. They are all the same thing. It is into this "Glory as a Person" idea that John later writes, "Isaiah saw his Glory" (Isa 12:41).

But it isn't merely John. For example, a verse translated by the ESV as, "[Stephen], full of the Holy Spirit, gazed into heaven and saw the glory of God, and Jesus standing at the right hand of God" (Acts 7:55), if taken epexegetically (that is, with the addition of words to clarify the meaning), could just as well be translated, "He ... saw the glory of God, that is Jesus standing at the right hand of God."[190]

And then there is Philippians 2:6-11. Christ exists "in the form of God" and the "likeness of men" (6-7). In the OT, Moses beheld the "form [Heb: *temunah*; GK: *doxa*] of the LORD" (Num 12:8). *Temunah* was translated as "glory" by the LXX and the Targums. This same Hebrew word is translated as "likeness" (*homoioma*) in the Second Commandment (Ex 20:4). That is, you shall not make any "likeness" of things in your worship of God. This happens to be the word used for

Art, and Thought in the Twelfth Century (Riverside, CA: Cambridge University Press, 2014), 92.
[189] See for example, John Ronning, *The Jewish Targums and John's Logos Theology* (Grand Rapids, MI: Baker Academic, 2010); John L Ronning, "The Targum of Isaiah and the Johannine Literature," *WTJ* 69 (2007): 247-78; esp. 259-62.
[190] Ralph P. Martin, "A Hymn of Christ: Philippians 2:5-11," in *Recent Interpretation & in the Setting of Early Christian Worship* (Downers Grove, IL: InterVarsity Press, 2009), 111 n. 3.

"likeness" in Php 2:7. We are not to make any likenesses of God, because the Living Christ is the only True Likeness! The old hymn that is Philippians 2 is not saying that Christ only *appeared* to be one of us, but really wasn't. Rather, it is saying that he *is* the Glory of God. Thus, "'Taking the form of a slave', 'becoming in the likeness of men'; and 'being found in the fashion as a man' (vv 7-8) ... Phil 2:6 would seem to say that Christ is the divine Glory. The same idea is expressed by the title, 'image of the invisible God', in the beginning of the hymn of Christ in Col 1:15-20."[191]

Paul is clear about this in other places, as he takes his ideas straight out of the OT. In the incarnation, "God who said, 'Let light *shine* out of darkness,' has *shone* in our hearts to give the light of the knowledge of the *glory of God in the face of Jesus Christ*" (2Co 4:6). Where does this come from? Isaiah: "Arise, shine, for your light has come, and *the glory* of the LORD has risen upon you" (Isa 60:1). "Therefore," Paul concludes, "'Awake, O sleeper, and *arise* from the dead, and *Christ* will *shine* on you'" (Eph 5:14).

So, what is "glory" (Heb. *kabod*; Gk. *doxa*)? Most people probably think of it as God in a very abstract sense, like God's reputation or his honor. "Glory" literally means "to be weighty, full of good things." Certainly "praise" is not far removed from glory either. Each of these are good and right to ascribe to the glory of God. But more than something we ascribe to God, Glory is properly something that God simply is. That is why the word can be used as a substitute for the Angel of the LORD (or the Spirit, or the Father).

---

[191] J. E. Fossum, "Glory," ed. Karel van der Toorn, Bob Becking, and Pieter W. van der Horst, *Dictionary of Deities and Demons in the Bible* (Leiden; Boston; Köln; Grand Rapids, MI; Cambridge: Brill; Eerdmans, 1999), 351 [348-52]. This entire entry is extremely helpful in grounding our discussion.

11

THE ANGEL AND THE DIVINE COUNCIL

The Angel in Heaven

The Story of The Angel

T HE FOLLOWING PUTS INTO AN EASY TO DIGEST STORY-FORM the significance of this chapter for our study. At this early point, there may be some things here that are unfamiliar, perhaps strange. Some may even seem wrong. That's alright. By the end of the chapter, it should all make sense. But it is important to grasp upfront that what we are dealing with in this chapter is in fact vital to the overall study of the Angel. In fact, more than perhaps any other, this chapter may very well explain why he is such an important figure in the OT.

In the very beginning, as God was creating, before there was any man to plow the land, the sons of God watched in amazement as the foundations of the earth were laid. They watched and sang and shouted for joy. Then God made man in his image and announced to his divine council of heavenly beings that this creature would have dominion over the earth.

Tragically, this enraged at least one of the heavenly beings who believed this right should be his. So, when he had the chance to interact with Eve, he tempted our mother and our first parents fell into sin. When the Angel of the LORD came to them, he punished them and kicked them out of the Garden, but not before clothing them in sacrificial skins and giving them the promise that her Seed would one day crush the head of the serpent.

Many long centuries passed, and after a terrible wickedness was spawned upon the earth at the instigation of the heavenly sons of God, the LORD flooded the earth and destroyed all flesh that walked upon it. Having saved only eight people, the children of Noah had offspring and soon there were enough of them to hatch a plan to build a tower to the heavens. This ziggurat structure was a microcosm of the Edenic paradise, a mountain-stairway to link heaven and earth, thereby contacting the sons of God in an attempt to thwart Yahweh's sovereignty.

For their treachery, God divided mankind into seventy nations and gave to each of these nations a member of the heavenly council to rule over them. The entire world fell into complete spiritual darkness and slavery to evil powers. But that promise remained, and with Abram, the Angel of the LORD took for himself a man whom he would turn into a nation—Israel, the people of his own inheritance.

The sons of God ruled wickedly, and the LORD announced to them that they would be punished. At this moment, the promise given to Abraham that he would be "the father of many nations" took form and shape in a prophecy that would center on the Angel of the LORD ruling over not only one nation, but all the nations while the other sons would be disinherited. The kings of the earth would rise up and the heavenly rulers would take counsel together against the LORD and against his Anointed Messiah. But the promise would not be eclipsed.

To the heavenly council it was announced by the LORD that a son of David would rule the kingdoms forever. This covenant was witnessed in the clouds by the Cloud-Rider, a Son who strangely and shockingly looked like a son of Adam!

At just the right time, the Son of God emptied himself of his divine prerogatives and his angelic power and took the lowly form of a human. Born under law, the Second Adam obeyed where the First Adam failed. One man lost his full dominion. The other Man gained it back through his temptation, as he cast away the serpent of old—a reversal of the events of Eden, thereby securing hope for our race as one of us.

Through his obedience even to death, he made a way possible for God's elect to have forgiveness of sin, but more, adoption into the very family of God. They would be called "sons of God." Simultaneously, on an old Roman cross, he would triumph over the principalities and rulers of this present darkness by putting them to open shame as he cancelled the record of debts that stood against us; and before the divine council with all of its courtly rules, he legally made it possible for the Son of God to pluck any that were predestined out from under the grip of Satan.

Satan, thus bound and powerless, became a mere roaring but toothless lion. No longer can he deceive all peoples when this gospel goes forth in power for, "In these last days, God has spoken to us by his Son, whom he appointed the heir of all things, through whom he also created the world."

Today, the creation itself groans in eager expectation for the earthly sons of God to be revealed in all their future glory. On that day, these meek shall inherit the earth, as brothers of Christ, sons of the living God. They will take their seats around the symbolic 24 thrones of heaven, replacing the fallen watchers. They will judge the angels who will be punished in the lake of fire, forever. From their position on the newly reconstituted council, they will begin their eternal dominion which was fully reclaimed by the Second Adam through his obedience. And the new heavens and new earth will remain without end.

Amen! Amen!

The Council of God

Eliphaz the Temanite was one of Job's good friends. At least, he was until Job got sick and Eliphaz came with some others to "comfort him." The wisest thing Eliphaz ever did was sit quietly with Job in his misery, silent. But eventually, comforters must try to comfort with their words.

This man has a fairly typical view of evil: "Job, you get what you deserve. What goes around comes around. Figure out what you did, repent, and God will restore you." But Job insists he has done nothing wrong. He did nothing to deserve the evils that had come upon him.

Soon, Eliphaz becomes indignant (never the way to treat a suffering man!), "Are you the first man who was born? Or were you brought forth before the hills? Have you listened in the council of God? And do you limit wisdom to yourself?" (Job 15:7-8). His point is that Job hasn't listened in on the heavenly rulings, and he can't possibly know why God was doing this to him. But it's the way he puts it here that makes for an interesting segue into the exegetical meat of this chapter.

There are some questions about who Eliphaz is talking about here. Who is this "first man?" Some who try to deal with the verse in its original context admit, "He may be referring to Adam."[192] Certainly, Adam is the first man in Scripture. A problem may be that he was "fashioned" rather than "born."[193] Many commentators today believe that Eliphaz, who is not a Jew, is probably referring to some primordial myth of a first man—*a heavenly man*.[194] In this light, it is interesting that the language of being "brought forth before the hills" is identical to that which describes Wisdom in Proverbs 8:25. We have seen how this, in turn, is a passage describing the Son of God, who is "begotten, not made."

Whether referring to Adam or the Son of God or some other unknown myth circling around Eliphaz's head, what is certain is that this person had access to a heavenly "council [Hb: *sôd*] of God." A "council" is an assembly of people that meets for some purpose. However, some translations render it "counsel." "Counsel" is a word usually associated with giving advice (sometimes that advice is legal advice). This translation does fit within the semantic range of the word. However, what would the counsel of God refer to? If it means something like God is trying to counsel Job but he didn't listen, why mention this First Man? If it refers to the secret counsel of the Godhead, why bring this man up at all, for "the secret things belong to the LORD" (Dt 29:29), and neither Job nor Eliphaz nor anyone else is privy to it. For this and other reasons that we will delve into, the ESV and other translations properly render it "council."

---

[192] John E. Hartley, *The Book of Job*, The New International Commentary on the Old Testament (Grand Rapids, MI: Wm. B. Eerdmans Publishing Co., 1988), 245.

[193] Some lexicons like *BDB* give a possible meaning of *yalad* as "bring forth," which might fit the idea of Adam being fashioned or made. But the overwhelming use of this word is to "be born." Of course, the genealogy in Luke 3:38 does call Adam "the son of God," so at least in a metaphorical sense, God "bore" him.

[194] Cf. Hartley, ibid.; David J. A. Clines, *Job 1–20*, vol. 17, Word Biblical Commentary (Dallas: Word, Incorporated, 1998), 349-50; John H. Walton, *Zondervan Illustrated Bible Backgrounds Commentary (Old Testament): The Minor Prophets, Job, Psalms, Proverbs, Ecclesiastes, Song of Songs*, vol. 5 (Grand Rapids, MI: Zondervan, 2009), 269.

One of those reasons occurs at the beginning of Job. This council actually starts off the book, thereby providing the context for understanding Eliphaz's remarks. In fact, it shows that his comments are quite ironic, since it becomes apparent that Eliphaz hasn't sat in on the council either, for if he had, he would not have made these accusations against Job. It says, "Now there was a day when the sons of God came to present themselves before the LORD, and Satan also came among them" (Job 1:6).

The scene takes place in heaven, for that is where God is enthroned. It is not an earthly scene before a temple with Jewish rulers. There is no temple yet and there is almost certainly no Israel, as Job is the earliest book of the Bible, and predates the existence of Israel. Besides, the characters here give this away.

Importantly, we have the LORD here. This is not some priest standing in the place of the LORD. It is Yahweh himself, and Yahweh speaks directly to Satan (literally, "the satan," see our Appendix on this). Satan does not come with people while they worship God. Finally, there are those called "the sons of God." While a detailed defense of their identity is not feasible here,[195] the sons of God return later in the book and their identity is clear.

Talking about the very beginning of creation, God asks Job where he was, "When the morning stars sang together and all the sons of God shouted for joy?" (Job 38:7). Here, "morning stars" is parallel with "sons of God." Since the context speaks of God laying "the foundation of the earth" (4) and "determining its measurements" (5) and "sinking its bases" and "laying its cornerstone" (6), and this is described as the time "when"[196] the sons of God shouted, it is simply not possible for this to be humans. There were no humans around at this point in history. It has to refer to heavenly beings. This is among the reasons that in at least half of the 10 occurrences of the phrase in the OT, the LXX translates

---

[195] See more below, but for a detailed exegesis of the phrase see Douglas Van Dorn, *Giants: Sons of the Gods* (Erie, CO: Waters of Creation Publishing, 2012), 1-48; Michael Heiser, "Deuteronomy 32:8 and the Sons of God," *BibSac* 158:629 (Jan-Mar 2001): 52-74; Jacob Johannes Theodoor Doedens, "The Sons of God in Genesis 6:1-4" (Ph.D. diss. Theologische Universiteit Kampen, 2013).

[196] Nearly all English translations take the preposition בְּ temporally ("when" or "as" or "while"). This includes the LXX, the Vulgate, and the Targum which even adds, "in the time."

"sons of God" as "angels." This is the oldest and frankly only interpretation that we find in the church for its first several hundred years after Christ, and in Judaism until long after the destruction of its temple.[197]

"Sons of God" Passage	Heb/Gk Phrase	LXX Translation
Genesis 6:2	beney ha-'elohim	"sons of God"
Genesis 6:4		"sons of God"
Job 1:6		*"angels* of God"
Job 2:1		*"angels* of God"
Job 38:7		"my *angels*"
Psalm 29:1	beney 'elim	"sons of God"
Psalm 89:6		"sons of God"
Psalm 82:6	beney 'elyon	"sons of the Most High"
Deut 32:8	aggelōn theou*	*"angels* of God"
Deut 32:43	uioi theou*	(some manuscripts) *"angels* of God"

* signifies only found in LXX

What Is the Divine Council?

This idea of a heavenly council is not well-known outside of OT scholarship, though that is beginning to change. I have vague memories reading about it in semi-popular OT scholarly literature, yet those authors very often just mention it, never explaining anything about it, seemingly assuming that the reader knows exactly what they are talking about. Here's an example that we will return to later:

> The very form of the creative fiat of Genesis 1:26 calling for the making of man in God's image tells us that we have to do here with the Glory-theophany, and thus with the heavenly assembly or council.

---

[197] See Doedens, "The Sons of God," 89–180; Robert C. Newman, "The Ancient Exegesis of Genesis 6:2,4," *Grace Theological Journal* 5:1 (1984): 13–36; Doedens, "The Indecent Descent of the Sethites: The Provenance of the Sethites-Interpretation of Genesis 6:1-4," *Sárospataki Füzetek* 16:3–4 (2012): 47–57.

> For the Creator speaks in the deliberative plural idiomatic of the council: "Let us make man in our image, after our likeness" … [This is] the Lord of Glory enthroned as King of kings in the midst of the angelic hosts of the divine council.[198]

Without knowing what I was reading, I just blasted my way past these references. It wasn't until being introduced to the subject in a direct and blunt way that I finally understood the concept and was then able to go and read the breadth of literature out there on it.[199] It was then that I realized that I had read about it many times before, I just didn't notice it.

So, what is this "divine council?" Scholars define it as a council of heavenly beings that meet in assembly in order to administer the affairs of the cosmos.[200] Titles and words used to describe those who serve here are *elohim*,[201] stars, sons of God, thrones, rulers, princes, principalities, authorities, dominions, powers, the host of heaven; and some of these came to be encapsulated in the biblically morphing catch-all word "angels" even as early as the NT (words change in meaning over time, and

---

[198] Meredith G. Kline, *Kingdom Prologue: Genesis Foundations for a Covenantal Worldview* (Eugene, OR: Wipf & Stock Publishers, 2006), 42–43. For more, see Meredith Kline, *Glory in our Midst: A Biblical-Theological Reading of Zechariah's Night Visions* (Eugene, OR: Wipf and Stock, 2001), 4, 12, 24, etc.; Richard S. Hess, *Israelite Religions: An Archeological and Biblical Survey* (Grand Rapids, MI: Baker Academic, 2007), 14, 296; John Walton, *The Lost World of Genesis One: Ancient Cosmology and the Origins Debate* (Downers Grove, IL: InterVarsity Press, 2009), 177 n. 2.

[199] The best technical introductions to it include dictionary entries like Michael S. Heiser, "Divine Council," ed. Tremper Longman III and Peter Enns, *Dictionary of the Old Testament: Wisdom, Poetry & Writings* (Downers Grove, IL; Nottingham, England: IVP Academic; Inter-Varsity Press, 2008), 112-16; E. Theodore Mullen Jr., "Divine Assembly," ed. David Noel Freedman, *The Anchor Yale Bible Dictionary* (New York: Doubleday, 1992), 214-17. Also journals and dissertations like H. Wheeler Robinson, "The Council of Yahweh," *Journal of Theological Studies* 45 (1944): 151-157; Michael S. Heiser, "The Divine Council in Second Temple Literature" (Ph.D. diss., University of Wisconsin, 2004). Also books like E. Theodore Mullen, *The Divine Council in Canaanite and Early Hebrew Literature*, Harvard Semitic Monographs 24 (Missoula, MT: Scholars Press, 1980).

[200] M. S. Heiser, "Divine Council," ed. Tremper Longman III and Peter Enns, *Dictionary of the Old Testament: Wisdom, Poetry & Writings* (Downers Grove, IL; Nottingham, England: IVP Academic; Inter-Varsity Press, 2008), 112; E. Theodore Mullen Jr., "Divine Assembly," ed. David Noel Freedman, *The Anchor Yale Bible Dictionary* (New York: Doubleday, 1992), 213; Brian P. Gault, "Job's Hope: Redeemer or Retribution?," *Bibliotheca Sacra* 173:690 (2016): 157.

[201] "Elohim" is a generic term for a heavenly being.

while "angel" did not really describe these beings early on, it certainly did later).[202]

There are all kinds of questions people might have about this council. Who is its leader? What is his relationship to the others who rule on it? Does it include fallen heavenly beings? If God uses a council to carry out events, what is the relationship between divine sovereignty and their ruling? Many more could be added. Some of these questions have to remain in the realm of speculation. Others we can answer with at least some degree certainty by looking at various passages that speak to the issue of the divine council. Of course, our main focus in all of this will be to relate how the council is important to the Angel of the LORD and, later, to the incarnated Christ. Let's turn to some of these passages to see what they have to say about this council.

The Divine Council in Scripture

1 Kings 22

One of the most direct passages is found in the rather strange story in 1 Kings 22:

> And Micaiah said, "Therefore hear the word of the LORD: I saw the LORD sitting on his throne, and all the host of heaven standing beside him on his right hand and on his left; and the LORD said, 'Who will entice Ahab, that he may go up and fall at Ramoth-gilead?' And one said one thing, and another said another. Then a spirit came forward and stood before the LORD, saying, 'I will entice him.' And the LORD said to him, 'By what means?' And he said, 'I will go out, and will be a lying spirit in the mouth of all his prophets.' And he said, 'You are to entice him, and you shall succeed; go out and do so.' Now therefore behold, the LORD has put a lying spirit in the mouth of all these your prophets; the LORD has declared disaster for you."
>
> (1 Kings 22:19-23)

The text sounds foreign to a modern way of viewing the world, but it is self-explanatory. Clearly, the setting is heaven, not earth. The players are

---

[202] On many of the terms used by Paul as members of the divine council see Ronn Johnson, "The Old Testament Background for Paul's Principalities and Powers" (PhD Dissertation, Dallas Theological Seminary, 2004).

obviously spirit-beings, not human beings—except for the prophet who is seeing this all in a vision. These beings are deliberating over affairs on earth, making decisions, carrying out actions, and so forth. One thing is made crystal clear here. Yahweh is the head of the council, and nothing gets done without his permission.

We want to make three points from this passage. The first concerns the question about God using other creatures to do his will. We believe we should view God's role and the (other)[203] council members much the way we view God working things out on earth through mankind (including our forms of government). On earth, we know that God uses human agency to accomplish his will. His people are responsible to carry out his will, knowing that ultimately, it is God who works in us both to will and work for his pleasure. Why should it unsettle us that God works similarly in heaven, using the agency of heavenly beings to accomplish his will, giving them responsibility? God is Sovereign and nothing is done apart from his decretive will. However, he has given real wills[204] to these creatures and made them responsible agents to act rightly upon them. Therefore, there is a dance between God's sovereignty and human or angelic responsibility where both are real and simultaneously true. God uses real creatures to carry out his will through secondary causes; yet creatures cannot thwart God's decrees.

---

[203] Clearly, God is part of the council. We will have more to say about this as we move to other passages.

[204] We intentionally stay away from the term "freewill" here because of how it is used in very different, sometimes contradictory senses by Christians. Most Christians believe in freewill, but it is often defined very differently from one group to another. One view of freewill believes that the will of man is "indifferent" and has a power of "contrary choice" whereby he in fact can thwart God's secret, decretive, or divine will. This is sometimes called Libertarian Freedom. This is the classic view of the will held by Christians from Pelagius to Arminius to Wesley and probably the majority of Christians today. We do not believe that *any* being can have this kind of will, not even God. Rather, we believe all wills are wrapped up in that person or being's nature, that all act based on their chief desires. So, for example, if there is no desire to sin as is the case with God, there will never be a choice to sin. If someone is a slave to sin, then they will sin, for they are in slavery to it. Yet, all choices are real and proceed from true desires of free agents (in God's case, he is the freest of all beings, doing all his good pleasure all the time). Sometimes this is called Compatibilism from the idea that divine sovereignty and responsibility are "compatible" ideas; there is no contradiction between them.

Second, notice how the spirit says he will "go out." Basically, he is being "sent" by Yahweh, much like we see in Genesis 28:12 where angels "ascend and descend" the ladder-stairway to carry out God's directives. They are responsible agents, and God charges them with tasks. This is very interesting, for the Angel of the LORD is one of those beings who has a seat on this very council. Furthermore, he is often said to be "sent" by Yahweh:

- The LORD, the God of heaven ... he will *send his Angel* before you, and you shall take a wife for my son from there (Gen 24:7).
- Behold, I *send an Angel* before you to guard you on the way and to bring you to the place that I have prepared. Pay careful attention to him and obey his voice; do not rebel against him, for he will not pardon your transgression, for my Name is in him (Ex 23:20-21).
- I will *send an Angel* before you, and I will drive out the Canaanites, the Amorites, the Hittites, the Perizzites, the Hivites, and the Jebusites (Ex 33:2).
- When we cried to the LORD, he heard our voice and *sent an Angel* and brought us out of Egypt (Num 20:16).
- And the LORD *sent an Angel*, who cut off all the mighty warriors and commanders and officers in the camp of the king of Assyria (2Ch 32:21).

On the most basic level, even though he is the uncreated Creator of all things, like the Lord Jesus incarnate in his relations to men, the Angel of the LORD, like any angel or spirit who carries out tasks, functions rather ordinarily as a member of the council. He is The Emissary sent from Yahweh (even though he is also Yahweh), usually (though not always) to his own people.

Where is he being sent from? Certainly not from the Post Office or the I.R.S. He is being sent *from heaven*, just as Jesus was (John 6:38, etc.). This is not just the Father sending the Son, though of course it is that. This is the Father doing things according to the good and proper order, according to the procedures which he set up in heaven with the sons of God. They are involved in our affairs, though, when the Ancient of Days renders his verdict, the court is closed. If the Angel is sent from heaven, then obviously he exists in heaven, just like the other beings on the council do. The Angel comes from the council and is sent by Yahweh.

Third, returning to Micaiah, we want to ask what is a prophet of God doing here? The answer is that this was essential to his very calling, and it gave him his authority. In Jeremiah 23, the LORD calls out false prophets saying, "For who among them has stood in the council of the LORD to see and to hear his Word, or who has paid attention to his Word and listened? ... I did not send the prophets, yet they ran; I did not speak to them, yet they prophesied" (Jer 23:18, 21). The answer is only the prophets of Yahweh have that privilege. "But if they had *stood in my council*, then they would have proclaimed my words to my people, and they would have turned them from their evil way" (22). As Michael Heiser says, "The implications are clear: true prophets have stood and listened in Yahweh's divine council; false prophets have not."[205]

"Word" (Heb. *Debar*; Gk. *Logos*) in these verses is doing double duty. It refers both to words (it is plural in vs. 22) and to the Person called the Word of God (it is singular in vs. 18). Not only do they hear his words, they also "see" (*ra'ah*) the Word. This is exactly what we saw with people like Abraham (Gen 18:1), Samuel (1Sa 3:21), and importantly here, Jeremiah (Jer 1:11, 13). The Jews perceived it this way as well, for the Targum inserts the Memra here. "They have not attended *to his Memra*, and they have not heeded him/it."[206]

If this is right, then we have a clear example that the Word of God, that is the Angel of the LORD, speaks to the prophets from the divine council itself. He speaks before other heavenly beings to his earthly representative. Thus, his place on the council must be very exalted. This is such an important point that Jeremiah says if someone claims to be a prophet and has not been taken into the council chambers to see and hear the Word, then they are false prophets and should not be heard or trusted.

We believe that this fact also accounts for the diminishing of "the Angel of the LORD" phrase as we move through the history of the OT. As a general rule, we do not see "The Angel of the LORD" as much later in the OT as we do in, say, Genesis. Again, it's not that we don't see the

---

[205] Michael S. Heiser, *The Unseen Realm: Recovering the Supernatural Worldview of the Bible* (Bellingham, WA: Lexham Press, 2015), 239.

[206] The note in the Cathcart, Mahaer, McNamara edition of Targum Jeremiah suggests that this is one of the rare translations of *dabar* where Memra is found and then cites an article on Jewish theology of Intermediaries. See Kevin Cathcart, Michael Maher, and Martin McNamara, eds., *The Aramaic Bible: The Targum of Jeremiah*, trans. Robert Hayward, vol. 12 (Collegeville, MN: The Liturgical Press, 1990), Jer 23:18; G. F. Moore, "Intermediaries in Jewish Theology," *Harvard Theological Review* 15 (1922) 41–85.

Person (who is virtually omnipresent in the OT), but we don't see the *phrase*. Why? Someone explains, "The fundamental authority undergirding the prophetic message in ancient Israel is the fact that the prophet has stood in the council of Yahweh, has listened in on the decisions of the heavenly assembly ... The prophet has access to the council and is sent to declare the divine decisions."[207]

When a prophet hears from God directly in the divine council, he is hearing from The Angel himself. Hence, we have discussed how in almost every prophetic book, the prophet receives and often even sees the Word of God. This becomes his divinely commissioned authority.

Isaiah 6

Prophets are "sent," just like the Angel. A great example of this is the divine council scene of Isaiah 6, a passage we looked at in an earlier chapter where we focused on the "glory." Isaiah sees the Lord (*Adonai*) sitting upon a throne, high and lifted up; and the train of his robe filled the temple (Isa 6:1). John tells us explicitly that "Isaiah said these things because he saw [*Christ's*] glory and spoke of him." The scene is in heaven, and there are heavenly seraphim attending (2). After a short while, the purpose of the vision becomes clear. "Whom shall I send, and who will go for us?" (Isa 6:8). "Us" is the same kind of plurality we mentioned earlier in that divine council quote from Genesis 1:26. Isaiah speaks up. "Then I said, 'Here I am! Send me'" (Isa 6:8). Isaiah son of Amoz sees Christ and then, with a similar change from the plural to the singular pronoun found in Genesis 1:26-27, through the words "whom shall I send," *Christ* speaks to Isaiah who is thus sent from the heavenly court by Christ's authority, to go and speak on the LORD's behalf. This is the way it was with all the prophets.

The same idea is true in the NT, except that the word used is now "apostle" rather than "prophet." An "apostle" in Greek is one "who is sent on a mission with full authority, a messenger, an envoy" (Friberg).

---

[207] Patrick D. Miller, Jr. , "Eridu, Dunnu, and Babel: A Study in Comparative Mythology," *Hebrew Annual Review* 9 (1985): 230, reprinted in Richard S. Hess and David T. Tsumura, eds., *I Studied Inscriptions from Before the Flood: Ancient Near Eastern, Literary, and Linguistic Approaches to Genesis 1-11*, SBTS 4 (Winona Lake, IN: Eisenbrauns, 1994), 146.

It is the same idea as a prophet who receives his commission from the LORD. Apostles are those who knew and spoke with Jesus Christ. But the Apostle Paul is a special case. He heard from the Lord Jesus in visions, like the prophets of old. He went to the "third heaven." But he was received by the Apostles themselves and his word became the very words of God in thirteen books of the NT.

In the places where we find "the Angel of the LORD" phrase appearing multiple times, prophets being sent to speak God's message are few and far between. Instead, the Angel himself is sent from heaven by the Father, and that is why he is so prominent with this title. Later, when the prophets and apostles see and hear the Angel-Son (or incarnated Son), the title "Angel" is less appropriate, because they are the ones giving the message rather than the Angel directly. Hence, other titles such as "Word" become much more common for the Angel, even though both refer to the same Divine Person.

One final point is appropriate here. If God is sending messengers who speak his very words, then people do not need direct encounters with him in order to have contact with the Word. Thus, what becomes ordinary today, since the Angel isn't coming, and Jesus has ascended to heaven, and prophets and Apostles have ceased as roles, is preaching. "The Word is near you, in your mouth and in your heart (that is, the word of faith that we preach)" (Rom 10:8). In this way, that special role of the Angel early on in the Scripture and later taken by the Incarnate Christ, is granted, by the Second Person, to those who deliver his word in his stead, until that day comes when he will return to judge the living and the dead. We find that word in Holy Scripture.

Daniel 4

While the Micaiah story anticipates the soon to be carried out plans of God in the council, perhaps an even better place to see the deliberation *carried out* is Daniel 4. Nebuchadnezzar has a dream of a huge tree. This troubles him greatly. He says, "I saw in the visions of my head as I lay in bed, and behold, *a watcher, a holy one*, came down from heaven. He proclaimed aloud..." (Dan 4:13-14). What did this "watcher" proclaim? It was a message of judgment upon him saying, "This sentence is *by the decree* of the watchers, *the decision by* the word of the holy ones, to the end that the living may know that the Most High rules the kingdom of men and gives it to whom he will" (17). Immediately, the sentence is carried out, and Nebuchadnezzar loses his mind, becoming wild like an animal for a period of seven years until he is restored to give praise to the Most High.

What is a watcher? As one scholar puts it, "The 'Watchers' are widely attested in Jewish literature of the Hellenistic and early Roman periods.[208] The most famous attestation is in the 'Book of the Watchers' (1Enoch 1-36) where the term is used for the fallen angels."[209] Thus, where the Hebrew reads "watcher," the Old Greek has "angel."[210] There

---

[208] (This is our note, not Collins'.) For example, Hesiod in the 8th century B.C., "You princes, mark well this punishment; for the deathless gods are near among men and mark all those who oppress their fellows with crooked judgements. . . For upon the bounteous earth Zeus has thrice ten thousand spirits, watchers of mortal men, and these keep watch on judgements and deeds of wrong as they roam, clothed in mist, all over the earth" (Hesiod, *Works and Days* 248-53).

[209] J. J. Collins, "Watcher," ed. Karel van der Toorn, Bob Becking, and Pieter W. van der Horst, *Dictionary of Deities and Demons in the Bible* (Leiden; Boston; Köln; Grand Rapids, MI; Cambridge: Brill; Eerdmans, 1999), 893. Daniel 4 is the only unquestioned place in the OT where the Watchers are mentioned. Other passages have been proposed such as Micah 5:13; Jer 2:28, and Jer 19:15. The most interesting suggestion is Isa 33:7-9. The first line "Their heroes (*'er'el*) cry" (vs. 7) was thought in Jewish midrash to refer to "death-spirits howling" (Margaret Barker, "Isaiah," in James D. Dunn; J.W. Rogerson (eds.), *Eerdmans Commentary on the Bible* [Grand Rapids, MI: Eerdmans, 2003], 520). From here, the LXX reads, "Behold the … angels of peace weep bitterly." Finally, vs. 9 mentions Lebanon, Bashan, and Carmel, three places associated with Watchers in other literature (see Gregorio del Olmo Lete, "Bashan," *DDD*, 161-163; Wolfgang Röllig, "Lebanon," *DDD*, 506-507). Thus the reading, "Behold the Arielites [angels] cry aloud, the angels of peace weep bitterly. Highways are desolate, Wayfarers have ceased, a covenant has been renounced, the Watchers rejected," This has been defended by several scholars (cf. Michael S. Heiser, "The Divine Council in Late Canonical and Non-Canonical Second Temple Jewish Literature," A Dissertation at the University of Wisconsin-Madison, 2004, 227-28; Robert Murray, "The Origin of Aramaic 'îr, Angel." *Orientalia* 53 (1984), 307-308.

[210] The Aramaic word for watcher is ʿîr (עִיר). A Hebrew word for a "city" is ʿîr (עִיר). Through bilingualism, these words are homographs (Murray, "Origen"). Given that watchers are the same beings that are put over nations in more than one ancient book, it is curious that we find such an overlap in the meaning of these words. Further, the LORD is sometimes said to "watch" over Jerusalem or Israel (Gen 31:49; Ps 141:3; Dan 9:14; Jer 31:28; 44:27; etc.). While the technical word used is not this word, there seems to be a conceptual overlap, especially if we keep this in mind from the perspective of the Angel of the LORD. For more on this and other fascinating connections of watchers and angels and various biblical texts see Basil Lourié, "A Danielic Pseudepigraphon Paraphrased by Papias: A New Translation and Introduction," in

are actually many other terms that are familiar (see the list above that includes "dominions" and "authorities"), but they are not often put into a context that makes sense of them. This first portion of the book of Enoch is an expansion of Genesis 6:1-4. It uses the term "watchers" for Genesis' "sons of God," which we also saw in Job, and will see in other divine council scenes. Therefore, watcher is a term used for the ruling members of the divine council. These watchers of Daniel 4 are delivering the message not only of the whole court of watchers, but of the Most High himself (Dan 4:34-35). In other words, they are also sent by the LORD.

Their title here as "holy ones" seems to imply that these beings are good, or at the very least, they are loyal to Yahweh and are not seeking to usurp him. For, evil watchers, which is what the majority of the tradition of this term refers to, are not usually called "holy ones."[211] Given scenes like Isaiah 6 (above) where Isaiah sees wonderful beings surrounding the throne, it is certain that at least some of those on this divine council are deeply loyal to Yahweh.[212] This is the very point in Daniel 4. These watchers here are decreeing and deciding the fate of Nebuchadnezzar, and the LORD approves.

The Apostles and all biblical writes believed these creatures were real, and that they exist as members of a divine council. It is possible that Yahweh (which in context of the term would mean the Angel-Yahweh) himself is likened to a Watcher in places like Ps 121:4 or Zech 4:10,[213] and if so, this would almost certainly refer to the role of the Son of God "watching" over Israel.

Old Testament Pseudepigrapha: More Noncanonical Scriptures, ed. Richard Bauckham, James R. Davila, and Alexander Panayotov, vol. One (Grand Rapids, MI; Cambridge, U.K.: William B. Eerdmans Publishing Company, 2013), 437-40.

[211] There are a few exceptions. For example, 1 En 15:9, "Evil spirits went out from their body, since they came from the higher places, and from the holy watchers—the beginning of their creation beginning of a foundation—they will be called evil spirits."

[212] Of course, even these beings are calling God "holy, holy, holy," which means, by comparison, they are not like him. Who is like God?

[213] "Some biblical precedents for the notion of angelic beings as 'watchful ones', but with different terminology, have been proposed. The most noteworthy is Zech 4:10 which refers to seven 'eyes of the Lord which range through the whole earth.' ... [Another] biblical passage is found in Ps 121:4: "Behold, he neither slumbers nor sleeps, the guardian of Israel", with reference to Yahweh himself." J. J. Collins, "Watcher," ed. Karel van der Toorn, Bob Becking, and Pieter W. van der Horst, *Dictionary of Deities and Demons in the Bible* (Leiden; Boston; Köln; Grand Rapids, MI; Cambridge: Brill; Eerdmans, 1999), 894. See also n. 199 above.

Daniel 7

Daniel 7 is another great place to see the divine council in the OT.

> As I looked, thrones were placed, and the Ancient of Days took his seat; his clothing was white as snow, and the hair of his head like pure wool; his throne was fiery flames; its wheels were burning fire. A stream of fire issued and came out from before him; a thousand thousands served him, and ten thousand times ten thousand stood before him; the court sat in judgment, and the books were opened.
>
> (Daniel 7:9-10)

Again, the setting is heaven. There is a river of fire and the Ancient of Days (the Father) is presiding. But his is not the only throne here. He is surrounded by "thrones," upon which sit heavenly beings as they begin to deliberate and to judge. Just a couple verses later it tells us about "one like a son of man" coming "on the clouds" to be presented before the Ancient of Days, whereupon he is handed an everlasting kingdom.

There is good reason to believe that this is more than a vision (but not less than one). It is also a strong polemic against other religions, specifically the god Baal. This is because there are so many nearly identical parallels between this passage and the so-called *Ba'al Cycle* that it seems impossible for it to be a coincidence (see chart below).

The Baal Cycle is an Ugaritic (Canaanite) story about Ba'al, the storm god, ascending to the throne over his brother Yam (the sea god). It was discovered on clay tablets buried beneath the sands of an ancient site in western Syria in the 1920s.

Daniel 7:9-13	Ba'al Cycle
7:2a I saw in my vision by night, and behold b the four winds of heaven were c stirring up the great sea [yam].	[Baal], take your clouds, your winds, your lightnings, your rains (KTU I.5.v:6-9)
7:3a Four great beasts came up out of the sea There are a total of seven heads	Yam sent messengers. . . With great rejoicing they flew heavenwards Their nostrils flaring (KTU I.2.i.11-13) Yam is described as a seven headed sea-monster with four names: Dragon, Leviathan (L-t-n), Arsh, and Atick (KTU I.3.iii:38-44)

7:9 As I looked, thrones were placed,	The gods raise their heads from the thrones of their princeships (KTU I.2.i:29)
and the Ancient of Days took his seat; his clothing was white as snow, and the hair of his head like lamb's wool;	El: The Father of Years. (KTU I.3.v:8) I shall make ['El's] gray hair run with blood, The gray hair of his beard (KTU I.3.v.2)
his throne was fiery flames; its wheels were burning fire.	
7:10 A stream of fire issued and came out from before him;	She set her face towards El At the source of the rivers, At the midst of the springs of the two deeps. (KTU I.3.v:7).
thousand thousands served him, and ten thousand times ten thousand stood before him	
the court sat in judgment, and	Set your faces towards the convocation of the Council; Towards the divine mountain (KTU I.2.i:14)
the books were opened.	The tablets of Yam (KTU 1.2.i:26)
7:11a I looked then because of the sound of the great words that the horn was speaking.	Message of Yam, your master, Of your lord, Ruler Nahar: "Give up the god whom you obey, The one whom you obey, Tempest! Give up Baal and his retinue, The Son of Dagan, whose gold I shall seize!" (KTU I.2.i.34-36)
b And as I looked, the beast was killed, and its body destroyed and given over to be burned with fire.	Then Baal went out [ ] Valiant Baal dried him up Yam is indeed dead! (KTU I.2.iv.31-32)
7:12 As for the rest of the beasts, their dominion was taken away,	You [Ba'al], your name is 'Expeller." Expeller of Yam [the sea god]. Expel Yam from his throne Nahar from the siege of his dominion! (KTU I.2.iv:12-13)
but their lives were prolonged for a season and a time.	
7:13 I saw in the night visions, and behold, with the clouds of heaven there came one like a son of man, and he came to the Ancient of Days and was presented before him.	O Charioteer of the Clouds O Prince Baal (KTU I.2.iv:8) Baal stood by El (KTU I.2.i.22)
7:14 And to him was given dominion and glory and a kingdom, that all peoples, nations, and languages should serve him; his dominion is an everlasting dominion, which shall not pass away, and his kingdom one that shall not be destroyed.	Take your everlasting kingdom, your eternal dominion! (KTU I.2.iv.10)

Why would Daniel seem to borrow such imagery to describe what he saw? Besides the fact that he surely saw what he described, Daniel is showing the true reality in heaven, as opposed to the counterfeit Baal story. This Old Testament Person "like a son of man" is High Prince, not Baal (see the comparison on 7:13). Baal is a usurper, a supplanter, an imposter. His will never be the Kingdom. But this polemic is enough to prove beyond a reasonable doubt that we have here a heavenly vision of the divine council, for that is exactly what is going on in the Baal Cycle.

Amazingly, Jesus cites this very passage at his trial, and for what he says about it, he is put to death. The high priest asked him under oath, "I adjure you by the living God, tell us if you are the Christ, the Son of God" (Matt 26:63). Jesus answered him, "You have said so. But I tell you, from now on you will see the Son of Man seated at the right hand of Power and coming on the clouds of heaven" (64). "Then the high priest tore his robes and said, 'He has uttered blasphemy. What further witnesses do we need? You have now heard his blasphemy'" (65). Jesus was claiming that he was the son of man who was receiving a kingdom as he rode to the ancient of days on the clouds of heaven. He is the Cloud-Rider, a title that belongs everywhere else in the OT only to Yahweh.

Psalm 89

Psalm 89 explains the council this way,

> Let the heavens praise your wonders, O LORD, your faithfulness in the assembly of the holy ones! For who in the skies can be compared to the LORD? Who among the heavenly beings is like the LORD, a God greatly to be feared in the council of the holy ones, and awesome above all who are around him?
>
> (Psalm 89:5-7)

Again, we are in the skies or the heavens. This is not on the earth. This is an "assembly" of "heavenly beings," literally the *beney 'elim* or as the Psalm Targum translates it, "the multitude of angels." The LXX renders it more literally: "sons of God."

Here they are again. "Sons of God" is technical language used in the OT and around the ancient near east.[214] This particular Psalm begins

---

[214] See n. 194.

with the divine council for a reason. It prepares the setting for a series of prophecies about the coming Messiah, the son of David. Those prophecies begin with remembering the covenant God made with David, "You have said, 'I have made a covenant with my chosen one; I have sworn to David my servant: 'I will establish your offspring forever, and build your throne for all generations'" (Ps 89:3-4). Then, a long series of prophecies about one particular son of David are given (vv. 20-36). These are clearly about the Messiah to come.

They conclude with a remarkable verse, "Like the moon it [this covenantal promise] shall be established forever, a faithful witness in the skies" (37). This translation is unfortunate, because we miss what is actually being said. More literally, it says a witness "in the cloud" (the same word is found in vs. 6 where it is translated as "skies," but in both cases the word is singular in form). There is a witness in the cloud.

We would argue that this witness refers to the Cloud-Rider of Daniel 7. "Who in the cloud can be compared to Yahweh?" (Ps 89:6). E. Theodore Mullen writes, "Both occurrences presuppose some figure who stands before Yahweh in his court, one of the *qedoshim beney-elim* [holy sons of God]."[215]

In the OT, there is a heavenly figure that comes this way. At the Exodus, which is in view in this very song, it is Yahweh himself who is "in a pillar of cloud" (Ex 13:21; 16:10; etc.). He is clearly identified as The Angel of the LORD (14:18). In Revelation we see the same thing. "I saw another mighty angel coming down from heaven, wrapped in a cloud" (Rev 10:1). This refers to Christ.[216]

The verse as it reads in the ESV seems to suppose that the covenant itself is the witness in the clouds. The covenant is "a faithful witness in the skies." This is certainly theologically possible as the idea is found in other places (Gen 31:44; Dt 31:26). But the verse can be translated more literally, "... a witness in the clouds will be faithful."[217] *Thus, it would not be a thing but a Who that is in the clouds.* In other words, God is

---

[215] E. Theodore Mullen, Jr., "The Divine Witness and the Davidic Royal Grant: Ps 89:37-38," *JBL* 102:2 (1983): 215-16.

[216] See Ch. 14.

[217] See the NAS, along with Mullen, "The Divine Witness," 207-218; Mullen, *The Divine Council*, 253ff. P. G. Mosca, "Ugarit and Daniel 7: A Missing Link," *Biblica* 67 (1986): 508-517; Mosca, "Once Again the Heavenly Witness of Ps 89:38," *JBL* 105 (1986): 27-37.

going to make a covenant in heaven before all the heavenly beings, and One Being in the clouds will be its faithful witness. As Heiser puts it, this is God's co-signer of the covenant.[218]

Who is that co-signer? It is none other than Revelation's, "Faithful Witness," language that comes straight out of this verse. The book starts off, "...from Jesus Christ the faithful witness, the firstborn of the dead, and the ruler of the kings on earth. To him who loves us and has freed us from our sins by his blood" (Rev 1:5). And again, to the church at Laodicea, "The words of the Amen, the faithful and true witness, the [Chief] of God's creation" (Rev 3:14).

The divine council is in this Psalm, therefore, to teach us that God is going to swear an oath before the heavenly beings (the sun and the moon represent heavenly beings). But a Faithful Witness, who can be no less than Yahweh himself, is going to witness to the fact that what is sworn will come to pass. He is its Guarantor. But not only is he the Guarantor, he is also the focus of the prophecy and covenant, and he will make sure that all comes to pass by coming down as a human in the virgin's womb to bring about all the promises given to David.

Genesis 1-3

Another important divine council scene is, believe it or not, Genesis 1-3. We saw this hinted at earlier when we saw the quote about God speaking to the divine council when he created man in "our" image. It is possibly also hinted at in Job when that "first man" is discussed in relation to the council. Isaiah and Ezekiel confirm that this is a divine council scene.

Isaiah refers to a heavenly figure called, "Day Star, son of Dawn" (Isa 14:12). Notice, he is called a "son." The Hebrew here is *Helel ben-Shachar*, and it refers to a shining seraphim type being. The Latin translates it famously as Lucifer. Genesis 3 also has a shining being present. He is called "the serpent."

The word in Gen 3:1 is *nachash*. Nachash is a word that can act as a noun, an adjective, or a verb. As a noun it means "serpent" or "snake" or "divination" or "omens." As a verb it means "one who practices

---

[218] Michael Heiser, "Does God Need a Co-Signer?" *LogosTalk* (Oct 24, 2017), https://blog.logos.com/2017/10/god-need-co-signer/.

divination" such as a witch or sorcerer. As an adjective it means "shining" or, if that adjective is standing in the place of a noun (for example the movie "The Good, The Bad, and The Ugly), it means "Shining One." It is perfectly plausible grammatically to translate "the serpent" of Genesis 3:1 as "The Shining One." This would provide a perfect parallel to Isaiah.

The prophet continues, "You said in your heart, 'I will ascend to heaven; above the stars of God I will set my throne on high; I will sit on the mount of assembly in the far reaches of the north; I will ascend above the heights of the clouds; I will make myself like the Most High'" (Isa 14:13-14). Here we have the divine assembly or council mentioned yet again, as well as the clouds we just saw. When compared with Ezekiel, there is good reason to believe that Isaiah is using the story of Eden to talk about the fall of Satan.

Ezekiel preaches against the king of Tyre with strange, almost mythical language. "Because your heart is proud, and you have said, 'I am a god, I sit in the seat of the gods, in the heart of the seas...'" (Ezek 28:2). The reference here is identical to the description of El's abode in pagan stories. It is also symbolic of Eden.

Hence, the prophet begins talking about him as "the signet[219] of perfection, full of wisdom and perfect in beauty" (12) and adds, "You were in Eden, the garden of God; every precious stone was your covering ... on the day that you were created they were prepared" (13). So, we have someone who calls himself a god present *in Eden*.

He finishes by calling him the "anointed guardian cherub" who was "placed on the holy mountain of God; in the midst of the stones of fire"[220] (14). This idea of a holy or cosmic mountain being described

---

[219] There may be a hint in this word "signet" that the figure in Gen 3:1 is in mind, as this word can also mean "serpent." See Michael S. Heiser, *The Unseen Realm: Recovering the Supernatural Worldview of the Bible*, First Edition. (Bellingham, WA: Lexham Press, 2015), 79-82.

[220] The idea of "precious stones" has been understood for centuries to be a reference to the divine council. One of the earliest says, "He gave the names of nine stones, since there are nine ranks of angels. The first angel was adorned and covered with these nine since when it was set ahead of the whole multitude of angels, it was more illustrious in comparison with them." Gregory the Great, "Forty Gospel Homilies 34," cited in Kenneth Stevenson and Michael Gluerup, *Ezekiel, Daniel, Ancient Christian Commentary on Scripture OT 13* (Downers Grove, IL : InterVarsity Press, 2008), 95. See also George W. E. Nickelsburg and Klaus Baltzer, *1 Enoch: A Commentary on the Book of 1 Enoch*, Hermeneia (Minneapolis,

here is the headquarters of the divine council (think Mt. Olympus),[221] and it is certainly the reason why Jesus takes his apostles to a specific mountain to give them their "sending" Great Commission.

Clearly, this figure in Ezekiel is a heavenly being (a cherub) and in both Ezekiel and Genesis he is surrounded by other heavenly beings.[222] Then, Ezekiel describes a fall reminiscent of Isaiah, "You were blameless in your ways from the day you were created, till unrighteousness was found in you" (15). For these and many more reasons, the Garden of Eden has often been seen as the meeting place of the divine council.

We bring this up here, and now relate it to something we saw earlier with the prophets. There is one (in fact two) humans that are here in the midst of these heavenly beings. Adam and Eve were put here by God. Psalm 8 comments on their relationship saying, "What is man that you are mindful of him … you have made him a little lower than the *elohim* …" (Ps 8:5-6). The LXX and Hebrews' citation of this both read "angels" (Heb 2:7). And yet for some reason, God "crowned him with glory and honor. You have given him dominion over the works of your hands; you have put all things under his feet" (6-7).

This remarkable song clearly remembers the story of Genesis 1-2, and in it actually provides a biblical reason for the fall of Satan. God made man lower than the heavenly beings, and yet crowned him with honor and gave him dominion. The idea is that Satan was the glorious ruler. But then, God did the unthinkable and made a ball of mud the ruler of the earth! Hence, we read things in the Jewish tradition like this, "For God created us for incorruption, and made us in the image of his own eternity, but through the devil's envy death entered the world"

MN: Fortress Press, 2001), 286; Richard Clifford, *The Cosmic Mountain in Canaan and the Old Testament*, Harvard Semitic Autographs 4 (Cambridge, MA: Harvard University Press, 1972), 173; Kelley Coblentz Bautch, *A Study of the Geography of 1 Enoch 17-19* (Boston: Brill, 2003), 114-20; Millard C. Lind, *Ezekiel, Believers Church Bible Commentary* (Scottdale, PA: Herald Press, 1996), 237; Walther Zimmerli, *Ezekiel 2: A Commentary on the Book of Ezekiel, Chapters 25-48*, Hermeneia (Philadelphia: Fortress Press, 1983), 93.

[221] See especially Richard Clifford, *The Cosmic Mountain in Canaan and the Old Testament*, Harvard Semitic Autographs 4 (Cambridge, MA: Harvard University Press, 1972).

[222] See For Ezekiel, see notes 218 and 219 above. See also Ezek 31 and the "trees of Eden." In Genesis, besides Satan, these include Yahweh who walks with Adam, and the two(?) cherubim that guard the gate of Eden.

(Wis 2:23-24 NRS).[223] That's the theory anyway, and it is the only one we've ever heard that actually makes sense of the context, not to mention provides a reasonable motive for Satan's fall.

Psalm 82

Of all the divine council passages, Psalm 82 may be the most important, though it also one of the most disputed. The reason we call it the "divine council" is probably because of Psalm 82:1. "God (*elohim*) has taken his place in the divine council; in the midst of the gods (*elohim*) he holds judgment." Though other translations say things like, "his own congregation" (NAS) (thereby leading to a non-supernatural interpretation) or "in the company of God" (YLT), the ESV is giving an informed theological rendering of the phrase *ba'adat-'el* (lit. "the assembly of El"). This is based on at least three things.

First, "El" is a term used often in the OT for God, and importantly, also by Israel's neighbors. These neighbors refer especially to the Canaanites who wrote, among other things, the Ba'al Cycle we saw earlier.

Second, and related to the first point, these people had almost the exact same phrase for the assembly of El. They talk about it as the *dr bn*

---

[223] Ephrem the Syrian (306 – 373 AD), in what is called the *Cave of Treasures* (a book in the NT Apocrypha) merges various traditions into the best summary of the view we have.

"On the sixth day … God the Father said to the Son and Holy Spirit: 'Come, Let us make man in our image, according to our likeness." When the heavenly host heard this voice they were afraid, saying to one another, 'We will see an awesome sight today, the likeness of God our maker" … And God created him by his holy hands in his image and according to his likeness. When the angels saw his image and the glorious appearance of Adam, they trembled at the beauty of his likeness. The wild and domestic animals and birds were assembled and passed before Adam and he game them their names. They bowed their heads and prostrated themselves before him. The angels heard the voice of God which said: 'I have made you king … and I have made you ruler over all which I have created.' [And when the heavenly host heard this voice, they all blessed him and prostrated themselves before him.] And when the chief of that lower order saw that great dominion had been given to Adam, he was envious of him from that day and did not wish to worship him with the angels, and said to his host: 'Don't worship him or give him praise with the angels. It would be [more] proper that he worship me, for I am made of fire and spirit. I cannot worship dust which is made from soil." (*Cave of Treasures*, "The Creation of Adam").

'il ("assembly of the sons of El") or *'dt 'ilm* ("assembly of El/the gods").[224] No one questions that in Canaanite literature this phrase refers to a council of heavenly beings (gods). The way they conceived of this was that El, the high god, presided over a council consisting of his seventy sons (one of whom was Baal). Some scholars have concluded from these parallels that the Bible was copying and borrowing from the peoples around Israel, and that Israelite religion was originally polytheistic. We believe the Bible argues the opposite—that the other ANE religions were copying and twisting the true revelation of God.

Third, God takes his place before a group called "gods" (*elohim*). These "gods" are identified in vs. 6 as "sons of God" (lit. "sons of Elyon, the Most High) where there is more than one "son." As we saw with the phrase "divine council," sometimes translations will take this term "gods" and render it differently. Sometimes it is taken in the singular. For example, "God hath stood in the company of God, in the midst of God doth judge" (YLT).

The word *elohim* appears twice in Ps 82:1. For reasons of grammar, the first occurrence is necessarily singular. There must be agreement in the translation between *elohim* and the singular verbs "takes his place" (lit. "to stand;" *nissab*) and "to judge" (*yispot*). Hence, the universal translation "God." There is no disagreement on this translation.

The second is necessarily plural ("gods"). There must be agreement between how this *elohim* is translated with the preceding preposition "in." While the Bible can and does speak of two Persons in the Godhead being next to each other, it never does this with the term *elohim* used twice. Rather, it will use the names of God to differentiate such as "the LORD [Yahweh] said to my Lord [Adonai]" (Ps 110:1) or in the parallel to Genesis 19:24, "I overthrew some of you, as when God (Elohim) overthrew Sodom and Gomorrah … declares the LORD" (Amos 4:11). Furthermore, the language of "standing" in a divine council most likely refers to the function of a plaintiff in the divine court (cf. Ps 109:6).[225] The term "judging" certainly shows us that we have a court scene. But who is being judged and for what? When we see the answer to this, it is very clear that the second *elohim* cannot refer to God.

---

[224] Cf. Heiser, "Divine Council," *Dictionary of the OT: Wisdom, Poetry & Writings*, 113.
[225] See Jacob Johannes Theodoor Doedens, "The Sons of God in Genesis 6:1-4," 227.

The judgment begins in Ps 82:2 and is directed towards "you," in other words, towards the second *elohim*. In vv. 2-4 the judgment is for bad things. "You" "judge unjustly," "show partiality to the wicked," do not "give justice to the weak or fatherless," do not "maintain the right of the afflicted or destitute," do not "rescue the week and needy," and "do not deliver them from the wicked."

In vv. 5-7, the foundations of the earth are shaken and these persons are punished. There is a parallel here to Isaiah. "The earth is utterly broken, the earth is split apart, the earth is violently shaken … On that day the LORD will punish the host of heaven, in heaven, and the kings of the earth, on the earth" (Isa 24:19, 21). All of this clearly rules out "God" as a translation for the second *elohim*. God has never sinned. In fact, it is the opposite, for these very things are exactly what Yahweh is praised for doing as Israel's God (Ex 3:7-8; Dt 10:17-18; Ps 12:5; 68:4-5; 103:6; 146:5-7; Prov 22:22-23; etc.). Given what we will argue below, that this Psalm is all about the Son of God, this would mean that these verses are a direct contrast between these wicked heavenly sons doing the opposite in their rule to what the Son of God, that is the Angel of the LORD, did for Israel.[226]

But sometimes the translation is rendered as "judges" (NAS) instead of "gods." This non-supernatural interpretation fits with the other that we saw above ("his own congregation"). The problem here is that it is the same word, *elohim*. On what basis do we interpret this term so radically different? Furthermore, this "human rulers" interpretation fails to account for how the judgment is that, "You will die like men" (vs. 7). It is a tautology to tell men that they are going to die like men. However, there is a parallel in Revelation. "The devil who had deceived

---

[226] This idea of ruling creating beings is found in other places in the Bible. Besides the many titles for these creatures that tells us about their ruling authority (see above), Satan himself tells Jesus that he has "all the kingdoms of the world" at his disposal (Matt 4:8-9). What kind of a temptation would it be if this were not actually true? Furthermore, why wouldn't Jesus just call his bluff, "Satan, you don't have any kingdoms, so stop it with this nonsense." Along other lines, we have pagans like Plato saying this very thing of the sons of God that were placed over the ancient peoples. After a time, they "became diluted" and "behaved unseemly" and "were full of avarice and unrighteous power" failing to rule the peoples in the "order of government" and "wisdom and virtue" that they once did. See Plato's *Critias* 109.

them was thrown into the lake of fire and sulfur where the beast and the false prophet were, and they will be tormented day and night forever and ever" (Rev 20:10).

It is sometimes assumed that the term *"elohim"* refers to human judges. Of the over 2,600 occurrences of the word in the OT, no one questions that the vast majority of them refer to either God or deities like Baal. Nevertheless, this did not stop the famed Brown-Driver-Briggs Lexicon (1907) from having as is first definition "ruler, judges." The lexicon gives only eight verses to support this claim (Ex 21:6; 22:7-8; 1Sa 2:25; Jdg 5:8; Ps 82:1, 6; 138:1), even though all of them have some kind of supernatural attestation in the manuscripts (God, gods, or angels). In other words, none of them are clearly "humans." Given this, there is good reason (as some scholars have argued) to believe that *elohim* never refers to living humans anywhere in the entire Bible (humans are *not* gods!), which is why newer lexicons such as HALOT and TWOT don't even offer human judges as a possibility.[227] For these reasons, unless a person has a preconceived bias against the possibility of this translation, the most natural interpretation is that of the ESV.[228] This song is talking about a heavenly divine council scene with heavenly beings identified as "sons of the Most High" being judged for their wicked rule on earth.

John 10 and Psalm 82

We need to address one other reason why our interpretation seems controversial to some. This has to do with Jesus' words in John 10:24. We believe that Jesus' words and Psalm 82 have often been misunderstood because of a lack of understanding (or acceptance of) of the Divine Council.

Jesus is having a confrontation with the Pharisees and his identity had come to a head. *"If you are the Christ, tell us plainly"* (John 10:24). He explains that he has, like the Angel of the LORD of old and opposite of the *elohim* of Psalm 82:2-4, been doing works in his Father's name that bear witness about his testimony (John 10:25). So his first argument

---

[227] Cyrus H. Gordon, " 'elohim in Its Reputed Meaning of Rulers, Judges," *Journal of Biblical Literature* 54 (1935): 139–44.
[228] For an extensive treatment of this translation, including why a human interpretation makes no sense see Michael S. Heiser, "You've Seen One Elohim, You've Seen Them All? A Critique of Mormonism's Use of Psalm 82," *FARMS Review* 19/1 (2007): 221-66.

is about his righteous works done for the people of Israel. But they do not believe, because they are not his sheep (26). The Father has given him others who do believe (27-29). Who are these "others"? In the context, these are the poor and suffering, which also connects us at least conceptually to Psalm 82:2-4.

Just then, he makes a startling claim, "I and the Father are one" (30). This is an idea that we have seen throughout our study where both the Angel and the Father are simply: Yahweh. They are One. This time it isn't The Angel, but the God-Man.

The Jews know exactly what he is claiming. He—a man (recall our discussions on the "son of man" and Daniel 7 and Ezekiel 1)—is making himself God (33). Then, in the focus of our attention here, attempting to stone him for making himself God (John 10:31), Jesus says, "Is it not written in your Law, 'I said, you are gods?'" His meaning has often been misunderstood. What is Jesus quoting and what does he mean in quoting it?

First, where does it come from? Many think that this is just a general teaching of the OT, where "law" (*torah*) is taken in the broadest possible sense of the whole OT. Thus, any time you find *elohim* referring to human rulers (an assumption very difficult to prove as we have seen), Jesus is invoking this principle.

Sometimes it is admitted that this does in fact refer directly to Psalm 82:6. The Psalms are sometimes simply called "law" (cf. John 15:25). This verse says, "I said, 'You are gods, sons of the Most High, all of you." Jesus said, "Is it not written in your Law, 'I said, you are gods?'" This extremely rare phrase is only found in one other place (Isa 41:23), and no one says Jesus has that in mind.

Immediately after quoting the Psalm, Jesus says something just as important, but often missed. "If he called them gods to whom the word of God came—and Scripture cannot be broken—do you say of him whom the Father consecrated and sent into the world, 'You are blaspheming,' because I said, 'I am the Son of God?" (John 10:35-36). It is difficult to try and understand Jesus's reasoning here, no matter which view you take. But we would propose it is absurd for Jesus to be saying, "Look fellas, I'm a god, you're a god, we're all gods. That's what your own book teaches. Can't we all just get along?" Some will argue that he isn't claiming that the text is calling Jewish rulers divine, merely that it is saying that they stand "in the place of" God.

But think about it, neither point helps Jesus in the discussion even slightly, at least not according to the way the Pharisees took his meaning. For after he says all this, they want to kill him *for blasphemy*. If he wasn't calling them divine, then why would they get so angry? If he is, by equating himself to them, then how does this help his cause at all? Are we really to think that he is appealing to their own sense of inner-*elohim*? Of course not! No. Something he said here differentiated himself from *them*. What that is is his identification of himself with the title Son of God. Somehow, he is something *other* than they are.

Our view is thus that the "I said" of John 10:34 refers to Elohim-God who has taken his place in the midst of the *elohim*-gods from Psalm 82:1). It is these beings, the gods of vs. 1, whom the speaker of that verse later calls "gods, sons of the Most High" in vs. 6. So, Jesus is not saying that the Scripture is calling the *Pharisees* "gods," but that Elohim who has taken his stand is calling *the heavenly sons of God* "gods."

The "He" who called them gods still refers to the God who stands in the divine council. It is tempting to think that this refers to the Father. We believe that it has to refer to the Son. Here, we need to remember that this is *John's* Gospel. John began his Gospel in the very first verse with the Logos—the Word. The burden of his entire book has been to prove to you that Jesus Christ is this Word.

So, let's return to what we just read. "If he called them gods to whom *the word* of God came..." Some might think that this word refers to something like the Father *speaking* to the *elohim*. We would argue that John's "Word of God" here is not merely speech, but a Person who speaks, a Person who is called the Word. In other words, Psalm 82:1's first Elohim is now being called The Word. This is Johannine Prologue language through and through. "In the beginning was the Word, and the Word was with God, and *the Word was God*" (John 1:1). In other words, Jesus is interpreting Psalm 82:1 as saying that the Word of God came to the sons of God and identified them as gods. The Son is the Elohim-God of vs. 1.

The next part of the John verse is, "... and the Scripture cannot be broken." This strange statement seems quite out of place in the normal interpretation. Usually we think of Scripture being "broken" in terms of prophecy, not statements of fact. What would it mean that the word of God called them gods and the Scripture cannot be broken? Shouldn't it have said something like, "And Scripture does not lie" or "and

Scripture is perfectly trustworthy. Yes, they are gods because the Bible is true?" But if you understand that he is talking about the judgment that was pronounced *against the gods* throughout the Psalm, it makes perfect sense. That judgment is firm. They will die. This prediction cannot be broken. The Logos has taken his place in the council and he has spoken. His council (it is a Triune Council) shall stand! It has been written in The Book. *So let it be written. So let it be done.*

Jesus goes on to make a comparison with the Pharisees. If the Word of God came among the sons of God, and the Father sent me to you, then why do you charge me with blasphemy for saying, "I am the Son of God?" In this comparison, Jesus references Psalm 82 even more. First, he says, "If I am not doing the works of my Father, then do not believe me" (John 10:37). Why would he say this? Because he is referencing the very thing the sons of God were supposed to be doing in the Psalm, but he is saying that he is doing them.

This in turn presupposes that Jesus is one of the heavenly sons of God, for it was *their* task to do these works. In fact, he is Israel's God and he is doing what he has always done as Israel's God—take care of the orphan, destitute, and pitiable. Jesus is telling the Pharisees that in Psalm 82 there was a very special Son of God—the Word—and that this Son has now come among them. This is why he can call himself the Son of God. He is taking a title perfectly fitting a heavenly being. It's an argument from the lesser to the greater. If they were called "sons of God," how much more "him whom the Father consecrated and sent into the world" - i.e. the Logos himself!

At this point they should start asking what works is Jesus doing? Works of injustice or works of mercy and compassion? Is Jesus like one of the unjust "sons of God"? If they understood the works Jesus was doing, they would see "that the Father is in me and I am in the Father." In other words, they would see that Jesus is the "sent" mediator who truly represents God and mediates God's goodness because he is one with the Father, he is Yahweh. He is not "given" the title 'son of God,' it is his birthright as the true, only-begotten Son of God. But there was huge cognitive dissonance going on, not in the claim itself, but in his actually being right about it. So instead of asking these questions, they simply want to kill him.

Psalm 82:8; Psalm 2:8; and Deuteronomy 32:7-9

Psalm 82:8 concludes with a startling claim, and it fits right in with our interpretation that the first Elohim in Psalm 82:1 is the Son of God. In fact, it confirms that Jesus is the Son of God. "Arise, *O God*, judge the earth; for you shall inherit all the nations!" (Ps 82:8). We would argue that someone new is now speaking. The Son (the first Elohim of vs. 1) has been pronouncing judgment in the heavenly court against the fallen sons of God. The judgment is that they will die like men. In their place, God will inherit all the nations.

Who is saying this, and why? It is the Father, the Ancient of Days, who is making this pronouncement upon the Son because of his true and just judgment (among other things). We argue this because there is a very clear parallel to this verse earlier in the Psalms.

Psalm 2 may be the most fundamental of all OT passages that the Disciples tell us explicitly refer to Christ. It has the Father speaking to his *Son*. "As for me, I have set my King on Zion, my holy hill" (Ps 2:7). Then, the Son speaks. "I will tell of the decree: The LORD [that is the Father] said to me, 'You are my Son [Jesus]; today I have begotten you. Ask of me, and I will make *the nations your inheritance*, and the ends of *the earth your possession*." The end of this is the exact same language as Psalm 82:8.

It is also the same language that we saw in Daniel 7 when the son of man inherits a kingdom. Daniel 7:14 says, "And to him was given dominion and glory and a kingdom, that all peoples, nations, and languages should serve him; his dominion is an everlasting dominion, which shall not pass away, and his kingdom one that shall not be destroyed." Who is given these things? "One like a son of man" who comes *riding on the clouds of heaven* (13). We've seen how this refers to a man as Yahweh. The Ancient of Days is the Father who now bestows upon his Son this great blessing.

Notice that in both passages, what he receives are the nations! He receives them as one like a son of man and as the Son of God. This is Jesus Christ coming in the flesh. All this confirms that Jesus is using Psalm 82 to prove to the Pharisees that he is the Son of God even as other parts of the NT use Psalm 2 for the same purpose. Yet, this language is actually telling a very old story, and this story becomes the central reason why we needed to include this chapter. This story centers on the Angel when it first begins to unfold. For as Daniel 7 and Psalm 82 had origins in Psalm 2, so Psalm 2 has origins in Moses.

Let's ask a basic question at this point. Why would Yahweh of Israel need to "inherit" anything? Were the nations not already "his?" At this point, we need to explain another important idea that is often missed in the OT alongside this idea of the divine council. This is the idea of the inheritance (and giving over) of the nations to evil fallen supernatural beings.

The forerunner of Psalm 2 (and therefore also Psalm 82) is found in the monumentally important Deuteronomy 32:7-9. The passage reads,

> Remember the days of old; consider the years of many generations; ask your father, and he will show you, your elders, and they will tell you. When the Most High [Elyon] gave to the nations their inheritance, when he divided mankind, he fixed the borders of the peoples according to the number of the sons of God. But the LORD's portion is his people, Jacob his allotted heritage.

There are several points of contact between Psalm 82 and this passage. First, there is the word Elyon or "Most High" (cf. Dt 32:7 and Ps 82:6). This is a relatively rare epitaph given to God, at least compared to some names. But it is found in both passages alongside of the same phrase, "sons of God" (cf. Dt 32:8 and Ps 82:6). This phrase is a second connection between the passages. A third is the language of a "heritage" or inheritance (cf. Dt 32:9 and Ps 82:8).

"Heritage" (or "inheritance") is the word *nachalah*. This same noun is also found, not coincidently, in Psalm 2:8, "... I will make the nations your *heritage*." The verbal form is found in Psalm 82:8, "... you shall *inherit* all the nations."

Deut 32:9	Psalm 2:8	Psalm 82:8
But the LORD's portion is his people, Jacob his allotted *heritage*."	I will make the nations your *heritage*.	you shall *inherit* all the nations.

To understand the background and the reason for the Son inheriting in the above passages (and thus the story we began this chapter with), we have to understand this passage in Moses.

Moses says, "Remember the days of old." What days does he have in mind? They were a long time ago. He gives them an event that occurred that their sages and elders would still remember, because it was passed down to them from generation to generation. Those days were, "When Elyon gave to the nations their inheritance." "Inheritance" is that same word that we just saw in the two psalms.

This in turn is explained as happening when, "he divided mankind" and "fixed the borders of the peoples." To what does this refer? In using the word "divided" (*parad*), Moses is going back to the tower of Babel story as summarized by Genesis 10:32. "These are the families of the sons of Noah, after their generations, in their nations: and by these were the nations divided [*parad*] in the earth after the flood" (KJV; cf. Acts 17:24, 26-27).

The final piece of this passage is the most controversial. It says that God did this, "according to the number of the sons of God." The controversy surrounds the phrase "sons of God." We've seen it enough now to know what it probably refers to. So, what is the controversy? "Sons of God" has a variant reading: "sons of Israel." If sons of God are heavenly beings, you can see the problem. Sons of Israel clearly are not those.

There are several ways to figure out which was the original phrase.[229] We could survey all the early and relevant manuscripts. While the Masoretic text reads, "sons of Israel," our oldest copies really only go back 1,000 years. Far older are our copies of the Greek translations.[230] While a few of these also have "sons of Israel," the large majority read "angels of God," and several others have "sons of God." The Dead Sea scrolls do not attest to the "sons of Israel" reading.[231]

---

[229] The best treatment of this is Michael Heiser, "Deuteronomy 32:8 and the Sons of God," *BibSac* 158:629 (Jan-Mar 2001): 52-74.

[230] Some may think that the Hebrew manuscripts are purer *de facto*, simply because this was the original language. However, besides presupposing that it is more difficult to make copiest errors in Hebrew than it is to make a translation error in Greek (any introductory story of textual critic will show how naïve that is), this view also presupposes that that Jesus hating Jewish Rabbis who were mainly responsible for preserving the Hebrew text were not tampering with it, a fact that we know is simply not true given the existence of this and other variants which both come from Jews.

[231] We would add to the manuscript evidence the testimony of Plato in the *Critias* (n. 226), who has a passage that is virtually identical with Deuteronomy 32:7-8. Where Moses says, "Remember the days of old ... when the Most High divided

The phrase "number of" is the next important thing to investigate in trying to discern the original. This "number" refers to the number of nations at Babel given in the Table of Nations. It has seventy names.[232] Of course, Israel is not among them. They were not at Babel, so it makes no sense for God to divide the nations according to the seventy nations of Babel according to one nation that wouldn't even exist for hundreds of years.

Furthermore, as Tigay notes, "Verse 9, which states that God's portion was Israel, implies a contrast: Israel was God's share while the other peoples were somebody else's share, but verse 8 fails to note whose share they were."[233] Here, we have a possible translation difficulty that can prevent us from noticing the contrast. Almost all translations read something like the ESV's, "When the Most High gave to the nations their inheritance," implying that the nations are inheriting, not the sons of God. Of course, there is no comparison with the LORD receiving Israel as his portion and the nations receiving divisions of land. There might be with the nations receiving an inheritance of gods, which as we

---

the nations … according to the sons of God," Plato reads, "In the days of old the gods had the whole earth distributed among themselves by allotment," adding, "different gods had their allotments in different places which they set in order. Hephaestus and Athene … both obtained as their common portion this land…" The entire passage is fascinating for its parallels with Deuteronomy 32 and Psalm 82. Here the key parallel is "the gods." This parallels the "sons of God" reading and if it is connected to Moses would antedate even the Dead Sea Scrolls by hundreds of years.

But could Plato, writing in Greece, have had access to the writings or thinking of Moses? Yes, he could have, through his ancestor Solon who travelled to Egypt, and surely could have gone through Israel on his journeys (in fact, he necessarily would have, unless he had taken a boat both ways across the Mediterranean). This idea has been suggested before. Peter Allix remarks, "It is certain, that Plato himself, by conversing with the Jews in Egypt, borrowed of them the best notions he had of God." Peter Allix, *The Judgment of the Ancient Jewish Church Against the Unitarians*, second edition (Oxford: Clarendon Press, 1821), 2. In fact, going all the way back to Justin Martyr we read, "Plato clearly and openly alludes to the law of Moses, but, fearing the hemlock, he did not dare mention him by name whose teaching, he well knew, was hateful to the Greeks."(Justin Martyr, *Exhortation to the Greeks* 25).

[232] Umberto Cassuto, *A Commentary on the Book of Genesis: From Noah to Abraham* (Jerusalem: Magnes Press, 1964), 177–180; Allen P. Ross, "Studies in the Book of Genesis - Part 2: The Table of Nations in Genesis 10 - its Structure," *Bibliotheca Sacra* 137:548 (Oct-Dec 1980): 342.

[233] Jeffrey H. Tigay, *Deuteronomy*, JPS Torah Commentary (Philadelphia Jewish Publication Society, 1996), 302.

will see below, is in fact part of the Deuteronomy worldview. However, the text can also be read, "When the Most High gave the nations as an inheritance," implying that the sons of God are the ones inheriting, thus filling out the parallel with vs. 9.[234]

At any rate, "seventy" is clearly the "number" that is in mind in the passage, as the traditions all inform us.[235] Now, it isn't like Israel doesn't become wrapped up in this number. There is good reason to see this number related to Israel, as Moses brought "seventy" elders up Mt. Sinai (Ex 24:1) and the later Sanhedrin was composed of seventy men (plus the high priest). It is incorrect, however, to see this as related to the number of the sons of Israel that went down into Israel as the variant reading seems to presuppose (cf. Gen 46:27; Ex 1:5), because this, too, is a textual variant. As Stephen (Acts 7:14), the LXX, and the Dead Sea Scrolls all attest, the actual number was seventy-five.[236]

What is happening here in Deuteronomy 32:7-9 is thus quite unknown in today's anti-supernatural materialistic world. Vs. 8 is basically saying that God gave the nations as an allotment to the heavenly sons of God so that they might be ruled over by them.[237] But the LORD's

---

[234] Understanding the "nations" (*goyim*) as the object of the infinitive constructive "to give as an inheritance" so that the non-existent word "their" in the ESV is not added to the translation. See Heiser, "Deuteronomy 32:8 and the Sons of God," 71, n. 79.

[235] This is remembered in Targum Pseudo-Jonathan Deut 32:8; 1 Enoch 89:59; 3 Enoch 17:818:2-330:2; b.Sukk 55b; NumR 14:12; Midraš Tehillim 68:6 [to Ps 68:12]; m.Soṭ 7:5; b.Shab 88b; and importantly the "seventy sons of El" at Ugarit (KTU 1.4:VI.46; CTA 4.6.38-59; 12.2.44-49; etc.) and probably Ex 15:24, where immediately prior to the wilderness temptation (Ex 16:4ff; cf. Satan tempting Jesus in the antitype in Matthew 4) the Israelites go to a place called Elim (elim means "gods") and there are 70 palm trees and 12 springs of water, both of which are clearly symbolic numbers, the larger of which, in being connected to palm trees, has symbolic association to the stuff they made idols with as well as several Hebrew words for "trees" which all have '*el* as their root. Sometimes the number is "72" rather than "70." This is not a significant change, as 72 comes from the LXX's two extra nations in Genesis 10.

[236] We know that the rabbis could not tolerate the new Christian "heresy" as they called it and thus outlawed any kind of "two-powers" thinking. It is not a stretch, therefore, to postulate that this same hatred was behind these otherwise innocuous textual variants, for they strike at the heart of a supernatural Jesus Christ as found in the OT. An interesting discussion is Nathan Hoffman, "Were the Pyramids Built Before the Flood? (Masoretic Text vs. Original Hebrew)," *Youtube* (May 28, 2017): https://www.youtube.com/watch?v=VI1yRTC6kGE.

[237] The Egyptians believed the same thing, "Grant [Merneptah] a lifetime like that of Re (Ra), to avenge those injured by any land; Egypt has been assigned him as

portion, his allotment, is Israel. Two more things need to be said here.

The first is that referring back to Babel makes it abundantly clear that this was punitive. The whole world was to be given over to darkness (Acts 17:27; Rom 1:21ff; Eph 2:1-3, etc.) because they refused to love the Creator. Second, as was hinted at above, this giving-over was a two-way street. In Deuteronomy 4:19-20, for example, we have a virtual parallel, except in that passage, the heavenly beings are given to the nations (two other parallel passages make it clear that it is, in fact, supernatural entities that are in view, see table below).

Deuteronomy 32 Worldview			
32:8-9	4:19-20	17:3	29:26
"When the Most High gave to the nations their inheritance, when he divided mankind, he fixed the borders of the peoples according to the number of the sons of God. ⁹ But the LORD's portion is his people, Jacob his allotted heritage."	"And beware lest you raise your eyes to heaven, and when you see the sun and the moon and the stars, all the host of heaven, you be drawn away and bow down to them and serve them, those that the LORD your God has allotted to all the peoples under the whole heaven. ²⁰ But the LORD has taken you and brought you out of the iron furnace, out of Egypt, to be a people of his own inheritance."	"... and has gone and served other gods and worshiped them, or the sun or the moon or any of the host of heaven, which I have forbidden..."	"... and went and served other gods and worshiped them, gods whom they had not known and whom he had not allotted to them."

portion, He owns it forever to protect its people." (*Poetical Stela of Merneptah* 15). Also, see Plato in the note 231. Also, the Jews outside of the Old Testament taught this. "And he sanctified them and gathered them from all of the sons of man because (there are) many nations and many people, and they all belong to him, but over all of them he caused spirits to rule so that they might lead them astray from following him. But over Israel he did not cause any angel or spirit to rule because he alone is their ruler and he will protect them and he will seek for them at the hand of his angels and at the hand of his spirits and at the hand of all of his authorities so that he might guard them and bless them and they might be his and he might be theirs henceforth and forever" (Jub 15:31-33).

Elyon giving an inheritance of human nations to the "sons of God" combined with Psalm 2, 82, and Daniel 7 becomes the necessary background to identifying the Person in Deut 32:9. It says that "the LORD" receives Israel as an inheritance and portion. The context demands that the LORD here can only be one Person. He can't be the Father, for the Father is Elyon giving things away. Nor does it make sense that it is the Spirit, much less God in his bare Essence. The LORD here *must* refer to the Son of God, who is one of the sons of God—only infinitely greater, because he is himself God. *Sons* receive inheritances. "Yahweh" in Deuteronomy 32:9 must therefore refer to the Angel of the LORD, who is the greatest of all the angels of the divine council because he *is* Yahweh. This may be what the translators of the LXX were getting at when they render the very famous Messianic prophecy of Isaiah 9:6 as the quite unexpected, "Angel of the Great Council,"[238] rather than the normal "Wonderful, Counselor" (literally "wonder of a counselor").[239]

It is impossible to overstate the importance of this point. For here we have Moses telling us that the Son of God inherits Israel as his portion. The sons of God get their nations. The Son of God gets his. Who

---

[238] English LXX translations render it "counsel" rather than "council." This is how it is usually translated into English in the Church Fathers as well (for hundreds of years and on a regular basis the Fathers cite the LXX's version in their defense of Christ's deity, though it wasn't until Origen that the term began to be used as more than a function). But the word *boule* can mean "counsel" (as in advice) or "council" (as in a group meeting). See Joseph W. Trigg, "The Angel of Great Counsel: Christ and the Angelic Hierarchy in Origen's Theology," *Journal of Theological Studies* 42:1 (April 1991): 42 [35-51]; Michael S. Heiser, "The Divine Council in Second Temple Literature" (Ph.D. diss., University of Wisconsin, 2004), 218-20.

[239] This very strange translation from "wonderful, counselor" or "wonderful counselor" to "The Angel of the Great Council," has a couple of possible explanations. First, it could be the original reading a now lost version of the Hebrew text. The idea would be that later Jews corrupted our inherited Hebrew text because it was linking the coming Messiah too directly to a heavenly figure. "Wonderful counselor" seemed a way to lessen this connection. Without question, the rabbis were known to have done this in other (though few in number) key places from time to time. Second, it could be an interpretive decision to help the Greek readers understand what the translator of the LXX felt was the meaning. Certainly, there is a conceptual link between "wonderful," the God who does "wonders" (Ex 15:11) and the name of the Angel which is "wonderful" (Jdg 13:18). There is also a direct link between the words translated as counsel or council.

did he get Israel from? His Father (called "the Most High" or *Elyon*), the same as all the others, though it should also be noted that he takes it for himself, which is his divine prerogative as Yahweh. This is why he is called Israel's Angel and following some scholars and Fathers, it is quite possible that the proper name of this angel is Michael, for Michael "the great prince," is Israel's Angel (Dan 12:1; cf. Dan 10:21).[240]

Before concluding, we want to take a moment to address the question raised by Gerald McDermott, "Doesn't a lot of this seem awfully pagan? Especially talk about a divine council with Yahweh consulting with other supernatural beings?" His answer is well worth heeding,

> Not when you consider the immense differences between pagan and biblical cosmology (view of the cosmos or what we would call ultimate reality). First of all, among Israel's pagan neighbors, the gods were roughly comparable in stature and power so that there were many rivalries and assorted relations (often sexual) among them. But for Israel, Yahweh brooked no rivals. There was only a single council of the ruler and the ruled. There were no other relations among the gods. Furthermore, Yahweh had no consort, no sexual partner, no children conceived by sexual acts. The Old Testament rejected the Canaanite symbolism of El (its god) as a bull and Asherah as his wife. The Bible shifted the paradigm 'from the model of the divine couple in charge of the four-tiered pantheon to a single figure surrounded by minor powers, who are only expressions of that divinity's power.'
>
> Second, while for ancient Near Eastern pagans, monsters and gods challenge the high god for mastery, Yahweh is depicted in the Old Testament as having conquered them all. Some still challenge, but there is no doubt that in future fights Yahweh will win again. The monsters are subservient to Yahweh in Psalm 148:7 ('Praise Yahweh from the earth, you sea monsters and all deeps'), Leviathan is a 'tamed pet' in Job 41 and Psalm 104:26, and in Genesis 1 the cosmic forces are no longer divine—as they were for many of Israel's pagan neighbors.
>
> Finally, the Israelites believed there was only one true God. There were other 'gods,' but none had the power of Yahweh, and they were probably created by Yahweh anyway. What power they have is on loan from Yahweh. In fact, as some Old Testament texts proclaim,

---

[240] See our Appendix on Michael and Melchizedek.

Yahweh alone is the creator of all. He alone is therefore sovereign of all. And he alone is eternal.

So while there are some superficial similarities to pagan religions of the ancient Near East—in that both Israel and her neighbors believe in a cosmos animated by a variety of powers—they still display significant differences. And there are enough differences to sharply distinguish biblical religion from pagan religion.[241]

Inheritance of the Council

We now want to summarize these somewhat disparate parts in a way that will allow you to see clearly where the story at the beginning of the chapter comes from. This story actually becomes one of the major reasons we wanted to write this book. But without the divine council as background, it is very difficult to identify. With it, it shines as bright as the Glory-Angel himself who comes so many times to people in the Scripture, all for a single great overarching purpose which glorifies himself and his people.

- **Psalm 8:6.** What is man that you are mindful of him, and the son of man that you care for him? Yet you have made him a little lower than the heavenly beings and crowned him with glory and honor. You have given him dominion over the works of your hands; you have put all things under his feet.

- **Gen 1:26.** Then God said, "Let us make man in our image, after our likeness. And let them have dominion over the fish of the sea and over the birds of the heavens and over the livestock and over all the earth and over every creeping thing that creeps on the earth."

- **Deut 32:7-9.** Remember the days of old; consider the years of many generations; ask your father, and he will show you, your elders, and they will tell you. When the Most High gave to the nations their inheritance, when he divided mankind, he fixed the borders of the peoples according to the

[241] Gerald R. McDermott, *God's Rivals: Why Has God Allowed Different Religions? Insights from the Bible and the Early Church* (Downers Grove, IL: InterVarsity Press, 2007), 61-62.

number of the sons of God. But the LORD's portion is his people, Jacob his allotted heritage.

- **Deut 4:19-20.** Beware lest you raise your eyes to heaven, and when you see the sun and the moon and the stars, all the host of heaven, you be drawn away and bow down to them and serve them, things that the LORD your God has allotted to all the peoples under the whole heaven. But the LORD has taken you and brought you out of the iron furnace, out of Egypt, to be a people of his own inheritance, as you are this day.

- **Deut 29:6.** [Israel] went and served other gods and worshiped them, gods whom they had not known and whom he had not allotted to them.

- **Ps 2:7-8.** I will tell of the decree: The LORD said to me, "You are my Son; today I have begotten you. Ask of me, and I will make the nations your heritage [or "inheritance"], and the ends of the earth your possession.

- **Ps 82:1, 6-8.** God has taken his place in the divine council; in the midst of the gods he holds judgment ... I said, "You are gods, sons of the Most High, all of you; nevertheless, like men you shall die, and fall like any prince. Arise, O God, judge the earth; for you shall inherit all the nations!"

- **Dan 7:13-14.** I saw in the night visions, and behold, with the clouds of heaven there came one like a son of man, and he came to the Ancient of Days and was presented before him. And to him was given dominion and glory and a kingdom, that all peoples, nations, and languages should serve him; his dominion is an everlasting dominion, which shall not pass away, and his kingdom one that shall not be destroyed.

- **Heb 1:2.** In these last days he has spoken to us by his Son, whom he appointed the heir of all things, through whom also he created the world.

- **Matt 5:5.** Blessed are the meek, for they shall inherit the earth.

- **Rom 8:16-17.** The Spirit himself bears witness with our spirit that we are children [literally: "sons"] of God, and if children, then heirs-- heirs of God and fellow heirs with Christ.

- **Gal 4:7.** So you are no longer a slave, but a son, and if a son, then an heir through God.

We've placed these passages into four different sections. The first tells us about our God-given right to rule this earth as his human sons.

The second remember the fall of man and the giving over of the nations to the heavenly sons of God for their inheritance. These angels or created *elohim* of the divine council are paralleled with the Angel-LORD getting his own inheritance, which was announced to them in the same council. This inheritance is the very special nation of Israel. When the Son-Angel Yahweh took these people, he created them out of nothing, the same way he created everything else out of nothing, including the other sons of God. This is the whole point of the calling of Abram out of Ur of the Chaldees. He would become the father of the nation of Israel.

The third bring us to the prophecies of the Son of God inheriting all the earth. The context of these explain why. Two explain this was due to the wickedness of others. The last one explains it is because he will become a human who will rule in righteousness.

The fourth show how, through Jesus Christ, dominion is now being regained for those who are now called, not coincidently, sons of God.

Without this divine council worldview, this major storyline of the Bible, including the reason why Christians are called "sons of God" is completely lost on us. Passages such as "judging angels" are inexplicable. But most importantly, the glories that belong to Jesus Christ the God-man, glories which were announced, predicted, and came to pass are not understood as they ought to be. Without it, our Angel of the LORD theology suffers greatly and hence, our appreciation for exactly what Jesus Christ did for us in human flesh is significantly impoverished.

12

THE ANGEL AS "SHEPHERD"

The Angel in Psalm 23

A Mere Metaphor?

LIFE HAS CHANGED DRASTICALLY IN THE WESTERN WORLD during the past couple of centuries. For example, whereas at the founding of the United States, the vast majority of people owned land and were farmers, today it is the reverse. Many own no land and very few make their living off it. Our agrarian culture of green pastures has become a civilization of city lights and cold cement. This has taken us at least in some ways out of touch with metaphors the Bible uses to describe God.

One such metaphor is "shepherd." Jesus famously told the people, "I am the Good Shepherd" (John 10:11, 14). This is picked up later by his disciples. Peter calls Jesus "the Shepherd and Overseer of your souls" (1Pe 2:25) and "the Chief Shepherd" (5:4). Hebrews calls him "the Great Shepherd of the sheep" (Heb 13:20). But why did Jesus use this language of himself? Was he simply trying to capture a metaphor that the people of those days could relate to? Our guess is that this may be the default view of many Christians.

In fact, the language is taken from prophecies regarding the Messiah. The most explicit is probably Zechariah 13:7. "'Awake, O sword, against my shepherd, against the man who stands next to me,' declares the LORD of hosts. 'Strike the shepherd, and the sheep will be scattered; I will turn my hand against the little ones.'" We've already seen ("Angel as Man of War" chapter) that Jesus is "the man who stands next to me." Now we note that this man is called a "shepherd." This is confirmed by the NT, which directly quotes the last part of the verse. "Then Jesus said to them, 'You will all fall away because of me this night. For it is written, 'I will strike the shepherd, and the sheep of the flock will be scattered'" (Matt 26:31; Mark 14:27). Jesus directly applied this prophecy to himself.

There are other prophecies that speak of him as Shepherd. "But you, O Bethlehem Ephrathah, who are too little to be among the clans of Judah, from you shall come forth for me one who is to be ruler in Israel, whose coming forth is from of old, from ancient days ... he shall stand and shepherd his flock in the strength of the LORD, in the majesty of the name of the LORD his God. And they shall dwell secure, for now he shall be great to the ends of the earth" (Mic 5:2, 4). The first part of this passage is also quoted by the NT (Matt 2:6; cf. John 7:2) as referring to Jesus. Since it is the same person in view throughout, Jesus is thus predicted to be the shepherd here.

Notice how this shepherd stands "in the majesty of the Name of the LORD his God." We've discussed the Name in previous chapters and seen how it is a term that also hypostatically identifies the Son of God. We've seen the same with "arm." Thus, it comes as little surprise to see Isaiah predicting, "Behold, the Lord GOD comes with might, and his arm rules for him; behold, his reward is with him, and his recompense before him. He will tend his flock like a shepherd ..." (Isa 40:10-11). This passage is again cited in the NT as referring to Jesus (Rev 22:12). So we have established that the title of "Shepherd" comes from prophecies in the OT.

Shepherds, Kings, and Gods

But could there be more to it than the prophets simply taking a metaphor and applying it to the Messiah? Ezekiel predicts, "And I will set up over them one shepherd, my servant David, and he shall feed them: he shall feed them and be their shepherd" (Ezek 34:23). Again, this is a Messianic prophecy. Ezekiel is not predicting the reincarnation of David, but a future leader who comes from his line: "The Son of David" (Matt 9:27, etc.).

Now, kings of the ancient world were often called "shepherds." It's a rather ironic title, because shepherd is a lowly profession, filled with long hot days, dangers from animals and cliffs and thickets, mockery from townsfolk, and lots and lots of tedium. Why give such a glorious office as king a title like "shepherd?" The answer is that it gets at the difficult task they were assigned: to look over their people, who are often innocent but dumb as sheep.

But what do I mean "assigned"? Many ancient cultures taught in one form or another that kingship was given by the gods. For example, the ancient myth of Etana, a Sumerian antediluvian King of Kish says, "Scepter, crown, tiara, and (shepherd's) crook lay deposited before Anu in heaven | There being no counseling for its people. (Then) kingship descended from heaven." This is exactly what the Bible teaches when we learn that God himself chose Saul to be king, effectively, in his place. That is, Israel had rejected Yahweh as their king, therefore he chooses Saul and later David. They did not take this position of their own accord. God chose them. Kingship came from him, from heaven.

Notice how in the myth, king Etana is called a "shepherd." This is as we find it in the Bible too. God said to David, "You shall be shepherd of my people Israel, and you shall be prince over Israel" (2Sa 5:2). Curiously, Joshua (Greek: "Jesus!") is the first Israelite leader called a "shepherd" (Num 27:17-18). He, too, is chosen by the LORD. When kings like Jehoshaphat did not lead well, Israel was said to be "as sheep that have no shepherd" (1Kg 22:17).

Now let's put this idea of kingship coming down from heaven together with this notion that kings are called shepherds. Throughout the ancient world, the gods (or better, the sons of God) are called shepherds too. Baal (KTU 1.12.II), Adonis (Virgil, *Eclogues*), Osiris depicted often with his shepherd's crook staff, Tammuz (Babylon), and others are all called shepherds of the sheep.

Where this gets really curious is in the book of 1 Enoch. 1 Enoch 89:59 describes "seventy shepherds" of the nations. We've seen this number previously with the divine council of sons of God who rule the nations. Who are they here? Charles writes, "The 'seventy shepherds' raise the most vexed question in Enoch." Yet, while they may in a more immediate way represent humans, on another level, the level of paralleling heaven and earth, "They are certainly angels [which correspond to the seventy sons of God from Babel]."[242] We agree. With the Jews, seventy was always used in one way or another with this divine council theology in mind.

Christ is My Shepherd

Let's now take this over to our discussion of the Angel in the OT. We have seen that he is the Son of God who inherits the nations. Returning to a familiar text, there is a reason why Jacob says, "The God before whom my fathers Abraham and Isaac walked, the God who has been *my shepherd* all my life long to this day, *the angel* who has redeemed me from all evil, bless the boys" (Gen 48:15-16). This idea fits perfectly with the entire ancient world's conception of the sons of God as shepherds. Israel's God-Son is the Angel of Yahweh.

The Psalm says, "Give ear, O Shepherd of Israel, you who lead Joseph like a flock. You who are enthroned upon the cherubim, shine forth" (Ps 80:1). Who is it who comes to the Most Holy Place? Whose seat is the Mercy Seat? Yahweh, the Son of God (Lev 16:2).

And of course, in that most famous of all OT verses, David sings, "The LORD is my Shepherd" (Ps 23:1). What is he singing? Some barebones "divine essence"? He is singing about his Lord (Adonai), the Lord who stands between him and the Father Yahweh, yet as his own Lord, as Jesus taught the Pharisees (Matt 22:44-45). This is why Jesus takes the title of Shepherd upon himself. Every use of the term as it refers to God in prophecy or in history in the OT speaks of him.

Just as the Pharaohs knew Aman-Ra as their shepherd and Assurbanipal knew Shamash as his shepherd (*"Light of the great gods, resplendent illuminator of the universe, Lofty judge, shepherd of the celestial and earthly regions"*),[243] so also David knew the Son of God as his

---

[242] Robert Henry Charles, ed., *Commentary on the Pseudepigrapha of the Old Testament*, vol. 2 (Oxford: Clarendon Press, 1913), 255. For discussions see John J. Collins, *The Apocalyptic Imagination: An Introduction to Jewish Apocalyptic Literature* (Eerdmans, 2016), 87-89; and Margaret Barker, *The Revelation of Jesus Christ* (Edinburgh: T&T Clark, 2000), 226-29.

[243] *COS* 1.143:474. In T. Longman III, "Psalms 2: Ancient Near Eastern Background," ed. Peter Enns, *Dictionary of the Old Testament: Wisdom, Poetry &*

Shepherd. Except his Shepherd is not just a shepherd but The Shepherd, the Shepherd who would soon humble himself in the womb of a virgin, born at Bethlehem Ephrathah, come to shepherd his flock in the strength of the LORD, in the majesty of the name of the LORD his God, where the sheep shall dwell secure, and he shall be great to the ends of the earth. May none of us ever view "Shepherd" language in the OT apart from this worldview again.

In calling the LORD his Shepherd, he is effectively saying that the Angel of the LORD is his Shepherd; Christ is his Shepherd. All this in the Old Testament.

Christ in the Old Testament

This takes us to the end of our Old Testament study of the Angel of the LORD. While we will delve in the next few chapters into the NT, we would like to finish with a thought that we began this book with in our Prefaces. That is, simply, with these different perspectives that we have gained up to this point, it becomes overwhelmingly clear: The OT saints knew exactly who the Son of God was, they worshipped him, and he was at the very core of their religion. There is no OT Judaism without this.

To our shame, we have forgotten this. We hope to uncover more of that history a couple of chapters from now. In the meantime, it is our prayer that you might begin to have the veil lifted off of your eyes, just as the Apostle said when speaking of the Old Testament—"When they read the old covenant, that same veil remains unlifted, because only through Christ is it taken away" (2Co 3:13). Perhaps for the first time in your life, you are now able to see that the Israelites of old trusted not merely in the promises of the coming Christ, not merely in types of Christ, but they literally believed and trusted in him personally. May the Lord grant you such a vision as they had ... a vision that is satisfied in the God-man who is also the Angel of the LORD.

Writings (Downers Grove, IL; Nottingham, England: IVP Academic; Inter-Varsity Press, 2008), 601.

13

WHERE DID THE ANGEL GO?

The Angel in the New Testament
Part I: John's Gospel

Claims: Jesus and The Angel

THROUGHOUT THE OLD TESTAMENT, WE HAVE SEEN that the Angel of the Lord is God Himself, yet is also sent from God, someone who appears in visible form, who is the Word, the Name, the Presence, the Glory of God. He is Yahweh's Man of War, the Intercessor between people and God, who sits at the head of the heavenly council, yet who is promised to come one day to complete the covenant, to refine and purify his people, and to inherit the nations.

Yet what about the New Testament? Does it ever make any of these connections? Clearly, in several places, it identifies Jesus as present in the Old Testament. Speaking of Isaiah's vision of God in Isaiah 6, the Gospel of John says that Isaiah saw Jesus (John 12:42). Jude says that Jesus was the one who brought Israel out of Egypt (Jude 5). Paul says that Christ was the one who gave Israel water from the rock in the wilderness (1 Cor 10:4).

But does the New Testament really identify Jesus as "the Angel of the Lord"? In fact, the term is rarely used for Jesus,[244] probably for good

---

[244] There are several possible exceptions. One may be Galatians 4:14, "[You] received me as an angel of God, as Christ Jesus." Also, Revelation 10:1-7 and 20:1, where some scholars think the Seventh Angel is a description of Jesus. See our discussion of Revelation 10 below.

reason. The connotations of the term "angel" changed over biblical history. The term began to take on a more ontological meaning. In other words, it came to signify more about the *kind* of being than about a *function* the being was carrying out (i.e., a messenger). In some areas, angelic speculation and even angelic worship had become heterodox practices, followed by certain cults.[245] These tendencies would later develop into some of the Gnostic heresies and mystery cults. For these reasons, in order to avoid confusion, the New Testament seems to have avoided the term "angel" for Jesus. In fact, the opening chapter of the book of Hebrews specifically aims to argue from some of the Divine Angel passages in the Old Testament to prove that Jesus was more than simply an ontologically-created "angel."[246] But while the term "Angel" is used sparingly for Jesus, *every other name and title connected with the Divine Angel in the Old Testament is claimed for Jesus.* Jesus is the Word, the Glory, the Face-Presence, the Name, the Mediator, the Divine Warrior, the Son of Man.

Over the next three chapters, we will only be able to explore a small sampling of these connections. First, we will look at some of the claims Jesus himself made, connecting himself to the Old Testament. Then, in the next chapter, we will look at the connections between the Angel of the Lord and Jesus' Transfiguration before his disciples, as well as his heavenly appearance to John in Revelation. Finally, we will look at three passages that give us a hint of Jesus' relationship with other angels.

What the High Priest Knew About "The Son of Man"

Consider first the question that the high priest asks Jesus at his trial. Apparently, the Jewish leaders seem to have known what Jesus had

---

[245] The role of Gnostic "angel" speculation and its relation to the development of the NT is discussed in many works. For instance, Loren T. Stuckenbruck, *Angel Veneration and Christology: A Study in Early Judaism and in the Christology of the Apocalypse of John*, Wissenschaftliche Untersuchungen zum Neuen Testament 2/70 (Tübingen: J. C. B. Mohr, 1995); Margaret Barker, *The Great Angel: A Study of Israel's Second God* (Louisville, KY: Westminster / John Knox Publishers, 1992); Darrel D. Hannah, *Michael and Christ: Michael Traditions and Angel Christology in Early Christianity*. Wissenschaftliche Untersuchungen zum Neuen Testament 109 (Tübingen: Mohr-Siebeck, 1999).

[246] Of course, such an argument would only have been needed if Jesus' preincarnate status was something of a debate (see below).

been claiming about himself. At Jesus' trial before the Sanhedrin, many false witnesses were brought to accuse him. Finally, the high priest asked him outright, "Are you the Christ, the Son of the Blessed?" Jesus answered, "I am, and you will see the Son of Man seated at the right hand of Power, and coming with the clouds of heaven." The high priest then "tore his garments and said, 'What further witnesses do we need? You have heard his blasphemy'" (Mark 14:61-62).

What did the high priest mean by "Are you the Christ, the Son of the Blessed?" And when Jesus answered by reference to the "cloud rider" and "Son of Man" from Daniel 7, why did the high priest see that as blasphemy?[247]

We have seen hints that there was a pre-Christian Jewish conception of Two Powers in heaven (we will discuss this more thoroughly in Chapter 16). There were two different strands of Messianic speculation. One saw the Messiah as a coming Davidic, *human* king. Consider Jesus' question to the Pharisees in Matthew 22:42, "What do you think about the Christ? Whose son is he?" This was a provocative question because it was a matter for debate among the Jews. In this case, the Pharisees answered for the *human* side, "The son of David." Another strand saw the Messiah as an angelic, supernatural figure, connected with "Lesser Yahweh."[248] When the high priest asked Jesus outright, "Are you the Christ, the Son of the Blessed?," his question referenced this second divine Messianic theory.[249] Where else would he have gotten the idea that the "Christ" was also the "Son of the Blessed"? He was asking whether Jesus was claiming

---

[247] Daniel's "Son of Man" was clearly a different figure than the "Ancient of Days." So how was this blasphemy?

[248] This was a title the Jews themselves used. For example, Segal writes about the speculation of Enoch and the angel Metatron in 3 Enoch. "Metatron is set on a throne alongside God and appointed above angels and powers to function as God's vizir and plenipotentiary ... This is clearly dependent on the ancient "son of man" traditions which appear in Ethiopian Enoch 70 and 71, but they have been expanded in Jewish mysticism so that Enoch and Metatron are now alter egos, which neither the titles "son of man" nor "son of God" appear at all. Instead the principle angel is given the title 'YHWH HQTWN' (YHWH the lesser)." Segal, 65. Any passage with two Yahwehs such as Genesis 19:24 would have been fodder for this Greater and Lesser Yahweh discussion amongst the Jews.

[249] See the discussion in Ernst Wilhelm Hengstenberg, "The Deity of the Messiah in the Old Testament," in *Christology of the Old Testament and a Commentary on the Predictions of the Messiah by the Prophets* vol. 1, trans. Reuel Keith (Andover: William M. Morrison, 1836), 161-187.

to be this supernatural Son of God from the Old Testament. And when Jesus answered with one of the clear Two Powers texts, even saying, "I Am," and then using "Son of Man," "right hand," and "Power," the high priest knew exactly where Jesus' answer came from. He accuses Jesus of blasphemy—not because Jesus was claiming to be a human Messiah, but because Jesus was claiming to be the divine Second Power from the Old Testament—an idea with which they were familiar. They did not believe that someone who was clearly a human being, unimpressive flesh and blood,[250] could also be the Divine Son. The point is that they were familiar with the concept because of *the Old Testament*, and the high priest had heard by reputation, through Jesus' teachings and language, that Jesus used such passages and titles for himself.

The Divine Messiah of John's Prologue

Perhaps no book makes these connections more explicit than the Gospel of John. In fact, as we have already seen repeatedly, John's Gospel is a veritable apologetic for Jesus as the Old Testament Divine Angel.[251] A full exploration would take a whole book in its own right. There are just too many passages in John's Gospel connecting the Divine Angel with Jesus to be fully explored. However, several major themes must be discussed.

John begins his book with the famous claim, "In the beginning was the Word, and the Word was with God, and the Word was God" (John 1:1). The background to John's title, as we have seen, was not Greek philosophy, but Biblical and Jewish theology. In the Jewish Targums, the

---

[250] Consider Isaiah 53:2, "He had no form or majesty that we should look at him, and no beauty that we should desire him." Isaiah predicted they wouldn't recognize the Divine Servant because he would not appear in his Divine Form.

[251] One of the best books we have seen on the *Logos* of John is John Ronning, *The Jewish Targums and John's Logos Theology* (Grand Rapids, MI: BakerAcademic, 2010). Ronning does not deal directly with the "Angel of the Lord," and he does not seem to be exposed to Segal's work on Jewish Two Powers theology. But he traces the Gospel's use of texts and terms correctly to the Jewish Targums and makes some of the same connections we have made with the Word, the Glory, the Son of Man, the Man of War, the Name, etc. Another helpful work is Daniel Boyarin, "The Gospel of the Memra: Jewish Binitarianism and the Prologue to John," *Harvard Theological Review* 94:3 (2001): 243-84.

word *memra* (Aramaic for "word") was already used as "a divine title de-noting the name of God,"[252] even being used as a separate hypostasis and distinct Divine Person.[253] But the justifications for such a use are not found in the Targums, but in the Bible itself. The Old Testament already used "the Word" as a title for the mediating Divine Angel.

In vs. 9-10, John writes, "The true light, which gives light to every-one, was coming into the world. He was in the world, and the world was made through him, yet the world did not know him." Why does John say he was "*coming* into the world" and then also that he was "*in the world*"? John seems to be saying that he was *going to be coming* in a new way, but also that he was *already active* in the world, even in the Old Testament. Indeed, he was the Angel of God, who had come to his people, even in the Old Testament, and yet "his own people did not receive him" (11).

John Ronning has pointed out the parallels between vs. 11-13 and passages in the Targums concerning "the Word."[254]

Biblical Text	Targums
Psalm 106:25, "They did not listen to the voice of the Lord."	TgPs 106:25, "They did not receive the Word of the Lord."
Numbers 14:22, "None of the men who have seen my glory and my signs that I did…and have not obeyed my voice."	TgOnq and TgPsJon Num.14:22, "The men who have seen my glory and my signs which I have done…and have not received my Word."
Numbers 14:11, "How long will they not believe in me, in spite of all the signs that I have done among them?"	TgNeof Num 14:11, "How long will they not believe in the name of my Word, in spite of all the signs of my mir-acles which I have performed among them?" (cf. John 12:37)

---

[252] Ronning, 9.
[253] See Boyarin, 254.
[254] Ronning, p.28-32.

Deuteronomy 9:23, "You rebelled against the commandment of the Lord your God and did not believe him or obey his voice."	TgNeof Dt 9:23, "You rebelled against the decree of the Word of the Lord your God, and you did not believe in the holy name of the Word of the Lord, and you did not listen to the voice of his Word."
Exodus 19:5-6, "If you will indeed obey my voice and keep my covenant, you shall be my treasured possession among all peoples, for all the earth is mine; and you shall be to me a kingdom of priests and a holy nation.'"	TgOnq and TgPsJon Ex 19:5-6, "If you will diligently receive my Word…you shall be before me…a holy people."
Jeremiah 7:23, "Obey my voice, and I will be your God, and you shall be my people."	TgJer Jer 7:23, "Receive my Word, and I will be your God and you shall be a people before me."

So in the Old Testament, the Word had been seen as active among the people of God. He was "in the world" (John 1:10). He had been repeatedly rejected by the people of God, but "all who did receive him, who believed in his name, he gave the right to become children of God" (1:12). In vs. 9-13, John is speaking of the Word working and the Word being rejected, not in the New Testament era, but in the Old Testament era. He was already there, in the Old Testament, working as the mediating Word—the Divine Angel.

But *now*, John is saying, that mediating Word is "coming into the world" (1:9) in a whole new way—because now, "the Word became flesh and dwelt among us, and we have seen his glory, glory as of the only Son from the Father, full of grace and truth" (1:14). What was new was not the manifestation of the Word in creation; he had been there all along. What was new was he had now become "flesh." The 'ish became 'adam. The Son of God became Son of Man. He entered wholly into the physical world of dust. This is utterly new and completely astonishing; whether you're a Greek philosopher or a Jewish sage, it doesn't matter.

What is more—for the first time, "the glory of God" could be truly "seen"! The desire of Moses (Ex 33:18) finally came to fruition. The full revelation of God's glory and character became knowable through the incarnation and work of the God-man.

This is why John goes on, "For the law was given through Moses; grace and truth came through Jesus Christ. No one has ever seen God; the only God, who is at the Father's side, he has made him known" (John 1:17-18). Even Moses did not see God in his invisible, unapproachable light. Nobody in the Old Testament saw God in his essence. Frankly, no one ever has; it simply isn't possible. But all along, it was the Word who was God who had been making God known, and was now making God known fully and completely, though clothed in human flesh.

The Son Who Ascended and Descended

Later in John, while speaking to Nicodemus, Jesus makes a remarkable statement, "No one has ascended into heaven except he who descended from heaven, the Son of Man" (John 3:13). Commentators have struggled over Jesus' meaning, since it comes *before* his historical resurrection and ascension. When, to that point, had he "ascended into heaven"? If one only considers the period after his incarnate birth, it never happened until much later. But, if it is read as a claim to pre-incarnate deity, a claim John has already made in chapter one, then it makes perfect sense. Who else has made a habit of ascending and descending from heaven (Gen 17:22, 35:13; Jdg 13:20, *et al*)? Who else but the Angel of the Lord, who has now descended as the promised "Son of Man"?

Proverbs 30:4 powerfully asks, "Who has ascended to heaven and come down? Who has gathered the wind in his fists? Who has wrapped up the waters in a garment? Who has established all the ends of the earth? What is his name, and *what is his son's name?* Surely you know!"[255] Jesus is the divine Son of God, who has now descended in a whole new way and is being "given" to the world (John 3:16).

---

[255] Consider also Acts 2:34-35, "For David did not ascend into the heavens, but he himself says, 'The Lord said to my Lord, Sit at my right hand, until I make your enemies your footstool.'" Or Ephesians 4:9-10, "In saying, 'He ascended,' what does it mean but that he had also descended into the lower regions, the earth? He who descended is the one who also ascended far above all the heavens, that he might fill all things."

The Testimony to Jesus

In John 5, Jesus chides the Jewish leaders for not receiving the testimony about him.

> But the testimony that I have is greater than that of John. For the works that the Father has given me to accomplish, the very works that I am doing, bear witness about me that the Father has sent me. And the Father who sent me has himself borne witness about me. His voice you have never heard, his form you have never seen, and you do not have his word abiding in you, for you do not believe the one whom he has sent. You search the Scriptures because you think that in them you have eternal life; and it is they that bear witness about me, yet you refuse to come to me that you may have life. I do not receive glory from people. But I know that you do not have the love of God within you. I have come in my Father's name, and you do not receive me. If another comes in his own name, you will receive him. How can you believe, when you receive glory from one another and do not seek the glory that comes from the only God? Do not think that I will accuse you to the Father. There is one who accuses you: Moses, on whom you have set your hope. For if you believed Moses, you would believe me; for he wrote of me. But if you do not believe his writings, how will you believe my words?
> (John 5:36-47)

We have already seen the Jewish connection between God's miracles and his Word. Targum Neofiti of Numbers 14:11 says, "How long will they not believe in *the name of my Word*, in spite of *all the signs of my miracles* which I have performed among them?" John himself says in John 12:37, "Though he had done so many signs before them, they still did not believe in him." When Jesus says, "The works that the Father has given me to accomplish, the very works that I am doing, bear witness about me that the Father has sent me" (5:36), he is referencing the divine wonders that he is performing. They should make very clear that he is the Word sent from the Father to whom they must listen. This language of "sending" echoes the "sent" Angel of the LORD from the OT (see Ex 23:20; Gen 24:7, 40, 42; Num 20:16).

But Jesus goes on to say, "The Father who sent me has himself borne witness about me" (5:37). Where is this witness? Jesus refers them to the Old Testament. Using language from Exodus, Jesus says, "His voice you have never heard, his form you have never seen, and you do not have his word abiding in you, for you do not believe the one whom he has sent. You search the Scriptures because you think that in them you have eternal life; and it is they that bear witness about me, yet you refuse to come to me that you may have life" (5:37-40). Jesus argues that, if they had understood the Scriptures, they would have known that the Scriptures bear witness about him and would have come to him to have life.[256] Because they don't believe Jesus, they've never heard God's voice, they've never seen God's form, and they do not have his abiding word. Ronning writes,

> If we take "never" to mean that Jesus is speaking to the Jews collec-
> tively throughout history, the meaning would be that Israel never
> heard the Father's voice—not even from Mt. Sinai. The point could
> be that they heard the voice of the Son from Sinai … The context of
> this passage confirms that Jesus is saying not that he is just another
> in the line of those sent by God, but that he is the one who spoke to
> Israel from Mt. Sinai.[257]

In other words, Jesus is the "voice," is the "form," is the "word" from the Old Testament. He is the one who has always been "sent" from the Father. The "form" of the Lord, the "voice" of the Lord, the "word" of the Lord was always through the one "sent," who bore the name (see Exodus 23:21). Jesus says, "I have come in my Father's name" (John 5:43). He says that he is "the glory that comes from the only God" (5:44). These are references to the Divine Angel who revealed God. If they do not hear him, they have never heard from the Father either.[258]

This is confirmed when Jesus says, "If you believed Moses, you would believe me; for he wrote of me" (5:46). Was Jesus saying that Moses *predicted* him or was Jesus saying *more*? In fact, Moses didn't just predict Jesus; Moses wrote about his actual interactions with Jesus in

---

[256] See also Isaiah 55:3, "Come to me, listen, so that your soul may live." Tg. Isa. 55:3 says, "Receive my Word, listen, so that your soul may live."
[257] Ronning, 59-60.
[258] 1 John 2:23, "No one who denies the Son has the Father. Whoever confesses the Son has the Father also."

the first place.[259] Ronning writes:

> There is very little written in the law of Moses about a man who was to come in the future that would justify the statement, "it was about me that he wrote." Moses wrote about the Lord, full of grace and truth (Ex 34:6), which is how John describes Jesus (John 1:14). Moses wrote about the Lord who revealed the meaning of his name to him, and through him, to Israel (Ex 3:14; 34:5-7), as did Jesus to the disciples, and through them, to believers today (John 17:6, 26). Moses wrote about the Lord who came down from heaven (Ex 3:8; 34:5), as John did about Jesus (John 6:38)…"[260]

In other words, if the Jews really followed and believed Moses, how much more should they follow the one Moses spoke to and wrote about? Exodus 14:31 says, "They believed in the LORD and in his servant Moses." Targum Neofiti of Exodus 14:31 says, "They believed in *the name of the Word of the LORD* and in the prophecy of his servant Moses." *Mekilta* Exodus14:31 says, "If they believed Moses, how much more did they believe the LORD."[261]

According to Jesus, the testimony to his identity is found in the Old Testament, as the one sent from the LORD, who works divine wonders, who bears the divine name, who is the divine glory, who spoke to Moses, who has always revealed the LORD, and who is the only way to know the LORD. Could John be clearer?

The "I Ams" of John

Biblical interpreters have often drawn attention to the "I Am" (*Ego Eimi*) sayings of Jesus in John's Gospel. This Greek translation of the divine name is made more powerful by its use in the Septuagint.[262]

- LXX of Deuteronomy 32:39, "See, see that *I am* (*Ego Eimi*), and there is no god except me."

---

[259] See Acts 7:38, "This is the one who was in the congregation in the wilderness *with the angel* who spoke to him at Mount Sinai, and with our fathers."
[260] Ronning, 160.
[261] Cited in Ronning, 160.
[262] See Ronning, chs. 3, 8, and 9.

- LXX of Isaiah 43:10, "'Be witnesses to me, and I am a witness,' says the Lord God... 'in order that you may know and believe and understand that *I am* (*Ego Emi*); before me there is no other God, and there will be no one with me.'"

- LXX of Isaiah 52:6, "Because of this, my people will know my name in that day, that *I myself am* the one who speaks (*Ego Eimi autos o lalōn*)."

Isaiah 52:6 is especially relevant given Jesus' words to the Samaritan woman in John 4:25-26, "The woman said to him, 'I know that Messiah is coming (he who is called Christ). When he comes, he will tell us all things.' Jesus said to her, 'I who speak to you am he.'" Literally, he says, "I am, the one speaking to you" (*Ego Eimi autos o lalōn soi*). Jesus' words are a deliberate echo of the Septuagint of Isaiah 52:6.

There are, in fact, twenty-three "I Am" statements of Jesus in John's Gospel (John 4:26; 6:20, 35, 41, 48, 51; 8:12, 18, 24, 28, 58; 10:7, 9, 11, 14; 11:25; 13:19; 14:6; 15:1, 5; 18:5, 6, 8). Six of these are noteworthy as stand-alone, absolute statements.

1) John 6:20, "But he said to them, '*I am* (*Ego Eimi*); do not be afraid."

This statement occurs as Jesus comes walking to his disciples on a stormy sea. Likely, John is making a deliberate connection to Isaiah 43:1-3, which begins, "Fear not, for I have redeemed you ... When you pass through the waters, I will be with you ... For I am the LORD your God, the Holy One of Israel, your Savior." Just a few verses later, Isaiah 43:10 records, "You are my witnesses ... and my servant whom I have chosen, that you may know and believe me and understand that I am he. Before me no god was formed, nor shall there be any after me." The LXX records, "... in order that you may know and believe and understand that I am (*Ego Eimi*)." [263]

2) John 8:23-25, "'You are from below; I am from above. You are of this world; I am not of this world. I told you that you would die in

---

[263] The disciples' reaction and their arrival at their destination is probably also a deliberate connection to Psalm 107:30, "Then they were glad that the waters were quiet, and he brought them to their desired haven."

your sins, for unless you believe that *I am* (*Ego Eimi*) you will die in your sins.' So they said to him, 'Who are you?' Jesus said to them, 'Just what I have been telling you from the beginning.'"

The whole of John 8 is concerned particularly with the identity and origin of Jesus. The crowds echo Moses from Exodus 3 when they ask, "Who are you?" They wonder whether Jesus is really claiming what they think they are hearing. Jesus' words, this time, parallel Isaiah 43:10, "that you may know and believe and understand that I am (*Ego Eimi*)." Interestingly, the Targum of Isaiah 43:10, says, "I am he who was from the beginning," thus echoing Jesus' answer to the crowds in John 8:25, "Just what I have been telling you from the beginning."

3) John 8:28, "When you have lifted up the Son of Man, then you will know that *I am* (*Ego Eimi*), and that I do nothing on my own authority, but speak just as the Father taught me."

The phrase, "you will know that I am," is one of the most common pronouncements of God in the Old Testament, usually followed by "the LORD" or some statement of identity.

4) John 8:58, "Jesus said to them, 'Truly, truly, I say to you, before Abraham was, I am (*Ego Eimi*).'"

By 8:58, the crowds are left in no doubt that Jesus means exactly what they are hearing.[264] He preexisted Abraham as Yahweh himself.

5) John 13:19, "I am telling you this now, before it takes place, that when it does take place you may believe that *I am* (*Ego Eimi*)."

Like Isaiah 43:10, here, Jesus is giving a prediction to his disciples, so that, when it comes true, they will know truly that he is the Lord.

---

[264] Ronning goes on to point out that the Targums of Isaiah 43:12, 48:15, Ex 12:42, as well as the Genesis passages, mention the Divine Word appearing to Abraham with covenant promises, explaining how "Abraham rejoiced that he would see my day" (John 8:54) - see Ronning, 210-211.

6) John 18:5-8, "Jesus said to them, '*I am (Ego Eimi)*' … When Jesus said to them, '*I am (Ego Eimi)*,' they drew back and fell to the ground. So he asked them again, 'Whom do you seek?' And they said, 'Jesus of Nazareth.' Jesus answered, 'I told you that *I am (Ego Eimi)*. So, if you seek me, let these men go.'"

Jesus' prediction of his betrayal comes true in John 18:5-8, as he is confronted by the soldiers who ask for his identity. When he answers, "I am," they draw back and fall to the ground. Many have noted the connection with Psalm 9:3, "When my enemies turn back, they stumble and perish before your presence." Once again, Jesus speaks the divine name, and though the soldiers do not understand, they are still affected because Jesus is the divine "presence."

With each of these statements in John, Jesus is clearly claiming to bear the divine name, and even to have borne it "from the beginning" (John 8:25). He is the one "sent" from the Father, whether in the Old Testament or in the New Testament. He has now come to bear the divine name and carry out the divine will "*in the flesh*." For those familiar with the Divine Angel and Two Powers theology, Jesus' language is crystal clear.

14

ANGEL-GLORY AND A MOUNTAIN

The Angel in the New Testament
Part II: The Transfiguration

Appearances: More than Meets the Eye

T HE THEME SONG FROM THE CHILDREN'S CARTOON "Transformers" includes the suggestive phrase, "More than meets the eye." Things that appeared as everyday objects were actually hiding something else entirely. Children ever since have wished for their dad's sedan to turn into a giant, friendly robot. Even more, his sports car or truck!

Similarly, when Jesus walked on the earth, he looked like just a man ("He had no form or majesty that we should look at him" - Isaiah 53:2), but his disciples quickly got the sense that there was more to Jesus than "meets the eye." Like Moses before them, they wanted to see more of Jesus' "glory." On at least two occasions, some of the disciples did: On the Mount of Transfiguration and then later, when the Apostle John is given a glimpse of the ascended Christ in Revelation.

Interestingly, both the Transfiguration and Jesus' glorified appearance in Revelation reveal several important connections to the Divine Angel of the Old Testament.

Jesus' Transfiguration

The Transfiguration is recorded in each of the Synoptic Gospels (Matthew 17:1-8, Mark 9:2-8, Luke 9:28-36). Matthew's Gospel is especially helpful in making the Old Testament connections. In Matthew 16, Peter confesses Jesus' identity as the "Son of God," but the disciples still don't understand what that means (Matt 16:16, 23). Immediately after Peter's confession, Jesus begins to teach that he is the "Son of Man" who is "going to come with his angels in the glory of his Father," and that some would "not taste death until they see the Son of Man coming in his kingdom" (16:27-28). He begins to make connections for them with the Old Testament "Son of Man" commanding the angels of heaven and receiving a kingdom.[265] As we have seen, the disciples would have been familiar with these "Son of Man" references from the Old Testament—as references to the "Prince of heaven" who commanded the host of the LORD. Matthew then records,

> And after six days Jesus took with him Peter and James, and John his brother, and led them up a high mountain by themselves. And he was transfigured before them, and his face shone like the sun, and his clothes became white as light. And behold, there appeared to them Moses and Elijah, talking with him. And Peter said to Jesus, "Lord, it is good that we are here. If you wish, I will make three tents here, one for you and one for Moses and one for Elijah." He was still speaking when, behold, a bright cloud overshadowed them, and a voice from the cloud said, "This is my beloved Son, with whom I am well pleased; listen to him." When the disciples heard this, they fell on their faces and were terrified. But Jesus came and touched them, saying, "Rise, and have no fear." And when they lifted up their eyes, they saw no one but Jesus only.
>
> (Matthew 17:1-8)

The story has obvious parallels with the mountain encounters with God's glory in the Old Testament—of "seeing" God on the mountain. Exodus 24 records,

> Then Moses and Aaron, Nadab, and Abihu, and seventy of the elders of Israel *went up*, and *they saw the God of Israel*. There was under his feet as it were a pavement of sapphire stone, like the very

---

[265] See especially Chs. 6 and 11.

> heaven for clearness. And he did not lay his hand on the chief men of the people of Israel; they beheld God, and ate and drank ... Then Moses went up on the *mountain*, and the *cloud covered the mountain*.
>
> (Exodus 24:9-11, 15)

The parallels are obvious, but what really was happening here with Jesus? What does it mean that *he* was "transfigured" with his face shining "like the sun" and his clothes "white as light"? Commentators all agree that something of his divine glory was being revealed, that the veil of the flesh was being lifted to show his true glory. But what does that *really* mean? Was the veil of the flesh being removed to show merely an *anthropomorphism* of God? Was the *physical reality* of the flesh giving way to a *semblance* of the essence? It can't be his glorified human body, because he hadn't earned that yet; he had to be raised from the dead to receive this body. In fact, what the Apostles saw was what Moses and the elders of Israel and others in the Old Testament saw of the divine glory. They all saw the Angel of the Lord—the Son of God in a supernatural form, with a supernatural body.[266]

In fact, Jesus' description is very similar to the descriptions of other angels in the Bible.

- Judges 13:6. "His appearance was like the appearance of the angel of God, very awesome."

- Matthew 28:2-3. "Behold, there was a great earthquake, for an angel of the Lord descended from heaven and came and rolled back the stone and sat on it. His appearance was like lightning, and his clothing white as snow."

- Luke 24:2. "While they were perplexed about this, behold, two men stood by them in dazzling apparel."

- Luke 2:9. "And an angel of the Lord appeared to them, and the glory of the Lord shone around them, and they were filled with great fear."

---

[266] As Paul reminds us, "There are heavenly bodies and earthly bodies, but the glory of the heavenly is of one kind, and the glory of the earthly is of another" (1Co 15:40). It is speculative to try and insist what the body of the person they saw was like or dislike in terms of things like facial features, the Angel of the OT. We simply don't know what either the Angel or Christ looked like and the Scripture is silent on this question.

In other words, the Apostles were being shown Jesus in a typical super-natural form, similar to the way he manifests in the heavenly realm, as other supernatural beings from the heavenly realm appear from the per-spective of those on earth.

And yet the Gospels are careful to make clear that Jesus was not just an angel. Nor was he just on par with Moses and Elijah. Matthew records, "[Peter] was still speaking when, behold, a bright cloud overshadowed them, and a voice from the cloud said, 'This is my beloved Son, with whom I am well pleased; listen to him'" (Matt 17:5). The bright cloud and the voice were another demonstration of Jesus' identity.

- Exodus 13:21. "And the Lord went before them by day in a pillar of cloud to lead them along the way, and by night in a pillar of fire to give them light, that they might travel by day and by night."

- Exodus 14:19. "Then the angel of God who was going before the host of Israel moved and went behind them, and the pillar of cloud moved from before them and stood behind them."

- Exodus 16:10. "And as soon as Aaron spoke to the whole congregation of the people of Israel, they looked toward the wilderness, and behold, the glory of the Lord appeared in the cloud."

- Exodus 19:9. "And the Lord said to Moses, 'Behold, I am coming to you in a thick cloud, that the people may hear when I speak with you, and may also believe you forever.'"

- Numbers 12:5-8. "And the Lord came down in a pillar of cloud and stood at the entrance of the tent and called Aaron and Miriam, and they both came forward. And he said, 'Hear my words: If there is a prophet among you, I the Lord make myself known to him in a vision; I speak with him in a dream. Not so with my servant Moses. He is faithful in all my house. With him I speak mouth to mouth, clearly, and not in riddles, and he be-holds the form of the Lord.'"

- Exodus 23:20-21. "Behold, I send an angel before you to guard you on the way and to bring you to the place that I have prepared. *Pay careful attention to him and obey his voice*; do not rebel against him, for he will not pardon your transgression, for my name is in him."

In other words, the pairing of the "bright cloud" (a manifestation of the Spirit), the voice of the Father, and the transfigured Son deliberately identify Jesus as the Divine Angel of the Old Testament, the one who had spoken to Moses and Elijah before, coming to them in cloud and glory as the divine mediator who also bore the divine name. Moses and Elijah appear as the representatives of the Law and Prophets, serving as witnesses to Jesus' identity. The words from heaven confirmed the interpretation, not only echoing Exodus 23:21, but also likely Isaiah 42:1, "Behold, my servant, whom I uphold, my chosen, in whom my soul delights."

Even Matt 17:7—when "Jesus came and touched them, saying, 'Rise, and have no fear'"—is an echo of the Old Testament.

- Judges 6:22-23. "And Gideon said, 'Alas, O Lord God! For now I have seen the angel of the Lord face to face.' But the Lord said to him, 'Peace be to you. Do not fear; you shall not die.'"[267]

- Daniel 10:10, 12. "And behold, a hand touched me and set me trembling on my hands and knees ... Then he said to me, .Fear not, Daniel.'"

- (See also Gen 15:1; 21:17; Luke 1:13, 30, etc.)

The Angelic Son of Revelation and Daniel

The disciples' vision of Jesus' transfigured glory has important parallels in the Old Testament book of Daniel and the New Testament book of Revelation. In chapters 8-12 of Daniel, the prophet has an encounter with several angels. In 8:16, he hears "a man's voice between the banks of the Ulai, and it called, 'Gabriel, make this man understand the vision.'" The "voice" he hears apparently was the Lord himself sending the angel Gabriel to speak to Daniel. Daniel is then visited by "one having the appearance of a man," the angel Gabriel.

In ch. 10, Daniel has a vision of a second figure—apparently the one who had spoken previously (in 8:16) "between the banks"...

> On the twenty-fourth day of the first month, as I was standing on the bank of the great river (that is, the Tigris). I lifted up my eyes and

---

[267] See also 1 Kings 19:5.

looked, and behold, a man clothed in linen, with a belt of fine gold from Uphaz around his waist. His body was like beryl, his face like the appearance of lightning, his eyes like flaming torches, his arms and legs like the gleam of burnished bronze, and the sound of his words like the sound of a multitude. And I, Daniel, alone saw the vision, for the men who were with me did not see the vision, but a great trembling fell upon them, and they fled to hide themselves. So I was left alone and saw this great vision, and no strength was left in me. My radiant appearance was fearfully changed, and I retained no strength. Then I heard the sound of his words, and as I heard the sound of his words, I fell on my face in deep sleep with my face to the ground.

(Daniel 10:4-9)

This is a different figure than the angel Gabriel. It is very much like the supernatural vision John sees of Jesus in Revelation 1.[268]

Then I turned to see the voice that was speaking to me, and on turning I saw seven golden lampstands, and in the midst of the lampstands one like a son of man, clothed with a long robe and with a golden sash around his chest. The hairs of his head were white, like white wool, like snow. His eyes were like a flame of fire, his feet were like burnished bronze, refined in a furnace, and his voice was like the roar of many waters. In his right hand he held seven stars, from his mouth came a sharp two-edged sword, and his face was like the sun shining in full strength. When I saw him, I fell at his feet as though dead. But he laid his right hand on me, saying, "Fear not, I am the first and the last, and the living one. I died, and behold I am alive forevermore, and I have the keys of Death and Hades."

(Revelation 1:12-18)

Because of the parallels between Daniel 10 and Revelation 1, many identify Daniel's description as a vision of the Son of God in his divine angelic form, as the Angel of the Lord. When Daniel describes his "radiant appearance [as] fearfully changed" (Dan 10:8), he seems to be echoing the encounters of Moses with the Divine Angel (Exodus 34:29-30).

Others, however, disagree because, in Dan 10:13, the person speaking to Daniel says, "The prince of the kingdom of Persia withstood me

---

[268] See also Rev 14:2, 19:11-16; Ezek 43:2.

twenty-one days, but Michael, one of the chief princes, came to help me, for I was left there with the kings of Persia." For obvious reasons, commentators have doubted that the Son of God would need help from other angels or could be resisted by other supernatural beings.

But there are two possible ways to resolve this complication. First, it is possible that there is a condescension on the part of the Divine Son to interact in his creation according to the rules of his creation, and that, when he interacts in the created heavenly plane, he interacts according to the rules of the created heavenly plane. So it is a presupposition to assume that the Son could not be engaged in spiritual warfare, be delayed, and need help.

However, there is a second possibility. It is possible that the figure who touches Daniel in vs. 10, 16, 18, and who speaks to him, is different from the figure in the vision of vs. 4-7. Remember that in 8:16, the man over the stream had sent Gabriel to speak to Daniel. Gabriel is described as "one having the appearance of a man" (8:15). In 8:18, it is Gabriel who, when Daniel "fell into a deep sleep with his face to the ground … touched" him and made him stand. So likewise, in 10:10, when the hand touches him and raises him up and speaks to him, later described as "one in the likeness of the children of man…one having the appearance of a man" (10:16, 18),[269] it is possible that, after Daniel's incredible vision of the man over the stream, this is again Gabriel coming to more directly interpret to Daniel.[270]

The Man Above the Waters	The Angel Gabriel (?)
And I heard a man's voice between the banks of the Ulai, and it called, "Gabriel, make this man understand the vision." (Dan 8:16)	So he came near where I stood. And when he came, I was frightened and fell on my face. But he said to me, "Understand, O son of man, that the vision is for the time of the end." And when he had spoken to

---

[269] "One in the likeness of the children of man (כִּדְמוּת בְּנֵי אָדָם, *kidmut beney adam*)" (vs. 16) and "one having the appearance of a man" (כְּמַרְאֵה אָדָם, *kemar'e adam*)" (vs. 18) is a different construction than the "Son of Man (כְּבַר אֱנָשׁ, *kebar enash*)" from Daniel 7:13, and should not necessarily be connected.

[270] If the angel in 10:10ff is different from the majestic vision, this leaves open the possibility of identifying Jesus with the Archangel Michael of 10:13, 21 and Revelation 12:7, as some scholars do.

	me, I fell into a deep sleep with my face to the ground. But he touched me and made me stand up. (Dan 8:17-18)
As I was standing on the bank of the great river ... I lifted up my eyes and looked, and behold, a man clothed in linen. (Dan 10:4-5)	And behold, a hand touched me and set me trembling on my hands and knees. (Dan 10:10)

Another problem, however, poses itself for interpreting Daniel's vision as the Divine Son. Later on we are told.

> Then I, Daniel, looked, and behold, two others stood, one on this bank of the stream and one on that bank of the stream. And someone said to the man clothed in linen, who was above the waters of the stream, "How long shall it be till the end of these wonders?" And I heard the man clothed in linen, who was above the waters of the stream; he raised his right hand and his left hand toward heaven and swore by him who lives forever that it would be for a time, times, and half a time, and that when the shattering of the power of the holy people comes to an end all these things would be finished. I heard, but I did not understand. Then I said, "O my lord, what shall be the outcome of these things?" He said, "Go your way, Daniel, for the words are shut up and sealed until the time of the end."
>
> (Dan 12:5-9)

Daniel now describes three men: two on the banks, *as well as* the "man clothed in linen, who was above the waters of the stream" (the man from 10:5). But the man clothed in linen "raised his right hand and his left hand toward heaven and swore by him who lives forever." The figure is described as distinct from the eternal God in heaven. Is the connection between Jesus in Revelation 1 and the man clothed in linen from Daniel 10 and 12 then wrong? Not necessarily. In the economy of redemption, can the Divine Persons act independently of one another without contradicting their unity? We know they can in the New Testament. And now we are seeing the same in the Old Testament.

This is confirmed by another connection to the book of Revelation. In Revelation 10:1-7, John has a vision of a mighty angel coming down from heaven that directly echoes Daniel 12.

> Then I saw another mighty angel coming down from heaven, wrapped in a cloud, with a rainbow over his head, and his face was like the sun, and his legs like pillars of fire. He had a little scroll open in his hand. And he set his right foot on the sea, and his left foot on the land, and called out with a loud voice, like a lion roaring. When he called out, the seven thunders sounded. And when the seven thunders had sounded, I was about to write, but I heard a voice from heaven saying, "Seal up what the seven thunders have said, and do not write it down." *And the angel whom I saw standing on the sea and on the land raised his right hand to heaven and swore by him who lives forever and ever,* who created heaven and what is in it, the earth and what is in it, and the sea and what is in it, that there would be no more delay, but that in the days of the trumpet call to be sounded by the seventh angel, the mystery of God would be fulfilled, just as he announced to his servants the prophets.
>
> (Revelation 10:1-7)

Some commentators are adamant that this angel is not Jesus. Leon Morris writes, "The swearing of an oath 'by him who lives forever and ever' (vs. 6) does not look like an action of Christ."[271] Joel Beeke, however, disagrees, "Some commentators question whether the angel is really Christ. They say, 'God cannot swear by God.' But that is precisely what God does. When God established His covenant with Abraham, He did so by swearing by Himself" (Heb 6:16-18).[272] Similarly, in Deuteronomy 32:40 (a passage mentioned for its *Ego Eimi* connections above), God himself says, "For I lift up my hand to heaven and swear, As I live forever..." So in Daniel 12 and Revelation 10, the Divine Son uses the same action in speaking to the Father. Beeke explains, "When the pre-incarnate Christ appears in human form in the Old Testament, he is often called the angel of the Lord ... So it is legitimate to identify the mighty angel of Revelation 10:1 as Jesus Christ. This identification is confirmed by how John describes the appearance of this mighty angel."[273]

Beeke is strong on identifying this Angel as Jesus, but he does not make the connection to Daniel 12. His "right foot on the sea, and his left

---

[271] Leon Morris, *Revelation*. Tyndale New Testament Commentaries (Grand Rapids, MI: Intervarsity Press and Eerdmans, 1987), 134.

[272] Joel R. Beeke, *Revelation* (Grand Rapids, MI: Reformation Heritage Books, 2016), 298.

[273] Ibid, p. 291-292.

foot on the land" (Rev 10:2) is not exactly the same as being "above the waters of the stream" (Dan 12:6), but the posture is similar enough. When he "raised his right hand to heaven and swore by him who lives forever and ever" (Rev 10:5-6), the vision obviously echoes Dan 12:7. When the Angel says, "Seal up what the seven thunders have said, and do not write it down" (Rev 10:4), he echoes Daniel 12:9, "The words are shut up and sealed until the time of the end." Later in the Revelation passage, when the Angel tells John to "eat" the scroll (Rev 10:8-10), it echoes the Angel of the Lord's appearance and command to Ezekiel in Ezekiel 3:1-3.

If this is all correct, that the description of Jesus in Revelation 1 is a deliberate reference to Daniel 10, that Daniel 10 and 12 (and Ezekiel 1-3) are the same figure as Revelation 10, *then this clearly confirms the New Testament identification of Jesus with the Angel of the Lord*. After discussing the connections between these passages, Greg Beale agrees, "The figure in 10:1 is probably equivalent to 'the angel of Yahweh' in the OT, who is referred to as Yahweh himself ... Since the Son of Man figure in Revelation 1 is clearly Jesus, he is also to be identified with the angel of the Lord figure in 10:1."[274]

On this basis, we are then allowed to make some connection between these descriptions as descriptions of the Divine Son in an angelic, supernatural, heavenly form. We are told then that the Person of the Son has a form in the heavenly realms—a form that was manifested prior to the incarnation. This has implications for our theology, for our identification of the Persons of the Trinity interacting separately in the Old Testament economy of redemption, and for our understanding of Jesus' appearances in both the Old Testament and New.

Conclusion

Jesus' appearance at the Transfiguration in Revelation 1 and Revelation 10 are not merely an appearance of his post-resurrection body. They

---

[274] Beale goes on to note the "Son of Man" connections between Revelation 1:13, 14:14, and the "angel" of 10:1, confirming the identification of the angel with Jesus appearing in an angelic interaction. The rest of Beale's discussion of Revelation 10 is also very helpful... G. K. Beale, *Revelation*, NIGTC (Grand Rapids, MI: Eerdmans, 1999), 523.

are very similar to his pre-incarnate supernatural form. To be sure, the New Testament is clear that Jesus has a resurrected *human* body that is glorified. But this resurrected body is able to transcend the physical realm. Paul describes it as "imperishable...raised in glory...raised a spiritual body... As is the man of heaven, so also are those who are of heaven. Just as we have borne the image of the man of dust, we shall also bear the image of the man of heaven" (1Co 15:42-49). Jesus' resurrection body was a heavenly body! Its glorified human attributes are parallel to his pre-incarnate, heavenly, angelic attributes. Though for a little while he was made "lower than the angels" (Psalm 8:5, Heb 2:6-8), he has been restored to the heavenly glory he had before (John 17:5, 24). When he was on the earth, there was still "more to him than meets the eye"!

In other words, the Person of the Son of God was known, was active, and was manifest in the Old Testament—in his Personhood!—as a supernatural figure known to angels in the heavenly realm and appearing to men. In the incarnation, he was made "for a little while lower than the angels"; he became flesh; he took the form of a servant; he was born in the likeness of men (Php 2:7). But now he has returned to the glory that he had before with the Father in the heavenly realms—in fact, an even greater glory, because of his incarnation, death, and resurrection, uniting all things in heaven and earth (Eph 1:10). This view, specifically that the Son appeared and was active in the Old Testament in his Personhood, is the New Testament view.[275] They were not the actions and appearances of a monad God. They were not actions and appearances of the One Essence of God. The New Testament teaches that the Divine Son of the Godhead worked personally in both Testaments.

---

[275] It should be stated and understood that, when we say that the Person of the Son acted in his Personhood in the OT, that does not exclude the real union and participation of the Father and the Spirit, but it highlights the Son's prominent role as the "sent" mediator. Interestingly, the work of the Spirit is also often connected to the OT Angel and united with the work of the Son - see Isa 63:9-10; Neh 9:19-20; Hag 2:5. See also in the NT, where the Spirit is connected with the angel and called the Spirit of the Son - Acts 8:26, 29; 16:7; Rom 8:9; 1Pe 1:11.

PROBLEM PASSAGES

The Angel in the New Testament
Part III: Three Examples

A Jewish Tradition

T HERE ARE THREE MORE NEW TESTAMENT PASSAGES that need to be explored that are sometimes thought to raise questions about the Jesus-Angel thesis, as well as the relationship between Jesus and other angels. Acts 7:52-53, Galatians 3:19, and Hebrews 2:2-3 each mention a prominent Jewish tradition that the Sinai covenant had been instituted by God with the help of angels.

- Acts 7:52-53. "Which of the prophets did your fathers not persecute? And they killed those who announced beforehand the coming of the Righteous One, whom you have now betrayed and murdered, you who received the law as delivered by *angels* and did not keep it."

- Galatians 3:19. "Why then the law? It was added because of transgressions, until the offspring should come to whom the promise had been made, and it was put in place through *angels* by an intermediary."

- Hebrews 2:2-3. "For since the message declared by *angels* proved to be reliable, and every transgression or disobedience received a just retribution, how shall we escape if we neglect such a great salvation?"

This tradition has posed problems for interpreters who don't see much evidence of the idea in the Old Testament.[276] But some have seen these verses as references to "angel of the Lord" appearances, and have used them to support the idea that the Old Testament "angel" passages referred to God speaking through or inhabiting a lesser angelic messenger, and thus denying that the angel of the Lord was God (or Jesus) himself.[277] They see these NT passages as supporting the idea that God merely used different "angels" as intermediaries and spokesmen. But as we will see, the details of these passages actually support the opposite conclusion.

Stephen's Historical Vision of Jesus

In Acts 6:8-15, the martyr Stephen is hauled before the Jerusalem council for purportedly "speaking blasphemous words against Moses and God" (6:11) and for saying "Jesus of Nazareth will destroy [the Temple] and will change the customs of Moses" (6:14). In defense, Stephen gives a speech tracing the story of God's covenant *appearances* in the Old Testament and showing the historical rebellion of the people. He argues that God's presence was not limited to the Temple (7:2) or even the Promised Land (7:47-50), that God's presence required only the revealed Law and faithfulness to his appointed messengers. His speech touches on numerous deep areas of Old Testament theology, theophany, and typology, pointing forward to the Messiah. It was a very subtle, very Jewish apologetic. At the end of the speech, he declares a vision he has of Jesus (7:56-57). We can't explore all the elements of his speech, but we do need to focus on his discussion of theophanies.

He begins by saying, "The God of glory appeared to our father Abraham when he was in Mesopotamia" (7:2). Much of his speech

---

[276] The tradition was common among rabbis. See, for instance, *Josephus, Jubilees* 1:27, 2.:1, 49-50. The only apparent Scriptural support for multiple angels accompanying the Sinai revelation can be found in Dt 33:2 or Ps 68:17-18 (see below).
[277] See John Peter Lange et al., *A Commentary on the Holy Scriptures: Acts* (Bellingham, WA: Logos Bible Software, 2008), 122-126. Also Augustine, *On the Trinity*. For an evaluation of Augustine's perspective, see Bogdan Bucur, "Theophanies and Vision of God in Augustine's *De Trinitate*: An Eastern Orthodox Perspective." *St. Vladimir's Theological Quarterly* 52:1 (2008): 67-93.

focuses on God's "appearances." In vs. 30, he says,

> Now when forty years had passed, an angel appeared to [Moses] in the wilderness of Mount Sinai, in a flame of fire in a bush.

Whereas in vs. 2, he says that "the God of glory appeared," here he says "an angel appeared." But he immediately notes, "as he drew near to look, there came the voice of the Lord" (7:32). Stephen is using the standard interpretation that the angel speaking is God speaking. He mentions the angel two (and possibly three) more times:

- Acts 7:35. "This Moses, whom they rejected, saying, 'Who made you a ruler and a judge?'—this man God sent as both ruler and redeemer by the hand of the angel who appeared to him in the bush."

- Acts 7:38. "This is the one who was in the congregation in the wilderness with the angel who spoke to him at Mount Sinai, and with our fathers."

- Acts 7:44. "Our fathers had the tent of witness in the wilderness, just as he who spoke to Moses directed him to make it, according to the pattern that he had seen."

In each of these cases, Stephen proleptically (and without much explanation) mentions the Angel of the Lord appearing to Moses and yet speaking as God. In 7:35, he introduces a distinction between God and the Angel (notice also that he mentions the "hand of the angel" - see below). In 7:38 (and apparently 7:44) he mentions this Angel speaking to Moses at Mount Sinai, even though the Sinai episodes do not explicitly mention the Angel. Yet, this agrees with the overall Angel theology of the Exodus, as Moses says in Numbers 20:16, "When we cried to the LORD, he heard our voice and sent an angel and brought us out of Egypt."

Why does Stephen emphasize the OT story these ways? Why does he bring up the angel and what does it add to his defense? We have to remember that Stephen is interacting in a Jewish context with a lot of theological tradition behind these questions. He's being charged with attacking the Temple and Moses. He's emphasizing "the God of glory" appearing as an angel to key figures in the OT, regarding whom Moses "trembled and did not dare look at" (Acts 7:32). He emphasizes the people's rejection of Moses despite the favor God showed him. Towards the end, he emphasizes how God is not limited to a building made with hands, though the people tried to limit him there (7:48-51).

Many commentators think that Stephen is subtly asking who this angel is and implying that it was Jesus all along who was the "appearance" and "voice" of "the God of glory." After all, this is the view that is taught in the rest of the NT: "Now I want to remind you, although you once fully knew it, that Jesus, who saved a people out of the land of Egypt, afterward destroyed those who did not believe" (Jude 5); "Our fathers were all under the cloud, and all passed through the sea, and all were baptized into Moses in the cloud and in the sea, and all ate the same spiritual food, and all drank the same spiritual drink. For they drank from the spiritual Rock that followed them, and the Rock was Christ" (1Co 10:1-4).[278] Consider the following commentators from church history...

> When Moses was looking after the sheep of his maternal uncle in the land of Arabia, our Christ in the shape of fire from a bush talked with him, and said, "Loose thy sandals and come near and listen." He, loosing them and approaching, heard that he must go down to Egypt and lead out from there the people of Israel; and he received mighty strength from Christ, who spoke to him in the form of fire.
>
> (Justin Martyr, *Apology* 1.62)

> [Stephen] calls the Son of God an angel as one who is also a man ... not only does he show here that the angel who appeared to Moses was the Angel of Great Counsel, but he also shows how great was the compassion God manifests through his appearance... There is no Temple as yet, so the place is holy by the appearance and activity of Christ. This is much more wonderful than the place in the holy of holies.
>
> (Chrysostom, *Commentary on Acts 7:30-33*)

> It is first demanded who this angel was? and, secondly, why he appeared in such a form? For after that Luke had called him an angel, he brings him in immediately speaking thus: *I am the God of Abraham, &c.* Some answer, As God doth sometimes attribute and impart unto his ministers those things which are most proper to himself, so

---

[278] Cf. John 12:43, speaking of Jesus, "Isaiah said these things because he saw his glory and spoke of him."

it is no absurd or inconvenient thing, if they have his name given them; but seeing this angel affirms manifestly that he is the eternal God, who alone is, and in whom all things have their being, we must needs restrain this title unto the essence of God; for it can by no means agree to the angels. It might be said more fitly, that because the angel speaks in the name of the Lord, he taketh upon him his person, as if he declared his commandments word for word, as out of the mouth of God, which manner of speaking is usual in the prophets; but when Luke shall say afterwards, that this was the same angel through whose assistance and guiding Moses delivered the people: and Paul, in the 10th chapter of the First to the Corinthians (1 Cor. 10:4), doth affirm that Christ was that guide, there is no cause why we should now wonder that the angel taketh to himself that which is proper to God alone.

Therefore, let us, first of all, set down this for a surety, that there was never since the beginning any communication between God and men, save only by Christ; for we have nothing to do with God, unless the Mediator be present to purchase his favor for us. Therefore, this place doth plentifully prove the divinity of Christ, and teaches that he is of the same essence with the Father. Furthermore, he is called an angel, not only because he had the angels always to bear him company, and to be, as it were, his apparitors: but because that deliverance of the people did shadow the redemption of us all, for whose sake Christ was to be sent of his Father, that he might take upon him the shape of a servant together with our flesh. It is certain, indeed, that God did never appear unto men as he is, but under some shape agreeable to their capacity; notwithstanding, there is another reason why Christ is called by this name, because he being appointed by the eternal counsel of God to be unto men the minister of salvation, doth appear unto Moses to this end.

(John Calvin, *Commentary on Acts 7:30*)

It is quite possible...that the author of the speech, like the author of [Hebrews], envisages Christ as present with the people of Israel in the critical moments of their history under the old dispensation."

(R. P. C. Hanson)[279]

---

[279] R. P. C. Hanson, *Allegory & Event: A Study of the Sources and Significance of Origen's Interpretation of Scripture* (Louisville: Westminster John Knox Press, 2002), 94.

That *he was with the angel that spoke to him in the mount Sinai, and with our fathers* ... of this God speaks (Ex 23:20), *I send an angel before thee*, and Ex 33:2. And see Num 20:16. He was in the church with the angel, without whom he could have done no service to the church; but Christ is himself that angel which was with the church in the wilderness, and therefore has an authority above Moses."

(Matthew Henry, *Commentary on Acts 7:30*)

An angel; not a created, but the uncreated Angel; the Angel of the new covenant, as may be seen ver. 32, and by Moses putting off his shoes because the place was holy, Exod. 3:2, 5; he is also in the 4th verse of that chapter called the Lord."

(Matthew Poole, *Annotations on Acts 7:30*)

I admire the expression *Stephen* uses, when he calls the Lord, *the* God *of glory*. And I would humbly ask, whether *Stephen* did not mean the same glorious Person as appeared to *Moses* in the bush, and which he takes notice of in his discourse, (verse 30.) ... Now that angel which spoke to *Moses* in the mount, expressly called himself Jehovah. See Exod. 3:6. And Christ is both the covenant himself, and the angel or messenger of the covenant. Isaiah 42:6. Mal. 3:1.

(Robert Hawker, *Poor Man's NT: Acts*)[280]

Stephen is not openly identifying Christ with the angel of the bush, or with 'he who spoke' in vs.44, but he is hinting at it... According to Stephen's argument here God was to have no permanent dwelling place until the coming of the Word. One could take this further and express it thus: God always dwelt in the Word, and Moses saw and heard the Word on Mount Sinai and therefore realized that God would never dwell in a house made with hands.

(A. T. Hanson, *Jesus Christ in the Old Testament*)[281]

In other words, Stephen is emphasizing that God's presence is mediated through his Angel, not the Temple. He is emphasizing that the patriarchs and Moses followed the directions of that Angel who speaks as God himself. Therefore, Moses himself is a servant of that Angel. Calvin agrees, "To this end tends that which Stephen says, that this charge

---

[280] Robert Hawker, *Poor Man's New Testament Commentary: Acts–Ephesians*, vol. 2. (Bellingham, WA: Logos Bible Software, 2013), 56.

[281] A. T. Hanson, *Jesus Christ In the Old Testament* (London: SPCK 1965), 89.

was committed to Moses in the hand of the angel. For by this means Moses is made subject to Christ, that under his conduct and direction he may obey God. For *hand* is taken in this place not for ministry, but for principality."[282]

What then do we do with the mention of multiple "angels" in Acts 7:53 - "You who received the law as delivered by angels and did not keep it"? A. T. Hanson says we should make a distinction between these angels (pl.) and the angel Stephen mentions earlier - "Stephen speaks about an angel on Sinai, whom we have good reason to believe he identified with Christ, and later about the services of angels on the same occasion. We must keep the angel of the bush, 'he who spoke', 'the voice of the Lord', distinct in our minds from the angels of vs. 53, for, as we shall find, they are very far from being identical."[283]

Hanson and others are quick to cite the Jewish interpretive tradition on Deuteronomy 33:2-5, showing the hosts of heaven present with the Lord on Sinai:

> The LORD came from Sinai
>   and dawned from Seir upon us;
>   he shone forth from Mount Paran;
> he came from the ten thousands of holy ones,
>   with flaming fire at his right hand.
> Yes, he loved his people,
>   all his holy ones were in his hand;
> so they followed in your steps,
>   receiving direction from you,
> when Moses commanded us a law,
>   as a possession for the assembly of Jacob.
> Thus the Lord became king in Jeshurun,
>   when the heads of the people were gathered,
>   all the tribes of Israel together.

The LXX makes the connection even clearer:

> The Lord came from Sinai
>   and displayed *himself* to us from Seir

---

[282] Calvin, J., & Beveridge, H. (2010). *Commentary upon the Acts of the Apostles*, vol. 1. (Bellingham, WA: Logos Bible Software), 283-84.
[283] Hanson, 94.

and made haste from Mount Paran together with myriads of Kadesh,
>   from his right, angels with him.
And he spared his people,
>   and all those who have been sanctified beneath your hands,
>   even these *who* are beneath you,
>   and it received of his words
a law, which Moses commanded you,
>   an inheritance of the congregations of Jacob.
And he shall be a ruler with the beloved one;
>   rulers of people have been gathered
>   with the tribes of Israel.

Remember that Stephen has been describing "the God of glory" appearing on Sinai as "an Angel." Deuteronomy 33:2 describes God appearing on Sinai with multitudes of angels. It would not be surprising, when the Lord appears, for the heavenly host to appear with him.[284] The question is: Who did Stephen see as "the Lord" who came from Sinai? Stephen has already cited him appearing as an "Angel" (sing.). But now he acknowledges that he also appeared with the other angels - the host of heaven. Hanson writes,

> He would see a clear distinction between the pre-existent Christ and the angels. The latter are under Christ, he is superior to them... Indeed, the words as they stand in the LXX may even have suggested to him that Moses only rules in Christ ... Thus, we have a clear distinction in Stephen's mind between the angel whom he identifies with the pre-existent Christ, and who was the author of the Law, and the angels who accompanied the theophany.[285]

(We see the same principle at work in Hebrews 1:6, which cites Deuteronomy 32:43 as a reference to Christ and the angels - see below).

---

[284] In fact, this was expected. Hengstenberg cites a passage in the Jewish Zohar that reads, "When the divine majesty dwells [appears] with regard to man, there is also present at the same time an innumerable holy army of others." Hengstenberg comments, "When Stephen, after the example of the OT, Deut. 33:2, Ps. 68:18, speaks in the plural number of angels who were concerned in giving the law, he does not intend to deny, that one among them infinitely exceeded in power above the rest took the lead as the highest revealer of God." See Hengstenberg, *Christology of the Old Testament*, 185.

[285] Hanson, 95. In the original, Hanson says "theodicy." But this seem impossible and must be a typo.

Stephen is describing the "angel of the Lord" who manifested God, and then describing his heavenly host with him,[286] adding to the glory of the moment - which the people, in their stubbornness of heart, ignored.

What Stephen sees and says next confirms this interpretation! In Acts 7:55-56, after ending his speech, Stephen has a vision into heaven:

> But he, full of the Holy Spirit, gazed into heaven and saw the glory of God, and Jesus standing at the right hand of God. And he said, 'Behold, I see the heavens opened, and the Son of Man standing at the right hand of God.

In other words, Stephen, like those mentioned in his speech, *sees* Jesus. Notice the familiar OT themes he highlights: "glory," "right hand," and "Son of Man." These were ideas familiar to his Jewish hearers. They were words connected in OT theology to the Angel who manifested God. Stephen has already mentioned "the God of glory" (7:2). He's already mentioned "the hand of the angel" (7:35), the "hand" by which God created the world (7:50), who in the OT was "commander of the host."[287] The Jewish Sanhedrin would have been very familiar with "the Son of Man" speculations from the OT and Jesus' own use of them during his life. In fact, vs. 55 is possibly mistranslated. As asked in the Glory chapter, "May the καὶ be epexegetical in this reference? If so, we should read: '[Stephen] saw the glory of God, that is, Jesus standing at the right hand of God."[288] In other words, by this vision, Stephen is confirming that Jesus is the glory of God who is in heaven. He was that Divine Angel from the OT who came with the hosts of heaven. Stephen charges the Jews with failing to recognize Jesus, as well as rejecting and rebelling against Jesus, throughout Jewish history.

Paul's View of Angels and the Intermediary at Sinai

Galatians 3:19-20 provides another possible hint of the relationship between Jesus and angels at Sinai:

---

[286] See again 2Th 1:7-8, Rev 19:7-16.
[287] See ch. 6, "The Angel as a Man of War."
[288] Ralph P. Martin, *A Hymn to Christ*, 111.

Why then the law? It was added because of transgressions, until the offspring should come to whom the promise had been made, and it was put in place through *angels* by an intermediary. Now an intermediary implies more than one, but God is one.

In this passage, Paul is explaining that the Sinai covenant was provisional and temporary but was preceded by a prior covenant promise to Abraham and superseded by the new covenant fulfillment of that promise in the coming of Christ. But why, in explaining the intent of the Sinai covenant, does he bring up "angels" and an "intermediary?" It is possible that the Judaizers themselves emphasized the important role of angels in the OT Law. Back in Galatians 1:8, Paul had said, "Even if we *or an angel from heaven* should preach a gospel contrary to the one we preached, let him be accursed." Angelic speculation was also mentioned as part of the false teaching in Colossians 2:18. Apparently, angels highlighted to the Jews the importance and authority of the Law (as in Stephen's speech above). They were part of the glory and administration of the Law. So Paul says, Yes, the Law was put in place through angels, but also by an "intermediary." There was someone else involved, more important than angels.

Who is this "intermediary?" There are two possible interpretations. First, many scholars see the "intermediary" as a reference to Moses as the mediator between God and the people (see Exodus 20:19-21), who received the Law from God in the presence of "angels." In this interpretation, Paul is pointing out the difference between how God gave the Law and how God gave the "promise" (Gal 3:17-18) to Abraham. God did not give the Law "directly," God to man; he gave it through the mediator Moses. But the "promise" was given directly to Abraham, so the "promise" is superior. But in this interpretation, many of those same scholars don't know what to do with vs. 20, "An intermediary implies more than one, but God is one." They admit that Paul's meaning is unclear.[289]

But the other interpretation, favored by the early church fathers, is that Paul is talking about *Jesus himself* as the intermediary. Paul is acknowledging the role of angels in giving the Law, but pointing out the more important role of the Divine Angel intermediary. And under this

---

[289] For instance, see Leon Morris, *Galatians: Paul's Charter of Christian Freedom* (Downers Grove, Il: InterVarsity Press, 1996).

interpretation, vs. 20 makes much more sense. Paul is making a Christological statement: the OT "Angel of the Lord" acting as an intermediary
for God "implies more than one, but God is one." He is saying, there was
someone there even more important than the angels - the Divine Son of
God himself, the "Angel of the Lord" who made the "promise" to Abraham (see Gen 15:1; Gen 22:11, 15-17), who promised an "offspring," and
who was going to come himself as the "promised offspring" (see Gal 4:4).
The intermediary, who revealed God, who was God himself, the Son of
God, was going to come into the world, and he gave the Sinai Covenant
as a provisional protection for his people until he comes.

In other words, rather than undermining the Christ-Angel interpretation, this comports completely with the rest of the NT, seeing the
Son of God as the OT Divine Angel, who leads the heavenly host.

The Angelic Polemic of Hebrews

The last passage highlighting Jesus' relationship to the angelic host
and the giving of the Law at Sinai is found in Hebrews. In fact, Jesus'
relationship to angels is the main subject of the opening two chapters
of the book. Hebrews begins with a statement of Jesus' superiority over
Old Testament revelation and over the angels.

> Long ago, at many times and in many ways, God spoke to our
> fathers by the prophets, but in these last days he has spoken to us by
> his Son, whom he appointed the heir of all things, through whom
> also he created the world. He is the radiance of the glory of God and
> the exact imprint of his nature, and he upholds the universe by the
> word of his power. After making purification for sins, he sat down
> at the right hand of the Majesty on high, having become as much
> superior to angels as the name he has inherited is more excellent
> than theirs.
>
> (Hebrews 1:1-4)

As we have noted, widespread speculation and emphasis on the
importance of angelic mediation existed in the first century. The Jewish
authorities emphasized the role of angels in the revelation and administration of the Mosaic covenant. For this reason, the New Testament
writers were always careful to affirm Jesus' superiority and exaltation

over angels. For example, 1 Peter 3:22 says that Christ "has gone into heaven and is at the right hand of God, with angels, authorities, and powers having been subjected to him" (see also Eph 1:20-21). But some still questioned the Son's pre-incarnate status. They knew the NT assertion that Jesus existed and was present and active in the Old Testament era. But was he just "a really important angel" in the Old Testament? Was he the principal angel, the first among the *created* beings, like the Essenes described the archangel Michael? These questions seem to be exactly what Hebrews is seeking to answer: was the divine "Angel of the Lord," at the end of the day, ontologically simply the first created angel among the angels?

Hebrews answers very strongly and clearly, using language and divine angel texts that are now very familiar. In Heb 1:2-4, it uses seven notable (now familiar) words to identify Jesus: Son, Heir, Glory, Word, Power, Right Hand, and Name—all words that we have seen clearly used in the Old Testament for "the Angel of the Lord." He further identifies Jesus as the one "through whom [God] created the world" who "upholds the universe."

Then, in vv. 5-14, the author of Hebrews cites seven Old Testament passages to underscore Jesus' superiority over angels.

First, he quotes Psalm 2:7 and 2 Samuel 7:14 to show that Jesus' is *the unique and special "Son"* of the Father. As we have seen, sometimes the angels are called "Sons of God" (Job 1:6, 2:1, 38:7; Psalm 29:1, 82:6, 89:6). Deuteronomy 32:8 talks about Yahweh giving over the nations to the angelic "Sons of God" (Gen 6:2, 4) and claiming Israel as his special inheritance. But Psalm 2 looks forward to the day when God would judge the rulers over the nations and would reclaim *all* the nations as the inheritance of his "Son."[290] Jesus' is declared to be the "begotten" Son. Angels may have been *given* the *title* "sons of God" (Psalm 82:6), but Jesus was God's Son in his very nature, and he comes into his inheritance when he is brought forward and acknowledged to be who he always was - the "Son" of the Father. No created angel was ever given such an illustrious honor.

Next, Hebrews quotes from Deuteronomy 32:43 and Psalm 104:4 to show that angels themselves are *worshipers and servants of the Son*. The end of Deuteronomy 32 in the LXX, Dead Sea Scrolls, and the

---

[290] See also Psalm 82.

Targums, as we have already seen, make several connections to the Angel of the Lord as the bearer of the divine name (see Dt 32:39). Vs. 43 then looks forward to the heavenly beings bowing down and worshiping him. (The LXX specifically records, "Let all the sons of God worship him.") Similarly, Psalm 104:4 speaks of the angels as "servants" or "ministers." The point is, they are servants, not sons or heirs.

Heightening the point, Hebrews quotes then from Psalm 45:6-7 and 102:25-27 to proclaim the Son himself *as eternal God*. Psalm 45 is one of the classic Two Yahweh texts, where the Messianic king is himself called "God, anointed by God" whose throne is everlasting. In Psalm 102, Hebrews interprets Jesus as the one addressed as the Lord who laid the foundation of the earth, who never changes.

Hebrews concludes the argument with another classic Two Powers text—using Psalm 110:1 to name Jesus as David's "Lord" who is at the "right hand of the father." The verse is one of the most often cited verses in the New Testament to identify Jesus (see again Jesus' own use of it in Luke 20:41-44).

The conclusion from these passages is clear. Hebrews assumes the Son was pre-existent, present, and active in the Old Testament. It uses the titles regularly attributed to the Divine Angel in the Old Testament. Yet, Hebrews argues that these titles were never attributed to simply a *created* angel. He was the only true and eternal Son from the Father, who was always superior to the angels.

As we saw at the end of the last chapter, Hebrews then goes on to use this point to highlight the astounding mystery of the Son's condescension and incarnation. The eternal Son, who was always superior to the heavenly beings, who appeared in the OT at the head of the heavenly host, remarkably was made "for a little while lower than the angels" (Heb 2:7). He took on "flesh and blood" to become the representative and mediator of fallen humanity, to defeat death and the claims of the devil (2:14-15). He has now been exalted again above the heavenly beings, crowned with glory and honor, and given authority over all (2:7-8). Therefore, his New Testament appearing represents a greater revelation, an even greater salvation, a greater covenant, with a greater mediator. The Son, who reveals the Father to us, became a man to represent us to his Father.

In Part II we want to turn our attention to demon-strating from history that indeed this has always been the position of the church. There is nothing novel about our thesis. This is important to us to establish with you because we believe that orthodox Christianity, that is the Faith once-for-all delivered to the saints, is the way all good theology should develop. Not by creating brand new ideas, but in developing or recovering old ideas in ways that ever more closely fit the biblical data which our forefathers in the Faith knew to be true.

THE ANGEL AND CHURCH HISTORY

Chapters: 16-18

Historical Theology: *The branch that studies the historical development of the understanding and statement of Christian doctrine in the Church.* ~ *Alan Cairns*

In Part II we will look at how the Angel of the LORD as Christ may have first developed by looking at Jewish antecedents, then moving into the early church. We will see how the earliest views have remained with us through the Reformation and on into today

16

$$\text{\Large \ding{96}\ding{96}\ding{96}}$$

THE ANGEL IN THE JEWISH CHURCH

The Angel and Historical Theology
Part I

The Big Picture

I N HIS DISSERTATION ON THE ANGEL OF THE LORD, Joel Huffstutler has an Appendix listing those who take the Angel as Christ vs.
those who do not. The history covers the early church through
the Reformation. We want to reduplicate it here (see next page). The purpose is to visually highlight how few there are that have taken the non-
Christological view. While we find many more who have taken the Christological view in Part II, we want to focus in this chapter the Jewish interpretation of the Angel of the LORD.

A Jewish Puzzle

How could Jews who believe in the Shema—a verse found in Deuteronomy 6:4 that is the pillar of modern and ancient Judaism, most
commonly translated as "Hear, O Israel: The LORD our God *is* one
LORD" (KJV)—how could these Jews have come so easily to believe
that Jesus Christ was God in the flesh in such great numbers in the days

TWO PRIMARY VIEWS OF THE ANGEL OF YAHWEH[291]		
Period of Church History	Christological or Ante-Nicene View	Non-Christological or Augustinian View
Ante-Nicene Period A.D. 90-325	Justin Martyr Irenaeus of Lyons Clement of Alexandria Tertullian of Carthage Novatian Cyprian	Jews
Nicene and Post-Nicene Period A.D. 325-787	Eusebius of Caesarea Athanasius of Alexandria* Hilary of Poitiers Gregory of Nyssa Ambrose of Milan Arians (denied Christ's deity) Eunomius of Mysia (denied Christ's deity)	Augustine of Hippo
Medieval Period to the Present A.D. 787-present	Reformed tradition John Calvin* Charles Hodge Lutheran tradition Martin Luther* Calovius Methodist tradition John Wesley Richard Watson John Miley Independent/Baptists tradition Jonathan Edwards John Gill W.G.T. Shedd Louis Berkhof *Allows generic use of the term Angel of Yahweh/Angel of God (i.e., can also be a finite creature)	Thomas Aquinas Roman Catholic Church* *Allows Christological Interpretation

[291] Joel Ira Huffstutler, "He Who Dwelt in the Bush: A Biblical and Historical Theology of the Angel of the LORD," (PhD Dissertation, Bob Jones, 2007), Appendix B, 286.

of the New Testament and earliest church? This is a vital question. It is not often asked. But its answers are simply life-changing in the way we read our Old Testaments and understand the claims Jesus was making about himself in light of his own ancient Jewish context.

By "easy" we don't mean that it was a simple thing, humanly speaking, to do. For conversion like this is always a gift from God. Left to ourselves, no one would convert, even with a preexisting worldview that could "handle" the theology. But that's just it. Modern Judaism does not have a worldview that can handle the claims of Jesus to be God in the flesh, because modern Judaism is openly and blatantly Unitarian. Any kind of divine plurality is, by default, impossible.

What is Unitarianism? We've brought up the word several times in our study. The current entry on *Wikipedia*—that bastion of truth that anyone can edit at will—states that "Unitarianism is historically a Christian theological movement named for its belief that God is one entity, as opposed to the Trinity which defines God as three persons in one being; the Father, Son, and Holy Spirit."[292] While giving a rather simplistic definition of the Trinity, the language is good enough for our purposes here. What we want to make crystal clear, and where we find the entry historically lacking, is that Unitarianism as a heresy against a Triune God did not begin in Christianity. Rather, nearly 2,000 years ago, sometime soon after the Second Temple was destroyed in A.D. 70, the rabbis created a much more formal form of Unitarianism within their ranks, and it has stuck for nearly two millennia.

But believe it or not, prior to that some Jews saw some form of a *Godhead*,[293] and it was a perfectly acceptable belief to hold, though not all of them

---

[292] "Unitarianism," Wikipedia, last accessed June 19, 2018, **https://en.wikipedia.org/wiki/Unitarianism.**

[293] The seminal work on this is Alan Segal, *Two Powers in Heaven: Early Rabbinic Reports about Christianity and Gnosticism* (Leiden: E. J. Brill, 1977). After that, an explosion of material has come out. Here is a short bibliography (with thanks to Michael Heiser): Daniel Abrams, "The Boundaries of Divine Ontology: The Inclusion and Exclusion of Metatron in the Godhead," *Harvard Theological Review* 87:3 (July 1994): 291-321; Margaret Barker, *The Great Angel: A Study of Israel's Second God* (Louisville, KY: Westminster / John Knox Publishers, 1992); Richard Bauckham, "The Throne of God and the Worship of Jesus," in *The Jewish Roots of Christological Monotheism: Papers from the St. Andrews Conference on the Historical Origins of the Worship of Jesus*, ed. C. Newman, J. Davila, and G. Lewis (Leiden: E. J. Brill, 1999): 43-69; Richard Bauckham, *God Crucified: Monotheism & Christology*

did. In other words, some Jews at the time of Christ had a view of God that held to the Shema while simultaneously holding to beliefs such as there being (at least) two Persons in the OT called Yahweh or two Persons such as the Ancient of Days and "one like a son of man" who were both separate and, yet, not separate. Several "Angel of the LORD" passages are intimately involved in this very *Jewish* theology (such as Exodus 23:20-22), a theology that was only labeled a heresy by the rabbis *after* the NT books had been completed. In fact, the emergence of Christianity as a threat to Judaism was precisely the catalyst for this strict circling of the theological wagons.

---

in the New Testament (Grand Rapids, MI: Eerdmans, 1998); Daniel Boyarin, "The Gospel of the Memra: Jewish Binitarianism and the Prologue to John," *HTR* 94:3 (July 2001): 243-284; Daniel Boyarin, "Two Powers in Heaven; or, The Making of a Heresy," in *The Idea of Biblical Interpretation: Essays in Honor of James L. Kugel* (Leiden: Brill, 2003): 331-370; Jarl E. Fossum, *The Image of the Invisible God: Essays on the Influence of Jewish Mysticism on Early Christology* (Göttingen: Vandenhoeck and Ruprecht, 1995); Simon Gathercole, *The Pre-Existent Son: Recovering the Christologies of Matthew, Mark, and Luke* (Grand Rapids: Eerdmans, 2006); Darrell D. Hannah, *Michael and Christ: Michael Traditions and Angel Christology in Early Christianity*, Wissenschaftliche Untersuchungen zum Neuen Testament 109 (Tübingen: Mohr-Siebeck, 1999); Michael S. Heiser, "The Divine Council in Late Canonical and Non-Canonical Second Temple Jewish Literature," A Dissertation at the University of Wisconsin-Madison, 2004; Michael S. Heiser, *The Unseen Realm: Rediscovering the Supernatural Worldview of the Bible* (Bellingham, WA: Lexham Press, 2015); Larry W. Hurtado, "What Do We Mean by 'First-Century Jewish Monotheism'?" in Society of Biblical Literature 1993 Seminar Papers, ed. E. H. Lovering Jr. (Atlanta: Scholars Press, 1993): 348-368; Larry W. Hurtado, *One God, One Lord: Early Christian Devotion and Ancient Jewish Monotheism* (Philadelphia: Fortress, 1988); Larry W. Hurtado, *Lord Jesus Christ: Devotion to Jesus in Earliest Christianity* (Grand Rapids: Eerdmans, 2003); Larry W. Hurtado, "First-Century Jewish Monotheism." *Journal for the Study of the New Testament* 71 (1998): 3-26; Larry W. Hurtado, "Jesus' Divine Sonship in Paul's Epistle to the Romans," in *Romans and the People of God*, ed. N. T. Wright and S. Soderlund (Grand Rapids: Eerdmans, 1999): 217-23; Larry W. Hurtado, "The Binitarian Shape of Early Christian Worship," in *The Jewish Roots of Christological Monotheism, Papers from the St. Andrews Conference on the Historical Origins of the Worship of Jesus*, ed. Carey C. Newman, James R. Davila and Gladys S. Lewis, *Supplements to the Journal for the Study of Judaism*, ed. John J. Collins. Leiden: E. J. Brill, 1999): 187-213; Larry W. Hurtado, *How on Earth Did Jesus Become a God?: Historical Questions about Earliest Devotion to Jesus* (Grand Rapids: Eerdmans, 2005); Aquila H. I. Lee, *From Messiah to Pre-existent Son*. Wissenschaftliche Untersuchungen zum Neuen Testament 192 (Tübingen: Mohr-Siebeck, 2005; reprinted Wipf and Stock, 2009); Alan F. Segal, *Two Powers in Heaven: Early Rabbinic Reports about Christianity and Gnosticism* (Leiden: E. J. Brill, 1977).

What this means is that there actually was, within ancient Judaism, a worldview capable (unlike Unitarianism would be) of accepting the claims of Jesus Christ to be *Theanthropos* (a term coined by the Church Father Origen which means God in human flesh) without giving up the commitment to the Shema. And that is how so many of them were able to digest his claims and by the grace of God come away believing them.

In Part III, which consists of three chapters, we move into what is called historical theology. What is historical theology? One popular dictionary defines it as "The branch of theology that studies the historical development of the understanding and statement of Christian doctrine in the church."[294] Alister McGrath explains that because of this, it is closely linked to the disciplines of church history and systematic theology in that it identifies factors within the history of the church that are important to understanding how different aspects of systematic doctrines developed over time.[295] Nothing could be more helpful, save the exegesis of Scripture itself, to understanding and appreciating the conversion of so many Jews to Christianity in those early days. It also has a remarkable side-effect of utterly helping reorient us in the way we think about the Bible ourselves.

Our discussion will not be exhaustive. We aren't going to look at the entire history of beliefs on the Angel. But we will start, in this chapter, with three extremely early tributaries of doctrine that poured into the reservoir of Christian thought that immediately saw the Angel of the LORD as the preincarnate Christ. Scholars have labeled them as a form of Binitarian Jewish theology, which means exactly what you think it means: One God with one Person less than a Trinity. However, we will point out that recent scholarship is starting to notice the Spirit's involvement in many of the early "binitarian" ways of speaking, meaning that Trinitarian thinking has been there all along at least in the Christian church's reflection.[296] We will also look at how these

---

[294] Alan Cairns, *Dictionary of Theological Terms* (Belfast; Greenville, SC: Ambassador Emerald International, 2002), 211.

[295] Alister E. McGrath, *Historical Theology: An Introduction to the History of Christian Thought*, Second Edition (Malden, MA: John Wiley & Sons, Ltd., 2013), 8-9.

[296] Bucur writes, "Is binitarian monotheism the first step to Christian Trinitarian theology? In my opinion, 'binitarianism' is less an early Christian phenomenon than it is a scholarly phenomenon: a term that alerts us to a built-in blind spot in the academic approach to sacred texts." Bogdan G. Bucur, "Scholarship on the

tributaries dried up, and how this may have contributed to the lowering of that reservoir in the understanding of some Christians. These are Philo, the Targums, and finally, the rabbis.

But first, a caveat. It has become popular in some scholarly circles in recent decades to conclude from the material we will be looking at (and subjects we do not have time to discuss) that Israelite religion was originally some kind of polytheistic syncretism of Yahweh and El and other deities. Then, over time and especially after the captivity, this began to morph into the monotheism we know today. We reject this view. In its place, primarily because of our exegesis of the OT, we hold that the Jewish Scriptures themselves contain an implicit trinitarianism by the inspiration of the Holy Spirit, and that at least some Jews (especially the biblical writers, but even those who came after) understood this quite explicitly. To these three examples we now turn.

A Jewish Trinity?

Philo and the Second God

Julius Philo, better known simply as Philo, was a Jew from a wealthy and noble family, a highly educated Roman citizen and philosopher, who lived during the time of Jesus, though he almost certainly never heard of him because he lived 315 miles as the crow flies in Alexandria, Egypt.

As a philosopher, Philo was grounded in the great Greek thinkers such as Plato and Aristotle. As he tried to think about God as a Hellenized (that is Greek-ized) Jew, he incorporated certain Greek views of God into his thinking. One of these is the view adopted by the church that God is a "simple" being. By simplicity, we do not mean that God is a *simpleton* or that he isn't immensely complicated in his thoughts or something like that. Rather, simplicity refers to the idea that God is not a composite being. Put more "simply," God is not made of pieces. He is not a group of parts that are more basic than God.

Old Testament Roots of Trinitarian Theology: Blind Spots and Blurred Vision," in *The Bible and Early Trinitarian Theology*, ed. Christopher A. Beely and Mark E. Weedman (Washington, D. C.: The Catholic University of America Press, 2018), 34 [29-49].

The doctrine of simplicity is a rather strange way of getting into a discussion of the Angel of the LORD in Philo, but it is also very important to think about in this regard. Aristotle explains that there was a debate in his own day "as to whether one should refer to 'parts' of the soul (*mere, moria*) or regard it as undivided but exercising a variety of functions, *dunameis*."[297] In other words, is the human soul simple or composite? This question was not only asked of God.

Dunameis comes from the Greek word for "power" (from which we get things like dynamite). Explaining Philo on simplicity and power, Christopher Stead writes, "To speak of parts would suggest the picture of God in human form, which the scriptures introduce only as a concession to human weakness (Philo, *On Dreams* 1.234-6). It follows that God must be seen as operating through his powers."[298] "Powers" then became a way of trying to figure out how a simple God could actually do things like be in an "eternally frozen pose," as J. I. Packer has put it.[299]

Philo often discussed God's powers. Alan Segal explains, "When discussing God's powers, Philo maintains that they are infinite. But, for convenience, Philo allows them to be categorized into two different kinds [creative power and merciful power] ... But this aspect of God can be identified with the Greek word for God, *theos*, which was the standard LXX translation of Elohim."[300] If you think you read that wrong, you didn't. He is identifying "power" with God himself. This actually makes sense in light of the idea that the attributes of a simple God simply are God, because "power" cannot be something more basic than God of which he is composed. But it is more complicated than this kind of Greek Unitarian thinking.

> From one point of view, divine powers are abstractions—like the *logos*, only convenient ways of discussing vast capabilities of God. However, since their characteristics are fixed, Philo often describes them as *living creatures*. For instance, the two angels who guard the gates of paradise and the angels who enter Sodom are allegorized as the two powers of God.

---

[297] Cited in Christopher Stead, "Divine Simplicity as a Problem for Orthodoxy," in Rowan Williams (ed.), *The Making of Orthodoxy: Essays in Honour of Henry Chadwick* (Cambridge: Cambridge University Press, 1989), 259-60.
[298] ibid.
[299] J. I. Packer, "God," in Sinclair B. Ferguson and J. I. Packer (eds), *New Dictionary of Theology* (Downers Grove, IL: InterVarsity Press, 2000), 276.
[300] Alan Segal, *Two Powers in Heaven*, 174.

How these powers relate to the *logos* is ambiguous. Since the *logos* can also signify the sum of all the powers, it logically stands above the two powers in the ascent from concrete to abstract. Yet sometimes Philo uses *kyrios* and *theos* to refer to the two powers of God and other times to refer to the *logos* and the highest God, being-in-itself.[301]

Now we are starting to move into how this touches on the Angel of the LORD. Philo called the two angels God's "powers," though he also believed they were created beings and not "part" of God himself. But the other—that third Angel—what about him?

While not using "power," here are a couple of fascinating examples using perhaps an even better-known idea. Commenting on Genesis 9:6, Philo poses the question, "Why is it that he speaks as if of some other god, saying that he made man after the image of God, and not that he made him after his own image?" His answer? "No mortal thing could have been formed on the similitude of the supreme Father of the universe, but only after the pattern of the second deity (*deuteros theos*), who is the *logos* of the supreme Being" (Questions on Genesis 2.62). What does this mean? He sums this up in another place, saying,

> And even if there be not as yet anyone who is worthy to be called a son of God, nevertheless let him labour earnestly to be adorned according to his first-born logos, the eldest of his angels, as the great archangel of many names; for he is called, the authority, and the name of God, and the Word [logos], and man according to God's image, and he who sees Israel ... Even if we are not yet suitable to be called the sons of God, still we may deserve to be called the children of his eternal image, of his most sacred logos; for the image of God is his most ancient word [logos]."
>
> (Philo, *Confusion of Tongues* 146)

For Philo, the *logos* is "neither uncreated as God, nor yet created as you, but between these two extremities" (*Heir of Divine Things* 206). He could have been at Nicaea, had he lived later and trusted in Christ. The Creed is very similar, "Begotten, not made." Did Philo believe in a Trinity? This is doubtful (though there is no evidence that Philo had ever heard of Jesus Christ and the claims of the Christians). Did he worship more than one God? Perish the thought! Did he believe in a plurality in a Godhead?

---

[301] Ibid., 175.

Segal's work, while not answering Philo definitively on this question, nevertheless concludes that some Jews in his day and earlier very much did! At any rate, compare this to Philo now talking about the "power":

> Akin to these two is *the creative power called God* (ἡ ποιητικὴ δύναμις, ἡ καλουμένη θεός) because through this the Father, who is its begetter and contriver, made the universe; so that "I am thy God" is equivalent to "I am thy maker and artificer." And the greatest gift we can have is to have *Him* for our architect, who was also the architect of the whole world ... And therefore we read "Let us make man after our image" (Gen 1:26), so that according as the wax received the bad or the noble impress it should appear to be the handiwork of others or of Him who is the framer of the noble and the good alone.
>
> (Philo, *On the Changing of Names* 29-31)

Segal explains more clearly,

> Philo maintains that one of God's two powers descends— in one case, to create man; in another, to punish those building the tower. He explains that these powers are angels and that their presence has so impressed some people (even Moses) that they feel no shame in calling them gods. In other words, Philo depends on his concept of the powers of justice and mercy to explain scriptural plurals, calling them both angels and divine. Therefore in *On the Change of Names*, Philo can offer another interpretation of what the patriarchs saw when scripture says they saw God (6-7). First, he remarks that they saw the same creative power of God which Moses saw on Sinai for the first time, having already been privileged to see God's ruling power. We remember that he has previously said that the elders saw the image of God or the *logos*.[302]

These quotations make it easy to see how the angel of the LORD (he even mentions the Angel, or at least an Angel being associated with the *Logos* in one of the quotations) and *logos* (that "second God) are connected to the Power. Whatever else we want to make of Philo on these things, one thing is clear. A strict unitarian like you find in Islam or contemporary Judaism does not talk like this. This fountainhead of thought of a kind of plurality of a Godhead is something we will take a step further as we consider the Jewish Targums.

---

[302] Segal, 177.

The Targums and the Memra[303]

One of our earliest points in the book was to associate the Angel of the LORD with the Word (see Ch. 2). Here, we want to explain more of the historical development that went on within at least some circles within Judaism, which saw God's "Word" in a rather unique way.

First, in the same way that the Greek word "*logos*" is the same as the English word "word," "*memra*" is the counterpart in the Aramaic language. Coming from the word *mmr'*, meaning "to say," it means "word."

Memra is found in the Jewish Targums and is "The designation for God most characteristic of all the Targums."[304] There are other terms, such as Shekinah (Presence) or Yeqara (Glory), which we have looked at that act the same way, but we will not deal with them more here. Memra suffices to demonstrate the point.

A Targum is an Aramaic translation/interpretation of a book of the OT. They are important because 1. Aramaic was the language of Jesus and, 2. They were in use during the time of Jesus' ministry, especially in the liturgy of the synagogues.[305] Though we do not know the exact dates of their being written down, he and the disciples certainly would have been familiar with them, and scholars have suggested that they may even have used them as they wrote their own books.

---

[303] For scholarly studies see G. H. Box, "The Idea of Intermediation in Jewish Theology. A Note on Memra and Shekinah," *The Jewish Quarterly Review* 23:2 (Oct 1932): 103-119; Daniel Boyarin, "The Gospel of the Memra: Jewish Binitarianism and the Prologue to John," Harvard Theological Review 94:3 (2001): 243-84; Craig A. Evans, "Philo, Memra, Targums, Logos," chapter 4 in *Word and Glory: On the Exegetical and Theological Background of John's Prologue*, Journal for the Study of the New Testament Supplement Series 89 (Sheffield Academic Press, 1993), 100-145; Adam Joseph Howell, "Finding Christ in the Old Testament Through the Aramaic Memra, Shekinah, and Yeqara of the Targums," A Dissertation at The Southern Baptist Theological Seminary, 2015; George Foot Moore, "Intermediaries in Jewish Theology: Memra, Shekinah, Metatron," *Harvard Theological Review* 15:1 (Jan 1922): 41-85; John L. Ronning, *The Jewish Targums and John's Logos Theology* (Grand Rapids, MI: Baker Academic, 2010); John L. Ronning, "The Targum of Isaiah and the Johannine Literature, *Westminster Theological Journal* 69:2 (2007): 247-78.

[304] Kevin Cathcart, Michael Maher, and Martin McNamara, eds., *The Aramaic Bible A: Targum Neofiti 1: Genesis*, trans. Martin McNamara, vol. 1 (Collegeville, MN: The Liturgical Press, 1992), 37.

[305] See Martin McNamara, *Targum and Testament Revisited: Aramaic Paraphrases of the Hebrew Bible* (Grand Rapids, MI: Eerdmans, 2010), 249.

Memra is used in a very strange way. As one scholar put it a century ago, these Jews:

> ... were sufficiently advanced to find difficulty in the more star-tlingly anthropomorphic expressions of the Old Testament like "The Lord God walked in the garden." Wherever anything of this kind occurs in the original, the Targum replaces it by some inoffensive substitute; the "Dwelling of the Lord" (*Shekinta* = Heb. *Shekinah*) or the "Word of the Lord" (*Memra*) are the most common.[306]

In other words, Memra shows up as more than a *translation*. It is also a theological *explanation* for unlearned Jews, even when the Hebrew equivalent isn't in the text. It is used as "a buffer word ... to avoid anthropomorphisms, to avoid making God the direct object or subject of actions connected with creation."[307] As you may be able to sense already, this is a rather strange thing. It is not something most of us feel free to do when we make even very loose paraphrases of the Bible in English.

But it gets stranger, especially when you consider what Judaism is like today and has officially been for more than 1,900 years! Yet, as we just saw in our discussion of Philo, things were not always like this. Even before the more modern studies, this was understood.

> It seems clear that [the idea of mediation between man and God by a celestial being or beings] was implicit in some forms of popular Judaism, which are reflected in certain phenomena of the Targums, and which the Rabbis had every reason to regard as highly danger-ous to the pure conception of God. In order to safeguard the ortho-dox religion it was found necessary to revise the Targums, which were accordingly done. The importance of this fact deserves to be emphasized. It is of considerable significance.[308]

Indeed. We wish to shout it from the rooftops! There were some Jews who were clearly viewing the Memra as essentially a divine

---

[306] Burnett Hillman Streeter, The Four Gospels: A Study of Origins Treating of The Manuscript Tradition, Sources, Authorship, & Dates (Macmillan & Co., 1924).

[307] Cathcart, 38.

[308] Box, 105.

person.[309] Consider the following passages. Whereas Genesis 6:6 says, "And the LORD regretted that he had made man…," a Targum says, "And the Lord regretted in his Memra that he had made man on earth, and he debated in his Memra about them" (Gen 6:6 TgPsJon). Whereas Isaiah 63:10 says, "But they rebelled and grieved his Holy Spirit…," the Targum says, "But they rebelled and incited to anger against the Memra of his holy prophets…" (Isa 63:10 TgIsa). "I have established my covenant between me and you" (Gen 17:7) becomes, "I have established My covenant between my Memra and you" in the Targums.[310] "They heard the sound/voice of the LORD God" (Gen 3:8) becomes, "They heard the voice of the Memra of the Lord God."[311]

These kinds of things are found all over the place. What sense do they even make as pure personifications or anthropomorphisms?[312] The idea behind them is clearly to distance God from certain interactions, not simply to find another way of saying he has them. This language has led scholars to say such things as the Memra is "the Word conceived as a person, the logos"[313] or, "The Memra has a place above the angels as that agent of the Deity who sustains the course of nature and

---

[309] This is disputed by some scholars. For example, Hurtado, *Binitarian Shape of Early Christianity*. But it is accepted as fact by others. For example, Fossum, *The Name of God and the Angel of the LORD*.

[310] Abelson writes, "It is the Memra who is always the subject of swearing or oathtaking. Either the Memra takes the oath, or God swears by His Memra." J. Abelson, *The Immanence of God in Rabbinical Literature* (London: Macmillan and Co., 1912), 157.

[311] There are so many of these that they could take up a book to discuss. In fact, someone has, and long ago. Peter Allix, *The Judgment of the Ancient Jewish Church Against the Unitarians*, second edition (Oxford: Clarendon Press, 1821). We have republished a portion of this book with the relevant material as a companion to this volume called *The Angel of the LORD in Early Jewish, Christian, and Reformation History*.

[312] Abelson explains, "The Rabbis personified [Memra], speaking with the greatest freedom of [it] as the visible manifestation of Deity in the objective world … [But] left no stone unturned to prevent any belief in anything but the unique and incomparable unity of God … That there was a danger lest the personification should be carried too far, is clear; that the Rabbis were alive to this danger is obvious from various indications. The official Targum was revised, and in the most dangerous cases Memra was eliminated from the text (as in the creation passages in Gen. 1 ff), and literal renderings were substituted." Abelson, 161 in Box, 112.

[313] Levy, *Wörterbuch*, cited in Box, 105.

personifies the Law."[314] Or, "If words have any meaning, the Memra is a hypostasis."[315] Rabbis as famous as Akiba ben Yosef (50-135 AD) have been identified as holding to "belief in a hypostatic Memra."[316]

The key thing to wrap your mind around here is simply to reinforce from the previous section that early Judaism was not monolithic regarding divine personhood, even though it was universally *monotheistic*. The Memra is a key way they developed this theology, which, thankfully, we still have available for us to study today.

The Rabbis and Two Powers in Heaven

With Philo and the Targums as background, we now want to discuss the Rabbis more specifically. In recent decades, scholars have made tremendous strides uncovering and thinking through something the Rabbis disparagingly called "'Two Powers in Heaven' heretics."[317] "Powers." Does this sound familiar? We raised this point in Philo on purpose to help prepare the soil for this final section of the chapter.

The idea, first brought to modern light by Alan Segal, explains that there was an undercurrent of alternative readings of the OT Scripture during the Second Temple era (roughly 450 B.C. through A.D. 70, which obviously includes much of the writing of the NT). These pertained to certain "dangerous" passages, as they themselves called them. These included Exodus 15:3, Exodus 23:20-23; and Daniel 7:9, all of which some taught spoke of "two powers in heaven." These Powers were both good, both divine, yet distinct from one another. For example, of Daniel 7 Segal explains,

> Not only does the passage allow the interpretation that God changes aspect, it may easily be describing two separate, divine figures. More than one throne is revealed and scripture describes two divine

---

[314] M. J. Edwards, "Justin's Logos and the Word of God," *JECS* 3 (1995): 263 [261-80], cited in Boyarin, "The Gospel of the Memra," 254.

[315] Robert Hayward, *Divine Name and Presence: The Memra* (Oxford Centre for Postgraduate Hebrew Studies; Totowa, NJ: Allanheld, Osmun, 1981), 3, cited in Boyarin, ibid.

[316] Samuel Zinner, The Gospel of Thomas: In the Light of Early Jewish, Christian and Islamic Esoteric Trajectories (London: The Matheson Trust, 2011), 40.

[317] On the 12 rabbinical passages see the list in Segal on p. 310.

figures to fill them. One sits and the other seems to be invested with power, possibly enthroned.[318]

They used the language of "powers," and putting these sections together in their own way, Kohler concludes,

> Just as the references to God's appearing to man suggested luminous powers mediating the vision of God, so the passages which represent God as speaking suggest powers mediating the voice. Hence arose the conception of the Divine Word (capital W), invested with divine powers both physical and spiritual.[319]

Indeed, it is abundantly clear from the Rabbis themselves that some Jews (which included Christians) were in fact reading these texts this way. It was the context of this minority opinion that allows us to understand certain Christological passages such as John 1:1-14, Colossians 1, and Hebrews 1 in their historical situation. The Christians were claiming that Jesus Christ come in the flesh was the Second Power, the Word, the Firstborn, the "Son of the Blessed," and all the other things that Jews in that day were suggesting had to be true if the OT was to make sense. Because he proved himself by being perfectly obedient to God and being raised from the dead, he *is* God and therefore worship of him is obligatory.

And now you can understand why the Rabbis had to put a stop to such thinking. They were losing their own people left and right to this "new" religious sect called Christianity. With their temple gone and their people scattered, it was more important than ever to create a unified, written set of beliefs that all Jews would heretofore follow. They have been so successful that, today, very few realize the actual history on how many Jews were interpreting their Scriptures with a Godhead. The heresy of Jesus would be squashed one way or another.

Or would it?

---

[318] Segal, 35.

[319] K. Kohler, *Jewish Theology Systematically and Historically Considered* (New York: The Macmillan Company, 1918), 198.

1 7

THE ANGEL IN THE CHURCH FATHERS

The Angel and Historical Theology
Part II

The Council of the Angel

A MAN NAMED PAUL HAD GROWN UP IN SAMOSATA, an ancient hilly village just off the Euphrates, 60 miles northwest of Abram's old stomping grounds in Haran. It is now the year A.D. 268. Paul had been bishop of Antioch for eight years, the church where followers of Jesus were first called Christians (Acts 11:26).

Suddenly, a letter arrived from six regional bishops, headed by Hymenaeus of Jerusalem.[320] Along with a full complement of seventy elders, the churches will soon be holding a synod to decide the fate of Paul. Why? Paul had begun preaching an early form of Unitarianism called Monarchianism. The churches had been through enough with the persecutions from the Caesars. Now, heresy was striking at the very seat of Gentile Christianity in what may be to this day the oldest surviving church in the world. This letter was meant to steer Paul back into orthodoxy so that drastic measures could be halted.

---

[320] It is now called "The Letter of Six Bishops" or "The Letter of Hymenaeus." The six who signed it are Hymenaeus, Theophilus, Theoteknus, Maximus, Proclus, and Bolanus. We have provided a full translation of the letter, until now unavailable in English as far as we can tell, in an appendix at the end of the book. It is a fascinating read, and we will only be presenting portions of it in this chapter.

For our purposes, what is so remarkable about this letter is how it calls upon Paul to confess Jesus Christ as the Second Person of a Holy Trinity (long before Nicaea had taken place). Bogdan Bucur explains, "Paul is challenged 'to think and to teach' in concert with the signatories on a few points. Part of *the doctrinal litmus test* is the Christological interpretation of Genesis 18, 22, 32 and Exodus 3 and 33, which takes up an entire section (5) of the letter" [emphasis mine].[321] In rapid-fire succession, these bishops hit the high points of Angel of the LORD theology in the books of Moses. The "Son" who created the world they say, "was the one who descended and showed himself to Abraham at the oak of Mamre as one of the three, with whom, as 'lord' and 'judge,' the patriarch held conversation."

They go on to cite the now familiar Genesis 19:24 and the Son raining fire and sulfur on Sodom and Gomorrah. He does this "as the angel, the angel of the Father, the Son." He spoke to Sarah and promised her a son. He appeared on Mt. Moriah. He came to Jacob in a dream. He was there in the bush with Moses and gave the law to him on the mountain. He told all Israel that he was the God of Abraham, Isaac, and Jacob. He showed his glory to Moses. All this was the only-begotten Son, whom the NT calls the King eternal, immortal, invisible, and only wise.

What is astonishing is that these examples are presented as if this is what all true Christians affirm. Everyone believes them, except Paul. Heretics were only just beginning to take these passages to "prove" that the Son was created. But from the oldest days these passages were read as proving the immortality, absolute sovereignty, incomparability, pre-existence, and equality of Jesus with the Father in the Godhead.

Bucur helpfully summarizes the importance of this in the early church in a couple of different ways. "Theologically, the identification of Christ with the Glory, Name, Angel, or Son of Man manifested to the patriarchs and prophets is *a constitutive element* of early Christology"

---

[321] Bogdan G. Bucur, "The Early Christian Reception of Genesis 18: From Theophany to Trinitarian Symbolism," *Journal of Early Christian Studies* 23:2 (2015): 251, n. 19 [245-72].

[emphasis added].[322] And, "God's intelligible providences are defined as his gifts, appearances, powers, attributes, allotments, abodes—in short ... the traditional understanding of Old Testament theophanies as Christophanies" which "went unchallenged until Augustine, and ... remained as traditional in Eastern theology and liturgy as the doctrine of created theophanies became to the post-Augustinian West."[323] In other words, this was very important stuff and no new theology! In fact, as this *Letter of the Six* (which became a precursor to Nicaea) demonstrates, it is at the very heart of what it means to read the Bible as Christians.

This chapter is an historical chapter on the Early Church Fathers. Its purpose (as well as the next chapter) is mostly to give a handy reference guide to some who have held to the same doctrines we do in this book. We will divide the chapter into two sections. First, we will list the Fathers in chronological order (biographies are provided at the end of the book for all the Fathers cited in this book) with some of the passages where they discuss the Angel-Son in the OT.

While the list is not exhaustive, it does provide a significant number of passages that taken together should be a death-blow to anyone who doubts the orthodoxy of our thesis.[324] Then we provide some of the more interesting quotations. Then we switch our attention to more modern writers, beginning with the Reformers and moving into our own day. Our hope is that you will discover just how mainstream Angel of the LORD theology really is and always has been.

---

[322] Bogdan Bucur, "Gregory Nazianzen's Reading of Habbakuk 3:2 and Its Reception: A Lesson from Byzantine Scripture Exegesis," *Pro Ecclesia* 20 (2011): 89 and n. 28.

[323] Bogdan Bucur, "Foreordained from All Eternity: The Mystery of the Incarnation According to Some Early Christian and Byzantine Writers," in *Dumbarton Oaks Papers Number Sixty-Two 2008* (Washington, D.C.: Harvard University Press, 2009), 202.

[324] A more comprehensive list is given in Joseph Barbel, Christos Angelos: Die Anschauung von Christus als Bote und Engel in der gelehrten und volkstümlichen Literatur des christlichen Altertums (Bottrop: 1941), 315-24. A summary is found in Summary: Joseph Barbel, "Christos Angelos: Die frühchristliche und patristische Engelchristologie im Lichte der neueren Forschung," in T. Bogler, ed., Die Engel in der Welt von huete: Gesammelte Aufsätze (Maria Laach: 1960): 89ff. See also Charles A. Gieschen, Angelomorphic Christology: Antecedents & Early Evidence (Boston: Brill, 1998), esp. 187-228.

A List of Church Fathers Who See the Angel as Christ

Shepherd of Hermes (first-second century)
 Similitude 7.5, 8.1.2, 8.1.5.[325]
Justin Martyr (100-165)
 Dialogue with Trypho, 56.1, 58.3, 59.1, 60, 61, 62, 76, 86, 116, 126, 127, 128.
Theophilus of Antioch (late second century)
 To Autolycus 2.22.
Melito (d. 190)
 New Fragments, 15.
Irenaeus (135-202)
 Against Heresies, 3.6.1-5 ; 4.10.1; *Fragments,* 53; *Proof of Apostolic Preaching*
 (44-46).
Clement of Alexandria (150-215)
 The Instructor, 1.7.
Tertullian (155-225)
 Against Praxeas, 16; *On the Flesh of Christ,* 14; *Against Marcion* 2.27, 3.9.6.
Origen (185-254)
 Against Celsus, 5.53, 8.27.
Hippolytus (fl. 222-245)
 Fragments from Commentaries, On Daniel Frag. 25; *Apostolic Tradition* 4.4.
Cyprian (200-258)
 Against the Jews 2.5.
Novatian (fl. 235-258)
 On the Trinity, 18, 19, 31; *Apostolic Constitutions,* 5.3.20.
Letter of the Six Bishops[326] **to Paul of Samosata (aka Letter of Hymenaeus)**
Methodius (d. 311)
 Symposium, 3.4.
Lactantius (260-330)

---

[325] The Shepherd is the oldest of our non-biblical documents. It is saturated with angel language and other terms (Shepherd, The Angel of Repentance, The Angel of Punishment, The Most Revered Angel, The Glorious Angel, etc.) that are clearly Christological at times. But it is an apocalyptic book with difficult symbols and its exact understanding of the Angel of the LORD and Christ can be difficult to nail down. Here are a couple of places to start: Charles A. Gieschen, *Angelomorphic Christology: Antecedents & Early Evidence* (Boston: Brill, 1998), 214-28; Bogdan G. Bucur, "The Son of God and the Angelomorphic Holy Spirit: A Rereading of the Shepherd's Christology," *ZNW* 98 (2007): 120-42.
[326] Hymenaeus, Theophilus, Theotecnus, Maximus, Proclus, and Bolanus. Full Latin and Greek text (Mansi, *Sacrorum Conciliorum Nova et Amplissima Collectio,* Vol. I, pp. 1033-40):
https://babel.hathitrust.org/cgi/pt?id=njp.32101078252002;view=1up;seq=557

The Divine Institutes 4.6.1.

Constantine (d. 337)

Eusebius, *Life of Constantine* 3.52.3.

Eusebius (260-340)

The Proof of the Gospel, 1.5, 4.10, 5.10; *Church History*, 1.2.7-8; *Preparation for the Gospel*, VII. 5, 14-15.

Pseudo-Clementine (third-fourth century)

Rec 1.52.

Hilary of Poitiers (315-367)

On the Trinity 4.25.

Athanasius (325-373)

Against the Arians, 1.38, 2.13, 3.25.12-14.

Cyril of Jerusalem. (313-386)

Catechetical Lectures 12.16.

Gregory of Elvira (fl. 359-85)

On Faith 80; *Tractates on the Books of Holy Scripture* 2.10-11.

Basil the Great (329-379)

Against Eunomius 2.18.

Ambrose (330-397)

Exposition of the Christian Faith, 1.13.83.

Gregory of Nyssa (335-394)

Against Eunomius, 11.3.

Council of Sirmium (351).

Chromatius of Aqueilea (fl. 400)

Sermon on the Washing of the Feet 15.2-3.

Chrysostom (344-407)

Homily on Gen 41.3, 42.2, *Against Theater* 3.

Augustine (354-430)

Jerome (347-420)

Commentary on Daniel 8:15.

Apostolic Constitutions (381-394)

5.20.

Theodoret of Cyrus (393-466)

Questions on the Octateuch Q. 90 on Genesis; Q. 5 On Exodus.

Sozomen (Salminius Hermias Sozomenus) (400-450)

Church Histories 2.4.2-3.

Fulgentius (467-532)

To Monimus, 2.3.3.

Pseudo-Dionysius the Areopagite (5th-6th century)

Corpus Areopagiticum 7-9; *Epistle* 9.1 (1105A)

The Angel in Various Stories According to the Fathers

Adam in the Garden

The God and Father, indeed, cannot be contained, and is not found in a place, for there is no place of His rest; but His Word, through whom He made all things, being His Power and His Wisdom, assuming the role of the Father and Lord of all, went to the garden and conversed with Adam [...]. John says, *"In the beginning was the Word, and the Word was with God"* (John 1:1), showing that at first God was alone, and the Word was in Him. Then he says, *"The Word was God; all things came into existence through Him; and apart from Him not one thing came into existence"* (John 1:1-2). The Word, then, being God, and being naturally produced from God, whenever the Father of the universe wills, He sends Him to any place; and He, coming, is both heard and seen, being sent by Him, and is found in a place.

(Theophilus of Antioch, *To Autolycus* 2.22)

And first, in that which is written in Genesis, *viz.*, that God spoke with man whom He had formed out of the dust; if we set apart the figurative meaning, and treat it so as to place faith in the narrative even in the letter, it should appear that God then spoke with man in the appearance of a man ... For I do not see how such a walking and conversation of God can be understood literally, except He appeared as a man ... Who then was He? Whether the Father, or the Son, or the Holy Spirit? [Augustine seems to think the best option is that it is the Father, but adds] ... possibly, it might be that the Scripture passed over in a hidden way from person to person, and while it had related that the Father said, *"Let there be light,"* and the rest which it mentioned Him to have done by the Word, went on to indicate the Son as speaking to the first man.

(Augustine, *On the Trinity* 2.10)[327]

---

[327] We put Augustine here to let his words speak for themselves. However, it needs to be pointed out that Augustine really changed the discussion on theophanies, inserting into the tradition a "revolutionary proposal" (Bogdan G. Bucur, "Scholarship on the Old Testament Roots of Trinitarian Theology: Blind Spots and Blurred Vision," in *The Bible and Early Trinitarian Theology*, ed. Christopher A. Beely and Mark E. Weedman [Washington, D. C.: The Catholic University of America Press, 2018]: 36-37). What was the proposal? We mentioned it earlier. Essentially, a created angel was "used" by the *Logos*, but was not the *Logos*. "Theophanies may (1) take the form of an angel, or (2) angels may change material bodies to facilitate the theophany, or (3) theophanies may involve a

The LORD First Meets with Abram

[Genesis 12:1]. It is not clear whether a voice alone came to the ears of Abraham, or whether anything also appeared to his eyes. But a little while after, it is somewhat more clearly said, "And the Lord appeared unto Abraham, and said, 'Unto thy seed will I give this land'" (Gen 12:7). But neither there is it expressly said in what form God appeared to him, or whether the Father, or the Son, or the Holy Spirit appeared to him. Unless, perhaps, they think that it was the Son who appeared to Abraham, because it is not written, God appeared to him, but "the Lord appeared to him." For the Son seems to be called the Lord as though the name was appropriated to Him; as *e.g.* the apostle says, "For though there be that are called gods, whether in heaven or in earth, (as there be gods many and lords many,) but to us there is but one God, the Father, of whom are all things, and we in Him; and one Lord Jesus Christ, by whom are all things, and we by Him."

(Augustine, *On the Trinity* 2.10)

Therefore, let it be altogether verified that they are sharers in the divine blessing and participants in the spiritual grace who, it is apparent, are followers of the faith of Abraham in sacrifice. In the book of Genesis we read: "Then the Lord appeared to Abraham and said, 'To your offspring I will give this land.' So he built there an altar to the Lord who had appeared to him. From there he moved on to the hill country

---

purpose-made body that is discarded after use (like the Burning Bush or the Pillar of Fire). Exodus 3:6 involved, Augustine considered, a real created angel. God's presence, however, was really only in him inasmuch as the Angel speaks *ex persona Dei* (III.10.20) (but on the other hand, it may be said the Word of God was in the angelic manifestation on Sinai in the sense that he was present in the Laws and that the theophany anticipated the Incarnation). Fundamentally, the stuff of theophanies was created and then discarded, and thus different from the divine essence ... So, unlike the earlier writers, who saw the angel as a reference to Christ in the form of an angel, Augustine held that the theophany involved both a real created angel and God, who spoke through him. God was not present himself but was impersonated by the angel" (Robert J. Wilkinson, T*etragrammaton: Western Christians and the Hebrew Name of God: From the Beginnings to the Seventeenth Century* [Boston: Brill, 2015], 144). What accounts for this? "Augustine, under the pressure of the Arian controversy and fearing that such identification might lead to the Son being considered a creature, considered the angel merely to *represent* the Son and to speak in his name" (144-145). See also Bogdan G. Bucur, "Augustine on Theophanies: An Orthodox Perspective," St. *Vladimir's Theological Quarterly* 52.1 (2008): 67-93.

on the east of Bethel and pitched his tent with Bethel on the west ...
and there he built an altar to the Lord God and invoked the name of
the Lord God." Now let the heretics choose what they want, that either they confess that the Father was seen by Abraham or certainly
agree that the altar was built by Abraham to the Son. The reading of
the Old Testament frequently indicates that the altar was built for no
other reason than that sacrifice must be offered to God.

(Fulgentius, To Monimus 2.3.3)

The Angel and Hagar

It is the Angel of God Who speaks, and speaks of things far beyond
the powers which a messenger, for that is the meaning of the word,
could have. He says, *I will multiply your seed exceedingly, and it shall
not be numbered for multitude.* The power of multiplying nations lies
outside the ministry of an angel. Yet what says the Scripture of Him
Who is called the Angel of God, yet speaks words which belong to
God alone? *And she called the Name of the Lord that spoke with her, You
are God, Who hast seen me.* First, He is the Angel of God; then He is
the Lord, for *She called the Name of the Lord;* then, thirdly, He is God,
for *You are God, Who hast seen me.* He Who is called the Angel of
God is also Lord and God. The Son of God is also, according to the
prophet, the *Angel of great counsel.*

(Hilary of Poitiers, On the Trinity 4.22)

Abraham and the Three Visitors

And again Moses tells how the Son of God drew near to converse
with Abraham: And God appeared unto him by the oak of Mamre
in the middle of the day. And looking up with his eyes he beheld,
and, lo, three men stood over against him. And he bowed himself
down to the earth, and said: Lord, if indeed I have found favor in
thy sight. And all that which follows he spoke with the Lord, and
the Lord spoke with him. Now two of the three were angels; but one
was the Son of God, with whom also Abraham spoke, pleading on
behalf of the men of Sodom, that they should not perish if at least
ten righteous should be found there. And, while these were speaking, the two angels entered into Sodom, and Lot received them. And
then the Scripture says: And the Lord rained upon Sodom and Gomorrah brimstone and fire from the Lord out of heaven: that is to
say, the Son, who spoke with Abraham, being Lord, received power
to punish the men of Sodom from the Lord out of heaven, even from

the Father who rules over all...

(Irenaeus, Proof of Apostolic Preaching 44)

Angels, after all, are not actually men by nature, but they resemble men in appearance. For example, three persons appeared as men to Abraham at the oak of Mamre (Gen 18:1), and yet they certainly were not men, for one of them was worshipped as the Lord. And so the Savior also stated in the Gospel: "Abraham beheld My day; he beheld it and rejoiced" (John 8:56).[328]

(Jerome, Commentary on Daniel 8:15)

Abraham Sacrifices his Son

While the Father does not serve as anyone's messenger, the Son is both God and "angel of great counsel." It was he who announced to us the mysteries of the Father: "All I have heard from my Father I have revealed to you." Likewise, the one who called out to Abraham is referred to as both "angel" (Gen 22:11) and "God" (Gen 22:1).

(Theodoret, On Genesis Question 5)

It is recorded that here [at Mamre] the Son of God appeared to Abraham with two angels ... then there appeared to the godly man he who in later times showed himself clearly of a virgin for the salvation of the human race.

(Sozomen, Church Histories 2.4.2-3)

Christ appeared to you, O wondrous one, flanked by two angels; and through [your] care for strangers you become a messmate to God and angels. O, blessed tent, which by condescension housed God accompanied by angels! Christ appeared to you in human form, disclosing to you the mystery of the divine advent of himself and [his] salvation."

(Chrysostom, Against Theater 3)

Jacob and His "Ladder"

Now, note that after reporting that an angel had appeared from above, Jacob indicated that this was none other than God himself: "I am God, who appeared to you on the way." He had seen angels ascending and descending the ladder and God set firm at the top,

---

[328] Jerome, *Jerome's Commentary on Daniel*, trans. Gleason L. Archer Jr. (Grand Rapids, MI: Baker Book House, 1958), 87.

whom he here called both "angel" and "God": "God" as to his nature, and "angel" so we would know that it was not the Father who appeared to him but the only-begotten Son.

(Theodoret, *On Genesis* Question 90)

Jacob' Wrestles a Man

No doubt the Almighty Son of GOD could have appeared for the purpose of teaching, and justifying men in exactly the same way that He appeared both to patriarchs and prophets in the semblance of flesh; for instance, when He engaged in a struggle, and entered into conversation (with Jacob), or when He refused not hospitable entertainment, and even partook of the food set before Him.

(Leo the Great, *Letter* 31.2)

Jacob Blesses Joseph

[Note: This passage (Genesis 48:15-16) is the subject of a great deal of an old book by the French Reformer Peter Allix. His treatment of the Angel of the LORD is so masterful that we have reproduced chapters from his book, along with a list of quotations from this text by the Church Fathers, as a companion volume to our own book on the Angel. For more, see *A Dissertation Concerning the Angel Who is Called the Redeemer*, published by Waters of Creation Publishing, 2020. In order to save space, we have only provided a single quotation from Athanasius here].

None of created and natural Angels did [Jacob] join to God their Creator, nor rejecting God that fed him, did he from any Angel ask the blessing on his grandsons; but in saying, 'Who delivered me from all evil,' he showed that it was no created Angel, but the Word of God, whom he joined to the Father in his prayer, through whom, whomsoever He will, God does deliver. For knowing that He is also called the Father's 'Angel of great Counsel,' (Isa 9:6 LXX) he said that none other than He was the Giver of blessing, and Deliverer from evil."

(Athanasius, *Against the Arians* 3.25.12)

Moses and the Burning Bush

Wherefore, as I have already stated, no other is named as God, or is called Lord, except Him who is God and Lord of all, who also said to Moses, "I AM THAT I AM. And thus shalt thou say to the children of Israel: He who is, hath sent me unto you" (Ex 3:14); and His Son Jesus Christ our Lord, who makes those that believe in His name the sons of God. And again, when the Son speaks to Moses, He says, "I am come down to deliver this people" (Ex 3:8).

(Irenaeus, *Against Heresies* 3.6.2)

"*And the Angel of the Lord appeared unto him in a flame of fire, out of the midst of a bush; and he looked, and, behold, the bush burned with fire, and the bush was not consumed. And Moses said, I will now turn aside, and see this great sight, why the bush is not burnt. And when the Lord saw that he turned aside to see, God called unto him out of the midst of the bush, and said, I am the God of thy father, the God of Abraham, the God of Isaac, and the God of Jacob*" (Ex 3:1-6). He is here also first called the Angel of the Lord, and then God. Was an angel, then, the God of Abraham, and the God of Isaac, and the God of Jacob? Therefore He may be rightly understood to be the Saviour Himself, of whom the apostle says, "*Whose are the fathers, and of whom as concerning the flesh Christ came, who is over all, God blessed forever*" (Rom 9:5). He, therefore, "*who is over all, God blessed forever*," is not unreasonably here understood also to be Himself the God of Abraham, the God of Isaac, and the God of Jacob. But why is He previously called the Angel of the Lord, when He appeared in a flame of fire out of the bush? Was it because it was one of many angels, who by an economy [or arrangement] bare the person of his Lord? or was something of the creature assumed by Him in order to bring about a visible appearance for the business in hand, and that words might thence be audibly uttered, whereby the presence of the Lord might be shown, in such way as was fitting, to the corporeal senses of man, by means of the creature made subject? For if he was one of the angels, who could easily affirm whether it was the person of the Son which was imposed upon him to announce, or that of the Holy Spirit, or that of God the Father, or altogether of the Trinity itself, who is the one and only God, in order that he might say, "*I am the God of Abraham, and the God of Isaac, and the God of Jacob?*" For we cannot say that the Son of God is the God of Abraham, and the God of Isaac, and the God of Jacob, and that the Father is not; nor will anyone dare to deny that either the Holy Spirit, or the Trinity itself, whom we believe and understand to be the one God, is the God of Abraham, and the God of Isaac, and the God of Jacob. For he who is not God, is not the God of those fathers. Furthermore, if not only the Father is God, as all, even heretics, admit; but also the Son, which, whether they will or not, they are compelled to acknowledge, since the apostle says, "*Who is over all, God blessed forever;*" and the Holy Spirit, since the same apostle says, "*Therefore glorify God in your body;*" when he had said above, "*Know ye not that your body is the temple of the Holy Ghost, which is in you, which ye have of God?*" (1Co 6:19-20), and these three are one God, as catholic soundness believes: it is not sufficiently apparent which person of the Trinity that angel bare, if he was one of the rest of the angels, and whether any person, and not rather that of the Trinity itself. But if the creature was assumed for the purpose of the business in hand, whereby both to appear to human eyes, and to sound in human ears, and to be called the Angel of the Lord, and the Lord, and God; then cannot God here be understood to be the Father, but either the Son or the Holy Spirit. Although I cannot call to mind that the Holy Spirit is anywhere else called an angel, which yet may be understood from His work; for it is said of Him, "*And He will show you things to come*" (John 16:13); and "angel" in Greek is certainly equivalent to "messenger" in Latin: but we read most evidently of the Lord Jesus Christ in the prophet, that He is called "*the Angel of Great Counsel*" (Isa 9:6), while both the Holy Spirit and the Son of God is God and Lord of the angels.

(Augustine, *On the Trinity* 2.13)[329]

I Send My Angel

And accordingly it is agreed that the Son of God Himself spoke to Moses, and said to the people, "Behold, I send mine angel before thy"—that is, the people's—"face, to guard thee on the march, and

---

[329] We supply this longer excerpt from Augustine in order to demonstrate how he wrestled mightily with the question of whether or not the Angel is the Son. Most scholarship believes he did not ultimately think the Angel was the Son, but the few excerpts we have given in this chapter from him seem to point in the other direction. Whatever the case, the comment by William Shedd here on Augustine are certainly worth pondering. "The theophanies of the Pentateuch are trinitarian in their implication. They involve distinctions in God—God sending, and God sent; God speaking of God, and God speaking to God. The trinitarianism of the Old Testament has been lost sight of to some extent in the modern construction of the doctrine. The patristic, mediæval, and reformation theologies worked this vein with thoroughness, and the analysis of Augustin in this reference is worthy of careful study." W. G. T. Shedd, in Philip Schaff, ed., *St. Augustin: On the Holy Trinity, Doctrinal Treatises, Moral Treatises*, vol. 3, A Select Library of the Nicene and Post-Nicene Fathers of the Christian Church, First Series (Buffalo, NY: Christian Literature Company, 1887), p. 47 n. 3.

to introduce thee into the land which I have prepared thee: attend to him, and be not disobedient to him; for he hath not escaped thy notice, since my name is upon him."

(Tertullian, Against the Jews 9)

Now, as he is also called "angel" we should realize that it was not God the Father who appeared to Moses. After all, is the Father anyone's messenger? Rather, it was the only-begotten Son, 'The angel of the great counsel," he who said to the sacred disciples, "All I have heard from my Father I have revealed to you." As Scripture uses the term "Angel," not to suggest a subordinate minister, but to indicate the person of the Only-begotten, so it goes on to proclaim his nature and authority when it relates that he declared "I am who am," and "I am the God of Abraham, the God of Isaac, and the God of Jacob. This is my everlasting name and memorial for all generations." This indicates his divinity and shows his everlasting eternity.

(Theodoret, Questions on the Octateuch: On Exodus Q.5)

Joshua 5: The Commander of the Hosts

'I shall give you another testimony, my friends,' said I, 'from the Scriptures, that God begat before all creatures a Beginning, [who was] a certain rational power [proceeding] from Himself, who is called by the Holy Spirit, now the Glory of the Lord, now the Son, again Wisdom, again an Angel, then God, and then Lord and Logos; and on another occasion He calls Himself Captain, when He appeared in human form to Joshua the son of Nave (Nun).'

(Justin Martyr, Dialogue 61)

Daniel 3: The Fiery Furnace

He who delivered the Young Men from the flames took flesh and came upon the earth. Nailed to the Cross, he granted us salvation, the God of our fathers, alone blessed and greatly glorified ... The Offspring of the Mother of God saved the innocent Youths in the furnace.

(Romanos the Melodist,
Canon of Holy Cross for Third Sunday in Lent, Ode 7 and
Canon of Akathist, Ode 8, Erimos)[330]

---

[330] Translated in Bogdan G. Bucur, "Christophanic Exegesis and the Problem of Symbolization: Daniel 3 (the Fiery Furnace) as a Test Case," *Journal of Theological Interpretation* 10.2 (Fall 2016): 229.

The Angel in Revelation

[The priest] offers this prayer for Christ's mystical body, which is signified in this sacrament, that the angel standing by at the Divine mysteries may present to God the prayers of both priest and people, according to Rev 8:4: *And the smoke of the incense of the prayers of the saints ascended up before God, from the hand of the angel* ... by the angel we are to understand Christ Himself, Who is the *Angel of great counsel* (Isa 9:6: *LXX*), Who unites His mystical body with God the Father and the Church triumphant.

(Thomas *Summa* III q. 83, a. 4, ad 9)

Various OT Angel Appearances Together

The Son of God is implanted everywhere throughout his writings: at one time, indeed, speaking with Abraham, when about to eat with him; at another time ... bringing down judgment upon the Sodomites; and again when He becomes visible and directs Jacob on his journey, and speaks with Moses from the bush.

(Irenaeus, *Against Heresies* 4.10.1)

He who hung the earth is hanging
He who fixed the heavens in place has been fixed in place
He who laid the foundations of the universe has been laid on a tree...
Today, He who hung the earth upon the waters is hung upon the
    Cross...
He who in the Jordan set Adam free receives blows upon His face...
He who rained manna down on the people in the wilderness is fed
    on milk from His Mother's breast.

(Melito of Sardis, *On Pascha* 96; *Antiphon* 15;
Ninth Hour of the Eve of Nativity: Glory Sticheron)

That Christ is at once Angel and God. In Genesis, to Abraham: "And the Angel of the Lord called him from heaven, and said to him, 'Abraham, Abraham!' And he said, 'Here am I.' And He said, 'Do not lay a hand upon the lad, neither do anything to him. For now I know that you fear God, and have not spared you son, you beloved son, for my sake." Also in the same place, to Jacob: "And the Angel of the Lord spoke to me in dreams, I am God, whom you saw in the place of God where you anointed a pillar of stone to me, and vowed to me a vow." Also in Exodus: "But God went before them by day indeed in a pillar of cloud, to show them the way; and by night in a pillar of fire." And afterwards, in the same place: "And the Angel of God moved forward, which went before the army of the children of Israel." Also in the same place: "Behold, I send my Angel before your face, to keep you in the way, that He may lead you into the land which I have prepared for you. Observe Him, and obey Him, and be not disobedient to Him, for He will not pardon your transgression. For my Name is in Him." As He Himself says in the Gospel: "I came in the name of my Father, and you received me not. But if another shall come in his own name, him you will receive." And again, in the 118th Psalm: "Blessed is He who cometh in the name of the Lord." Also in Malachi: "My covenant of life and peace was with Levi; and I gave him fear, that he should fear me, that he should go from the face of my name. The law of truth was in his mouth, and unrighteousness was not found in his lips. In the peace of the tongue correcting, he walked with us, and turned many away from unrighteousness. Because the lips of the priests shall keep knowledge, and they shall seek the law at His mouth; for He is the Angel of the Almighty."

(Cyprian, *Against the Jews* 2.5).[331]

It is the Son, therefore, who has been from the beginning administering judgment, throwing down the haughty tower, and dividing the tongues, punishing the whole world by the violence of waters, raining upon Sodom and Gomorrah fire and brimstone, as the LORD from the LORD. For He it was who at all times came down to hold converse with men, from Adam on to the patriarchs and the prophets, in vision, in dream, in mirror, in dark saying; ever from the beginning laying the foundation of the course *of His dispensations*, which He meant to follow out to the very last. Thus was He ever learning even as God to converse with men upon earth, being no other than the Word which was to be made flesh. But He was thus learning (or rehearsing), in order to level for us the way of faith, that we might the more readily believe that the Son of God had come down into the world, if we knew that in times past also something similar had been done.

(Tertullian, *Against Praxeas* 16)[332]

---

[331] This work is filled with gems on Christ in the OT.

[332] Foster writes, "Tertullian is extremely reluctant to identify Christ as an angel in the same way that Michael and Gabriel are angels. Additionally, Tertullian explicitly states that Christ is only an angel according to function and not with respect to His substance." Nevertheless, he does apply the term to Christ in his quotation of Isa 9:6 LXX, "Certainly he is described as an angel of great counsel, 'angel' meaning 'messenger', by a term of office, not of nature: for he was to

Was it without reason that Christ was made Man? Are our teachings ingenious phrases and human subtleties? Are not the Holy Scriptures our salvation? Are not the predictions of the Prophets? Keep then, I pray thee, this deposit undisturbed, and let none remove thee: believe that God became Man. But though it has been proved possible for Him to be made Man, yet if the Jews still disbelieve, let us hold this forth to them what strange thing do we announce in saying that God was made Man, when yourselves say that Abraham received the Lord as a guest? What strange thing do we announce, when Jacob says, For I have seen God face to face, and my life is preserved? The Lord, who ate with Abraham, ate also with us.

(Cyril, *Catechetical Lectures* 12.16)

When they assemble together, they read the Lamentations of Jeremiah, in which it is said, "The Spirit before our face, Christ the Lord was taken in their destructions" (Lam 4:20 LXX); and Baruch, in whom it is written, "This is our God; no other shall be esteemed with Him. He found out every way of knowledge, and showed it to Jacob His son, and Israel His beloved. Afterwards He was seen upon earth, and conversed with men" (Baruch 3:25-37) ... To Him did Moses bear witness, and said: "The Lord received fire from the Lord, and rained it down." Him did Jacob see as a man, and said: "I have seen God face to face, and my soul is preserved." Him did Abraham entertain, and acknowledge to be the Judge, and his Lord. Him did Moses see in the bush; concerning Him did he speak in Deuteronomy: "A Prophet will the Lord your God raise up" ... Him did Joshua the son of Nun see, as the captain of the Lord's host, in armor, for their assistance against Jericho; to whom he fell down, and worshipped, as a servant does to his master. Him Samuel knew as the "Anointed of God," and thus named the priests and the kings the anointed. Him David knew, and sung an hymn concerning Him, "A song concerning the Beloved" ... Concerning Him also Solomon spoke, as in His person: "The Lord created me the beginning of His ways, for His works: before the world He founded me, in the beginning before He made the earth, before the fountains of waters came, before the mountains were fastened; He begat me before all the

---

announce to the world the Father's great project, concerned with the restitution of man." Edgar G. Foster, *Angelomorphic Christology and the Exegesis of Psalm 8:5 in Tertullians' Adversus Praxean: An Examination of Tertullian's Reluctance to Attribute Angelic Properties to the Son of God* (New York: University Press of America, Inc., 2005), 7.

hills" … Him Daniel describes as "the Son of man coming to the Father," and receiving all judgment and honor from Him … Ezekiel also, and the following prophets, affirm everywhere that he is the Christ, the Lord, the King, the Judge, the Lawgiver, the Angel of the Father, the only-begotten God. Him therefore do we also preach to you, and declare him to be God the Word, who ministered to his God and Father for the creation of the universe.

(*Apostolic Constitutions* 5.20)

Know then that Christ, who was from the beginning, and always, was ever present with the pious, though secretly, through all their generations; especially those who waited for Him, to whom he frequently appeared.

(Pseudo-Clementines, *Rec* 1.52)

But our Instructor is the holy God Jesus, the Word, who is the guide of all humanity … when He speaks in His own person, He confesses Himself to be the Instructor: *"I am the Lord your God, who brought thee out of the land of Egypt."* Who, then, has the power of leading in and out? Is it not the Instructor? This was He who appeared to Abraham, and said to him, *"I am your God, be accepted before Me;"* and in a way most befitting an instructor, forms him into a faithful child, saying, *"And be blameless; and I will make My covenant between Me and you, and your seed."* There is the communication of the Instructor's friendship. And He most manifestly appears as Jacob's instructor. He says accordingly to him, *"Behold, I am with you, to keep you in all the way in which thou shalt go; and I will bring thee back into this land: for I will not leave you till I do what I have told thee."* He is said, too, to have wrestled with Him. *"And Jacob was left alone, and there wrestled with him a man (the Instructor) till the morning."* This was the man who led, and brought, and wrestled with, and anointed the athlete Jacob against evil. Now that the Word was at once Jacob's trainer and the Instructor of humanity [appears from this]—"He asked," it is said, *"His name, and said to him, Tell me what is your name." And he said, "Why is it that thou ask My name?"* For He reserved the new name for the new people—the babe; and was as yet unnamed, the Lord God not having yet become man. Yet Jacob called the name of the place, *"Face of God." "For I have seen,"* he says, *"God face to face; and my life is preserved"* (Gen 32:30). The face of God is the Word by whom God is manifested and made known. Then also was he named Israel, because he saw God the Lord. It was God, the Word, the

Instructor, who said to him again afterwards, *"Fear not to go down into Egypt."* See how the Instructor follows the righteous man, and how He anoints the athlete, teaching him to trip up his antagonist.

It is He also who teaches Moses to act as instructor. For the Lord says, *"If any one sin before Me, him will I blot out of My book; but now, go and lead this people into the place which I told thee."* Here He is the teacher of the art of instruction. For it was really the Lord that was the instructor of the ancient people by Moses; but He is the instructor of the new people by Himself, face to face. *"For behold,"* He says to Moses, *"My angel shall go before you,"* representing the evangelical and commanding power of the Word, but guarding the Lord's prerogative. *"In the day on which I will visit them,"* He says, *"I will bring their sins on them; that is, on the day on which I will sit as judge I will render the recompense of their sins."* For the same who is Instructor is judge, and judges those who disobey Him; and the loving Word will not pass over their transgression in silence. He reproves, that they may repent.[333]

(Clement of Alexandria, *The Instructor* 1.7)

Who is eager for distinction in piety in this way? Who has made as great a show of being a lover of Christ as these men have, even though they boast of their arrogant and dishonorable words that go so far as to destroy the glory of the Only-Begotten? You godless man! Please stop saying that he does not exist when he is the one who truly exists, the one who is the source of life, and the one who produces being for all that exists. Didn't he find a designation well-suited for himself and fitting for his own eternity when he named himself *He Who Is* in his oracle to Moses his servant? He said: *I am He Who Is.* No one will object when I say that these words were spoken in the person of the Lord, at least no one who does not have *the veil* of the Jews upon his heart *when he reads Moses* (2Co 3:15). It is written that the angel of the Lord appeared to Moses in the bush burning with fire. After mentioning the angel at the outset of the narrative, scripture introduces the voice of God when it says that he said to Moses: *I am the God of your father Abraham.* A little further on, the same one said: *I am He Who Is.* So, then, who is this one who is both angel and God alike? Isn't it he whom we have learned is called by the name *the angel of great counsel* (Is 9:6)?

---

[333] A good resource for Clement's view of Christ in the OT is Bogdan G. Bucur, "Clement of Alexandria's Exegesis of Old Testament Theophanies," *Phronema* 29:1 (2014): 61-79.

For my part, I don't think that this needs much demonstration; just mentioning it suffices for the lovers of Christ. But the incorrigible are not going to derive any benefit from a flurry of words. Even though *the angel of great counsel* comes later, it remains true that previously he did not disdain the designation 'angel.' You see, it is not only in this passage that we find the scriptures naming our Lord both 'angel' and 'God.' For when Jacob narrated an appearance to his wives, he said: *And the angel of God said to me* (Gn 31:11). And a little further on, it was said: *I am the God who appeared to you in the place where you anointed a pillar to me*. In addition, it was said to Jacob as he stood before the pillar: *I am the Lord, the God of Abraham your father and the God of Isaac* (Gn 28:13). The one who is called 'angel' in the former passage is the same as the one who said in the latter passage that he appeared to Jacob. So, then, it is clear to all that, where the same one is designated both 'angel' and 'God,' it is the Only-Begotten who is revealed, manifesting himself to human beings from generation to generation and announcing the will of the Father to his saints. Consequently, when he named himself *He Who Is* before Moses, he is understood to be none other than God the Word, who *was in the beginning with God* (Jn 1:2).

(Basil, *Against Eumonius* 2.18)

We will conclude this chapter with a thought about the heretics and perhaps one reason why some Christians are hesitant to link the Angel of the LORD with Christ. Without question, this is a topic little discussed today in most places. This may be a reason why the old heresies are still around today in groups like the Jehovah's Witnesses.

The Witnesses say that the Angel of the LORD is both Michael and Christ (a view also within mainstream orthodoxy from the beginning through today). Their deficiency is that they believe he is a *created* being rather than the eternally begotten Son of God. This idea has been around for at least 1,700 years in their predecessors the Arians. Because of the Arians and the Council of Nicaea (325), which was gathered to address it, the earlier freedom of citing the Angel as proof of Christ's pre-existence began to wane somewhat (though, as you can see from the extensive list of Fathers after Nicaea, it certainly never went away). Gieschen explains,

Unlike many of Arius' predecessors who used angel traditions to support Christ's pre-existence and divinity, he used them to argue for the created and subordinate aspect of the Son. In other words, traditions and texts that had been used to express a preexistent creator Christology were now being employed to assert a subordinate first-created Christology. This association with Arianism, through the emphasis on Christ having the created nature of an angel, is a primary reason that overt angel traditions no longer played a major part in Christological discussions after Nicaea."[334]

We should not let fear of heretics or their abuse and misuse of biblical texts keep us from employing their true and right meaning simply to avoid sounding like them. Rather, we believe we should take back the Scriptures from them and use them in the way that God intended them to be used, even as they were being used so prevalently as the *Letter of Six Bishops to Paul of Samosata* demonstrate, which led to the pre-ecumenical synods of Antioch seventy-five years earlier.

---

[334] Gieschen, 188.

1 8

THE ANGEL IN THE REFORMATION

The Angel and Historical Theology
Part III

Reforming but Keeping

THE PROTESTANT REFORMERS VIEWED THEMSELVES as seeking to recover the theology and practice of the early church, going back to the Church Fathers in order to reform later innovations and doctrines that had crept in and were detrimental to God's people. Since this is true, we would expect to find the Reformers and their heirs either uniformly rejecting the Angel as Christ theology as later novelties that had little to nothing to do with the Scripture (like they did so many of Rome's innovations), or else find them simply reflecting and utilizing it as helpful to our understanding of Jesus Christ. In fact, as we have already shown in quotations throughout this book, we find many of the Reformers as very supportive of the Angel-Christ interpretation. In this chapter, we will discuss briefly two key figures who utilized this tradition, and then give a survey of quotations from other Reformation figures. We certainly cannot be exhaustive. Our hope is simply to impress upon you the consensus over the identity of the Angel that has existed from the earliest times unbroken through today. If this third piece of the historical puzzle fits with the other two, then it is safe to say this theology must find its way back into the church in our day.

Two Key Figures

The Among the 17th-century Reformers, we have found three figures whose treatments of the Angel of the Lord stand out for their insight and clarity. In fact, all three men were very familiar with the Jewish Two Powers hermeneutic that we have discussed in this book. They
are each adamant that the Person and revelatory activity of the Son of
God was clearly revealed in the Old Testament and was known to the
Jews. We regard their work as so important that we have published parts
of their work in four volumes as companions to this book.[335] Since De
Gols overlaps so well with Allix, and for sake of brevity, we will only
look at Owen and Allix here.

John Owen

John Owen is a well-known theological giant of the Reformation,
a prolific writer, church leader, and professor among the English Non-
conformists until his death in 1683. One of Owen's best-known works
is his vast and exhaustive commentary on the Book of Hebrews. Despite
its popularity and likely due to its size, many are not familiar with
Owen's lengthy discussion of Christ in the Old Testament in Exercitation 10 of the commentary. An "exercitation" was a kind of preliminary
guide to understanding various aspects of the book of Hebrews. From
the beginning, Owen writes that Christ was revealed

> Through those visions and appearances of the Son of God…which
> were graciously given to the fathers under the Old Testament. These
> [instances]…are also eminently useful for the conviction of the Jews.
> For in them we shall demonstrate that a revelation was made of a
> distinct person in the Godhead, who in a peculiar manner managed

---

[335] John Owen, *Appearances of the Son of God in the Old Testament*, Christ in All
Scripture Series Book 1, ed. Douglas Van Dorn (Dacono, CO: Waters of Creation,
2019); Peter Allix, *A Dissertation Concerning the Angel Who is Called the Redeemer*,
Christ in All Scripture Series Book 2, ed. Douglas Van Dorn (Dacono, CO: Waters
of Creation, 2020); Gerard De Gols, *The Worship of the Lord Jesus in the Old Testament*, Christ in All Scripture Series Book 3, ed. Douglas Van Dorn (Dacono, CO:
Waters of Creation, 2020); Owen, Allix, De Gols, *The Angel of Yahweh in Jewish
and Reformation History*, Christ in All Scripture Series Book 4, ed. Douglas Van
Dorn (Dacono, CO: Waters of Creation, 2020).

all the matters of importance in the church after the entrance of sin. Here, also, according to our proposed method, we will inquire into what light was given regarding this truth that was then received by any of the Jewish masters, who also aptly demonstrate what confusion they are driven to, when they seek to evade the evidence that is in their own ancient writings.[336]

In fact, Owen explores some of the same texts we have explored in this book, coming to the same conclusions we have. He writes,

> By all these things the church was instructed in the person, nature, and office of the Son of God, even in the mystery of his eternal distinct subsistence in the Godhead, his future incarnation and condescension to the office of being the Head and Savior of his church... These manifestations of the Son of God to the church of old, as the angel or messenger of the Father, existing in his own divine person, are each of them *revelations* of the promised Seed, the great and only Savior and Deliverer of the church, in his eternal pre-existence prior to his incarnation; and *pledges* of his future taking our flesh for the accomplishment of all the word committed to him by the Father.[337]

Owen shows a wide knowledge of Jewish sources and traditions, quoting extensively from Philo and numerous other Jewish sources to show that a multiplicity in the Godhead and in the revelation of God was known in the Old Testament prior to Christianity. Consider his citation of the following Jewish writer:

One chief example of this, in the words of Moses Nachmanides Gerundensis, on Exodus 23, which has been taken notice of by many, shall suffice. His words are, "This Angel, if we speak exactly, is the Angel Redeemer, concerning whom it is written, 'My name is in him' (Ex 23:21); that Angel who said unto Jacob, 'I am the God of Bethel' (Gen 31:13); he of whom it is said, 'And God called unto Moses out of the bush' (Ex 3:4). And he is called an Angel because he governs the world: for it is written (Dt 6:21), 'The LORD brought

---

[336] John Owen, *An Exposition of the Epistle to the Hebrews*, ed. W. H. Goold, vol. 18, Works of John Owen (Edinburgh: Johnstone and Hunter, 1854), 216. The following citations are our shortening and modernizing of the original passages.
[337] Ibid., 229.

us out of Egypt'; and elsewhere (Num 20:16), 'He sent his Angel, and brought us out of Egypt.' Moreover, it is written (Isa 63:9), 'And the Angel of his face (presence) saved them,'—namely, that Angel who is the face of God; of whom it is said (Ex 33:14), 'My face shall go before you, and I will cause you to rest.' Lastly, it is that Angel of whom the prophet speaks (Mal 3:1), 'And the Lord, whom you seek, shall suddenly come to his temple, the Angel of the covenant, in whom you delight.'" His following words are to the same purpose: "Mark diligently what the meaning is of these words, 'My face shall go before you'; for Moses and the Israelites always desired the chief Angel, but who that was they could not truly understand, for neither could they learn it of any others nor obtain it by prophecy. But the 'face of God' signifies God himself, as all interpreters acknowledge. But no man can have the least knowledge of this unless he is skilled in the mysteries of the law." He adds moreover: "'My face shall go before you,' that is, 'the Angel of the covenant, whom you desire, in whom my face shall be seen'; of whom it is said, 'In an acceptable time have I heard you; my name is in him; I will cause you to rest, or cause that he shall be gentle or kind to you, nor shall lead you with rigor, but quietly and mercifully.'[338]

For those who would disagree with his conclusions, Owen is very strong: "Some of late interpreters would apply all these appearances to a created delegated angel. The conceit of this is irreconcilable with the sacred text, as we have already shown, and it is contrary to the sense of the ancient writers of the Christian church."[339] Earlier he says, "This is an invention crafted to evade the appearances of the Son of God in the Old Testament. It is against the interpretation of all antiquity. And it is contrary to any reason or instance produced to make it good."[340]

Peter Allix

Less well-known than John Owen, but certainly not less well-read, is the French Huguenot scholar Pierre (Peter) Allix. Allix was one of the leading Hebrew and Syriac scholars of the late 17th and early 18th

---

[338] Ibid., 230-31.
[339] Ibid., 229.
[340] Ibid., 221.

centuries. His knowledge of the ancient Jewish texts and writings was encyclopedic and astounding. (We consider him the Alan Segal before Alan Segal!) In fact, Allix wrote the most extensive treatment of the Angel of the Lord as Divine up to this point in history, in a work called *The Judgment of the Ancient Jewish Church Against The Unitarians in the Controversy Upon the Holy Trinity and the Divinity of Our Blessed Savior.*

In the late 17th century, a group of Millenarian and anti-Trinitarian sects threatened the church. Some were fascinated by the Jewish Talmud and other writings and were using the writings of the Jews themselves to deny the Trinity and to argue for a return to a so-called truly Jewish Christianity. Allix, as an expert on many of these writings himself, wrote to show that the writings of the Jews after Christianity were unreliable, but that the pre-Christian Jewish writings actually denied Unitarianism and supported a Trinitarian understanding. One historian summarizing Allix writes,

> By accepting a pre-Christian, Trinitarian oral law as authentic, Allix turns the rabbinical tradition from a source of antagonism for Christianity into an important 'proof' that the ancient Jews were Trinitarians... Some bits of the 'real' oral tradition have not been erased by the later Jews, and these can particularly be found in the oldest sources: Philo, The Apocrypha, the Chaldee Paraphrases, an occasional Midrash (of which the Tanchumah is one), and the Kabbalah. A careful search through these works reveals that the Jews formerly believed in a Trinity and a Christ who would arrive at the end of the Temple period. He would be the Son of God, the Word, and the Demiurge which Trinitarians had always detected at work in the Old Testament... The Jews had formerly believed in a Word which was a distinct person in the godhead, identical to the appearance of God and the Angel of the Lord found in the Old Testament. This Word, or *Logos*, was the same as the divine Name Yahweh of the Bible, and had been taken by the ancient Jews as identical to the messiah, who would be incarnated as the Son of God. The first Christians, as we find them in the New Testament, clearly believed and spoke in accordance with these same conceptions.[341]

---

[341] Matt Goldish, "The Battle for 'True' Jewish Christianity: Peter Allix's Polemics Against the Unitarians and Millenarians," in *Everything Connects: In Conference with Richard H. Popkin*, Brill's Studies in Intellectual History Online 91, ed. James E. Force and David S. Katz (Boston: Brill, 1999), 143-162.

Allix himself writes,

> I scruple not to assert that the ancient Christians ascribed all the appearances of God in Moses' writings to the eternal *Logos*, having the following authorities for my assertion. Justin Martyr, *Against Trypho*; Clement of Alexandria, *The Instructor* 1.7; Tertullian, *Against the Jews* 9; Origen, *On Isaiah* 6; Cyprian, *Against the Jews* 2.5; *Apostolic Constitutions*; Eusebius, *Church History* 1.3; Cyril, *Catechetical Lectures* 12.16; *The Council of Sirmium* (351), Canon 13; Gregory of Elvira, *On Faith*; Theodoret of Cyrus, *Questions on Exodus* 5; Leo, *Letter 31 to Pulcheria*, and many others. In like manner they refer to the Word those appearances of God, which he vouchsafed to Abraham, Isaac, and Jacob himself, as you may see in Justin Martyr, *Apology*, for those to Abraham and Isaac; and for those to Jacob, in Clement of Alexandria, *The Instructor* 1.7; Novatian, *On the Trinity* 26, 27; Procopius of Gaza in h. 1.
>
> The ancient Christians did in this no more than the ancienter Jews did before them, who by *Elohim* in this place did not understand a created angel, but the *Logos*, whom the Targumists and the strictest followers of their fathers' traditions are wont to express by the *Shekinah* (Glory) and the *Memra* (Word).[342]

Allix goes on in his book to explore and substantiate these conclusions, with exegesis of Scripture and extensive discussion of extrabiblical sources. For those interested, we encourage you to check out our companion volume.

The Angel in Various Stories in the Reformers

Now we return to our survey of church history, looking at other Reformers, Puritans, and Protestant Divines to show their support for identifying Christ as the Angel of the LORD.

Note: We have updated the language and punctuation from many of these earlier titles for ease of reading and harmony with the style of this book.

---

[342] Peter Allix, "A Dissertation Concerning the Angel," in *The Judgment of the Ancient Jewish Church Against the Unitarians* (London: R. Chiswell, 1699), 438-439.

Adam in the Garden

It is generally agreed among Divines, that Adam in the State of Perfection knew God in Trinity and Unity ... Jerome Zanchi thinks it very injurious to Adam, to believe that he had not as great favor shown him before the Fall, as Abraham, Moses, and others had since the Fall; and thereupon asserts, that Adam being then to be sure the beloved of God, Jehovah the Son exhibited himself visibly to him, and talked with him, and made himself known to him, as his God and Governor, before he gave him the precepts of obedience, as he did to the Jews, before he gave the law to Moses. And he tells us, that several of the ancients, Justin, Irenaeus, Tertullian, [Epiphanius], and many more, were of that mind, that it was Jehovah the Son who created Adam, placed him in Paradise, appeared visibly to him, discoursed with him, and whose voice he heard, and at which he trembled when he had transgressed.

Jerome Zanchi (1516-1590)[343]

Noah and Babel

When Jehovah saw the earth, it was corrupt; for all flesh had corrupted its way upon the earth. And this wickedness became so great ... in the days of Noah; it repented Jehovah that he had made man; and it grieved him to the heart. So, after having given warning by his preacher of righteousness for 120 years, till eight persons only were left uncorrupted, he destroyed that obstinate and impenitent generation; just time enough to save one family ... And from the Mosaic account of this Jehovah, that the sins of mankind grieved him to the heart, agreeable to what is said of him in other parts of Scripture; and from his making a covenant with Noah, we have reason to conclude; that it was not the Supreme Jehovah in Person, but the Angel of the Covenant.

After this all men lived together in Chaldea ... Jehovah (that is, Christ, the Jehovah Angel) came down to see the city and Tower (Gen 11:4), which the children of men built; and, in order to restrain them from their undertaking, he confounded their language; and scattered them abroad upon the face of all the earth.

Henry Taylor (1711-1785)[344]

---

[343] Zanchi, *de creat.* 1.I.c.i.§12. As discussed in Gerard De Gols, *A Vindication of the Worship of the Lord Jesus Christ as the Supreme God* (London: J. Darby and T. Browne, 1726), 115-116.
[344] Henry Taylor, *The Apology of Benjamin Ben Mordecai To His Friends, for Embracing Christianity* (London: J. Wilkie, 1771), 59-60. Taylor was not entirely orthodox, but you can find the same general idea in people like De Gols, 105.

Hagar

That God might make evident the exceeding care he had of them, he sent an Angel to Hagar, and willed her to return unto her Master: which Angel, some think was the Son of God, for he was called by the name of Jehovah (Gen 16) which name was not communicated to any created Angel.

Heinrich Bünting (1545-1606)[345]

Abraham

When Abraham believed ... God is so well pleased with his faith, that he swears ... *"I will bless you, and I will multiply your seed as the stars of the heaven, and as the sand which is upon the sea-shore"* (Gen 22:17). And the angel of the Lord, (viz. the Lord Jesus, as his own words show, vs. 12, 15, 16.) calls unto Abraham out of heaven and shows his admirable love in providing a ram for a burnt-offering. Thus, in believing times, the Lord reveals his love to his people.

Thomas Brooks (1608-1680)[346]

Jacob's ladder

Whosoever is assured of this Ladder (that reaches from Heaven to Earth) may well say with *Jacob*, 'Surely the Lord Jesus Christ is in this place;' here is nothing but the House of God, and here is the Gate of Heaven; as Christ himself testifies in the tenth of John, *I am the door, and whosoever enters not by me, &c.* So that Christ is the Head of his Church, the Ladder that ascends into Heaven, and the door whereby we may enter into eternal Life.

Heinrich Bünting (1545-1606)[347]

Jacob Blesses Joseph: Gen 48:15-16

The Angel which redeemed me ... Many of the ancient Fathers (as Athanasius L. IV. *Contra Arianos*, Cyril upon this place; Procopius Gazeus, etc.)

---

[345] Heinrich Bünting, Itinerarium totius Sacræ Scripturæ, or, The Travels of the Holy Patriarchs, Prophets, Judges, Kings, our Saviour Christ and his Apostles ... Collected Out of the Works of Henry Bunting; and done into English by R.B. (London, J. Harefinch for T. Basset, 1682), 67. Because Bünting only alludes to his view here, we have offered another quotation from him a little later.
[346] Thomas Brooks, *A Treatise on Assurance, A New Edition Considerably Amended and Abridged* (London: J. Mathews, and J. Buckland 1778), 69-70.
[347] Bünting, 73.

[348] understand this as an uncreated Angel, viz. the Second Person of the blessed Trinity. *"But the Discourse is not concerning the sending of the Son of God, in our Flesh to redeem Mankind ... and I do not know whether it be safe to call him an Angel, i.e. a Minister, or Messenger, lest we detract from his Divinity. For in conferring Blessings, he is not a Messenger or Minister, but a principle Cause together with the Father."* These are the words of that famous Divine Georg. Calixtus, who follows St. Chrysostom, who takes this angel to be one properly so called: And thus proves the heavenly Ministers take care of Pious People. And so does St. Basil in no less than three places of his Works: Which show it was his settled opinion. But it did not enter into their thoughts that Jacob here might have the angelic protection, by the special Favor of God to them. For it is just such an expression as that of David, to a contrary purpose (Ps 35:6).

Simon Patrick (1626-1707)[349]

The Burning Bush: Exodus 3

And the Angel of the Lord appeared to him ... For thus we must believe that God, as often as he appeared of old to the holy patriarchs, descended in some way from his majesty, that he might reveal himself as far as was useful, and as far as their comprehension would admit ... But let us inquire who this Angel was, since soon afterwards he not only calls himself Jehovah, but claims the glory of the eternal and only God. Now, although this is an allowable manner of speaking, because the angels transfer to themselves the person and titles of God ... the ancient teachers of the Church have rightly understood that the Eternal Son of God is so called in respect to his office as Mediator, which he figuratively bore from the beginning, although he really took it upon him only at his Incarnation. And Paul sufficiently expounds this mystery to us, when he plainly asserts that Christ was the leader of his people in the Desert (1Co 10:4).[350]

John Calvin (1509-1564)

---

[348] As we pointed out with the Fathers on this passage, we have included dozens of quotations on it in our supplemental book. We will only offer one here.

[349] Simon Patrick, *A Commentary upon the First Book of Moses, Called Genesis* (London: Chitwell, 1689), 596-97.

[350] Calvin, *Harmony of the Four Last Books of Moses*, Exod. 3:2 in loc. (CTS Harmony, I, pp. 60–61). Cited in Richard A. Muller, *Post-Reformation Reformed Dogmatics: The Rise and Development of Reformed Orthodoxy; Volume 4: The Triunity of God* (Grand Rapids, MI: Baker Academic, 2003), 291–292.

To this Angel is given the essential name of God: Jehovah. Therefore, it is certain that he also was God, even our Savior Christ, by whom and through whom the Lord communicates himself unto men, who otherwise could never have any access unto such Majesty. And he is called an Angel, because he was to be sent to be our Deliverer, whereof this Deliverance of the Jews out of Egypt was some shadow and figure. Theodoret is of the same mind, whose words are these [in Latin] … The whole place, he says, shows it was God: but he is called an Angel, that we might know, that he which was seen, was not God the Father (for whose Angel should the Father be) but the only begotten Son of God, which is the Angel of the great Council, which said to his holy Apostles; *All things which I have heard of my Father, I have declared unto you.* And even as he gave him the name of an Angel, not meaning thereby to note any other Minister or Messenger, but to show the person of the only begotten Son: so again he sets forth both his nature & power, saying he said: I AM THAT I AM, and I the God of Abraham, the God of Isaac, the God of Jacob, etc. Hillarie also speaks to this effect in his book on the Trinity.

Gervase Babington (1550-1610)[351]

Gideon

That Gideon worshipped Christ as God, is so plain, that anyone that reads Judges the 6th chapter must believe it, or must believe that Gideon was an idolater; for as vs. 12 we find that *"the Angel of the Lord appeared to him, and said to him, 'The Lord is with you, you mighty man of valor.'"* And it appears in vs. 13 that Gideon thought it was a created angel; but vs. 14 the Lord, the Jehovah, looked upon him, convinced him that he was not a created Angel, and commissioned him to be a judge and a deliverer of Israel. Here we have still the same person speaking first as an Angel, now as the Jehovah, and assuring him of his Presence, *"I will be with you,"* in the same manner as he had done to the Patriarchs before; and when Gideon had asked for a token of his Presence, and the Angel had wrought a miracle, and then departed from him, Gideon said, *"Alas, O Lord God!"* which was not an exclamation through fear or surprise, but was a recognition of his Divinity, and an act of Adoration paid to the divine Majesty.

Gerard De Gols (d. 1737)[352]

---

[351] Gervase Babington (1550-1610), *The Workes of the Right Reverend Father in God Gervase Babington, late Bishop of Worcester. Containing Comfortable Notes Upon the Five Bookes of Moses* (London, George Eld, 1615), 214-15.
[352] Gerard De Gols, *A Vindication of the Worship of the Lord Jesus Christ as the Supreme God* (London: J. Darby and T. Browne, 1726).

Samson's Birth: Judges 13

The glad tidings brought to his mother, that she should have a son. The messenger was an *angel of the Lord* (v. 3), yet appearing as a man, with the aspect and garb of a prophet, or man of God. And this angel (as the learned bishop Patrick supposes, on v. 18) was the Lord himself, that is, the *Word of the Lord*, who was to be the Messiah, for his name is called *Wonderful*.

Matthew Henry (1662-1714)[353]

And the angel of the LORD said to him, Why do you ask my name, seeing it *is* secret? Or, *hidden* from mortal men; or, *wonderful*, such as you cannot comprehend; my nature or essence (which is often signified by *name* in Scripture) is incomprehensible. This shows that this was the Angel of the covenant, the Son of God.

Matthew Poole (1624-1679)[354]

General Comments

Where the Person [in an OT passage] does not clearly identify itself by speaking and apparently only one Person is involved, you may follow the rule given above and be assured that you are not going wrong when you interpret the name Jehovah to refer to our Lord Jesus Christ, God's Son.

Martin Luther (1483 – 1546)[355]

Moreover, their inclination to think that in various of those *Apparitions of Angels* to the ancient *Patriarchs*, it was *Christ* himself that

---

[353] Matthew Henry, *Matthew Henry's Commentary on the Whole Bible: Complete and Unabridged in One Volume* (Peabody: Hendrickson, 1994), 356.
[354] Matthew Poole, *Annotations upon the Holy Bible*, vol. 1 (New York: Robert Carter and Brothers, 1853), 488.
[355] Martin Luther, *Luther's Works, Vol. 15: Ecclesiastes, Song of Solomon, Last Words of David, 2 Samuel 23:1-7*, ed. Jaroslav Jan Pelikan, Hilton C. Oswald, and Helmut T. Lehmann, vol. 15 (Saint Louis: Concordia Publishing House, 1999), 336. While Luther's quotation occurs in the middle of a barrage of OT passages, some of which he argues proves his point here, Gieshen explains, "Luther did not invent this understanding; it is found in the New Testament. There are Old Testament texts where YHWH is speaking that are applied to the Son by New Testmaent writers." For example, he cites Isa 45:23-24 cited in Php 2:10-11 and Rom 14:11 or Jer 9:24 cited in 1Co 1:31 and 2Co 10:17 or Zech 12:10 cited in John 19:37. Charles A. Gieschen, "The Real Presence of the Son Before Christ: Revisiting an Old Approach to Old Testament Christology," *Concordia Theological Quarterly* 68:2 (April 2004): 124-25.

appeared, would further have enticed them to retain this Doctrine of Preexistence of Souls, that that opinion of Christ's appearing then might be more entire and determinate; as it would be also in those that hold *Melchizedek* that blessed *Abraham* to have been *Christ:* which opinion *Cunaeus* looks upon as true; nor can *Calvin* look upon it as *strange*, if he does but hold to his own words in his readings upon *Daniel* ... And that the *Angel* that led the Israelites into the land of *Canaan* was *Christ*, seems plainly asserted 1Co 10:9. *Neither let us tempt Christ, as some of them tempted him, and perished by Serpents.* But Christ is a complexion of the Human nature with the Divine. Consider also Heb 11:26 which seems to imply that the Soul of the *Messiah* was a Patron and Protector of the *Holy seed* betimes, and had a special relation to the *Jews* above any other Nation. And therefore when he came into the world (i.e. was born, brought up and conversed among the Jews), he might the more properly be said to come to *his own*, though his own knew him not (Jn 1:11).

Henry More (1614-1687)[356]

Q. 20. *How was the will of God made known to the church, before it was committed to writing?*
A. By immediate revelations, Gen 2:16, 17, and 3:15; by frequent appearances of the Son of God, delighting, beforehand, to try on the human likeness, Gen 18:2, compared with vs. 3, Jdg 13:11, compared with verses 18, 19; by the ministry of the holy angels, Gen 19:1, 15; Heb 2:2, and of the patriarchs, Jude, vs. 14, 15; Heb 11:7.

Ebenezer Erskine (1680-1754) [357]

It is observable, that when Christ appeared to manage the affairs of his church in this period, he often appeared in the form of that nature which he took upon him in his incarnation. So he seems to have appeared repeatedly to Moses, and particularly at that time when God spoke to him face to face, as a man speaks to his friend, and he beheld the similitude of the Lord (Num 12:8), after he had besought him to show him his glory; which was the most remarkable vision that ever

---

[356] Henry More, An explanation of the grand mystery of godliness, or, A true and faithfull representation of the everlasting Gospel of our Lord and Saviour Jesus Christ, the only begotten Son of God and sovereign over men and angels (London, J. Flesher for W. Morden, 1660), 22-23.
[357] Ebenezer Erskine and James Fisher, *The Assembly's Shorter Catechism Explained By Way of Question and Answer* (Edinburgh: John Gray and Gavin Alston: MDCCLXV). Q. 2.20.

he had of Christ. There was a twofold discovery that Moses had of Christ: one was spiritual, ... another was external; which was that which Moses saw, when Christ passed by, and put him in a cleft of the rock. What he saw was doubtless a glorious human form, in which Christ appeared to him, and in all likelihood the form of his glorified human nature, in which he should afterwards appear. He saw not his face; for it is not to be supposed that any man could subsist under a sight of the glory of Christ's human nature as it now appears.

So it was a human form in which Christ appeared to the seventy elders, of which we have an account (Ex 24:9, 11). *"Then Moses and Aaron went up, Nadab and Abihu, and seventy of the elders of Israel. And they saw the God of Israel: and there was under his feet, as it were a paved work of sapphire-stone, and as it were the body of heaven in his clearness. And upon the nobles of the children of Israel he did not lay his hand: also they saw God, and ate and drank."* So Christ appeared afterwards to Joshua in the form of the human nature (Josh 5:13, 14). *"And it came to pass when Joshua was by Jericho, he lift up his eyes, and looked, and behold, there stood a man over against him, with his sword drawn in his hand: and Joshua went to him, and said to him, 'Are you for us, or for our adversaries?' And he said, 'No, but as captain of the host of the Lord am I now come.'"* And so he appeared to Gideon (Jdg 6:11ff). and so also to Manoah (Jdg 13:17–21). Here Christ appeared to Manoah in a representation both of his incarnation and death; of his incarnation, in that he appeared in a human form; and of his death and sufferings, represented by the sacrifice of a kid, and by his ascending up in the flame of the sacrifice; intimating, that it was he that was the great sacrifice, that must be offered up to God for a sweet savor, in the fire of his wrath, as that kid was burned and ascended up in the flame. *Thus Christ appeared, time after time, in the form of that nature he was afterwards to assume; because he now appeared on the same design and to carry on the same work.*

Jonathan Edwards (1703-1758)[358]

All the divine appearances of the ancient economy are referred to *one person.*—Compare Gen. 18:2, 17; 28:13; 32:9, 31; Ex. 3:14, 15; 13:21; 20:1, 2; 25:21; Deut. 4:33, 36, 39; Neh. 9:7–28. This one person is called Jehovah, the incommunicable name of God, and at the same time *angel,* or *one sent.*—Compare Gen. 31:11, 13; 48:15, 16;

---

[358] Jonathan Edwards, "A History of the Work of Redemption," in *The Works of Jonathan Edwards,* vol. 1 (Banner of Truth Trust, 1974), 551.

Hosea 12:2, 5. Compare Ex. 3:14, 15, with Acts 7:30–35; and Ex. 13:21, with Ex. 14:19; and Ex. 20:1, 2, with Acts 7:38; Isa. 63:7, 9. But God the Father has been seen by no man (John 1:18; 6:46): neither could he be an angel, or one sent by any other; yet God the Son has been seen (1 John 1:1, 2), and sent (John 5:36).

A. A. Hodge (1823-1886)[359]

(a) The angel of Jehovah identifies himself with Jehovah; (b) he is identified with Jehovah by others; (c) he accepts worship due only to God. Though the phrase "angel of Jehovah" is sometimes used in the later Scriptures to denote a merely human messenger or created angel, it seems in the Old Testament, with hardly more than a single exception, to designate the pre-incarnate Logos, whose manifestations in angelic or human form foreshadowed his final coming in the flesh. (a) Gen. 22:11, 16—"the angel of Jehovah called unto him [Abraham, when about to sacrifice Isaac]… By myself have I sworn, with Jehovah"; 31:11, 13—"the angel of God said unto me [Jacob]…. I am the God of Beth-el." (b) Gen. 16:9, 13—"angel of Jehovah said unto her … and she called the name of Jehovah that spoke unto her, You are a God who sees"; 48:15, 16—"the God who fed me … the angel who hath redeemed me."

Augustus Strong (1836-1921)[360]

It is another question, however, whether there may not exist in the pages of the Old Testament turns of expression or records of occurrences in which one already acquainted with the doctrine of the Trinity may fairly see indications of an underlying implication of it. The older writers discovered intimations of the Trinity in such phenomena as the plural form of the Divine name *Ĕlōhīm*, the occasional employment with reference to God of plural pronouns ("Let us make man in our image," Gen. 1:26; 3:22; 11:7; Isa. 6:8), or of plural verbs (Gen. 20:13; 35:7), certain repetitions of the name of God which seem to distinguish between God and God (Ps. 45:6, 7; 105:1; Hos. 1:7), threefold liturgical formulas Num. 6:24, 26; Isa. 6:3), a certain tendency to hypostatize the conception of Wisdom (Prov. 8), and especially the remarkable phenomena connected with the appearances of the Angel of Jehovah (Gen. 16:2–13, 22:11, 16; 31:11, 13; 48:15, 16; Ex. 3:2, 4, 5;

---

[359] A. A. Hodge, *Outlines of Theology: Rewritten and Enlarged* (New York: Hodder & Stoughton, 1878), 170.

[360] Augustus Hopkins Strong, *Systematic Theology* (Philadelphia: American Baptist Publication Society, 1907), 319.

Jgs. 13:20–22) … After all is said, in the light of the later revelation, the Trinitarian interpretation remains the most natural one of the phenomena which the older writers frankly interpreted as intimations of the Trinity; especially of those connected with the descriptions of the Angel of Jehovah no doubt.

B. B. Warfield (1851-1921)[361]

God … visits his people in personal beings … Among all these envoys of God the Messenger of the Lord (מלאך יהוה) occupies a special place. He appears to Hagar (Gen 16:6–13; 21:17–20); to Abraham (Gen 18; 19; 22; 24:7; 40); to Jacob (Gen 28:13–17; 31:11–13; 32:24–30; cf. Hos 12:4; Gen 48:15, 16); to, and at the time of, Moses (Ex 3:2f.; 13:21; 14:19; 23:20–23; 32:34; 33:2f.; cf. Num 20:16; Isa 63:8, 9; and further also Josh 5:13, 14; Jdg 6:11–24; 13:2–23). This *Malak YHWH* is not an independent symbol nor a created angel but a true personal revelation and appearance of God, distinct from him (Ex 23:20–23; 33:14f.; Isa. 63:8, 9) and still one with him in name (Gen 16:13; 31:13; 32:28, 30; 48:15, 16; Ex 3:2f.; 23:20–23; Jdg 13:3), in power (Gen 16:10, 11; 21:18; 18:14, 18; Ex. 14:19; Jdg 6:21), in redemption and blessing (Gen 48:16; Ex 3:8; 23:20; Isa 63:8, 9), in adoration and honor (Gen 18:3; 22:12; Ex 23:21) … The angel of the covenant again appears in prophecy (Zech. 1:8–12:3) and will come to his temple (Mal. 3:1). Theophany reaches its climax, however, in Christ who is the (Angel, Glory, Image, Word, Son of God) in whom God is fully revealed and fully given.

Herman Bavinck (1854-1921)[362]

The most important and characteristic form of revelation in the patriarchal period is that through 'the Angel of Jehovah' or 'the Angel of God'. The references are: Gen. 16:7; 22:11, 15; 24:7, 40; 31:11; 48:16 [cp. also *Hos.* 12:4, with reference to *Gen.* 32:24ff.].

The peculiarity in all these cases is that, on the one hand, the Angel distinguishes himself from Jehovah, speaking of Him in the third person, and that, on the other hand, in the same utterance he speaks of God in the first person. Of this phenomenon various explanations have been offered … We must assume that behind the twofold representation there lies a real manifoldness in the inner life of the

---

[361] Benjamin B. Warfield, *The Works of Benjamin B. Warfield: Biblical Doctrines*, vol. 2 (Bellingham, WA: Logos Bible Software, 2008), 140-41.
[362] Herman Bavinck, John Bolt, and John Vriend, *Reformed Dogmatics: Prolegomena*, vol. 1 (Grand Rapids, MI: Baker Academic, 2003), 328–330.

Deity. If the Angel sent were Himself partaker of Godhead, then He could refer to God as his sender, and at the same time speak as God, and in both cases there would be reality behind it. Without this much of what we call the Trinity, the transaction could not but have been unreal and illusory.

Geerhardus Vos (1862-1949)[363]

The mysterious "angel of the LORD" or "angel of God," who appears often in the early Old Testament story and is sometimes identified with the God from whom he is at other times distinguished (Gen. 16:7–13; 18:1–33; 22:11–18; 24:7, 40; 31:11–13; 32:24–30; 48:15–16; Exod. 3:2–6; 14:19; 23:20–23; 32:34–33:5; Num. 22:22–35; Josh. 5:13–15; Judg. 2:1–5; 6:11–23; 9:13–23), is in some sense God acting as his own messenger, and is commonly seen as a preincarnate appearance of God the Son.

J. I. Packer (1926-)[364]

He is the "angel" who redeems us (Gen. 48:16). He is not a creaturely angel, but the angel of the Lord with whom Jacob wrestled (32:22–32), a pre-incarnate manifestation of the Messiah, according to churchmen throughout history. Centuries after Jacob lived, God came to earth to defeat sin and reveal His faithfulness (John 1:1–18).

R. C. Sproul (1939-2017)[365]

Scripture is Clear

Elsewhere in this book and in the companion volume we have cited Martin Luther, Theodore Beza, William Perkins, John Wolleb, John Owen, Francis Turretin, Herman Witsius, John Gill, Thomas Ridgley, Nehemiah Coxe, Isaac Watts, Heinrich Schmid, R. L. Dabney, J. P. Boyce, Robert Reymond, Douglas Kelly, John Frame, and others. This is no new doctrine. Neither is it an undercurrent. Rather, it is and always has been the mainstream view of the Angel of the LORD in church history

---

[363] Geerhardus Vos, *Biblical Theology: Old and New Testaments* (Eugene, OR: Wipf & Stock Publishers, 2003), 72–73.

[364] J. I. Packer, *Concise Theology: A Guide to Historic Christian Beliefs* (Wheaton, IL: Tyndale House, 1993), 65.

[365] R. C. Sproul, *Tabletalk Magazine, November 2007: The English Reformation* (Lake Mary, FL: Ligonier Ministries, 2007), 47.

To conclude Part II, we offer a few choice words selected from among some who very clearly recognize the Angel, just so you can get a flavor for how important this topic was for some of them and how important it is for us.

> For my part, I don't think that this needs much demonstration; just mentioning it suffices for the lovers of Christ. But the incorrigible are not going to derive any benefit from a flurry of words.[366]
>
> (Basil, *Against Eunomius* 2.18)

> Indignation rushes into my heart and interrupts my discourse, and under this emotion arguments are lost in a turmoil of anger roused by words like these [denying the angel of the LORD is God, but saying he is only an angel].[367]
>
> (Gregory of Nyssa, *Against Eunomius* 11.3)

> What blind faithlessness it is, what dullness of an unbelieving heart, what headstrong impiety, to abide in ignorance of all this, or else to know and yet neglect it! Assuredly it is written for the very purpose that error or oblivion may not hinder the recognition of the truth.
>
> (Hilary, *On the Trinity* 4.26)

> And for this reason I think it is, the Holy Spirit is placed as it were without the veil, like a ministering angel. Many of the ancients knew this, as Victorinus of Pettau, Ambrose, Bede, Arethas, Autpert Ambrose, Walafrid Strabo, Haymo, Rupertus, from whom Thomas Aquinas, and Cælius of Pannonia, who rebukes those that understand it otherwise, and other elder Divines of the Roman Church learnt it, to say nothing of those of the Reformed Church…
>
> YOU SEE WHAT CONTRADICTIONS Bellarmine falls into, out of his zeal to promote the doctrine of *invocation of saints*. I wish there were not something as bad in our Divines [the Reformers were not in complete agreement on this], that carries them in the like contradictions. The best I can say for their excuse is only this, they have not carefully attended to the style of the holy Scriptures…

---

[366] Basil of Caesarea, *Against Eunomius*, trans. Mark DelCogliano and Andrew Radde-Gallwitz, vol. 122, *The Fathers of the Church* (Washington, DC: The Catholic University of America Press, 2011), 156.

[367] Gregory of Nyssa, "Gregory of Nyssa against Eunomius," in Gregory of Nyssa: Dogmatic Treatises, Etc., ed. Philip Schaff and Henry Wace, trans. William Moore et al., vol. 5, *A Select Library of the Nicene and Post-Nicene Fathers of the Christian Church*, Second Series (New York: Christian Literature Company, 1893), 234.

I have often wondered how it came to pass, that most of the Divines of the Church of Rome, who would seem to have the greatest veneration for antiquity, would so much despise it in this question, while the ancient Jewish and Christian Church agree. Sanctius in his notes on Acts 7 says, it is a difficult question among Divines, whether God's appearances in Scripture were performed immediately by God himself, or by his angels. And then having cited several ancient Fathers, who thought it was the *Logos* that appeared, he adds, "But currently, the Theologians prefer that judgment which states that in the ministry of angels a divine form was presented to ancient people; this is the judgment of Dionysius, etc." ...

But this is not the worst of it that they forsake the judgment of the ancients; for they also make bold to contradict the plain words of Christ himself in John 1:18. Christ says, *"No man has seen God at any time, the only-begotten who is in the bosom of the Father he has declared him."* And parallel to this text is John 6:46. Certainly he must be very blind who does not see that Christ in these words not only denies that the Father had showed himself in those appearances that were made to the ancient patriarchs, but that he also ascribes them to himself, and not to the angels.

Away then with such Divines, who, setting aside the authority of Christ, do choose to theologize in the principal heads of religion according to the sense and prejudices of the modern Jews. We do not desire to be wiser in these matters than the primitive Christians were, among whom it passed for an established truth, that the *Elohim* in Jacob's prayer was the very Jehovah of the Jews, termed by them sometime *Shekinah*, and sometime *Memra*.[368]

---

[368] Peter Allix, *Dissertation*, 31, 24-25, 10-11.

PART III

THE ANGEL IN APPLICATION

Chapters: 19-20

Systematic Theology: *Any study that answers the question, "What does the whole Bible teach us today?" about any given topic.*
~ Wayne Grudem and John Frame

Pastoral Theology: *All the varied activities of the pastor have a single center: life in Christ. Pastoral theology seeks to point to that center in credible contemporary language.* ~ Thomas Oden

In Part III we will look at how the Angel as Christ is relevant today. The first chapter will ask how the Angel of the LORD as Christ might impact the way we think about our theology as a whole. We will look at various components of systematic theology such as the doctrine of God, of Christ, of salvation, and of heaven. The second will seek more practical application as it pertains to everyday life.

19

ROOM IN THE SYSTEM

The Angel and Systematic Theology

Systematic Implications of the Angel

PART I OF THIS BOOK WAS TAKEN UP WITH a biblical theology of the Angel of the LORD. Part II was an historical survey of the past that sees the Angel as the Second Person of the Trinity. However, like any subject in God's word, it has implications for other disciplines. In Part III we want to explore some of these in regard to systematic and practical theology.

What is systematic theology? Wayne Grudem and John Frame give the simple definition, "Systematic theology is any study that answers the question, 'What does the whole Bible teach us today?' about any given topic."[369] Richard Gaffin compares biblical theology and systematic theology to a plot and character analysis in literature. Biblical theology traces the development of ideas over the scope of the Bible. Systematic theology asks the larger, more conclusive questions about what the Bible teaches. In systematic theology, broad questions about God's word, God's nature, Jesus Christ, mankind, salvation, the church, the

---

[369] Wayne A. Grudem, *Systematic Theology: An Introduction to Biblical Doctrine* (Leicester, England; Grand Rapids, MI: Inter-Varsity Press; Zondervan Pub. House, 2004), 21. Grudem cites Frame as his source for this definition.

future, and many other areas of inquiry are put down in a logical order to create a system of doctrine covering the whole counsel of God. While most systematics address the Angel, he often does not play much if any role in the overall development of a system. He just seems to be a curious novelty to be mentioned, often in passing.

Some examples may help. In Grudem's *Systematic Theology* he tells us, "Several passages of Scripture, especially in the Old Testament, speak of the angel of the Lord in a way that suggests that he is God himself taking on a human form to appear briefly to various people in the Old Testament."[370] With such a profound insight, one would think this would be brought up in other places. Yet outside of this brief discussion under "The Doctrine of God: What Are Angels?" almost nothing is mentioned at all.

Louis Berkhof, in his *Systematic Theology* under "The Doctrine of the Person and the Work of Christ: The Offices of Christ" says, "He [Christ] exercised His prophetical office immediately, as the Angel of the Lord in the Old Testament period, and as the incarnate Lord by His teachings and also by His example."[371] Again, an amazing insight. Yet, outside of this and one other reference in the same section, Berkhof is wholly silent on the Angel.

Again, Charles Hodge in his *Systematic Theology* under "Theology Proper: The divinity of Christ" writes things like, "Here [Genesis 22] God, the angel of Jehovah, and Jehovah are names given to the same person, who swears by Himself and promises the blessing of a numerous posterity to Abraham."[372] We've seen the very same thing in our treatment of the passage. Then, in the same chapter, he makes the vital connection that he says, "has been almost universally adopted in the Church, at least since the Reformation," that:

> The angel, who appeared to Hagar, to Abraham, to Moses, to Joshua, to Gideon, and to Manoah, who was called Jehovah and worshipped as Adonai, who claimed divine homage and exercised divine power, whom the psalmists and prophets set forth as the Son of God, as the Counsellor, the Prince of Peace, the mighty God, and whom they

---

[370] Ibid., 401.

[371] L. Berkhof, *Systematic Theology* (Grand Rapids, MI: Wm. B. Eerdmans Publishing Co., 1938), 359.

[372] Charles Hodge, *Systematic Theology*, vol. 1 (Oak Harbor, WA: Logos Research Systems, Inc., 1997), 486.

predicted was to be born of a virgin, and to whom every knee should bow and every tongue confess, of things in heaven and things on earth, and things under the earth, is none other than He whom we now recognize and worship as our God and Saviour Jesus Christ. It was the *Logos asarkos* [the Word without flesh or *sarx*] whom the Israelites worshipped and obeyed; and it is the *Logos ensarkos* [the Word in flesh or *sarx*] whom we acknowledge as our Lord and God.[373]

We are seeing a pattern here in the agreement on the identity of the Angel. But that same pattern of saying virtually nothing outside of a couple of remarks about the Angel also continues in Hodge. This is something we believe must change, because The Angel is not a novelty. Rather, he is the Second Person of the Holy Trinity and he is the main character in the entirety of the Old Testament, perhaps to be found on every single page of the text. How can he therefore not have more impact on our systems than just a brief mention in one or two places?

Before getting to some places where we think a doctrine of the Angel could have more impact upon our systematics, we want to say a word about how we will proceed in this chapter. Rather than undertake a systematic development, we have decided simply to make some observations about the Angel in relation to particular systematic categories. In a couple of instances, we will be dogmatic about our view. But in many more, we will simply raise what we think are some important questions. We have decidedly not undertaken to answer all the questions, and there are certainly more areas of inquiry than we are addressing. Space would never permit it, and we know that others are better equipped to answer some than we are. Our hope would be that others might take up the torch where we drop it off, and that the Angel of the LORD might begin to have the proper impact we believe he should have in an overall system of biblical thought, just as the incarnated Lord Jesus rightly does in those same systems.

The Doctrine of God

The doctrine of God is usually the first or second topic taken up in systematic theology, with only the doctrine of the word of God sometimes coming first. This is both good and natural. The doctrine of God

---

[373] Hodge, 490.

is an immense subject, consuming such questions as "How do we know that God exists?" or "Can we really know God?" or "What kinds of attributes does God have?" or "How can God be three persons, yet one God?" It seems to us that an informed view of the Angel of the LORD needs to be allowed to speak to these many kinds of questions as, after all, he is God!

The shortest comprehensive statement about the doctrine of God that we know is contained in a couple of Confessions of Faith. Regarding his existence and attributes, we read:

> The Lord our God is but one only living and true God; whose subsistence is in and of himself, infinite in being and perfection; whose essence cannot be comprehended by any but himself; a most pure spirit, invisible, without body, parts, or passions, who only hath immortality, dwelling in the light which no man can approach unto; who is immutable, immense, eternal, incomprehensible, almighty, every way infinite, most holy, most wise, most free, most absolute; working all things according to the counsel of his own immutable and most righteous will for his own glory; most loving, gracious, merciful, long-suffering, abundant in goodness and truth, forgiving iniquity, transgression, and sin; the rewarder of them that diligently seek him, and withal most just and terrible in his judgments, hating all sin, and who will by no means clear the guilty.
>
> (London Baptist Confession of 1689 2.1;
> see also the Westminster Confession of Faith 2.1)

This summary speaks directly to some of the issues we would like to raise for potential investigation.

The Divine Nature and Theophany

Theologians speak of things called "theophanies." A theophany is literally "a God-appearance" (from *theos* meaning "God" and *phaneros*, meaning "manifestation"). Therefore, in a theophany, the invisible God condescends and appears to man through some kind of created medium like wind, storm, fire, cloud, physical voice, etc.

Differing specificity concerning the nature of theophanies has created a bit of confusion. For example, some suggest that "The theophany par excellence, [is] the Incarnation of God."[374] This is a theophany generally considered as simply a "God-appearing." But when theologians get more exacting, they often say something very different about the incarnation such as, "The incarnation was no mere theophany; no transient wonder; no illusion exhibited to the senses..."[375] The key idea here is the transient nature of a theophany. If one defines a theophany this way, the incarnation is not included. If it is defined more broadly, it is the highest pinnacle of theophany.

We have only a little doubt that at least some of the theophanies of the OT are temporary manifestations. When they are gone from human sight, they are gone everywhere until they "poof" into existence again the next time. This would seem to fit the idea of a cloud or fire or wind.

We say, "only a little doubt," because we are not entirely sure what happens to many earthly manifestations when they vanish from human sight. Many (perhaps even most) may disappear altogether. Augustine was the true innovator of this view.[376] Speaking on behalf of Augustine's view (in a note in Augustine's *On The Trinity*), Shedd explains,

---

[374] Benedict Englezakis, *New and Old in God's Revelation: Studies in Relations Between Spirit and Tradition in the Bible* (Cambridge: James Clarke & Co., 1982), 63. This idea seems to be followed by Bavinck and Berkhof. Bavinck writes that God reveals himself in this "trio": "theophany (incarnation), prophecy, and miracle" (Herman Bavinck, John Bolt, and John Vriend, *Reformed Dogmatics: Sin and Salvation in Christ*, vol. 3 [Grand Rapids, MI: Baker Academic, 2006], 190). Berkhof says, "There is a constant coming of God to man in theophany, prophecy, and miracle, and this coming reaches its highest point in the incarnation of the Son of God" (Louis Berkhof, *Introductory Volume to Systematic Theology* [Grand Rapids, MI: Wm. B. Eerdmans Publishing Company, 1932], 137).

[375] John W. Nevin, *Mystical Presence: A Vindication of the Reformed or Calvinistic Doctrine of the Holy Eucharist* (Philadelphia: S. R. Fisher & Co., 1846), 210, 211. In Charles Hodge, *Systematic Theology*, vol. 3 (Oak Harbor, WA: Logos Research Systems, Inc., 1997), 203. Strong and Boettner are representative of this. Strong writes of the incarnation, "Nor can it be a mere theophany, in human form" (Augustus Hopkins Strong, *Systematic Theology* [Philadelphia: American Baptist Publication Society, 1907)], 686). Why? As Boettner says, "The sojourn of Christ on earth was therefore not a mere theophany or temporary appearance of God in human form, but a real and permanent incarnation" [Loraine Boettner, *Studies in Theology* (Grand Rapids, MI: Presbyterian and Reformed Publishing Company, 1947], 207).

[376] See Robert J. Wilkinson, *Tetragrammaton: Western Christians and the Hebrew Name of God: From the Beginnings to the Seventeenth Century* (Boston: Brill, 2015), 143-146.

A theophany, though a harbinger of the incarnation, differs from it, by not effecting a hypostatical or personal union between God and the creature. When the Holy Spirit appeared in the form of a dove, he did not unite himself with it. The dove did not constitute an integral part of the divine person who employed it. Nor did the illuminated vapor in the theophany of the Shekinah. But when the Logos appeared in the form of a man, he united himself with it, so that it became a constituent part of his person. A theophany, as Augustin notices, is temporary and transient. The incarnation is perpetual.[377]

But if we are too quick to answer this question, we risk doing great damage to the very real, permanent, and parallel reality we call heaven, the spiritual realm, which at least as it regards temple, theophany, and worship experiences, is the archetype of earthly counterparts. Heaven is a real, permanent place, populated with people and architecture that do not disappear. We've seen this with heavenly scenes such as Isaiah 6, Daniel 7, and 1 Kings 22.

While we can't be sure if something like the earthly fire, which seems to be a theophany of the Holy Spirit, somehow shifts to the heavenly world rather than "poofs" out of existence altogether, it does appear from our study of the Divine Council that this is exactly what the Angel of the LORD does. He goes somewhere, for he "came down" and "was sent." It does not say God sent a soulless husk of a body to impersonate himself, or that he sent Gabriel to speak for the Angel. It says God sent his Angel and that Angel is the LORD—Christ. Given that he is parallel in terms of ruling over nations to other sons of God, it would seem that he rules them from heaven; he does not poof in and out of existence. Further, if God is truly unknowable to all rational creatures, then it seems it would necessarily be true that *there are theophanies in heaven*, and that God is manifesting himself even to angels through created avenues in heavenly places.

This takes us into our thoughts regarding the Angel-theophanies of the OT. We do not believe that the Angel of the LORD "poofed" in and out of existence between appearances to man (see the section under

---

[377] W. G. T. Shedd, n. 6 in Augustine's *On The Trinity* 2.6.11, in Philip Schaff, ed., *St. Augustin: On the Holy Trinity, Doctrinal Treatises, Moral Treatises*, vol. 3, A Select Library of the Nicene and Post-Nicene Fathers of the Christian Church, First Series (Buffalo, NY: Christian Literature Company, 1887), 44.

"Heaven" below for our reasoning). The Angel of Israel no more ceases to exist when he is not appearing on earth than Gabriel ceases to exist when he is not appearing on earth. He simply retreats to the world of spirits, where he naturally (in this form) resides.

Now, there is some question about what becomes of the created angelic form once the Son of God assumes *human* flesh. Does it cease to exist? Does the Logos drop one nature while taking on a new nature? Could he (because he is omnipresent and exists in places his human form is now limited to) be simultaneously angel and man? We've seen how there are some reasons to see Christ in Revelation as "angel" even after the incarnation. What does this mean? We are not sure. But we think further reflection on this and how it might inform our understanding of theophanies would be a valuable area of research.

We also believe that considering the idea of theophany more often than is noticed by the overt appearances of "the Angel of the LORD" would be helpful. Here we can consider where "theophany" is usually discussed in systematics. The majority of treatments speak about it under the main heading of the divine nature of God (this is the topic we saw the confessions speaking to).[378]

Such discussions often speak of God apart from the Persons first, before moving logically to speak of the Persons and God as triune later in the chapter. We understand why this is done and do not necessarily have a problem with it. But this can be dangerous in that it makes Oneness either a logical or ontological priority over Threeness. Some have even said as much. But God wasn't first One only to "become" Three. Rather, he is always One and always Three—eternally. Neither is more ultimate. Both are equally ultimate, and both mutually and necessarily inform the other.

As we have made a point to explain at various times in the book, we Christians are not Unitarians. A good case can be made that the Trinity is the single most important doctrine that we hold. Yet we seem to default to a kind of Unitarian way of thinking as it regards "comings" of Yahweh in the OT—if they don't explicitly mention something like "The angel of the LORD came..."

---

[378] Some treat it under the heading of "Revelation" (i.e. special revelation) or under Christology, which is taken up after the doctrine of God more generally.

For example, when "God" appeared to Adam and Eve, what was it that was there with our parents? A thought? An idea? An unknowable Unitarian monad? A disembodied voice? Did a bare-naked "divine nature" walk through the garden after our parents sinned? What would that even mean? Was their bodies being clothed with the skins of a dead animal merely metaphorical? We don't think so. When God spoke to Noah and told him to build an ark, was it, as Aronofsky recently depicts in his blasphemous *Noah* movie, just a crazy man hearing things in his head? When God tested Abraham and told him to sacrifice his son, who was talking to him? Was it "the Father"? Was it "the Divine Nature?" Did Abraham see anything? We've addressed these three chapters already in the book. But now we want to make some theological applications.

The first application is learning to recognize the Angel-theophany, even when the text does not mention the word "Angel" (such as Genesis 1 or 6), or especially when it does (such as Genesis 22). We have seen that he goes by many other titles: Name, Word, Wisdom, Glory, Right Hand, and even just Yahweh.

There is a question we would like to see asked much more often, especially when theological debates like God's foreknowledge or impassibility or simplicity or the question of functional subordination within the Trinity threaten to tear the church into ever smaller pieces. Who is speaking in any given text? When it says something about "God" or "Yahweh," does it have in mind merely the Divine Nature, such as we found in the Confession's paragraph? Sometimes it does. But other times, perhaps it is the Son (or even the Father or the Spirit) speaking in a theophany.

The point here is not somehow to divide God into parts. We understand that there is, of course, a sense that when the Son speaks, the Father also speaks, and more, that when any Person speaks, the One God is speaking. Nevertheless, we can say different things about Jesus than we can say about the Divine Nature. Jesus died on the cross. The Divine Nature did not die on the cross, nor did the Father. Think of it like you might those red-letter Bibles. While we're not fond of them, because in one sense the entire Bible should be in red letters, at the same time it makes things clear that when, for example, Peter is talking to "God," he is not speaking to a voice in his head. He is talking to the incarnated Jesus, his friend who was known by everyone, and not as a bare-naked divine essence (even though he himself confessed that he is God).

What we are asking is that in a similar way, when Yahweh or Elohim is speaking in the OT, we need first to ask the question of whether we can be more specific than that regarding the Persons. Sometimes we can't. Sometimes it is just giving us things like attributes of the Divine Nature. Many other times, it isn't. If it isn't, would it have any bearing upon our interpretation of any given text? Let's consider some examples of how this might work as we continue thinking about things that belong in the Doctrine of God.

Anthropomorphism

Theologians and Confessions speak about God as "without body." A children's catechism teaches something similar. "*Q. What is God? A. God is a Spirit and has not a body like men.*" We want to be absolutely clear: *we firmly agree* that the Divine Nature has no body like men or anything else. As Jesus said, "God is spirit" (John 4:24). Amazingly, of course, Jesus is also God and, simultaneously, Jesus has a body. There is no contradiction, because we are speaking in terms of a hypostatic union or an incarnation or a theophany. But it highlights that the issue of a bodily manifestation is more complex than is sometimes explored.

Often, the OT depicts God in bodily terms. "The eyes of the LORD are toward the righteous" (Ps 34:15). "Then the LORD put out his hand and touched my mouth" (Jer 1:9). "I will take away my hand, and you shall see my back, but my face shall not be seen" (Ex 33:23). Because this is not the NT, it is a near given universal that a discussion of these passages must involve something called *anthropomorphism.*

An anthropomorphism is an attribution of human characteristics to God. It is a figure of speech not meant to be taken literal-physically. Clearly, the Bible uses human traits sometimes to describe God and they are not meant to be taken literally. "The eyes of the LORD" is often a good example. When it says, "Noah found favor in the eyes of the LORD" (Gen 6:8), it isn't talking about some kind of literal eyes inside eye-sockets on some kind of a huge heavenly head or something. The figure is an analogy that teaches that God sees all and knows and shows favor to people.

However, what often happens is that *any time* some kind of body part is ascribed to "God," it is *always* chalked off as anthropomorphism. Few do this with Jesus in the incarnation. When it says that Jesus reached out his hand and touched someone, we know he has hands and that it is meant to be taken physically. But since we are in the OT, what else could it possibly be but a figure of speech? *We all know it can't be physical!*

We want to suggest that at least some of the time it actually is physical. Not always. But sometimes. When it's a theophany. Not because the Divine Nature has a body, but because it is describing the Angel of the LORD who *does* have a body.

The Jeremiah reference above ("The LORD put out his hand and touched my mouth." We've also seen this physicality with Abraham, Manoah, Samuel, and many others) is an example. It was the Angel of the LORD who was talking to Jeremiah, not "The Divine Nature." Yes, the Angel of the LORD is God, and thus the Divine Nature is present. But the Divine Nature is coming *through* the Second Person who himself is coming *to* a man in the form of the Angel. In other words, the Eternal Nature is being mediated by the Eternal Person who is himself being mediated in the created form of an Angel that he has somehow assumed. When Abraham washed the LORD's feet and the LORD ate a meal with him and then went into his tent and Sarah overheard it and laughed ... this is meant to be taken physical-literally, not anthropomorphically.

It is our contention that some, perhaps many, of the proof-texts that systematics chalk off as anthropomorphic are, in fact, not. We would like to see more work done on this, so that exegesis of the Angel can play a higher role in making our talk about God without a body more precise. We want to see the doctrine derived from the correct texts rather than out-of-context proof texts.

Impassibility

Impassibility is the doctrine that deals with whether or not God has "passions." Generally speaking, a passion is a strong created emotion, usually (though not always) of the negative kind (like hatred or lust or greed or anger). Again, this idea is found in the Confessional paragraph above. Without getting into the technical discussion, consider Genesis 6:6, as it is often cited in this context. "The LORD regretted that he had made man on the earth, and it grieved him to his heart." "Grieving" and "regretting" are passions.

Classically, the church has affirmed that God is without passions.

We affirm this too. However, all have recognized that Jesus Christ, who is God, had strong emotions, and that these emotions came and went. "Jesus wept" (John 11:25). He was "consumed with zeal" (John 2:17). He was "full of compassion" (Matt 15:32). We even refer to his last days as "the passion" of Christ. Of course, in none of this did he ever sin.

Thus, we have an obvious dilemma when it comes to the God-man. How the church has dealt with this question has not always been the same,[379] but it shows that we all must deal with the question. It isn't as straightforward as just saying, "No, Jesus didn't have passions (or if you like, emotions)." Somehow, he both did and didn't.

Clearly, the language of Genesis ascribes passions to the LORD. Answers of what this means have usually fallen into one of two opposing sides. Either the language is anthropopathic (ascribing human passions to God) and is therefore not meant to be taken literally because God literally has no passions at all, or God has passions and impassibility is simply denied, which has its own set of problems.

What if this was a false dichotomy? Is it possible to maintain impassibility while affirming that "the LORD grieved" is not an anthropopathism simultaneously? Again, we've seen that something akin to it is certainly possible with the God-man, Jesus. To answer biblically, we must begin by asking, *who is talking?* Our exegesis has answered that it is almost certainly the Angel of the LORD speaking here. But does this matter?

It might; it might not. Throughout history, some have said that angels are also impassible. However, others have said they are quite passible. The Greeks were divided on this question regarding the gods; Christians have been divided on it regarding angels. But if it were to be granted that angels are passible, why should the Angel of the LORD necessarily be any different? There *might* be good reasons someone could conceive of as to why this could be so. However, it was not so regarding Christ's humanity. He simply was a human. He experienced all the frailties, movements, and passions that human experience (yet

---

[379] The Nestorian controversy is a good example. In this debate over secondary issues, Nestorius and Theodore of Mopsuestia did not want to live with the tension held by Cyril that "The Word suffered impassibly." Instead, they believed it was necessary to make sharp distinctions between the properties of the two natures of Christ (his human and divine natures) such that they were constantly dividing him up into parts. See for example Paul Gavrilyuk, "Theopatheia: Nestorius's Main Charge Against Cyril of Alexandria," *SJT* 56-2 (2003): 190–207.

without sin), because he became one of us.

Taking this further, it seems to us that most of the proof-texts about impassibility and immutability (where God seems to "change") involve not the Divine Essence, but the Angel of the LORD. If this is true, what impact would this have on the way we put together our systems of doctrine of God? For example, when it says, "The LORD regretted that he had made man on the earth" (Gen 6:6), does regret refer to the essence of God or to the manifestation of God's Presence in time, who soon speaks to Noah almost certainly through the Angel of the LORD? We are not suggesting that anything would or should change regarding "the Divine Nature." But might it at least cause us to be more careful in how we "prove" the doctrine from specific texts?

God's Relationship to Time

God's relationship to time is a very difficult question. The majority position in church history is that God is somehow outside of time (atemporal). Our feeling is that this is probably true in some sense. The recent trend, however, has been to challenge this assumption and say that God is actually temporal. Importantly, they would add, he is *not bound by time*, but somehow temporality belongs to his very essence. That is their position. But because the very idea of temporality seems to strike a blow to other classical doctrines such as immutability (the idea that God cannot change), any form of temporality is sometimes met with harshness or even ridicule or anathema.

Because the Bible often uses language of God being temporal, rather than chalk this off as some form of anthropomorphism again (which of course many do), some Christian philosophers and theologians have tried to deal with this by asserting that God prior to creation was atemporal, but after creation has become temporal. It seems to us that they speak here of the Divine Nature in both instances and this does severe damage to our understanding of God if we want to hold that he is simple (without parts) and immutable (cannot change), etc.

Again, we want to look at our theology of God first through the prism of Jesus Christ. Whatever people say about God outside of creation, there can be no question but that Jesus Christ, the Eternal Son of God, when he incarnated, was somehow temporal. He aged. He changed. He performed things "now" and then "later." While it is still difficult to figure out the exact relationship to time that God may have in all of this, there can be no question as to the person of Jesus in the incarnation. He was temporal, even though he was also God.

Again, we want to ask our question about the temporal language about God used in the OT. Is the Angel in view? If so, why would we take temporal language of him any differently than we would temporal language of Jesus in human flesh? Maybe there would be a good reason not to; maybe there wouldn't be. But our systematics need to do a much better job of dealing with how God relates to time through theophanies, especially through the theophany of the Angel. If we can do it with the theophany of the God-man, we can also do so with the God-Angel.

We would also suggest that this temporal relationship to creation does not merely extend to earth, but also to heaven, where the Angel goes when he leaves the earth. Not that heaven is somehow on some set earthly time zone (though, if it was, Doug has no doubt that it would be Mountain Standard Time, while Matt inexplicably insists that the entire world revolves around Eastern Standard Time). Yet it is a place of temporal succession of moments rather than an unchanging atemporal eternity.

The Trinity and Subordinationism

The Trinity is the cornerstone doctrine of the Christian Faith. Frankly, in our estimation, it should be where we begin rather than end our doctrine of God. We should not be starting as Unitarians only to later "arrive" at a trinitarian destination, like some high-schooler graduating into college. Certainly, the Angel helps us in this regard, and we will say more about this in the next chapter. However, there is at least one specific doctrine within trinitarianism on which perhaps the Angel can help us think more clearly. It is the doctrine of the eternal relationship of the Son to the Father.

One of the early Trinitarian heresies was called Subordinationism. This is the idea that that Son is eternally ontologically subordinate to the Father. In other words, he is somehow a lesser created being than the Father. That is, not merely the Angel-body (which was created), but the Son of God himself is inferior in his nature.

But another kind of subordinationism is not necessarily heretical. In fact, it is a way that the church has tried to describe at least some kind of relationship between the Son and the Father. This is sometimes called functional or economic subordination. This kind of subordination refers to the things the persons do rather than who they are. The Persons undergo these "functions" willingly, cooperatively, selflessly, according to their Persons rather than their Divine Nature.

Again, returning to Jesus, everyone admits that Jesus was "sent" by the Father. He also "submitted" to his Father's will. Some will say that this was a temporary form of functional subordination that is not part of the eternal relationship between the Two Persons. Others think there has to be some kind of eternal functional distinction between them, otherwise, what makes them differ?

While we could get into the more technical discussions of what it means to be "begotten" (or in the case of the Spirit, "spirated"), we simply want to note that very few look at the OT relationship between the Father and Son the same way they view it in the NT. In fact, it is quite common to hear people say that prior to the incarnation, there was no kind of subordination of role whatsoever. It is totally unique to Jesus coming in the flesh.

Here, we want to point out that the very same language used by Jesus of being "sent" is used of the Angel of the LORD. "He [the Father] will send his Angel before you…" (Gen 24:7). "Behold, I send an angel before you…" (Ex 23:20). This is exactly how Jesus speaks of himself. "The Father who sent me …" (John 5:37). "As the living Father sent me…" (John 6:57). If the Angel of the LORD is the Son of God, and if the sending is not unique to the incarnation, might this have any bearing upon our doctrine of functional distinctions within the Trinity? We believe such questions need to be asked.

Angels vs. Men

For whatever reason, angels are often discussed under the doctrine of God. Above, we saw a quotation from Wayne Grudem that is almost universally believed regarding the appearance of the Angel of the LORD in the OT "taking on human form" or coming "as a human." We want to make an observation here that we also made in Part I, and then suggest an application.

Is it true that the Angel of the LORD took *human* appearance? As far as we can tell, the text never says so. Here, we have to understand the distinction between two overlapping, but not identical Hebrew words. The words are *'ish* and *'adam*. Both words are usually translated as "man." Now, both words are used to describe human beings (humans can be either *'ish* or *'adam*). But *'ish* also describes angelic messengers. This is why angels are sometimes called "men" (Gen 19:5; Josh 5:13; Dan 8:15; cf. Luke 24:4, etc.). However, when it comes to *'adam*, angels are rarely and (as we have seen previously) arguably never given this description as being intrinsic to their essence. It only belongs to sons of Adam—human beings (male or female). In other words, the Hebrew sees overlap between the two kinds of beings, but also distinguishes between them using these words.

A problem comes when we fail to distinguish these terms in English. Thus, it is natural to think that when an angel appears, because he is called a "man" in an English Bible, this means he must be coming as a *hu*-man. Not so fast.

We saw that when Abraham saw three men (*'ish*), he instantly recognized that these were no ordinary men. This could have been because they simply appeared to him out of nowhere. It could also have been because there was something about their appearance that was instantly recognizable. That's what Manoah's wife said, "A man of God came to me, and his appearance was like the appearance of the angel of God, very awesome" (Jdg 13:6).

Now, it is possible that there is no difference in appearance of features between the species. "Some have entertained angels unawares" (Heb 13:2). This may mean that they do in fact look very much like us (or, at least that they *can*).[380] Yet how many times do we have a prophet seeing

---

[380] Here, the strange but ancient idea of shape-shifting comes into view. This is hardly a modern invention of fantasy and sci-fi literature, but was actually used as an explanation for the pregnancies of human women from the gods. For example, in the Testament of Reuben we read, "[The Watchers] were transformed into human males, and while the women were cohabiting with their husbands they appeared to them" (TestReub 5:6). 1 Enoch says, "Whenever they want, they appear as men" (1 Enoch 17:1). See Kelley Coblentz Bautch, *A Study of the Geography of 1 Enoch 17-19* (Boston: Brill, 2003), 46-49. On shape shifting in Greek mythology see Homer, *Odyssey* 4.315-462; Ovid, *Metamorphosis* 11.250-263. You

a heavenly being that is instantly recognizable as such: shimmering, glowing brightly, arrayed in brilliant clothing, having human-like faces, but also sometimes with things like wings? They often call them angels.

There are many different kinds of heavenly beings. There are curious descriptions of certain of them that we find in places like the Dead Sea Scrolls that are simply fascinating. We want to mention here one other place where "angel" appears in the Greek OT of the book of Genesis. It is found in the strange story of Genesis 6:1-4 where the "sons of God" see the "daughters of men."[381]

Most of our copies of the LXX retain the phrase "sons of God." However, some of them read "angels."[382] This is something we find the LXX doing in half of the ten places where the phrase is used in the OT. This includes Dt 32:8; 43; Job 1:6; 2:1; and 38:7. In each, "sons of God" is rendered as "angels." In this minority case of Genesis 6 where some translations of the LXX render the "sons of God" as "angels," other ancient texts call them "Watchers."[383] "Watchers" are mentioned three times in Daniel 4.

Watchers are heavenly beings of some kind. The context of the following quotations all deal with the fall of the Watchers in the days before the Flood according to Jewish tradition. In a strange Dead Sea Scroll called the Testament of Amram, manuscript B (Frag 1), it says something most interesting about the appearance of the Watchers, "[I saw Watchers] in my vision, the dream-vision. Two (men) were fighting over me, saying . . . and holding a great contest over me. I asked them, 'Who are you, that you are thus empo[wered over me?' They answered me, 'We] [have been em]powered and rule over all mankind.' They said to me, 'Which of us do yo[u choose to rule (you)?' I raised my eyes and looked.] [One] of them was terr[i]fying in his appearance, [like a serpent, [his] cl[oa]k many-colored yet*

---

can also see this in the recent Hollywood production *Clash of the Titans*, when Zeus comes to the human Queen Danaë in the form of her husband King Acrisius and from this union, the demigod Perseus is born.

[381] For a detailed exegesis of this passage, see Douglas Van Dorn, *Giants: Sons of the Gods* (Erie, CO: Waters of Creation Pub, 2013).

[382] Including codex Alexandrinus. See John William Wevers, ed., *Genesis*, vol. I, Vetus Testamentum Graecum. Auctoritate Academiae Scientiarum Gottingensis Editum (Göttingen: Vandenhoeck & Ruprecht, 1974), 108.

[383] The parallel texts with Genesis 6:1-4 include 1 Enoch (10, 12, etc.), Jubilees 10:1; TestReub 5:7; TestNaph 3:5.

very dark ... [And I looked again], and . . . in his appearance, his visage like a viper..."[384]

While the *Testament*, dating to a time before Christ, describes Watchers as having the appearance of serpents and vipers, wearing darkly colored cloaks, the *Book of Noah* found at Qumran as part of 1 Enoch adds to the description saying that they have bodies *"whiter than snow and redder than a rose,"* that *"every hair [is] white. . . curly and glorious"* (1En 106:2). Then there is the description found in a book that scholars have called the *Book of the Secrets of Enoch*. In it Enoch says, *"And there appeared to me two men very tall, such as I have never seen on earth. And their faces shone like the sun, and their eyes were like burning lamps; and fire came forth from their lips. Their dress had the appearance of feathers; their feet were purple, their wings were brighter than gold, their hands whiter than snow."*[385]

It is fascinating to see how the ancient Jews sometimes depicted Satan in this regard. For instance, in the very strange book *The Apocalypse of Abraham* (23:5-11), the Devil is the chief of the fallen angels whose *"portion is on earth."*[386] He is depicted behind the tree of knowledge, *"standing (something) like a dragon in form, but having hands and feet like a man's, on his back six wings on the right and six on the left."*[387] If Satan in the Garden is not a possessed snake, but actually a serpent-like seraphim being, then such descriptions at least make sense. As the Watchers are also described in similar terms, it is thus easy to see that at least some Jews did not think that these creatures looked exactly like human beings, at least not all the time. Far from it!

This evidence corroborates the idea that when Abraham saw the three heavenly beings come to his tent, he recognized them immediately. Perhaps at least one of them was a Watcher. While it is possible that the two "angels" were more ordinary looking (based on the Sodom and Gomorrah story), the Angel of the LORD himself could very well have been considered a Watcher, due to his being a "son of God" who

---

[384] *Test Amram*, 4Q543 Frag Bi: 9-14. See Robert H. Eiseman and Michael Owen Wise, *The Dead Sea Scrolls Uncovered* (New York: Penguin Books, 1993), 164.
[385] Milton S. Terry, *Biblical Apocalyptics: A Study of the Most Notable Revelations of God and of Christ in the Canonical Scriptures* (New York; Cincinnati: Eaton & Mains; Curts & Jennings, 1898), 491.
[386] ApocAbr 13:6.
[387] ApocAbr 23:7.

inherits Israel (the other two angels may or may not have looked different from him). Sons of God are Watchers.

This is obviously speculative, since it would truly be an extraordinary feat for Jacob to have beaten this Man in a wrestling match. Nevertheless, it can at least help us distinguish in our minds that when the Angel of the LORD appears to people, they are not mistaking him for a human being. Why? Because they are not seeing a human being. They are seeing an ʾish-man, a supernatural being who is often called just Yahweh or God. As such, it is at best an overstatement rooted in speculation to say that Christ as the angel "appeared as a human." At worst, it is flat-out wrong. He very probably didn't. This sets the stage for our next topic: the vitally important uniqueness of the incarnation.

Christology

The Incarnation

One of the vital questions that we must address and not leave to others to flesh out is the question of the uniqueness of the incarnation. Perhaps the chief question people raise to our proposal is that if we are right, if the Word of God has already come in the OT in the form of an Angel, then how does this not obliterate the uniqueness of the incarnation? This objection, it seems to us, actually misses the truly unique thing about the incarnation while majoring on minors. It creates a problem where none exists.

The incarnation is the doctrine that God (specifically the Second Person) became flesh, put so bluntly in the prologue of John's Gospel (John 1:14). "Flesh" is the term *sarx*, and it represents the "stuff" out of which we are made "down here." In other words, men are *sarx*, but angels are not. Here, two words in Greek function in a similar way to the ʾish /ʾadam Hebrew distinction. It isn't as though angels do not have *bodies*. They do. Those bodies are called *soma* (1Co 15:40) or sometimes "spirit" (*pneuma*).[388] Humans have *soma* and angels have *soma*; both are translated as "bodies." But of the two, only humans have *sarx*—flesh.

---

[388] 1 Enoch 15:8 describes the distinction as saying that "the giants" are "those who are born of spirits (*pneuma*) and flesh (*sarx*).

What Jesus did that was unique is not necessarily taking on a body (*soma*). As we saw in Part II, the church is nearly universal in its teaching that the Angel of the LORD is the preincarnate Christ. No one wants to say that this body was not real but purely imaginary. Some may think it was non-physical (but then, how does it wrestle, eat, grab, and other physical things?) or perhaps temporary (not that we can see how this would matter much to the point at hand).

More might want to say that the *Logos* was not united to this body in some kind of mystical union between the uncreated Word and a created angelic substance. We understand the trepidation. We have been taught our entire lives that the uniqueness of the incarnation is that nothing like it has ever happened before. Before answering this objection, it seems to us that any kind of unreal union idea would make it nearly impossible to affirm what they want to affirm, which is that the Angel of the LORD *is* the Second Person. If the Angel is akin to a mask that the Second Person puts on, how can this mask be called God and Yahweh? Only persons can be called God, not husks or shells. How much more if the whole thing was illusory? On the other hand, because we do not even fully understand what heaven "is," we do not understand what heavenly "bodies" are and cannot then make any firm conclusions about "nature."

Rather, what is unique in the incarnation is the "*car*" (Lat: *caro*) part of this borrowed word. What had never happened before, and has never happened since, is that God became *human* flesh (*sarx*) and dwelt among us. Jesus did not come here as an angel in the NT like he did in the OT. As we have seen, John himself says that he *was there* among the people in the OT (John 1:11), but this was as an angel, not as a human.[389]

---

[389] Commenting on John 1:1-14, Bavinck writes, "It is especially John in his prologue who brings out for us this preparation for the incarnation in a preceding history. Not only was the Logos in the beginning with God and himself God and not only were all things made by him, but from the moment of creation this Logos also communicated his life and light to creatures. For in him was life, and the life was the light of all people [John 1:4]. Even after the fall, this revelation did not stop. On the contrary, the light of that Logos shone in the darkness [5] and enlightened everyone coming into the world [9]. He revealed himself particularly in Israel [11], which he had chosen for his own inheritance and led and blessed as Angel of the covenant. He came continually to his own in theophany, prophecy, and miracle. In that manner the Son prepared the whole world, including Jews as well as Gentiles, for his coming in the flesh. The world

There is simply nothing about the Angel of the LORD theology that harms the incarnation. The uniqueness of the incarnation is something that we must hold tenaciously. For never before and never since has God become *sarx*, taken on our flesh, and become one of us. God the Son's manifestation through an angelic body does not have the same ontological and redemptive significance as his incarnation, no matter what that relationship is, for the simple reason that it is not *adam*-man. The saving significance of the incarnation was Christ becoming eternally one with earthly humanity and raising us up with him to heavenly glory. He was the Son of God, but more noteworthy was his coming as Son of Man. He was "in the world" prior to his incarnation as the eternal Logos (John 1:10), the Angel of Yahweh manifest in the OT (John 1:1). But now that Word has become "flesh and dwelt among us, and we have seen his glory" (John 1:14). Christ coming in the OT as the Angel does nothing whatsoever to harm this most treasured and precious doctrine.

Soteriology (Salvation)

Jesus' descent from his seat at the head of the angelic Divine Council to becoming incarnate as a man raises the question of the scope of Soteriology. Soteriology is the study of salvation—how God achieves the salvation of fallen humanity. Most discussions of salvation rightly focus on the "atonement" of human sin—particularly, penal substitutionary atonement: the idea that Christ achieved salvation by becoming a substitutionary sacrifice satisfying the eternal punishment due to sin. But while atonement is properly the central aspect of salvation, salvation has broader implications as well. Some theologians in history have focused more on a *Christus Victor* model of salvation, while often denying a model of substitutionary atonement. This has caused more conservative theologians to be wary of a

---

and humanity, land and people, cradle and stable, Bethlehem and Nazareth, parents and relatives, nature and environment, society and civilization—these are all components in the fullness of the times in which God sent his Son into the flesh. It was the Son himself who thus immediately after the fall, as Logos and as Angel of the covenant, made the world of Gentiles and Jews ready for his coming. He was in the process of coming from the beginning of time and in the end came for good, by his incarnation making his home in humankind. Bavinck, *Reformed Dogmatics: Sin and Salvation in Christ*, 280.

Christus Victor model. However, surely, a *Christus Victor* emphasis is evident in the NT. This does not need to be an either/or.

Christus Victor is the idea that Christ's salvation was a victory over spiritual forces of evil in the heavenly places who held dominion over the earth. We see it in texts like Eph 1:21-22; 3:9-10; Col 2:15; Heb 2:14, 1Co 15:24; etc. These texts can only be fully understood in light of the OT Divine Council. Through his work, Jesus reclaims rights to all the nations for himself (see Dt 32:8-9, Ps 82:8), removing the claims of the demonic forces of evil. In fact, in the end, he judges these forces of evil.

We believe this cosmic aspect of Christ's work of salvation has often been neglected. When Ephesians 1:10 says that God had "a plan for the fullness of time, to unite all things in him, things in heaven and things on earth," when Colossians 1:20 describes Christ's work as reconciling "to himself all things, whether on earth or in heaven, making peace by the blood of the cross," we need to understand the cosmic storyline from OT to NT. It was not just God and humanity that were alienated. There was alienation in the earth itself. There was alienation between heaven and earth. There was alienation even within heaven itself—a war that was going on.

We think Christ's role in the heavenly realms as God's unique Son on the Divine Council needs to be explored and developed more in our theology. Berkhof touches on the idea when he says, "That the atoning work of Christ also had significance for the angelic world would seem to follow from Eph 1:10, and Col 1:20 … Kuyper holds that the angelic world, which lost its head when Satan fell away, is reorganized under Christ as Head. This would reconcile or bring together the angelic world and the world of humanity under a single Head. Naturally, Christ is not the Head of the angels in the organic sense in which He is the Head of the Church."[390] Berkhof and Kuyper make some suggestions, but these ideas need to be further explored.

In the OT, the Son was the unique God of Israel (Dt 32:9) who had given over the nations to other "gods." In the NT, the Son is "made lower than the angels" (Heb 2:9); he "partook" of "flesh and blood … that through death he might destroy the one who has the power of death, that is the devil … For surely it is not angels that he helps" (Heb

---

[390] Berkhof, *ST*, 399.

2:14-16). Though he does not "help" angels, his work has significance for the angelic realm, as Berkhof notes. He was a ruler in the angelic realm, but not the mediator for it. He became a man as a mediator, to remove the devil's claims, and to purify and prepare his elect to occupy heaven and to dispossess the devil and his angels. In doing so, he also purifies heaven itself and unites heaven and earth. God clearly intends for our eyes to be opened to Christ's exaltation and work for us in heaven and their implications for our heavenly hope.

Doctrine of Heaven

This brings us again to contemplate the created reality that is heaven. Earlier we discussed one of the theories we have heard put forward to explain the appearance and disappearance of the Angel of the LORD (who is in the same breath agreed upon to be the Second Person of the Trinity). We called it the "poof-theory." As we have noted, the motive seems to be to safeguard the uniqueness of the incarnation, which, as we have seen, is not in jeopardy in the first place (see "The Incarnation" above).

There's a major problem with the poof-theory. Heaven is a supernatural but created plane of existence. It is real. It exists. It is permanent. It is inhabited by other beings that *exist*. The divine council on which some of them preside is enduring. These beings don't poof in-and-out of existence. They are simply in another place than we are.

Scripture clearly reveals that the Godhead, including the Persons of the Trinity, manifest and interact in both the earthly and the heavenly created realms. God is in the heavens. He is certainly also above the heavens (1Kg 8:27). The Son of God, we have seen, had an historical, supernatural mode of existence interacting in the heavenly realm prior to the incarnation. Christ sat in the OT at the head of the divine council of angelic beings, at the right hand of the Father.

This raises questions (perhaps unanswerable questions) about the nature and differences between heaven and earth. For instance, interaction between heaven and earth seems to require some transmigration in form of existence. Both angels and the Angel are described as going up or coming down (see Gen 28:12-13). Even when angels come down, they are not automatically visible or physically corporeal. But they can become visible and corporeal on the earthly plane of existence. This included the Son of God in his angelic form in the OT.

Similarly, there is some obvious parallel with the resurrected body of Jesus. His resurrected body remains identifiably and recognizably human, but exalted. His body is able to appear and disappear, to ascend and descend from heaven, to move to different planes of existence. Interestingly, as we have seen, the description of his heavenly manifestation in the book of Revelation shows more correspondence with his angelic form as described in the OT and revealed at the Transfiguration. Clearly, he was raised with "a spiritual body," equipped for heavenly dwelling (1Co 15:44). All of this shows again that heaven is a real, created "place." The exalted body of Jesus does not just exist in God's mind in the eternal realm of ideas; Jesus' body has ascended to heaven, where he now resides.

It is our conviction then that our systematic theologies have not always thought deeply enough about heaven, about the specifics of God's manifestation in heaven, or our own future exaltation in heaven. This supernatural perspective, with Christ as the eternal Right Hand of the Father, needs more emphasis in our understanding.

The point of this chapter has been to show that the theology of the Angel of the LORD touches upon many places in our systematic thinking about God. In some of these places, we need to do a better job incorporating this theology into our thinking. In others, we need to realize that this theology only supports the systems already in place or at other times is no threat to them. Given that the majority position has always been that the Angel of the LORD is the preincarnate Christ, this should be obvious.

20

THE ANGEL TODAY

The Angel and Practical Theology

Why is The Angel of the LORD Important?

ONE SUNDAY, MANY, MANY YEARS AGO, TWO DISCIPLES were walking down a road towards the Jewish village of Emmaus, dev-
astated and bewildered by the death of Jesus just two days
earlier. They were confused and frustrated by some women of their company who had claimed to have seen Jesus *alive*. While these men were
talking, an apparent stranger came up to them on the road and joined
their conversation. After a few minutes, the stranger said to them, "O
foolish ones, and slow of heart to believe all that the prophets have spoken! Was it not necessary that the Christ should suffer these things and
enter into his glory?" (Luke 24:25-26). Then the stranger, beginning with
the books of Moses and working his way through all the Jewish Scriptures, began to explain to them everything concerning the Messiah.

What kinds of things did he talk about? We can guess at some. Perhaps he talked about the typology of the Temple and purpose of the
sacrificial system—the barrier between us and God and the need for a
mediator. He probably talked about the typology of the wilderness wan-
derings of God's people—from the patriarchs to Joseph to the Exodus

to the Exile—asked to leave and to follow and to be a blessing to the world. He may have talked about the war in heaven, with the forces of the serpent ruling in wickedness throughout the world, and how the serpent with his rule and claims needed to be crushed. Or what about the need for a mediator and intercessor between heaven and earth to serve as a prophet, priest, and king? That's in the OT. He doubtless talked about sin and its consequences and the requirements of eternal justice. Certainly, he went to the promises of the Messiah and the Suffering Servant of Isaiah. Then there's God's pity on humanity, that there was no one to intercede, and so God undertook to accomplish salvation by his right hand by sending His special Son to become Immanuel, to fulfill all the requirements of justice that fallen humanity could not, to defeat death, and to reclaim all the nations for God's rule and glory. In all of this, they learned why

> *He left his Father's throne above,*
> *So free, so infinite his grace,*
> *Humbled himself because of love,*
> *And bled for Adam's helpless race.*

They learned that Jesus was the Word, who was with God in the beginning, and who was God himself, who was the Creator of all things and the Eternal Son from the Father. And they learned why he became flesh, to bring the fullness of God's promises to pass. In all of this, they learned that he was the Divine Angel, sent to reveal God to us, and now become man to represent us to God. Their minds were opened to understand how this man was the key to the whole Bible and the center of history.

Jesus actually kept these disciples from recognizing him visibly until they recognized him in the OT first! He wanted them to see him there and to understand! Why is seeing Jesus as active and present in the OT so important? What difference does it make to see the appearances of the Divine Angel as appearances of the Son of God? What relevance does this really have for Christians today? We hope, after making your way through this book, that some of these answers are self-evident. However, it may be helpful, in drawing this book to a close, to crystalize and summarize some final thoughts on the importance of this issue.

1. It's What the Bible Teaches

The more you understand the theology of the Old Testament and the role of the Angel in the Old Testament, the more you see that this is what the New Testament is claiming about Jesus. Jesus was not just predicted in the Old Testament; he was not just portrayed in types and shadows. "Typology" is an important aspect of the New Testament's reading of the Old Testament, but it is not the most important aspect. The most important way to understand the New Testament's reading of the Old Testament is the "real presence" of Christ in the Old Testament, and not just sacramentally. In other words, the New Testament sees Christ not merely as typified in the Old, but actually there.[391]

The Trinity is not a New Testament invention. Instead, the Old Testament already revealed a plurality in the Godhead, a God who acts through subsistent Persons. The God of the Old Testament is not a Unitarian God, but a Father who has a Son and a Spirit. As we have seen, in many places, there is a sent God who reveals God, who speaks for God and speaks of God. In the Old Testament, his coming is often described as accompanied by or synonymous with the Spirit of God. This "sent" God is called a "Man," an "Angel," the "Word," the "Glory," the "Name," the "Hand/Arm," the "Power," the "Prince/Commander," and "the Son." Even the Jews acknowledged these terms as describing a condescended revelation of God through a distinct being. The problem is that people have lost an understanding of how the Old Testament uses these terms. They often don't recognize the connections the New Testament is making when using these terms and the associated texts when identifying Jesus. But when this interpretive key is brought to bear, it becomes clear that the New Testament identifies Jesus as the "Son of the Blessed" who has always carried these attributes. He was *there* in the

---

[391] A. T. Hanson came to the same conclusion many years ago in his book, *Jesus Christ in the Old Testament* - "The main aim of this book is to examine one element in NT exegesis, and to suggest that this element, rather than typology as such, is the most important clue to the understanding of the NT exegesis of the OT. That element may be called the real presence of the pre-existent Christ in OT history—or, to be more accurate, the real presence of the pre-existent Jesus. 'Jesus in the Old Testament' is, in fact, the way in which the NT writers for the most part thought of it … The normative approach of the NT writers to the OT is not that of typology but rather of what we have called 'real presence.'" 7-8.

Old Testament! So this is the teaching of the Bible; this is the testimony of the Apostles; this was the understanding of the early Church Fathers; this has been the majority understanding of church history. This understanding needs to be recaptured and re-emphasized today.

Of the Father's love begotten ere the worlds began to be,
He is Alpha and Omega, he the Source, the Ending he,
Of the things that are, that have been, and that future years shall see,
Evermore and evermore!

2. It Helps You Understand the Unity of the Bible

If you fail to see Jesus as the primary actor in biblical history, in both Testaments, you lose the unity of Scripture, you fail to understand the activity and plan of God throughout history, and you lose something of the power and relevance of the whole Bible for life. Many Christians today struggle to understand and relate to the OT. They struggle to relate to the God of the OT. Some divide the Testaments between a God of wrath and a God of grace. Some have said that "Christians must 'unhitch' the OT from their faith," saying, "[First century] Church leaders unhitched the church from the worldview, value system, and regulations of the Jewish Scriptures."[392] Some believe that Jesus was not in the OT and that the Christian faith only needs to focus on the NT Jesus. Some view Jesus as a hippie-peacenik with flowing locks who believed that all we need is love. They miss that Jesus is the God of the OT. They fail to see that, in both Testaments, Jesus is actually a man of war, the commander of the army of the Lord, and the one who will bring final judgment on the earth. Seeing that Jesus is the Angel of the Lord who brings both God's grace (Ps 34:7) and judgment (Ps 35:5-6), and understanding his role as God's Son in both Testaments, helps us hold together the whole Bible.

O Word of God incarnate, O Wisdom from on high,
O Truth unchanged, unchanging, O Light of our dark sky;
We praise thee for the radiance that from the hallowed page,
A lantern to our footsteps, shines on from age to age.

---

[392] This statement was made in 2018 by the megachurch pastor Andy Stanley - https://www.youtube.com/watch?v=pShxFTNRCWI, last accessed July 26, 2018.

3. It's a Compelling Argument for Apologetics

Showing that the appearances of the Angel of the Lord are Yahweh himself and also a Second Divine Person—and showing that the Person is Jesus—is crucial for apologetic witness to Jews, but also to other sects like Jehovah's Witnesses or Mormons. We have shown that the Hebrew Old Testament itself clearly identifies this Angel with Yahweh himself (using all the various titles) and also shows him to be a distinct Divine Person. We have shown that pre-Christian Jewish traditions saw these same issues in the text, and only after Christianity did they become anathematized by the rabbis, who sometimes even manipulated the texts to protect from a Christian interpretation. But the texts still speak for themselves, and we believe that Jesus is the clear and only explanation that makes sense.

Similarly, this exegesis of the Angel is extremely relevant in appealing to Jehovah's Witnesses and Mormons. Jehovah's Witnesses have long identified Jesus as the first *created* Angel of the Lord (even identifying him as Michael), but they have not grappled sufficiently with those texts that identify the Angel as synonymous with "Jehovah," as essentially one with Yahweh. Mormons likewise have an extremely developed emphasis on angels and the angelic realm, but they have not grappled with a biblical theology of the divine council and the real distinction between the "gods" and "God."

Understanding the real presence of Jesus in the Old Testament clarifies the unity of the Bible and Christian theology and becomes a compelling argument for the authority of God's revelation.

> *Let all mortal flesh keep silence,*
> *And with fear and trembling stand;*
> *Ponder nothing earthly minded,*
> *For with blessing in his hand,*
> *Christ our God to earth descendeth*
> *Our full homage to demand.*

4. It Makes the God of the OT More Personal

Even those who believe in the covenantal unity of the Bible would have their understanding deepened and their hearts warmed to see the immediacy of Christ's presence in the Old Testament, that Jesus is the God who reveals God in both Testaments. This perspective helps us see his activity throughout history. It helps us see that the Old Testament saints knew Jesus, but also how we know Jesus differently. It changes how we read texts.

We noted in the preface: does it make a difference to know that, when the Angel of God is introduced as calling to Abraham in Genesis 22 to stop him from sacrificing Isaac, that the Angel's introduction into the text was on purpose, and that it was the Person of Jesus stopping Abraham from sacrificing his son? The text introduces the distinction on purpose. But we see even more than Abraham saw! We see a God "who did not spare his own Son but gave him up for us all" (Rom 8:32). We also see one "who is at the right hand of God, who indeed is interceding for us" (Rom 8:34). Suddenly, the story becomes that much more personal, tragic, beautiful, and amazing. We see that the Son has been working, from the very beginning, to intercede for us. We see that the Father *sent* the Son. The Father himself loves us and he has loved us by sending his Son—to lead his people in the Old Covenant, and to represent his people in the New. Now he has sent the Spirit of his Son into our hearts. And we rejoice to gaze upon that Son.

Majestic sweetness sits enthroned upon the Savior's brow
His head with radiant glories crowned, His lips with grace o'erflow.
No mortal can with Him compare among the sons of men;
Fairer is He than all the fair that fill the heav'nly train.

5. It Deepens Our Understanding of the Cross

Seeing Jesus' activity in the Old Testament increases our appreciation of the drama of his cross. We see even more the majesty and humility in his willing sacrifice. He was the eternal Son from the Father, in eternal union with the Father, who perfectly represented God to this world, who carried out the Father's will. He was the commander of the armies of the Lord, who bore the sword of the Lord, as the eternal right hand from the Father. And the Father "saw that there was no man, and wondered that there was no one to intercede; then his own arm brought him salvation, and his righteousness upheld him. He put on

righteousness as a breastplate, and a helmet of salvation on his head...
And a Redeemer will come to Zion" (Isa 59:16-17, 20). The eternal Son
from the Father set out to bear our griefs, to carry our sorrows, to be
pierced for our transgressions, crushed for our iniquities, to bring us
peace, to heal our wounds, to bear our iniquities (Isa 53:4-6). He would
do this by his own sword of judgment being turned against himself!
"Awake, O sword, against my shepherd, against the man who stands
next to me. Strike the shepherd" (Zech 13:7).

> *He saw me plunged in deep distress; He flew to my relief.*
> *For me He bore the shameful cross and carried all my grief.*
> *To Him I owe my life and breath and all the joys I have.*
> *He makes me triumph over death and saves me from the grave.*

6. It Deepens Our Understanding of the Cosmic Aspect of the Bible

Jesus' cross, resurrection, and ascension were not just a victory over
sin and death. They were a victory over spiritual forces of wickedness in
the heavenly places. Understanding the Son's role in the Divine Council
and the spiritual warfare in the heavenly realms helps us see the unfolding story in both Testaments, not just on earth but in heaven, how it's
important that Jesus became heir of all things, in both earth and heaven.

In the Old Testament, we have seen that the Person of Jesus was active
in the heavenly realms as the Son of the Most High, as the God who
claimed Israel as his special inheritance among all the nations, and who
gave over the nations to the control of other gods (*elohim*). As the Angel of
the Lord, he was both among the other "sons of God" and above them as
the eternally begotten Son of the Most High, seated on the throne of the
Most High. Yet, the Father and Son together were in judgment of the gods
of the nations for their oppression and wickedness and rebellion against
righteousness. They determined together that the Son would bring to an
end their rule and claims over the nations, that the Son would reclaim all
the nations of the earth as his inheritance (Psalm 2, 82, etc.), and would
judge and punish the principalities and powers in heaven.

To do this, the eternal Son became a perfect man to be our new
federal head and to offer himself as a sacrifice for sin in our place. By
the acceptance of his intercession, the record of debt that stood against

us was cancelled. "He disarmed the rulers and authorities and put them to open shame" (Col 3:15). Because of his worthiness, he was raised from the dead, exalted back to the right hand of the Father above all other principalities and powers, given the name above every name, and given all authority in both heaven and earth. As a result, he has united and reconciled to himself all things, things in heaven and things on earth (Eph 1:10; Col 1:20; Php 2:9-10). Further, he has raised believers up with him and seated us in the heavenly places as new heavenly sons of God (Eph 2:6), a new divine council to rule and judge over heaven and earth (1Co 6:3, 2Ti 2:12, Rev 2:26, 3:21).

Christians have often missed seeing this cosmic story and have not understand the supernatural world of the Old and New Testaments or recognized the work of the Persons of the Godhead in the heavenly realm. The Gospel is more far-reaching than my personal sin and forgiveness. It encompasses a cosmic purpose for the future.

> *Thou comest in the darksome night*
> *To make us children of the light,*
> *To make us, in the realms divine,*
> *Like thine own angels round thee shine.*

> *See, the Con-qu'ror mounts in triumph; see the King in royal state,*
> *Riding on the clouds, his chariot, to his heavenly palace gate:*
> *Hark! the choirs of angel voices joyful alleluias sing,*
> *And the portals high are lifted to receive their heavenly King.*

7. It Reminds Us That Jesus is Still All These Things ... and Has Come into His Full Rights as Son

We have seen that, in the Old Testament, Jesus is the mediating Divine Angel who is the Word, the Glory, the Name, the Power, the Face-Presence, the Hand-Arm, the Prince-Commander, and the eternally begotten Son. He was the one sent to guide Israel on the way and to bring them to the place prepared. He was the one against whom they sinned, and eventually, his presence and blessing were withdrawn from them, his covenant with them broken. But it was promised that he would come again as the Angel of the Covenant and return to his Temple and purify his people.

In the NT, Jesus comes in a startling and brand-new way—still as the Word, the Glory, the Name, the Presence, the Hand, etc., *but now made flesh* to dwell among us, not ashamed to call us brothers! After his death and resurrection, he has now ascended back into heaven as the firstborn from the dead that he might be preeminent in all things, both in earth and in heaven. He has been fully revealed as the Son of the Father and has entered into his inheritance. Now, in the NT, he has been given authority over earth and heaven and promises he will be with us always, to the end of the age. In other words, the new covenant has been inaugurated, the promise of the old covenants fulfilled. God has truly become our salvation. All that the Divine Angel was in the OT, he still is, with the added bonus that he calls us brothers. With all of these titles and in all of these ways, Jesus has been revealed in both Testaments. He is still all of these things, and more, because he has come into an exalted possession of them. So when we read and see Him in the Old Testament, we know that all he is there, he still is for us today and more!

> *Fear not, I am with you, O be not dismayed;*
> *For I am your God, and will still give you aid;*
> *I'll strengthen you, help you, and cause you to stand,*
> *Upheld by my righteous, omnipotent hand.*

8. This Calls You to Draw Near, Worship, and Follow Jesus

Our biggest problem is that we need a way back to God and the way is barred because of sin and because of fallenness. How can we draw near to God when the way is shut?

Amazingly, God sent his Son and that sending of the Son began in the OT, really at the very beginning of creation. He revealed himself to man in Adam. He revealed Himself to His chosen people. He came to provide covenants of promise—that there was a way back to God. The old covenant system provided a picture of the way. It pictured the barriers between us and God, the need for atonement, and a mediator who would go past the curtain and intercede for us, yet would come back out to assure us that God was with us and we had peace with him.

But then the most amazing act of history happened! Those pictures gave way to an even greater reality. One never before seen in all the long history of the world. Unique. Startling. Staggering. The God who was sent to reveal God to us was sent to become a man in human flesh in order to truly be "with us." Immanuel. He became himself our perfect mediator, able to represent us before God, to enter the heavenly holy places, to intercede for us. By his resurrection and ascension, we see that the way is no longer shut. We can have boldness to draw near to God. Like all of his saints throughout history, he calls us out of slavery, calls us to leave our hopes and desires for this world, to deny ourselves and to follow him in the pilgrimage of life wherever he leads, knowing that he is with us wherever we go, and he will finally bring us to his eternal home.

May God be pleased to open minds and hearts to the glory of his Son and to heed his call in all the Scriptures to draw near, to worship, and to follow Him.

Before the throne of God above,
I have a strong and perfect plea,
A great High Priest whose name is Love
Who ever lives and pleads for me.
My name is graven on His hands,
My name is written on His heart,
I know that while in heaven he stands,
No tongue can bid me thence depart.

None other Lamb, none other name,
None other hope in heaven or earth or sea,
None other hiding place from guilt and shame,
None beside thee!

Soli Deo Gloria

PART IV

APPENDICES

APPENDIX I

The Angel and the Satan

1 Chronicles 21:1 says, *"Then Satan stood against Israel and incited David to number Israel."* What has this to do with the Angel of the LORD? The answer may surprise you.

We begin with the word *"saṭan"* which the ESV, following most translations, renders as the proper noun: "Satan." But the word simply means "adversary." Thus, Young's Literal Translation reads, "And there standeth up an adversary against Israel…"

1Ch 21:1 has a parallel in 2Sa 24:1. *"Again, the anger of the LORD was kindled against Israel, and he incited David against them, saying, 'Go, number Israel and Judah.'"* Both verses teach about someone who instigated, or at least inspired, David to desire to number the people of Israel. But whereas in Chronicles it is some "adversary" (possibly Satan but not necessarily), in Samuel it is "Yahweh."

Now obvious questions are raised if one translates Chronicles as "Satan." Because suddenly, we have to explain how both Satan and Yahweh could be doing the very same thing? This in turn leads to potential questions about God's relationship to evil. While it is possible to give some good responses to these things assuming it is literally the person Satan in one passage and Yahweh in the other, it may very well be that we have created a tension where none existed for the ancient writer(s).

The word *satan* in Hebrew is not well understood in the broader Christian culture, as we use it almost exclusively for the great adversary of God: the Devil (the LXX translator seems to have thought it was Satan, as he translates the word as *diabolos*). But the word in the OT is most often used to describe a function rather than a personal name. This can be understood by looking at its Hebrew form which often puts the definite article (*ha*) in front of the word so that you get *ha-satan*, "the satan," or "the accuser."

Hebrew does not allow a definite article to go in front of a proper name (neither does English, unless you are "The Donald"). This is why, even though it may very well be the chief arch-rival of God that goes before the LORD in a place like Job 1:6 or Zech 3:1-2, it is still not good grammar to translate it as "Satan." Rather, it is simply "the accuser" or "the adversary" (again, see Young's Literal Translation), with no specially named individual in mind.[393] We see this in other places, for example when David confronts his own nephews and calls them *l'satan*, an adversary (2Sa 19:22).

There is no article in front of *satan* in 1 Chronicles 21:1. This has led to the majority translation "Satan." This is grammatically possible. Commentaries often run to this to mitigate the seemingly damaging effects of the Samuel passage where it is Yahweh who "incited" (*suth*) David against Israel. As such, it is possible that this translation is theologically rather than textually driven.

This word *suth* is variously translated in other places as "stimulate," "divert," "irritate," "entice," "incited," "mislead," "stir up," and "persuade." The Greek translation means "to stir up." These are obviously not all the same level of involvement as one another. Some are more direct. Some are more indirect. The perceived problem, of course,

---

[393] Even Jude doesn't call him Satan in the parallel to Zech 3:2. That said, though they do not have the same story in mind, and though Jude is likely borrowing from an intertestamental book called *The Testament of Moses* (sometimes called *The Assumption of Moses*), the language parallel between Zech 3:2 ("And the LORD said to *ha-satan*, 'The LORD rebuke you *ha-satan*") and Jude 1:9 ("When the archangel Michael, contending with the devil, was disputing about the body of Moses ... [he] said, 'The Lord rebuke you'") shows how the person we call the devil or Satan could on at least one occasion very easily be seen as the great antagonist of the LORD when the phrase *ha-satan* was used. But as we said, Jude doesn't call him Satan, but the devil. Also—and this is important (see the rest of the discussion below)—in Zechariah 3, *ha-satan's* enemy is very clearly called "the Angel of the LORD," meaning that the Angel cannot possibly be the *satan* in this story. For more on the background sources of Jude 1:9 see, "Excursus: The Background and Source of Jude 9," in Richard J. Bauckham, *2 Peter, Jude*, vol. 50, Word Biblical Commentary (Dallas: Word, Incorporated, 1998), 65-76.

comes from "who" does the "inciting" and whether the "inciting" is explicitly evil. To translate it as "Satan" doing the inciting in one passage doesn't actually solve the problem if the LORD is doing it in the other passage. If what the LORD does in Samuel is evil as some want to suggest, then it is evil. If what he does in Samuel is not evil, then what the *satan* does in Chronicles is not necessarily evil either, since they are doing the same thing.

Our take is that in neither case is the *suth*-ing ("inciting") of David an evil thing. Of course, what *David* does with it is evil. The text says as much. But that is different. God can have one motive for decreeing or even *suth*-ing a thing, while the person carrying it out has a completely different motive. Joseph said it best to his brothers, "As for you, you meant evil against me, but God meant it for good" (Gen 50:20). In this case, the "good" would be just judgment upon Israel. What had they done? We are not really told. What was David's exact sin? Again, we aren't really told. But the lack of detail does not change the fact that if what the LORD did is evil, then it is evil, and if what the LORD did is good, then it is not necessarily evil when the *satan* does it in the parallel.

What is so tantalizing about all of this is that *both* stories are replete with verses telling us that the Angel of the LORD was deeply involved in this whole affair (see 2Sa 24:16, 17; 1Ch 21:12, 15, 16, 18, 20, 27, 30), and this is quite unusual in both Samuel and Chronicles. There are more references to the Angel in this one story than there are in all the other stories of both 1-2 Samuel and 1-2 Chronicles combined! And for good measure, we also see "the Word of the LORD" speaking in one (2Sa 24:11) and the Name of the LORD in the other (2Ch 21:19). In other words, this entire story is supercharged with the Person we are studying in this book.

So what does any of this have to do with the *satan* of 1Ch 21:1? Just this. The only other instance in which *satan* is used of a non-human entity without the definite article just so happens to be when *the Angel of the LORD* is called *l'satan* in the Balaam story. "And the Angel of the LORD took his stand in the way as *his adversary*" (Num 22:22). In other words, there is explicit biblical precedent that the Angel of the LORD is the *satan* in at least one other instance. Again, he is not Satan. That would be blasphemy. He is the adversary—in this case, to Balaam, because the evil prophet stands against Yahweh.

This English word "stand" is a good segue to a curious choice of words that the Chronicler uses in his telling of the story. Whereas Samuel says, "Again the anger of the LORD was kindled against Israel, and he incited David against them," the Chronicler says, "Then Satan *stood* against Israel and incited David." The word "stood" (*amad*) is not in the Samuel account. It is in the Chronicles account. Could it be that this is a verbal clue as to who the *satan* is? How so?

Later in the same story we find the Chronicler saying, "And God sent the angel to Jerusalem to destroy it, but as he was about to destroy it, the LORD saw, and he relented from the calamity. And he said to the angel who was working destruction, 'It is enough; now stay your hand.' And the angel of the LORD was standing by the threshing floor of Ornan the Jebusite. And David lifted his eyes and saw *the angel of the LORD standing* (*amad*) between earth and heaven, and in his hand a drawn sword stretched out over Jerusalem. Then David and the elders, clothed in sackcloth, fell upon their faces" (1Ch 21:15-16). Previously the *satan* was standing; now it is the Angel.[394] In both instances, both persons are standing against Israel. In both cases, it is because Israel has sinned. In both instances, judgment is being carried out by God.

Scholars have long puzzled over this strange change from "Yahweh" (Samuel) to the *satan* (Chronicles), even as they puzzle long and hard over how—even in this very story—the Angel seems both to be God and yet be distinct from God. All of these problems are solved if the *satan* of Chronicles is the Angel of the LORD.[395]

This solution makes good sense of the repository of "Angel," "Word," and "Name" verses later on in both stories. It makes sense of

---

[394] "Yahweh's messenger" and *śāṭān* are sometimes identified elsewhere in Hebrew Bible, or at least associated as colleagues or opponents. And the verb associated with the *śāṭān* at the outset (*'āmad*, 1Ch 21:1) reappears later (21:16, 17)—and precisely with *mal'ak yhwh* as subject." A. Graeme Auld, *I & II Samuel: A Commentary*, ed. William P. Brown, Carol A. Newsom, and Brent A. Strawn, 1st ed., The Old Testament Library (Louisville, KY: Westminster John Knox Press, 2012), 605. This entire section in Auld makes the argument that the Chronicler was actually aware of a source ("the original text") that also knew the instigator as the *satan*. This implies that he isn't changing anything.

[395] For scholarship that comes close to this solution, seeing the *satan* as some kind of angelic entity, see Paul Evans, "Divine intermediaries in 1 Chronicles 21 an overlooked aspect of the Chronicler's theology," *Biblica* 85:4 (2004): 545-558.

the most common usage of *satan* in Hebrew. That is, the Chronicler would be doing this in order to highlight the function that the Angel has throughout this story: he is an adversary to Israel because of her sin. The Chronicler changes many parts of this story to fit its own teaching design, so this would be consistent with his practice. And it means that the Chronicler is not changing Samuel because he felt some sort of theological problem needed to be averted (whether Samuel has the Father Yahweh or the Son Yahweh in mind, it is irrelevant since they are both Yahweh). Read this way, there is no new theological problem that is introduced as some see if somehow the person in mind is the Devil (the problem would be if the Chronicler is trying to get Yahweh "off the hook" for the apparent "evil" that could be implied in Samuel, but even here we see no problem as it would be the LORD inciting David through the instrumental means of the temptation of the Devil).

Why has this solution so often escaped people's attention?[396] We believe it is most likely due to the same factors we have been seeing throughout this book. People do not realize that "Angel" and "LORD" are used synonymously throughout the Scripture. Nor do they realize that the Angel of the LORD can be someone's accuser (*satan*).

---

[396] It hasn't always. Recently, Michael Heiser argued a similar idea. See Michael S. Heiser, "1003 BC Census: Who Authorized It—God or Satan?," in *I Dare You Not to Bore Me with the Bible*, ed. John D. Barry and Rebecca Van Noord (Bellingham, WA: Lexham Press; Bible Study Magazine, 2014), 71-74. Originally published in *BibleStudy Magazine* Vol. 2 No. 5.

2 Samuel 24:1-25	1 Chronicles 21:1-30
[1] Again the anger of the LORD was kindled against Israel, and he incited David against them, saying, "Go, number Israel and Judah."	[1] Then Satan stood against Israel and incited David to number Israel.
[2] So the king said to Joab, the commander of the army, who was with him, "Go through all the tribes of Israel, from Dan to Beersheba, and number the people, that I may know the number of the people."	[2] So David said to Joab and the commanders of the army, "Go, number Israel, from Beersheba to Dan, and bring me a report, that I may know their number."
[3] But Joab said to the king, "May the LORD your God add to the people a hundred times as many as they are, while the eyes of my lord the king still see it, but why does my lord the king delight in this thing?"	[3] But Joab said, "May the LORD add to his people a hundred times as many as they are! Are they not, my lord the king, all of them my lord's servants? Why then should my lord require this? Why should it be a cause of guilt for Israel?"
[4] But the king's word prevailed against Joab and the commanders of the army. So Joab and the commanders of the army went out from the presence of the king to number the people of Israel. [5] They crossed the Jordan and began from Aroer, and from the city that is in the middle of the valley, toward Gad and on to Jazer. [6] Then they came to Gilead, and to Kadesh in the land of the Hittites; and they came to Dan, and from Dan they went around to Sidon, [7] and came to the fortress of Tyre and to all the cities of the Hivites and Canaanites; and they went out to the Negeb of Judah at Beersheba. [8] So when they had gone through all the land, they came to Jerusalem at the end of nine months and twenty days.	[4] But the king's word prevailed against Joab. So Joab departed and went throughout all Israel and came back to Jerusalem.
[9] And Joab gave the sum of the numbering of the people to the king: in Israel there were 800,000 valiant men who drew the sword, and the men of Judah were 500,000.	[5] And Joab gave the sum of the numbering of the people to David. In all Israel there were 1,100,000 men who drew the sword, and in Judah 470,000 who drew the sword.

	⁶ But he did not include Levi and Benjamin in the numbering, for the king's command was abhorrent to Joab.
¹⁰ But *David's heart struck him* after he had numbered the people.	⁷ But *God was displeased* with this thing, and he struck Israel.
And David said to the LORD, "I have sinned greatly in what I have done. But now, O LORD, please take away the iniquity of your servant, for I have done very foolishly."	⁸ And David said to God, "I have sinned greatly in that I have done this thing. But now, please take away the iniquity of your servant, for I have acted very foolishly."
¹¹ And when David arose in the morning, *the word of the LORD came to the prophet Gad*, David's seer, saying,	⁹ And *the LORD spoke to Gad*, David's seer, saying,
¹² "Go and say to David, 'Thus says the LORD, Three things I offer you. Choose one of them, that I may do it to you.'"	¹⁰ "Go and say to David, 'Thus says the LORD, Three things I offer you; choose one of them, that I may do it to you.'"
¹³ So Gad came to David and told him, and said to him,	¹¹ So Gad came to David and said to him, "Thus says the LORD, 'Choose what you will:
"Shall three years of famine come to you in your land? Or will you flee three months before your foes while they pursue you?	¹² either three years of famine, or three months of devastation by your foes while the sword of your enemies overtakes you,
Or shall there be three days' pestilence in your land?	or else three days of the sword of the LORD, pestilence on the land, with *the angel of the LORD* destroying throughout all the territory of Israel.'
Now consider, and decide what answer I shall return to him who sent me."	Now decide what answer I shall return to him who sent me."
¹⁴ Then David said to Gad, "I am in great distress. Let us fall into *the hand of the LORD*, for his mercy is great; but let me not fall into the hand of man."	¹³ Then David said to Gad, "I am in great distress. Let me fall into *the hand of the LORD*, for his mercy is very great, but do not let me fall into the hand of man."
¹⁵ So the LORD sent a pestilence on Israel from the morning until the appointed time. And there died of the people from Dan to Beersheba 70,000 men.	¹⁴ So the LORD sent a pestilence on Israel, and 70,000 men of Israel fell.
¹⁶ And when *the angel* stretched out his hand toward Jerusalem to destroy it, the LORD relented from the calamity	¹⁵ And God sent *the angel* to Jerusalem to destroy it, but as he was about to destroy it, the LORD saw, and he relented from the calamity.

and said to the angel who was working destruction among the people, "It is enough; now stay your hand." And *the angel of the LORD* was by the threshing floor of Araunah the Jebusite.	And he said to the angel who was working destruction, "It is enough; now stay your hand." And *the angel of the LORD* was standing by the threshing floor of Ornan the Jebusite.
¹⁷ Then David spoke to the LORD when he saw the *angel* who was striking the people, and said,	¹⁶ And David lifted his eyes and saw the *angel of the LORD* standing between earth and heaven, and in his hand a drawn sword stretched out over Jerusalem. Then David and the elders, clothed in sackcloth, fell upon their faces. ¹⁷ And David said to God,
"Behold, I have sinned, and I have done wickedly. But these sheep, what have they done? Please let your hand be against me and against my father's house."	"Was it not I who gave command to number the people? It is I who have sinned and done great evil. But these sheep, what have they done? Please let your hand, O LORD my God, be against me and against my father's house. But do not let the plague be on your people."
¹⁸ And Gad came that day to David and said to him, "Go up, raise an altar to the LORD on the threshing floor of Araunah the Jebusite."	¹⁸ Now *the angel of the LORD* had commanded Gad to say to David that David should go up and raise an altar to the LORD on the threshing floor of Ornan the Jebusite.
¹⁹ So David went up at Gad's word, as *the LORD commanded*.	¹⁹ So David went up at Gad's word, which he had spoken *in the name of the LORD*.
	²⁰ Now Ornan was threshing wheat. He turned and saw *the angel*, and his four sons who were with him hid themselves.
²⁰ And when Araunah looked down, he saw the king and his servants coming on toward him. And Araunah went out and paid homage to the king with his face to the ground.	²¹ As David came to Ornan, Ornan looked and saw David and went out from the threshing floor and paid homage to David with his face to the ground.
²¹ And Araunah said, "Why has my lord the king come to his servant?" David said, "To buy the threshing floor from you, in order to build an altar to the LORD, that the plague may be averted from the people."	²² And David said to Ornan, "Give me the site of the threshing floor that I may build on it an altar to the LORD– give it to me at its full price—that the plague may be averted from the people."
²² Then Araunah said to David,	²³ Then Ornan said to David,

"Let my lord the king take and offer up what seems good to him. Here are the oxen for the burnt offering and the threshing sledges and the yokes of the oxen for the wood.	"Take it, and let my lord the king do what seems good to him. See, I give the oxen for burnt offerings and the threshing sledges for the wood and the wheat for a grain offering; I give it all."
[23] All this, O king, Araunah gives to the king." And Araunah said to the king, "May the LORD your God accept you."	
[24] But the king said to Araunah, "No, but I will buy it from you for a price. I will not offer burnt offerings to the LORD my God that cost me nothing."	[24] But King David said to Ornan, "No, but I will buy them for the full price. I will not take for the LORD what is yours, nor offer burnt offerings that cost me nothing."
So David bought the threshing floor and the oxen for fifty shekels of silver.	[25] So David paid Ornan 600 shekels of gold by weight for the site.
[25] And David built there an altar to the LORD and offered burnt offerings and peace offerings. So the LORD responded to the plea for the land, and the plague was averted from Israel.	[26] And David built there an altar to the LORD and presented burnt offerings and peace offerings and called on the LORD, and the LORD answered him with fire from heaven upon the altar of burnt offering. [27] Then the LORD commanded *the angel*, and he put his sword back into its sheath. [28] At that time, when David saw that the LORD had answered him at the threshing floor of Ornan the Jebusite, he sacrificed there. [29] For the tabernacle of the LORD, which Moses had made in the wilderness, and the altar of burnt offering were at that time in the high place at Gibeon, [30] but David could not go before it to inquire of God, for he was afraid of the sword of the *angel of the LORD*."

APPENDIX II

Genesis 19:24 in Church History

Several passages mentioned in this book could actually be explored for entire chapters and might even deserve their own books. One of the more interesting is the continuous use of Genesis 19:24 in the early church (and even the Jewish church) all the way through the Reformation, as proof of Christ's presence in the OT. The verse reads, "Then the LORD rained on Sodom and Gomorrah sulfur and fire from the LORD out of heaven."

This verse is important on two counts. First, it is not well known or used today in discussions of Christ in the OT. Second, it was the opposite in the early church, including even among the Jews. The following are quotations showing the use of this verse in ancient days of the church. We will look at the Church Fathers first, then we will turn our attention to the early rabbis who were teaching this "heresy."

IGNATIUS (d. 107 AD), *Antiochians* 2 [397]

For Moses, the faithful servant of God, when he said, "The Lord thy God is one Lord (Deut 6:4; Mark 12:29);" and thus proclaimed that there was only one God, did yet forthwith confess also our Lord when he said, "The Lord rained upon Sodom and Gomorrah fire and brimstone from the Lord" (Gen 19:24).

---

[397] This is the longer version of Ignatius' epistle to the Antiochians. Therefore, it is sometimes called Pseudo-Ignatius. This quotation is in Pseudo-Ignatius of Antioch, "The Epistle of Ignatius to the Antiochians," in *The Apostolic Fathers with Justin Martyr and Irenaeus*, ed. Alexander Roberts, James Donaldson, and A. Cleveland Coxe, vol. 1, The Ante-Nicene Fathers (Buffalo, NY: Christian Literature Company, 1885), 110. While Ignatius died in 107 A.D., additions may date to the 4th century.

JUSTIN (100 – 165 AD), *Dialogue* 127 [398]

Therefore neither Abraham, nor Isaac, nor Jacob, nor any other man, saw the Father and ineffable Lord of all, and also of Christ, but [saw] Him who was according to His will His Son, being God, and the Angel because He ministered to His will; whom also it pleased Him to be born man by the Virgin; who also was fire when He conversed with Moses from the bush. Since, unless we thus comprehend the Scriptures, it must follow that the Father and Lord of all had not been in heaven when what Moses wrote took place: "And the Lord rained upon Sodom fire and brimstone from the Lord out of heaven" (Gen 19:24); and again, when it is thus said by David: "Lift up your gates, ye rulers; and be ye lift up, ye everlasting gates; and the King of glory shall enter" (Ps 24:7); and again, when He says: "The Lord says to my Lord, Sit at My right hand, till I make Thine enemies Thy footstool" (Ps 110:1).

IRENAEUS (135 – 202 AD), *Against Heresies* 3.6.1 [399]

Since, therefore, the Father is truly Lord, and the Son truly Lord, the Holy Spirit has fitly designated them by the title of Lord. And again, referring to the destruction of the Sodomites, the Scripture says, "Then the Lord rained upon Sodom and upon Gomorrah fire and brimstone from the Lord out of heaven" (Gen 19:24). For it here points out that the Son, who had also been talking with Abraham, had received power to judge the Sodomites for their wickedness.

TERTULLIAN (160 – 225 AD), *Against Praxeas* 13 [400]

I find in Scripture the name Lord also applied to them both: "The Lord said unto my Lord, Sit Thou on my right hand" (Ps 110:1). And Isaiah says this: "Lord, who hath believed our report, and to whom is the arm of the Lord revealed?" (Isa 53:1). Now he would most certainly have said *Thine Arm*, if he had not wished us to understand that the Father is Lord, and the Son also is Lord. A much more ancient testimony we have also in Genesis: "Then the Lord rained upon Sodom and upon Gomorrah brimstone and fire from the Lord out of heaven" (Gen 19:24). Now,

[398] Justin Martyr, "Dialogue of Justin with Trypho, a Jew," in *The Apostolic Fathers with Justin Martyr and Irenaeus*, ed. Alexander Roberts, James Donaldson, and A. Cleveland Coxe, vol. 1, The Ante-Nicene Fathers (Buffalo, NY: Christian Literature Company, 1885), 263.

[399] Irenaeus of Lyons, "Irenæus against Heresies," in *The Apostolic Fathers with Justin Martyr and Irenaeus*, ed. Alexander Roberts, James Donaldson, and A. Cleveland Coxe, vol. 1, The Ante-Nicene Fathers (Buffalo, NY: Christian Literature Company, 1885), 418.

[400] Tertullian, "Against Praxeas," in *Latin Christianity: Its Founder, Tertullian*, ed. Alexander Roberts, James Donaldson, and A. Cleveland Coxe, trans. Peter Holmes, vol. 3, The Ante-Nicene Fathers (Buffalo, NY: Christian Literature Company, 1885), 607–608.

either deny that this is Scripture; or else (let me ask) what sort of man you are, that you do not think words ought to be taken and understood in the sense in which they are written, especially when they are not expressed in allegories and parables, but in determinate and simple declarations?

CYPRIAN (200-258 AD), *Against the Jews* 3.33 [401]
That the Father judgeth nothing, but the Son; and that the Father is not glorified by him by whom the Son is not glorified. In the Gospel according to John: "The Father judgeth nothing, but hath given all judgment unto the Son, that all may honour the Son as they honour the Father. He who honoureth not the Son, honoureth not the Father who hath sent Him" (John 5:22, 23). Also in the seventy-first Psalm: "O God, give the king Thy judgment, and Thy righteousness to the king's son, to judge Thy people in righteousness" (Ps 72:1, 2). Also in Genesis: "And the Lord rained upon Sodom and Gomorrah sulphur, and fire from heaven from the Lord" (Gen 19:24).

NOVATIAN (200 – 258 AD), *On the Trinity* 18.15–17 [402]
That there might not remain any doubt that [God the Son] had been the guest of Abraham, it is written regarding the destruction of the Sodomites that "the Lord poured down on Sodom and Gomorrah fire and sulfur from the Lord out of heaven" (Gen 19:24). In fact, the prophet also says in the person of God, "I destroyed you as the Lord destroyed Sodom and Gomorrah." The Lord, therefore, destroyed Sodom; that is, God destroyed Sodom. In the destruction of the Sodomites, however, it was the Lord who rained fire from the Lord. This Lord was the God seen by Abraham (Gen 12:7; 18:1). This God is Abraham's guest (Gen 18:3-8) and was undoubtedly seen because he was touched. Now, since the Father, inasmuch as he is invisible, was assuredly not seen at that time, he who was seen and who was hospitably received and taken in was he who was willing to be seen and touched. This one then is the Son of God, "the Lord, who rained upon Sodom and Gomorrah fire and sulfur from the Lord" (Gen 19:24). But he is the Word of God, and the "Word" of God "was made flesh and dwelt among us" (John 1:14). This one then is Christ. Therefore it was not the Father who was the guest of Abraham but Christ. Nor was it the Father who was seen but the Son; therefore it was Christ who was seen. Consequently Christ is both Lord and God, who could be seen by Abraham only because he was God, the Word, begotten of God the Father before Abraham even existed (John 8:58).

---

[401] Cyprian of Carthage, "Three Books of Testimonies Against the Jews," in *Fathers of the Third Century: Hippolytus, Cyprian, Novatian, Appendix*, ed. Alexander Roberts, James Donaldson, and A. Cleveland Coxe, trans. Robert Ernest Wallis, vol. 5, The Ante-Nicene Fathers (Buffalo, NY: Christian Literature Company, 1886), 544.
[402] FC 67:70–71. Cited in Alberto Ferreiro, "Introduction to the Twelve Prophets," in *The Twelve Prophets*, ed. Alberto Ferreiro, Ancient Christian Commentary on Scripture (Downers Grove, IL: InterVarsity Press, 2003), 96.

EUSEBIUS (263 – 340 AD), *Ecclesiastical History* 1.2.9 [403]
Of him Moses speaks very clearly, calling him a second Lord after the Father, when he says, "The Lord rained upon Sodom and Gomorrah brimstone and fire from the Lord" (Gen 19:24).

FIRST CREED OF SIRMIUM (347 A. D.), Canon 17 [404]
17. Whoever shall explain, *The Lord rained fire from the Lord* (Gen 19:24) not of the Father and the Son, and says that He rained from Himself, be he anathema. For the Son Lord rained from the Father Lord."

ATHANASIUS (295 – 373 AD), *Discourses Against the Arians* 2.15.13 [405]
If then they [i.e. the Arians] suppose that the Savior was not Lord and King, even before he became man and endured the cross, but then began to be Lord, let them know

---

[403] Novatian, FC 19:40–41. Cited in Quentin F. Wesselschmidt, *Psalms 51–150*, Ancient Christian Commentary on Scripture OT 8 (Downers Grove, IL: InterVarsity Press, 2007), 254.

[404] Athanasius, *Select Treatises of S. Athanasius (Archbishop of Alexandria) in Controversy with the Arians*, trans. with notes and indices John Henry Parker (Oxford, F. and J. Rivington, 1853), 120-21.

A word of explanation on this little-known creed. In the intervening years after Constantine the Great's death there was a war for the heart of Christianity between the Orthodox and the Arians. The councils of Sirmium were convened by semi-Arians who sought a compromise between the two parties. While portions of their creeds were deemed heretical, other parts are perfectly orthodox (such is the nature of all heresy). Athanasius was heavily involved in those creeds, which is important since he will say the very same things about this text. Hence, one commentary states, "This and the [previous] Canon are Catholic in their main doctrine" (p. 120).

The very next canon (18) is more difficult, even though it continues with the Genesis 19 story. "Whosoever hearing that the Father is Lord and the Son is Lord and the Father and Son Lord, for there is Lord from Lord, says that there are two Gods, be he anathema. For we do not place the Son in the Father's order, but as subordinate to the Father; for they did not descend upon Sodom without the Father's will, nor did He rain from Himself, but from the Lord, that is, the Father authorizing it. Nor is He of Himself set down on the right hand, but He hears the Father saying, 'Sit Thou on My right hand.'" The first sentence is orthodox. The second is more difficult, especially in the context of Arianism. The Arians used "subordination" to refer to a lesser deity. But this very canon strictly condemns this view. Subordination of the Son in a functional (or economic) way was language used by some of the orthodox as a way of expressing the differences of the two Persons though there is only one God.

[405] NPNF 2 4:355. Cited in Quentin F. Wesselschmidt, *Psalms 51–150*, Ancient Christian Commentary on Scripture OT 8 (Downers Grove, IL: InterVarsity Press, 2007), 262–263.

that they are openly reviving the statements of the Samosatene [i.e., the heresy of Adoptionism]. But if, as we have quoted and declared above, he is the everlasting Lord and King, seeing that Abraham worships him as Lord and Moses says, "Then the Lord rained on Sodom and on Gomorrah brimstone and fire from the Lord out of heaven" (Gen 19:24); and David in the Psalms, "The Lord said to my Lord, 'Sit on my right hand'" (Ps 110:1); and "Your throne, O God, is forever and ever; a scepter of righteousness is the scepter of your kingdom" (Ps 45:6); and "Your kingdom is an everlasting kingdom" (Ps 145:13); it is plain that even before he became man, he was King and Lord everlasting, being Image and Word of the Father. And since the Word is everlasting Lord and King, it is very clear again that Peter did not say that the essence of the Son was made but spoke of his lordship over us, which "became" when he became man, and redeeming all by the cross, became Lord of all and King.

HILARY (315 – 367 AD), *On the Trinity* 5.16 [406]
I ask further, Who is this God Who overthrew Sodom and Gomorrah? For *the Lord rained from the Lord* (Gen 19:24); was it not the true Lord from the true Lord? Have you any alternative to this Lord, and Lord? Or any other meaning for the terms, except that in Lord, and Lord, their Persons are distinguished? Bear in mind that Him Whom you have confessed as *Alone true*, you have also confessed as *Alone the righteous Judge.* Now mark that the Lord who rains from the Lord, and slays not the just with the unjust, and judges the whole earth, is both Lord and also righteous Judge, and also rains from the Lord. In the face of all this, I ask you Which it is that you describe as alone the righteous Judge. The Lord rains from the Lord; you will not deny that He Who rains from the Lord is the righteous Judge, for Abraham, the Father of the Gentiles—but not of the unbelieving Gentiles—speaks thus: *In no wise shalt Thou do this thing, to slay the righteous with the wicked, for then shall the righteous be as the wicked. In no wise shalt Thou, Who judgest the earth, execute this judgment* (Gen 18:25). This God, then, the righteous Judge, is clearly also the true God. Blasphemer! Your own falsehood confutes you. Not yet do I bring forward the witness of the Gospels concerning God the Judge; the Law has told me that He is the Judge. You must deprive the Son of His judgeship before you can deprive Him of His true Divinity. You have solemnly confessed that He Who is the only righteous Judge is also the only true God; your own statements bind you to the admission that He Who is the righteous Judge is also true God. This Judge is the Lord, to Whom all things are possible, the Promiser of eternal blessings, Judge of righteous and of wicked. He is the God of Abraham, worshipped by him. Fool and blasphemer

---

[406] Hilary of Poitiers, "On the Trinity," in *St. Hilary of Poitiers, John of Damascus,* ed. Philip Schaff and Henry Wace, trans. E. W. Watson et al., vol. 9a, A Select Library of the Nicene and Post-Nicene Fathers of the Christian Church, Second Series (New York: Christian Literature Company, 1899), 89.

that you are, your shameless readiness of tongue must invent some new fallacy, if you are to prove that He is not true God.

GREGORY NAZIANZEN (330 – 389 AD), *Oration* 29:17 [407]
For we have learnt to believe in and to teach the Deity of the Son from their great and lofty utterances. And what utterances are these? These: God—The Word—He That Was In The Beginning and With The Beginning, and The Beginning. "In the Beginning was The Word, and the Word was with God, and the Word was God" (John 1:1), and "With Thee is the Beginning" (Ps 110:3), and "He who calleth her The Beginning from generations" (Isa 41:4). Then the Son is Only-begotten: The only "begotten Son which is in the bosom of the Father, it says, He hath declared Him" (John 1:18). The Way, the Truth, the Life, the Light. "I am the Way, the Truth, and the Life;" and "I am the Light of the World" (John 7:12; 9:5; 14:6). Wisdom and Power, "Christ, the Wisdom of God, and the Power of God" (1Co 1:24). The Effulgence, the Impress, the Image, the Seal; "Who being the Effulgence of His glory and the Impress of His Essence" (Heb 1:3), and "the Image of His Goodness" (Wisd 7:26), and "Him hath God the Father sealed" (John 7:27). Lord, King, He That Is, The Almighty. "The Lord rained down fire from the Lord" (Gen 19:24); and "A sceptre of righteousness is the sceptre of Thy Kingdom" (Ps 45:6); and "Which is and was and is to come, the Almighty" (Rev 1:8)—all which are clearly spoken of the Son, with all the other passages of the same force, none of which is an afterthought, or added later to the Son or the Spirit, any more than to the Father Himself.

BASIL (330 – 379 AD), *On Proverbs 7:22* [408]
The Lord Created Me (LXX.). According to them [the heretics he has in mind] the Saviour [Jesus] is not God nor the Father Lord, and it is written in vain, "the Lord said unto my Lord." False is the statement, "Therefore God, thy God, hath anointed thee." False too, "The Lord rained from the Lord." False, "God created in the image of God," and "Who is God save the Lord?" and "Who is a God save our God." False the statement of John that "the Word was God and the Word

[407] Gregory Nazianzen, "Select Orations of Saint Gregory Nazianzen," in *S. Cyril of Jerusalem, S. Gregory Nazianzen*, ed. Philip Schaff and Henry Wace, trans. Charles Gordon Browne and James Edward Swallow, vol. 7, A Select Library of the Nicene and Post-Nicene Fathers of the Christian Church, Second Series (New York: Christian Literature Company, 1894), 307.
[408] Basil, On Proverbs 7:22 in Blomfield Jackson, "Prolegomena: Sketch of the Life and Works of Saint Basil," in *St. Basil: Letters and Select Works*, ed. Philip Schaff and Henry Wace, vol. 8, A Select Library of the Nicene and Post-Nicene Fathers of the Christian Church, Second Series (New York: Christian Literature Company, 1895), xlii.

was with God" (John 1:1); and the words of Thomas of the Son, "my Lord and my God" (John 20:28).

AMBROSE (333 – 397 AD), *Exposition of the Christian Faith* 1.3.22-23 [409]
"In Thee," saith he, "is God"—forasmuch as the Father is in the Son. For it is written, "The Father, Who abideth in Me, Himself speaketh," and "The works that I do, He Himself also doeth" (John 14:10). And yet again we read that the Son is in the Father, saying, "I am in the Father, and the Father in Me." Let the Arians, if they can, make away with this kinship in nature and unity in work.
23. There is, therefore, God in God, but not two Gods; for it is written that there is one God (Isa 45:18; 1Co 8:4, 6), and there is Lord in Lord, but not two Lords, forasmuch as it is likewise written: "Serve not two lords" (Matt 6:24). And the Law saith: "Hear, O Israel! The Lord thy God is one God" (Dt 6:4); moreover, in the same Testament it is written: "The Lord rained from the Lord" (Gen 19:24). The Lord, it is said, sent rain "from the Lord." So also you may read in Genesis: "And God said,—and God made" (Gen 1:6-7), and, lower down, "And God made man in the image of God" (Gen 1:26-27); yet it was not two gods, but one God, that made [man]. In the one place, then, as in the other, the unity of operation and of name is maintained. For surely, when we read "God of God" (Nicene Creed), we do not speak of two Gods.

CHRYSOSTOM (344 - 407), *Homily* 3: 2 Tim 1:13-18 [410]
Here those who are infected with the heresy of Marcion assail this expression; but let them learn that this mode of speech is not uncommon in Scripture; as when it is said, "The Lord said unto my Lord" (Ps 110:1); and again, "I said unto the Lord, Thou art my Lord" (Ps 16:2); and, "The Lord rained fire from the Lord" (Gen 19:24). This indicates that the Persons are of the same substance, not that there is a distinction of nature. For we are not to understand that there are two substances differing from each other, but two Persons, each being of the same substance.

---

[409] Ambrose of Milan, "Exposition of the Christian Faith," in *St. Ambrose: Select Works and Letters*, ed. Philip Schaff and Henry Wace, trans. H. de Romestin, E. de Romestin, and H. T. F. Duckworth, vol. 10, A Select Library of the Nicene and Post-Nicene Fathers of the Christian Church, Second Series (New York: Christian Literature Company, 1896), 204.
[410] John Chrysostom, "Homilies of St. John Chrysostom, Archbishop of Constantinople, on the Second Epistle of St. Paul the Apostle to Timothy," in *Saint Chrysostom: Homilies on Galatians, Ephesians, Philippians, Colossians, Thessalonians, Timothy, Titus, and Philemon*, ed. Philip Schaff, trans. James Tweed and Philip Schaff, vol. 13, A Select Library of the Nicene and Post-Nicene Fathers of the Christian Church, First Series (New York: Christian Literature Company, 1889), 485.

AUGUSTINE (354 – 430 AD), *Tractates on John* 51.3 [411]
But when it is said, "Blessed is He that cometh in the name of the Lord, [as] the King of Israel" (Luke 13:35; Ps 118:26), by "in the name of the Lord" we are rather to understand "in the name of God the Father," although it might also be understood as *in His own name*, inasmuch as He is also Himself the Lord. As we find Scripture also saying in another place, "The Lord rained [upon Sodom fire] from the Lord."

CYRIL (375 – 444 AD), *Comments on* 1 John 1:2 [412]
The Divine Scripture says that the cities of the Sodomites were burned by the Anger of God, and explaining how the Divine wrath was brought upon them, and clearly describing the mode of the destruction, *The Lord, it says, rained upon Sodom brimstone and fire from the Lord* (Gen 19:24), since this too is *the portion of the cup* most befitting those who are wont to commit such sins (Ps 11:6). What Lord then from what Lord sent the fire on and consumed the cities of the Sodomites? It is clear that it was the Father Who worketh all things through the Son, since He is too His Might and His Arm, Who caused Him to rain the fire upon the Sodomites. Since therefore the Lord sends the fire from the Lord upon them, how is not the Father Other, in respect to His own Being, than the Son, and the Son again than the Father? For the One is here signified as being from One.

SOCRATES SCHOLASTICUS (380 – 450 AD), *Ecclesiastical History* 2.30 [413]
If any one says that it was not the Son that was seen by Abraham, but the unbegotten God, or a part of him, let him be anathema. If any one says that it was not the Son that as man wrestled with Jacob, but the unbegotten God, or a part of him, let him be anathema. If any one shall understand the words, "The Lord rained from the Lord" (Gen 19:24) not in relation to the Father and the Son, but shall say that he rained from himself, let him be anathema: for the Lord the Son rained from the Lord the Father.

---

[411] Augustine of Hippo, "Lectures or Tractates on the Gospel according to St. John," in *St. Augustin: Homilies on the Gospel of John, Homilies on the First Epistle of John, Soliloquies*, ed. Philip Schaff, trans. John Gibb and James Innes, vol. 7, A Select Library of the Nicene and Post-Nicene Fathers of the Christian Church, First Series (New York: Christian Literature Company, 1888), 284.
[412] Cyril of Alexandria, *Commentary on the Gospel According to S. John*, vol. 1 (Oxford; London: James Parker & Co.; Rivingtons, 1874), 19–20.
[413] Socrates Scholasticus, "The Ecclesiastical History, by Socrates Scholasticus," in *Socrates, Sozomenus: Church Histories*, ed. Philip Schaff and Henry Wace, trans. A. C. Zenos, vol. 2, A Select Library of the Nicene and Post-Nicene Fathers of the Christian Church, Second Series (New York: Christian Literature Company, 1890), 57.

CONSTITUTIONS OF THE HOLY APOSTLES (381 – 394 AD), 5.20 [414]
To Him did Moses bear witness, and said: "The Lord received fire from the
Lord, and rained it down" (Gen 19:24). Him did Jacob see as a man, and said:
"I have seen God face to face, and my soul is preserved" (Gen 32:30). Him did
Abraham entertain, and acknowledge to be the Judge, and his Lord (Gen 18:25,
27). Him did Moses see in the bush (Ex 3:2).

JEWISH

R. Ishmael b. Yosi (170-200 C.E.), Gen 19:24 (*b. Sanh.* 38b or 4:5, V.11 A-C) [415]
A min said to R. Ishmael b. R. Yosé, "It is written, 'Then the Lord caused to rain
upon Sodom and Gomorrah brimstone and fire from the Lord' (Gen 19:24). *It
should have said,* 'From him.'" *A certain laundryman said to him, "Let me answer
him. It is written,* 'And Lamech said to his wives, Ada and Zillah, Hear my voice,
you wives of Lamech' (Gen 4:23). *It should have said,* 'my wives.'" *"But that just
is how Scripture says things, and here too, that just is how Scripture says things."*

Genesis Rabbah 51.2
Abba Hilfi, the son of Samkai, said in the name of R. Judah [2nd c. A.D.]: *Then
the Lord caused to rain,* etc. refers to Gabriel; *From the Lord* (out of heaven, to the
Holy One, blessed be He). R. Leazar [1st – 2nd c. A.D.] said: Wherever 'And the
Lord' occurs, it means, He and His heavenly Court.

---

[414] Alexander Roberts, James Donaldson, and A. Cleveland Coxe, eds.,
"Constitutions of the Holy Apostles," in *Fathers of the Third and Fourth Centuries:
Lactantius, Venantius, Asterius, Victorinus, Dionysius, Apostolic Teaching and
Constitutions, Homily, and Liturgies,* trans. James Donaldson, vol. 7, The Ante-Nicene
Fathers (Buffalo, NY: Christian Literature Company, 1886), 448.
[415] Jacob Neusner, *The Babylonian Talmud: A Translation and Commentary,* vol. 16
(Peabody, MA: Hendrickson Publishers, 2011), 192.

APPENDIX III

Review of *Knowing Jesus in the OT*

Andrew Malone is an Australian scholar who has spent much of his career seeking to discount Old Testament Christophanies.[416] The culmination of his views is found in his 2015 book, *Knowing Jesus In the Old Testament?*[417] To his credit, Malone is a careful scholar, theologically orthodox and conservative, who is concerned to protect evangelicals from the charge of eisegesis and of being careless and simplistic in biblical interpretation. While acknowledging the historical and majority consensus of church history—that the appearances of the "Angel of the Lord" in the Old Testament were often appearances of God the Son—Malone believes that the historical arguments are based on wrong assumptions and hasty, over-eager eisegesis. Malone's work, therefore, represents a contemporary challenge to our thesis. However, after analyzing his views, we are convinced that Andrew Malone is wrong[418] and has not adequately dealt with all the data.

---

[416] Malone's articles on the subject include: *"Distinguishing the Angel of the Lord"*, Bulletin for Biblical Research 21 .3 (2011) 297–314; *"God the Illeist: Third-Person Self-References and Trinitarian Hints in the Old Testament"*, *JETS* 52/3 (September 2009) 499–518; *"The Invisibility of God: a Survey of a Misunderstood Phenomenon"*, EQ 79.4 (2007), 311–329; *"Is the Messiah Announced In Malachi 3:1?"*, Tyndale Bulletin 57.2 (2006) 215-228.

[417] Andrew Malone, *Knowing Jesus In the Old Testament?: A Fresh Look at Christophanies*. Intervarsity Press: Nottingham, England, 2015.

[418] Malone begins his book by saying, "Michael Bird is wrong!" and rejecting Bird's support for OT Christophanies found in *Evangelical Theology: A Biblical and Systematic Introduction* (Grand Rapids: Zondervan, 2013).

Malone divides his book into three parts. In the first, he discusses an historical misunderstanding about the New Testament's assertions of God's "invisibility." In the second, he analyzes three options for identifying the "Angel of the Lord." 1) It is simply a title for God himself (the option Malone supports). 2) He is a lesser supernatural, authoritative messenger. 3) He is the Person of the Son. In the final section, Malone analyzes what he sees as the relevant New Testament texts. Unfortunately, we don't have the space to do a full treatment of Malone's work. He touches on a lot of issues and talks about a number of the same texts we do. But we will have to let our discussion of those texts stand for themselves.

In our view, Malone offers some legitimate insights, particularly to the biblical understanding of God's "invisibility." However, he has failed to see the extent of the biblical and historical argument. Particularly, he shows no awareness of Jewish Two Powers Theology—again, that the idea of a mediating Divine Angel preceded Christian interpretation. He fails to see the ways the New Testament and the early church fathers reflected this pre-Christian Jewish tradition, and so he fails even to recognize much of the New Testament data. As we have argued, the Divine Angel appears more often than realized and is given different names and titles in the Old Testament, which are then given to Jesus in the New Testament. We have seen the Jewish tradition follow these same lines of argument concerning the mediating Angel. When the supernatural role of the Divine Angel in the heavenly realms is added to the equation, the role of the Divine Angel in the entire narrative of the Bible comes into focus. Malone hasn't even begun to scratch the surface of these issues.

"Invisibility" and Proper Foundations

On the positive side, Malone helpfully corrects what has been a historically simplistic approach to "invisibility." Texts such as John 1:18 ("No one has ever seen God; the only God, who is at the Father's side, he has made him known"), Colossians 1:15 ("He is the image of the invisible God"), or 1 Timothy 1:17; 6:16 ("Now to the King eternal, immortal, invisible, the only God...whom no one has ever seen or can see") have often been used as cut-and-dried proofs of the invisibility of the Father, and therefore as arguments for the visible appearances of the Son in both Testaments. Malone correctly argues that the issue of "visibility" is more complicated. There are times when the Father himself is said to be visible (certainly Daniel 7:13, Matthew 18:10; Revelation 4:3, 5:1-7; and others). Malone also notes "some passages that look forward to a time when God the Father *can* be seen (Matt 5:8; 1Co 13:12; Heb 12:14; 1Jn 3:2; Rev 22:4)."[419] Therefore, it is better to assume there are times when the Father, Son, and Spirit can each choose to be visible.

Instead, Malone argues that the Greek word *aoratos* is better translated "as something that is currently 'unseen,' not something that is permanently 'invisible.'"[420] For instance, Moses clearly saw *something* of God, but something of God also remained *unseen*; there was always more of him to see and know. In this sense, God's invisibility may have more to do with spiritual "incomprehensibility" than complete physical "invisibility." John Frame writes, "God is *essentially invisible*. This means, not that he can never be seen under any circumstances, but rather that, as Lord, he sovereignly chooses when, where, and to whom to make himself visible."[421] Malone explains, "The idea of 'invisibility' is best understood as a culturally appropriate way of depicting God as 'beyond common earthly experience.'"[422] Nevertheless, God is certainly able to reveal himself, even visibly, in whatever way he chooses. To this extent, we agree with Andrew Malone that the issue of God's visibility in the created plane, especially the visibility of the Persons of the Godhead, has not always been carefully explored.

However, Malone gets himself into major trouble in assuming that this misunderstanding of invisibility is (or should be) the main rationale for Christophanies in the Bible. He writes, "Contrary to popular perception and presentation, the NT is not at odds with the OT accounts of God's making himself visible to people. There's no dilemma that requires christophanies as the solution."[423] Early in the book, he says,

---

[419] *Ibid*, 65. However, in our opinion, it is extremely doubtful whether any of these specific passages can clearly be said to refer to the Father.
[420] *Ibid*, 50.
[421] John M. Frame, *The Doctrine of God, A Theology of Lordship* (Phillipsburg, NJ: P&R Publishing, 2002), 590.
[422] *Malone, Ibid.*, 79.
[423] *Ibid*, 44-45

Perhaps the most substantial rationale offered for christophanies boils down to a single assumption: that God the Father is permanently invisible to human eyes. The primary argument for christophanies incorporates this premise into a traditional three-stage syllogism:

1. Old Testament figures are said to have seen God.
2. But God the Father is invisible.
3. Therefore, Old Testament figures saw the Son, not the Father.[424]

To the extent that proponents make this argument, Malone is fine to critique them. It would be theologically wrong to pit the *invisibility* of the Father against the *visibility* of the Son. It's a very easy argument to fall into. But Malone himself expresses frustration when he finds some of the Christophany supporters being inconsistent about the argument from invisibility.[425] In fact, when Malone finds them being inconsistent, it may be because the argument for Christophanies is more involved than Malone realizes. A better syllogism would be:

1. The *Godhead* is essentially invisible, incomprehensible, and transcendent.
2. The Father, Son, and Holy Spirit are each able to manifest themselves clearly in the *created* plane (and may even be permanently manifest).
3. When God makes himself visible on *earth* to human beings, it is normally by means of the sent Second Person who eternally proceeds from the Father—in the Old Testament as a precursor to his incarnation, and in the New Testament by the incarnation itself.
4. This activity of the Son is both in the heavenly realms among the Divine Council and on the earth as the intermediary and Savior of Israel and the Church.

Malone writes, "What is the difference between God the Father and the preincarnate Son that supposedly renders one of them impervious to human sight while the other makes regular appearances?"[426] Maybe the issue is not "imperviousness," but the eternal generation of the Son! He goes on, "It's possible that the members of the Trinity might *choose* for the Son to be their visual representative. This, however,

---

[424] *Ibid*, 34.
[425] See his discussion of James Borland's supposed inconsistency on p.136-138.
[426] *Ibid*, 75.

is a line of argument not often pursued to support christophanies." On the contrary, the eternal generation of the Son and its relevance to Christ's appearing in both the Old Testament and New was a substantial line of thought in early Trinitarian discussions!

Throughout his work, Malone seems to assume that seeing Christ in the Old Testament is "at the expense" of the Father and the Spirit. But we have to ask: What does that even mean? Asserting a distinction in one sense without a difference in another sense is at the heart of the doctrine of the Trinity in the first place.[427] When we see the Angel, is it God or is it Christ? The answer is, of course: Yes! When the divine glory appears, of course all Three Divine Persons are involved. That is at the heart of the mutual indwelling (perichoresis) of the Godhead (and accounts for why it is so often that when the Son appears in the OT, he is accompanied by the Spirit-Cloud, for instance).

But we have to ask two questions: First, does the one essence of God ever work exclusive of the Divine Persons? Does the "essence" come to people? How would that even be possible? To put it another way, are there Three Persons *and* One Person? The One God is there necessarily every time any of the Three Persons show up. But is it possible that you can have the One God apart from the Persons? Our answer is an unequivocal "no!"

What is wrong with seeing a specific "appearing" of the Divinity in the Old Testament as one of the Persons (not separate from the others in essence, but acting in distinct Personhood)? Malone might say, "this begs the question." Can we show reasons for identifying distinctions among the active Persons in the biblical text itself? In fact, we believe we have.

Our second question is: How else would you write a text to describe such a transcendent and unfolding mystery of Oneness and Threeness in the Godhead other than what is recorded for us in the Old Testament, which we have explored—with hypostatic tendencies given to the "sent Angel," the "Word," the "Glory," the "Name," the

---

[427] In Malone's book, he argues that Christian commentators have not proven a distinction between the Angel and the Father in the relevant Old Testament texts. We will let our exegesis of these texts provide our answer. Especially in parallel places like 2 Samuel 24 and 1 Chronicles 21, we believe the distinction and unity between the Angel and God are obvious (see our ch. 6). Malone's own exegesis of those texts fails to explore fully the issue or to understand the meaning of "God's hand" - see his discussion on p. 112 of his book.

"Presence," the "Arm," with third-person self-referential speech, etc.? It would seem this is the only way you could try to express it. And, as we have seen, the Jews definitely wrestled with the same issues. The later Jewish refusal to accept the Old Testament arguments for Christ was to their discredit. The New Testament is clear that they should have understood!

In our view, Malone has not understood the extent of passages like John 1:18, 5:37, or 6:46.[428] He is correct that the "unseen-ness" of God cannot *only* apply to the Father. He is correct that "unseen" does not mean "incapable of being seen." But his exegesis of these texts has not grappled with their context. How does John use these texts to show the greater revelation of Jesus? Andrew Malone assumes that they only refer to the greater revelation of Jesus in the incarnation in the New Testament. But the context of the verses are referring to ideas from the Old Testament. We have seen that John 5:36 deliberately echoes wording from the Targums about miracles bearing witness.[429] Further, when Jesus says, "His voice you have never heard, his form you have never seen, and you do not have his word abiding in you, for you do not believe the one whom he has sent ... I have come in my Father's name ... How can you believe, when you ... do not seek the glory that comes from the only God?" (John 5:37-44), Malone fails to grapple with—or even recognize—the Old Testament language that Jesus is using: voice, form, word, sent, name, glory, arm! There is an historical content and background to these things. In other words, he hasn't explored half the argument and has in our view misunderstood the church's historical use of these texts.

The Problem with Christotelic Hermeneutics

Sadly, Malone repeatedly reveals a troubling hermeneutic in his writing and exegesis. This appears early in his 2006 article on Malachi 3:1, which he writes "should no longer be considered amongst the

---

[428] Malone accuses the Church Fathers of using the New Testament texts on "invisibility" simplistically. (Other texts include Col 1:15; 1Ti 1:17, 6:16; 1Jn 4:12.) We actually think that Malone has a simplistic understanding of how the Fathers were using those texts.
[429] See NT Chapter - Part One...

often-nebulous category of predictive messianic texts – a simplistic mould into which this verse cannot responsibly be squeezed. It is better counted amongst those Old Testament passages which are *appropriated* by the New Testament, whereby the attributes and activities of YHWH himself are recognized in and ascribed to Jesus."[430] Notice the word "appropriated." In other words, Malone believes that this verse doesn't *predict* Jesus, but that the New Testament "reads Jesus back" into this verse.

He uses similar language in his book. Concerning John 12:41 he says, "Once more we find the Son being *added to* the identity of God in the OT and recognized in his activities."[431] Speaking on 1 Corinthians 10:4, 9, he writes, "Paul is not *unmasking* Christ in the Old Testament. Rather, Paul *adds* the recently encountered Second Person of the Trinity to the identity of the Jewish God."[432] Commenting on the virgin giving birth in Isaiah 7:14, Malone argues, "There's nothing oddly supernatural envisaged. It's only when Matt 1:18-23 cites this verse … that we *rethink* what Isaiah understood and communicated."[433] Malone has some helpful things to say on each of these verses, but his overall conclusions are deeply troubling, for such interpretive moves on the part of the Apostles would not in fact be grounded in the meaning of the text, but in their subjective reinterpretation of it. On what basis should anyone trust that? How could this possibly be used as an apologetic against, of all people, their Jewish brothers who have not trusted in Christ?

Malone reveals his hand in the end when he writes,

> In what "order" do we approach the two testaments? Do we read the Bible from cover to cover like a novel, starting with God's initial revelation to Israel and then his fuller revelation to the church? Or do we begin at the end of the story and work backwards? I've already used the idea of a detective story or mystery thriller. Do we claim to be reading the "mystery" of the Old Testament for the first time, or are we rereading a favorite story knowing full well how it turns out?[434]

---

[430] Malone, "*Is the Messiah Announced In Malachi 3:1*," 228.
[431] Malone, *Knowing Jesus*, 168.
[432] *Ibid*, 173.
[433] *Ibid*, 179.
[434] *Ibid*. 184.

As a source for this idea, Malone cites Peter Enns' 2003 article, "Apostolic Hermeneutics and an Evangelical Doctrine of Scripture."[435]

In other words, Malone is following what has become known as a *christotelic* approach to Old Testament hermeneutics. The "christotelic" approach justifies Christ being "read back" into the Old Testament, stating that OT texts used by the NT do not, in their context, originally refer to Jesus, but are *appropriated* as referring to Jesus on the basis of the new revelation given in the NT. In fact, Malone calls them and justifies them as "*anachronisms*"![436]

Now, to be fair, there is some truth to the christotelic argument. The New Testament does bring greater light and revelation. There are elements to the Old Testament that are shadowy and obscure, mysteries that are made clear finally in the New Testament. We certainly read the Old Testament with greater light because of the New Testament and find things there made clear that weren't clear before.

However, and at the same time, Jesus and the New Testament repeatedly indicts the Jewish teachers and holds them responsible for misunderstanding the Old Testament and not recognizing Jesus—meaning: *Jesus thought that the Old Testament, by itself, was enough to lead to a recognition of Jesus and the necessity of his cross and resurrection.* The New Testament does not just *appropriate* Old Testament passages, but *cites* Old Testament passages as authoritatively predictive or revealing of Jesus.

Jesus himself lamented to his disciples on the Emmaus road, "'O foolish ones, and slow of heart to believe all that the prophets have spoken! Was it not necessary that the Christ should suffer these things and enter into his glory?' And beginning with Moses and all the Prophets, he interpreted to them in all the Scriptures the things concerning himself" (Luke 24:25-27; cf. John 5:39; Acts 3:18, 13:27, 17:11; 1Pe 1:11; 2Ti 3:15.) Jesus was not *reinterpreting* or *appropriating* the Scriptures. He taught that they led inevitably to him.

---

[435] Peter Enns, "Apostolic Hermeneutics and an Evangelical Doctrine of Scripture: Moving Beyond a Modernist Impasse," *Westminster Theological Journal* 65 (2003): 276-277. Enns was forced out of his teaching position at Westminster Theological Seminary because of his views. Since leaving WTS, he has significantly departed from biblical orthodoxy.

[436] See Malone's ch.10, "Issues of Working Backwards," 151-163.

Ironically for Malone, who decries eisegesis, the christotelic approach actually excuses its own high-level form of eisegesis, justifying reading Jesus back into texts in which he wasn't originally present and skirting any need for the Old Testament to be accountably revealing of Christ on its own terms. It divorces the NT from the OT. As Richard Gaffin writes,

> A reader, having read a novel in its entirety, is able, on a subsequent re-reading, to see how details in the plot leading up to its conclusion, which on an initial reading didn't seem to fit, in fact did fit all along. In the view of [Pete Enns and the christotelic hermeneutic, *our insertion*], however, not only on a "first" read but even when we re-read from the vantage point of the conclusion the NT provides, we are still unable to see how OT plot "details," *in their original contexts and when they were written by their human authors*, are in harmony with that NT conclusion or how the NT finds that harmony, other than by reading into the OT what is not there.[437]

Going Deeper

This proves to be a major problem. We actually think the New Testament writers understood their Old Testament better than many scholars today do. Jesus and the Apostles didn't need to read Jesus *"back"* into the Old Testament. There was already a hermeneutical tradition among the Jews about the Divine Angel and about the coming Messiah readily available. The interpretive traditions already existed prior to Christianity. The Jews already connected anthropomorphic appearances of God with the Divine Angel, with the Word, with the Glory, with the Name, with the Presence, with the Hand-Arm, etc., long before Jesus came in the flesh. The Jews themselves wrestled with self-

---

[437] Richard Gaffin, "Observations on a Controversy," http://nbatzig.google-pages.com/Gaffin_Critique1.pdf - accessed July 19, 2018. Gaffin's article provides an important critique of the christotelic hermeneutic. For more, read, "Covenantal, Christocentric and Christotelic Hermeneutics At Westminster Theological Seminary," https://d3h3guilcrzx4v.cloudfront.net/uploads/images/files/News/Christocentric/Christocentric,%20Christotelic%20Statement.pdf.

referential speech where God referred to himself in the third person.[438]

The Jews viewed these issues in the context of an entire theology of the heavenly realm and the divine council. They already wrestled with the same passages that the NT uses and wrestled with the connections between the Divine Angel and the Messiah. They wrestled with the theology of the Old Testament more deeply than many have today. And that Old Testament theology was the milieu in which the New Testament was written. What the New Testament is saying about Jesus cannot be explored apart from these issues.

In only one place in his book does Andrew Malone touch on the Jewish background. He writes, "It may be true that some strands of Jewish scholarship have seen divine tendencies in the Angel, but it's disingenuous to imply that non-Christian Jews have gone so far as to identify the divine Angel as Jesus Christ."[439] Of course not! But Malone's comment begs the historical question: What divine tendencies did the Jews see? How did they interpret the relevant texts? Why did so many convert so easily to Christianity if they were nothing but a Unitarian religion? And why did they come to reject later some of their own interpretive traditions?

We happen to *know why* the Jews rejected the Two-Powers theology that preceded Christianity. They didn't reject it until Christianity came into being, and they did so in response. But sadly, Malone doesn't know this and never explores the issue. And so he doesn't understand what the New Testament is actually saying because he doesn't understand how they read their Old Testament. In the end, Malone hasn't even skimmed the surface of an issue that goes far deeper than he realizes.

If, as Segal has clearly shown, a "Two Powers" minority-tradition existed in Judaism prior to Christianity and this tradition was later also used and adapted by the early church, then it becomes a distinct, even likely, possibility that this hermeneutical tradition influenced the New Testament writers themselves. What Segal's work shows definitively is that the Divine Angel Second-Power view predated Christianity, that arguments from the Angel of the LORD were crucial and central to Jewish evangelism in the first century, within the early generations after the

---

[438] Again, this is a glaring weakness to Malone's article, *"God the Illeist."* We don't believe Malone has grappled deeply enough with the uniqueness of Yahweh's third-person speeches.

[439] Malone, 138.

apostles. In other words, this was arguably the original Christian exegesis of the Old Testament and apologetic for the divinity of Christ that they received from Jesus and the Apostles themselves.[440] Malone's thesis is then counterproductive and hostile to the New Testament's own hermeneutic.

Sadly, Andrew Malone is not alone in his ignorance of these arguments. Many modern scholars have not grasped Old Testament theology. They have not fully understood what even the early church fathers were doing with the Old Testament and the traditions the early church fathers received from the Apostles themselves. But the material is out there for anyone to read. As we have argued, the "presence" of Jesus is not "read back" into the Old Testament by the New. The New Testament finds him already there, not even just predictively or typologically, but truly and actively. This is the interpretive tradition of the New Testament itself. For good reason, it's the interpretive tradition of most of church history. And it needs to be recovered.

---

[440] We are not saying that Jewish Two-Powers theology got everything right. It clearly did not. But they were much closer than scholars realize today. Jesus, we have seen, affirms what they got right and corrects what they got wrong.

APPENDIX IV

Short Biographies of Ancient Sources
In This Book

NOTE: Biographies of the Church Fathers come from *Ancient Christian Commentary on Scripture: Introduction and Biographic Information*. Downers Grove, IL: InterVarsity Press, 2005.

Shepherd of Hermas (second century). Divided into five *Visions*, twelve *Mandates* and ten *Similitudes*, this Christian apocalypse was written by a former slave and named for the form of the second angel said to have granted him his visions. This work was highly esteemed for its moral value and was used as a textbook for catechumens in the early church.

Justin Martyr (c. 100/110–165; fl. c. 148–161). Palestinian philosopher who was converted to Christianity, "the only sure and worthy philosophy." He traveled to Rome where he wrote several apologies against both pagans and Jews, combining Greek philosophy and Christian theology; he was eventually martyred.

Theophilus of Antioch (late second century). Bishop of Antioch. His only surviving work is *Ad Autholycum*, where we find the first Christian commentary on Genesis and the first use of the term Trinity. Theophilus's apologetic literary heritage had influence on Irenaeus and possibly Tertullian.

Melito of Sardis (d. c. 190). Bishop of Sardis. According to Polycrates, he may have been Jewish by birth. Among his numerous works is a liturgical document known as *On Pascha* (ca. 160–177). As a Quartodeciman, and one intimately involved in that controversy, Melito celebrated Pascha on the fourteenth of

Nisan in line with the custom handed down from Judaism.

Irenaeus of Lyons (c. 135–c. 202). Bishop of Lyons who published the most famous and influential refutation of Gnostic thought.

Clement of Alexandria (c. 150–215). A highly educated Christian convert from paganism, head of the catechetical school in Alexandria and pioneer of Christian scholarship. His major works, *Protrepticus*, *Paedagogus* and the *Stromata*, bring Christian doctrine face to face with the ideas and achievements of his time.

Tertullian of Carthage (c. 155/160–225/250; fl. c. 197–222). Brilliant Carthaginian apologist and polemicist who laid the foundations of Christology and trinitarian orthodoxy in the West, though he himself was later estranged from the catholic tradition due to its laxity.

Origen of Alexandria (b. 185; fl. c. 200–254). Influential exegete and systematic theologian. He was condemned (perhaps unfairly) for maintaining the preexistence of souls while purportedly denying the resurrection of the body. His extensive works of exegesis focus on the spiritual meaning of the text.

Hippolytus (fl. 222–245). Recent scholarship places Hippolytus in a Palestinian context, personally familiar with Origen. Though he is known chiefly for *The Refutation of All Heresies*, he was primarily a commentator on Scripture (especially the Old Testament) employing typological exegesis.

Cyprian (200-258). Martyred bishop of Carthage who maintained that those baptized by schismatics and heretics had no share in the blessings of the church.

Novatian of Rome (fl. 235–258). Roman theologian, otherwise orthodox, who formed a schismatic church after failing to become pope. His treatise on the Trinity states the classic Western doctrine.

Methodius of Olympus (d. 311). Bishop of Olympus who celebrated virginity in a Symposium partly modeled on Plato's dialogue of that name.

Lactantius (c. 260–c. 330). Christian apologist removed from his post as teacher of rhetoric at Nicomedia upon his conversion to Christianity. He was tutor to the son of Constantine and author of *The Divine Institutes*.

Constantine (d. 337). Roman emperor from 306, with his fellow-emperor Licinius. The two proclaimed religious tolerance in the *Edict of Milan* in 313, allowing Christianity to be practiced freely. He became sole emperor in 324 and sought to preserve the unity and structure of the church for the good of the state. Constantine issued decrees against schisms and summoned the Council of Nicaea (325) to settle the Arian controversy.

Eusebius of Caesarea (c. 260/263–340). Bishop of Caesarea, partisan of the Emperor Constantine and first historian of the Christian church. He argued that the truth of the gospel had been foreshadowed in pagan writings but had to defend his own doctrine against suspicion of Arian sympathies.

Pseudo-Clementines (third-fourth century). A series of apocryphal writings pertaining to a conjured life of Clement of Rome. Written in a form of popular legend, the stories from Clement's life, including his opposition to Simon Magus, illustrate and promote articles of Christian teaching. It is likely that the corpus is a derivative of a number of Gnostic and Judeo-Christian writings. Dating the corpus is a complicated issue.

Hilary of Poitiers (c. 315–367). Bishop of Poitiers and called the "Athanasius of the West" because of his defense (against the Arians) of the common nature of Father and Son.

Athanasius of Alexandria (c. 295–373; fl. 325–373). Bishop of Alexandria from 328, though often in exile. He wrote his classic polemics against the Arians while most of the eastern bishops were against him.

Cyril of Jerusalem (313-386). Bishop of Jerusalem after 350 and author of *Catechetical Homilies*.

Gregory of Elvira (fl. 359–385). Bishop of Elvira who wrote allegorical treatises in the style of Origen and defended the Nicene faith against the Arians.

Basil the Great (329-79). One of the Cappadocian fathers, bishop of Caesarea and champion of the teaching on the Trinity propounded at Nicaea in 325. He was a great administrator and founded a monastic rule.

Ambrose of Milan (c. 333–397; fl. 374–397). Bishop of Milan and teacher of Augustine who defended the divinity of the Holy Spirit and the perpetual virginity of Mary.

Gregory of Nyssa (c. 335–394). Bishop of Nyssa and brother of Basil the Great. A Cappadocian father and author of catechetical orations, he was a philosophical theologian of great originality.

Chromatius (fl. 400). Bishop of Aquileia, friend of Rufinus and Jerome and author of tracts and sermons.

John Chrysostom (344/354–407; fl. 386–407). Bishop of Constantinople who was noted for his orthodoxy, his eloquence and his attacks on Christian laxity in high places.

Jerome (c. 347–420). Gifted exegete and exponent of a classical Latin style, now best known as the translator of the Latin Vulgate. He defended the perpetual virginity of Mary, attacked Origen and Pelagius and supported extreme ascetic practices.

Augustine of Hippo (354–430). Bishop of Hippo and a voluminous writer on philosophical, exegetical, theological and ecclesiological topics. He formulated the Western doctrines of predestination and original sin in his writings against the Pelagians.

Apostolic Constitutions (c. 381–394). Also known as *Constitutions of the Holy Apostles* and thought to be redacted by Julian of Neapolis. The work is divided into eight books, and is primarily a collection of and expansion on previous works such as the *Didache* (c. 140) and the *Apostolic Traditions*. Book 8 ends with eighty-five canons from various sources and is elsewhere known as the *Apostolic Canons*.

Theodoret of Cyr (c. 393–466). Bishop of Cyr (Cyrrhus), he was an opponent of Cyril who commented extensively on Old Testament texts as a lucid exponent of Antiochene exegesis.

Sozomen (400-450). Church historian who wrote two books, only the second of which is known to exist.

Fulgentius of Ruspe (c. 467–532). Bishop of Ruspe and author of many orthodox sermons and tracts under the influence of Augustine.

Romanus Melodus (490–556). Born as a Jew in Emesa not far from Beirut, where after his baptism he later became deacon of the Church of the Resurrection. He later moved to Constantinople and may have seen the destruction of the Hagia Sophia and its rebuilding during the time he flourished there. As many as eighty metrical sermons (*kontakia*, sg. *kontakion*) that utilize dialogical poetry have come down to us under his name. These sermons were sung rather than preached during the liturgy, and frequently provide theological insights and Scriptural connections often unique to Romanus.

APPENDIX V

Michael, Melchizedek, and the Angel of the LORD

Throughout church history, the identity of two biblical figures has been debated in their relation to the Messiah. Both have been disputed amongst Christians *and early Jews*! The first is Michael. The second is Melchizedek. Doug and Matt aren't entirely sure about their identity, though Doug tends towards a view that both are probably proper names for the Second Person prior to the incarnation. We do not believe this is something to divide over, but given the ancient origin of both and their persistence to this day, we thought it would be interesting to give you some arguments for why they may or may not be Christ.

Reasons Why Michael Might be Christ

Argument #1 – The Prince of Israel

1. **Dt 32:7-9.** Vs. 8 talks about the "sons of God" being given to the nations. They are given to the nations by Elyon—the Most High, who must be the Father since he is giving the sons their inheritance. Fathers do not inherit; sons do. These sons are the national "princes" (Gk: archons) of Daniel 10, which include the "prince of Persia" and the "prince of Greece." Vs. 9 then talks about Yahweh taking Israel for himself, calling it his "inheritance" (nachalah). In context, given that it is the sons of God who inherit and the Father who gives the inheritance, Yahweh here could not be the Father, but must be the "Son," Second Yahweh, the Angel of the LORD.
2. **Psalm 2.** This Psalm uses the same language of "inheritance" (nachalah) as Dt 32:9 and is seemingly a prophetic expansion on that passage. This time,

"Son" language is explicit. This time, he will inherit not just a nation, but the whole world. This is obviously fulfilled in the Son of God in the NT.

3. **Gen 17:4**. The promise the Word-Son gave to Abraham was that through him, he would become the father of many nations, but this began as one nation, as the Son took Israel to be his own. This fits into both passages above.

4. **Dan 12:1**. Michael is the "prince" (Gk: aggelos) of that one nation: Israel. Could there be two princes of Israel: one the Angel of the LORD (Dt 32:9) and the other one of the highest-ranking archangels (Jude 1:9) in heaven? This would be very odd, and indicates strongly that Michael is in fact the Angel of the LORD.

5. **Ex 15:11**. Michael means either "He who is like God" (a statement) or "Who is like God?" (a question). It seems to originate in passages like Ex 15:11's "Who is like you among the gods, O LORD? Who is like you, majestic in holiness, awesome in praises, working wonders?" (Ex 15:11). The language of "gods" needs to be taken, again, not in the context of the Father, but the Son, who earlier in the song is the "man of war" (Ex 15:3). He is the one whose name is wonderful, whom no other god is like.

6. **Gen 32:29-30**. Jacob wrestled with the Angel of the LORD, and the same kind of language arises. "Then Jacob asked him, 'Please tell me your name.' But he said, 'Why is it that you ask my name?' And there he blessed him. So Jacob called the name of the place Peniel, saying, 'For I have seen God face to face, and yet my life has been delivered'" (Gen 32:29-30). The "face" (panim/paneh) of God is seen in the Angel of the LORD (Ex 23:20-21).

7. **Jdg 13:17-18**. The same language returns with Samson's father. "And Manoah said to the angel of the LORD, 'What is your name, so that, when your words come true, we may honor you?' And the angel of the LORD said to him, 'Why do you ask my name, seeing it is wonderful?'"

8. **Isa 9:6**. These titles (prince, wonderful, god) converge upon Jesus in the prophecy. "For to us a child is born, to us a son is given; and the government shall be upon his shoulder, and his name shall be called Wonderful Counselor, Mighty God, Everlasting Father, Prince of Peace." The LXX is even more interesting. "For a child is born to us, and a son is given to us, whose government is upon his shoulder: and his name is called the Angel of great counsel (or with Heiser in his dissertation, "Angel of the great council"): for I will bring peace upon the princes, and health to him."

Argument #2 – "The Lord Rebuke You"

1. **Jude 9**. "When Michael was contending with the devil, he did not blaspheme him, but instead said, 'The Lord rebuke you.'"

2. **Zech 3:1-2.** In this passage, we have the same language as Jude 9, but now it is not Michael but "the LORD" saying to Satan, "The LORD rebuke you, O Satan." This "LORD" (Yahweh) is not the Father (who will do the rebuking), but the "Angel of the LORD" (3:1). Jude seems to be incorporating Zechariah's language of the Angel and attributing it to Michael.

Argument #3 – "The Voice of the Archangel"

1. **1Th 4:16.** Christ "the Lord himself" descends with the voice of the archangel, the sound of the trumpet, and the dead in Christ will rise first. There is only one archangel known in the Bible: Michael (Note: This argument is weakened if we move beyond Scripture, for extra-testamental literature knows of several archangels. However, as someone writes, "It is not clear from the text who is shouting. GeCL makes it clear that it is God, and this makes good sense for receptor languages which prefer or require an explicit statement about the agent. Similarly, the text does not state explicitly that it is God who blows the trumpet, though this may be implied. The text states only that the trumpet belongs to God").[441]
2. **John 5:25.** In language that Paul seems to be using in 1 Thessalonians 4:16 for Michael, John records Jesus as saying, "The dead will hear the voice of the Son of God, and those who hear will live."
3. **Matt 16:27.** Another parallel says, "For the Son of Man is going to come with his angels in the glory of his Father" (cf. Matt 24:3; 25:31).
4. **2Th 1:7.** Paul seems to give another parallel in his second letter to the Thessalonians. This time it doesn't say archangel but, "When the Lord Jesus is revealed from heaven with his mighty angels in flaming fire..."
5. **Rev 1:10, 17.** The voice like a trumpet can certainly be the Lord Jesus.

Reasons Why Michael Might Not be Christ

1. **Daniel 10:13, 21.** We explored some of the difficulties with this passage in the book. If the figure Daniel sees in 10:4-6 is the Divine Angel and if the hand that touches Daniel and speaks to him in 10:10-14 is the same person, then the Divine Angel cannot be Michael, because he speaks of Michael helping him. However, it's possible that 10:4-6 is not the Divine Angel (though we argue that it is). It's also possible that the figure switches in 10:10-14 and is a

---

[441] Paul Ellingworth and Eugene Albert Nida, *A Handbook on Paul's Letters to the Thessalonians*, UBS Handbook Series [New York: United Bible Societies, 1976], 101).

different angel than in 4-6, in which case the identity of the Divine Angel as Michael is still possible.

2. **Revelation 12:7**. The imagery of this passage is also notoriously difficult. But since 12:5 references the birth of Jesus and a child who was "caught up to God and to his throne" and then separately mentions a war in heaven with "Michael and his angels fighting against the dragon," the plain reading of the text might suggest they are different figures. The writer John had the opportunity of making clear that the Christ child and Michael were the same person, but he did not.

3. **Jude 9**. Similarly, Jude has no problem identifying Jesus as active in the OT (Jude 5). When he cites the archangel Michael as "disputing about the body of Moses," the plain reading again suggests that he doesn't identify the two. If he wanted to make the identification between the two clear, he could have, but didn't. Also, when Jude says that Michael "did not presume to pronounce a blasphemous judgment, but said, 'The LORD rebuke you,'" he seems to suggest that Michael is a properly subservient creature who doesn't presume to pronounce judgment by his own authority. This does not seem to characterize the Angel of the LORD, who sometimes will speak of Yahweh in the third person, but will sometimes also speak as Yahweh himself and pronounce judgment directly.

Reasons Why Melchizedek Might be Christ

Psalm 110

1. **Psalm 110:1**. Psalm 110 is a psalm about the Messiah. "The LORD says to my Lord: 'Sit at my right hand, until I make your enemies your footstool.'" This OT verse is cited more than any other in the NT. It is always cited as Jesus being the second "lord" in the verse. The word is Adonai (YAHWEH says to David's Adonai). The song is also the song about a king (it is a Davidic, that is kingly psalm). Melchizedek is said to be "king of Salem" (Gen 14:18).

2. **Psalm 110:2**. Verse 2 continues the "king" theme of the prophecy. "The LORD sends forth from Zion your [Adonai's] mighty scepter. Rule in the midst of your enemies!" This verse bears striking resemblance to passages like Ps 2:1, 9; 82:6-9; 89:9-10; and importantly Dan 7:13-14 which the Jews and NT link to this passage. Perhaps more importantly, the verse describes the exact situation of Melchizedek after the battle when Abram comes to him.

3. **Psalm 110:3**. The king theme continues in vs. 3. "Your people will offer themselves freely on the day of your power, in holy garments; from the womb of the morning, the dew of your youth will be yours." Offering

himself freely is exactly what Abram does to Melchizedek. But there is a twist in the LXX's translation of the last part of the verse. "... I have begotten you from the womb before the morning." Somehow, "begotten" is now happening "before the morning." This again sounds like Psalm 2 language.

4. **Psalm 110:4**. This is the only OT verse outside of Genesis 14 that mentions Melchizedek. "The LORD has sworn and will not change his mind, 'You are a priest forever after the order of Melchizedek.'" Paul may link vv. 1 and 4 when he says, "Christ Jesus is the one who died—more than that, who was raised—who is at the right hand of God, who indeed is interceding for us." At the very least, there is some kind of relationship between this priest of vs. 4 and the king of vs. 1, both offices of which Melchizedek held.

Hebrews 7

1. **Heb 7:3**. This verse says that Melchizedek "continues as priest forever."
2. **Heb 7:24**. This verse seems to continue the thought from vs. 3, adding how Jesus holds his priesthood permanently, because he continues forever. This is linked to Melchizedek.
3. **Heb 7:8**. This verse says that the Levites received tithes because they were "mortal men." This is in contrast to Melchizedek, who must therefore be immortal. This is strongly implied when it later says of Melchizedek that "he lives" (a present active verb).
4. **Heb 7:16**. This verse takes the "he lives" from vs. 8 and adds that he had an "indestructible life." If this were merely talking about saints like Abraham being alive in spirit (Mark 12:26), the point wouldn't be nearly as strong.
5. **Heb 7:3**. Melchizedek has no father or mother. It doesn't say we have no record of his father and mother, but that "he is without father or mother or genealogy, having neither beginning of days nor end of life."
6. **Heb 7:4**. He is so great a man that even the mighty Abraham gave him a tenth of everything.

Isaiah 61:2

"The Spirit of the Lord God is upon me, because the LORD has anointed me to bring good news to the poor." This passage was read by Jesus who said he is the one who fulfills it (Luke 4:18-19). One of the Dead Sea Scrolls on this text, however, reads, "... the year of Melchizedek's favor" (11Q13 Col. ii.0).

His Name

The name "Melchizedek" means "King of Righteousness." This is a title given to the Messiah (Isa 32:1; Jer 23:5; Zech 9:9). He is also the King of Salem, which is Jerusalem, and this is the very place that the LORD desired to set "his Name" (Dt 12:5, 11, etc.).

Reasons Why Melchizedek Might Not be Christ

Hebrews 7

As we saw with some of the Michael referents, Hebrews has the opportunity to say simply and explicitly that Jesus is Melchizedek and doesn't. If the writer of Hebrews really saw them as the same, why dance around the issue? James Kugel suggests that Psalm 110:4 could be translated as a promise *to* Melchizedek ("I have made you a priest forever, *on my account*, O Melchizedek" rather than "*after the order of* Melchizedek").[442] But if Hebrews had interpreted the verse this way, it would have said so. Instead, Hebrews consistently talks about Jesus as "being made to resemble" (ἀφωμοιωμένος; *aphōmoiōmenos*) Melchizedek or being in the "likeness" (ὁμοιότητα; *omoiotēta*) of Melchizedek, interpreting the LXX τάξιν (*taxin*) as 'kind / type', as opposed to using the Hebrew דִּבְרָתִי as a reference to God's 'word.' As O'Brien confirms, "Hebrews refers to one in the 'likeness' of Melchizedek, not simply to an *ongoing order* of priests."[443] While Hebrews seems to accept the Jewish interpretation that Melchizedek was a supernatural, heavenly figure, not a mortal man (Heb 7:8), who perhaps was an angelic priestly figure of the heavenly Temple, it only argues that Jesus' priesthood was of a similar order, not that he was the same person.

---

[442] James L. Kugel, *Traditions of the Bible* (Cambridge, MA: Harvard University Press, 1998), 281.

[443] Peter T. O'Brien, *The Letter to the Hebrews*, The Pillar New Testament Commentary (Grand Rapids, MI; Nottingham, England: William B. Eerdmans Publishing Company, 2010), 262.

APPENDIX VI

The Letter of Six Bishops [444]

A Copy of the Letter

Sent to Paul, the Samosatan,

By the Orthodox Bishops, before he was Deposed.

Hymenaeus, Theophilus, Theoteknus, Maximus, Proclus, Bolanus, to Paul in Christ, greetings.

Now that we have reached the point of discussions with one another we shall demonstrate what we believe. And in order that it might be made abundantly clear what each one thinks and that those things which are in question might come to their most certain conclusion, *it seemed [good] to us to set forth a written account concerning this faith which we received from the beginning and so have what has been handed down and maintained in the universal and holy church until this very day through succession from the blessed apostles* who also "became eyewitnesses and

---

[444] For an introduction to this important third century letter stating how all the churches understood the Angel to be Christ, see the beginning Ch. 17: The Angel in the Church Fathers. Many thanks to Michael Emadi for the hard work of this translation. We are grateful for your professional work on this. This translation is taken primarily from the Greek text (the parallel Latin was also consulted) as found in Mansi, *Sacrorum Conciliorum Nova et Amplissima Collectio*, Vol. I, pp. 1033-40: https://babel.hathitrust.org/cgi/pt?id=njp.32101078252002;view=1up;seq=557.

ministers of the word",[445] being proclaimed in the Law and the Prophets and the New Testament. For God is unbegotten, one, without beginning, invisible, unchangeable, "whom no man has seen, nor is able to see,"[446] and any attempt to comprehend his glory or greatness or relate how they are in a way that does justice to the truth is humanly impossible. But we must also be content to receive a measured knowledge concerning Him as His Son reveals Him. Just as it says, "no one knows the Father except the Son, and anyone to whom the Son reveals [him]."[447]

This Son, begotten, the one and only Son, the image of the invisible God, the first-born of all creation,[448] the wisdom and word and power of God,[449] existing before the ages, not as to foreknowledge but as to being and nature God, Son of God, we confess and preach having come to a knowledge from both the Old and New Testaments. And whoever argues that the Son of God as God did not exist before the foundation of the world, [must] believe and confess [such] affirming that they proclaim two gods. If it is preached that the Son of God is not God, we shall lead this foreign [teaching] away from the ecclesiastical rule. And every catholic church is in agreement with us.

For concerning this it is written, "Your throne, O God, is forever and ever. A rod of equity is the rod of your rule; you loved righteousness and hated lawlessness. Therefore God, your God, anointed you with oil of rejoicing beyond your partners."[450] And again in Isaiah [it is written], "Our God is repaying judgment; yes, he will repay; he himself will come and save us. Then the eyes of the blind shall be opened, and the ears of the deaf shall hear; then the lame shall leap like a deer, and the tongue of stammerers shall be clear."[451] And again, "They will pray in you because God is in you."[452] And, "There is no God beside you. For you are God and we did not know it, O God of Israel, Savior."[453] And according to the apostle, "From whom is the Christ according to the flesh, who is

---

[445] Luke 1:2.
[446] 1Ti 6:16.
[447] Matt 11:27.
[448] Col 1:15.
[449] Possible citation of 1Co 1:24.
[450] LXX Psalm 44:7-8.
[451] LXX Is 35:4-6.
[452] LXX Is 45:14.
[453] LXX Is 45:14-15.

over all, God blessed forever. Amen."[454] Of this One [we read], "the one who is over all." And, "beside you," meaning over all created things.

Also in the writing of Hosea we read, "For I am God and not a man, holy in your midst, and I will not enter into a city. I will go after the Lord."[455] And every God-breathed Scripture reveals God to be the Son of God, which to set forth one by one we put off for another time.

We believe this One, being eternally with the Father, has brought to fruition the Father's will for all of creation. For He spoke and they came into existence. He commanded and they were created. Now the One who commands gives orders to another. We have been persuaded that this One is no other God than the One and Only Son of God, to Whom also He said, "Let us make man according to our image and likeness."[456]

Briefly stated, according to the Gospel, "All things were made through him and without him not one thing was made."[457] And according to the apostle, "In him all things were created: things in the heavens and things on the Earth, whether visible or invisible, whether thrones or rulers or dominions or authorities. Everything has been created through him and for him."[458] And thus He did as truly being and working, as both Logos and God, through Whom the Father has made all things - not as through a tool nor as through irresistible knowledge[459] - the Father having begotten the Son as a living Power and Subsistence who works all things in all things, not just by observing or by the Son only being present but also by being involved in the entire creative act, as it is written, "I was working alongside Him."[460]

We say that this One came down and appeared to Abraham by the Oaks of Mamre, one of the three, with Whom the patriarch conversed as with the Lord and Judge seeing that He has received from the Father all the judgment. Concerning Whom it has been written, "The Lord rained upon Sodom and Gomorra fire and sulphur from the Lord of heaven."[461] He is revealed to be the One who fulfils the Father's will to

---

[454] Rom 9:5.
[455] LXX Hosea 11:9-10a.
[456] LXX Gen 1:26.
[457] John 1:3.
[458] Col 1:16.
[459] Could also be "meaningless power."
[460] LXX Prov 8:30.
[461] LXX Gen 19:24.

the patriarchs and He speaks in the same passages and the same sections sometimes as an angel but other times as Lord and even at times being testified to as God. For to believe an angel to be called God of all is ungodly. But this angel is the Son of the Father, the Lord Himself, being also God. For it is written, "An angel of great counsel"[462] as [it is similarly written] in other places to Abraham, etc. "For now I know that you fear God" and "you did not spare your beloved son on account of Me."[463] And "he called the name of the place 'The Lord saw' that they might say today, 'On the mountain the Lord appeared.'"[464]

And concerning Jacob, "And the angel of God spoke to me while asleep saying, 'Jacob.' I said, 'Who is it?' And he said, 'Look up with your eyes … I am the God who appeared to you in a divine place where you anointed a pillar to me there and made a vow to me there.'"[465] Also after the struggle and the things concerning a man written about beforehand, it was added, "And Jacob called the name of that place 'Seeing-God.' 'For I have seen God face to face and my life has been preserved.'"[466]

The man written about beforehand, being the Son of God, whom the Scripture itself reveals [to be] God, we confess. Moreover, we also affirm that the law likewise was given to Moses by the ministry of the Son of God, as the apostle teaches saying, "Why then the law? It was added for the sake of transgressions, until the seed to whom the promise was made should come, having been ordained through angels in the hand of a mediator."[467] For we do not know another mediator between God and men other than this One.

What's more, Moses also teaches us the following: "now an angel appeared to him in a flame of fire out of the bush … Now when the Lord saw that he came near to see, the Lord called to him from the bush."[468] Again, "After you go, as you gather the elders of the sons of Israel, then you will say to them, 'The Lord, the God of our fathers has appeared to me, the God of Abraham, the God of Isaac, and the God of Jacob …' If then, they do not believe me, neither will they listen to my

---

[462] LXX Isa 9:6.
[463] LXX Gen 22:12.
[464] LXX Gen 22:14.
[465] LXX Gen 31:11-13.
[466] LXX Gen 32:30.
[467] Gal 3:19.
[468] LXX Ex 3:2, 4.

voice. For they will say, 'The Lord God has not appeared to you!' What shall I say to them?"[469]

And in the blessings, "According to the ordinances by the One who appeared in the bush, may *these things* come upon the head of Joseph."[470] And elsewhere, "And the Lord said to Moses, 'Even this word which you have spoken, I will do for you.'" So he said, "Show me your glory." And *the Lord* replied, "I will pass by before you in my glory. And I will call in the name 'Lord' before you and I will have mercy on whomever I have mercy and I will have compassion on whomever I will have compassion."[471] In this way it was indeed accomplished: "And the Lord descended in a cloud, and He stood beside him there. And he called in the name of the Lord. And the Lord passed by before his face. And he called 'the LORD God.'"[472]

For the One above who promised to pass by is the Son of God, the Lord. Yet he called in the name of the Lord, the Father. This One is the One who also speaks truth saying, "Not that anyone has seen the Father except He who is from the Father. This One has seen the Father."[473] And in the same gospel, "His voice you have never heard, nor His form have you seen."[474] And "No one has ever seen God. The only Son[475] who is in the bosom the Father, He has made him known." And in another place the apostle says, "Now to the King eternal, immortal, invisible, the only wise God."[476]

Now the Son, *who* is with the Father, being God and Lord of all creation and being sent by the Father from heaven and being enfleshed, became a man. For this reason also the body of the virgin held the fullness of deity in bodily form,[477] he was unchangeably united to deity and has been made divine. Therefore, the God and man himself, Jesus Christ, was prophesied about in the law and prophets, and in every

---

[469] LXX Ex 3:16.
[470] LXX Dt 33:16.
[471] LXX Ex 33:17-19.
[472] LXX Ex 34:6.
[473] John 6:46 (Codex Sinaiticus (א) and Didymus of Alexandria).
[474] John 5:37.
[475] John 1:18. This interesting textual variant differs from the NA27 text with the reading of υἱός rather than θεός. However, it agrees with many other mss which contain this reading. It appears the authors may not have known of the "the only God" variant, which surely would have doubled the power of this citation.
[476] 1 Tim 1:17.
[477] Col 2:9.

church under heaven it is believed that as God [He] emptied himself from being equal with God.[478] And as man [He was] also from the seed of David according to the flesh.[479]

The signs and wonders recorded in the gospels God accomplished by becoming flesh and blood [and] as One who has been tempted in all things [as we are, yet] without sin.[480] Thus also Christ in the divine Scriptures before he put on flesh was named as one and the same.

[We know that] in Jeremiah, "the breath[481] of our face"[482] is Christ. "The Lord is the Spirit,"[483] according to the apostle. "For they drank from the spiritual Rock and the Rock was Christ."[484] And again, "We must not put the Lord[485] to the test just as some tested Him and were destroyed by snakes."[486] And concerning Moses [it is written], "he considered the reproach of Christ greater riches than the treasures of Egypt."[487] So also Peter [wrote], "Concerning this salvation, the prophets who prophesied about the grace that was to be ours searched and made careful inquiry examining what person or time the Spirit of Christ in them was indicating."[488] Now if "Christ is the power of God and the wisdom of God,"[489] He has been so from eternity. Thus also with respect to Christ being one and the same in substance, even though these are lofty and high thoughts to be thinking.

Regarding these things which were written down from the greatest to the least, we want to know if you think and teach these things with us and will sign below [in agreement], [and] if [you are] in favor with that which has been written or not.

---

[478] Php 2:7.

[479] Rom 1:3.

[480] Heb 4:15.

[481] πνεῦμα (*pneuma*).

[482] LXX Lam 4:20.

[483] πνεῦμα; 2Co 3:17.

[484] 1 Cor 10:4.

[485] The text agrees with ℵ B C and other mss (see variant info in NA27/28) against the text of the NA27/28 which has Χριστόν (*Christon*).

[486] 1Co 10:9.

[487] Heb 11:26.

[488] 1Pe 1:10-11a.

[489] 1Co 1:24.

APPENDIX VII

Reference Guide to Titles of the Angel

This Appendix contains charts that give a brief recap of the OT titles for the Angel that find corresponding parallels in the NT. It is not meant to be exhaustive, only illustrative.

Ch.	Title	OT	NT
Intro	**Angel of the Covenant**	Ex 23:20-27, "Behold, I send an angel before you to guard you on the way and to bring you to the place that I have prepared. Pay careful attention to him and obey his voice; do not rebel against him, for he will not pardon your transgression, for my name is in him…" Mal 3:1-3, "Behold, I send my messenger, and he will prepare the way before me. And the LORD whom you seek will suddenly come to his temple; and the messenger of the covenant in whom you delight, behold, he is coming, says the Lord of hosts…" Num 20:16, "When we cried to the LORD, he heard our voice and sent an angel and brought us out of Egypt…"	Mt 11:10, "This is he of whom it is written, 'Behold, I send my messenger before your face, who will prepare your way before you." cf. Mk 1:2; Lk 1:17,76; 7:27 Jude 5, "Now I want to remind you, although you once fully knew it, that Jesus, who saved a people out of the land of Egypt, afterward destroyed those who did not believe."

Ch.	Title	OT	NT
1	The LORD or God	Gen 15:1-5, "The angel of the LORD said to her..." Gen 16:13, "So she called the name of the LORD who spoke to her, 'You are a God of seeing...'" Gen 48:15-16, "The God before whom my fathers Abraham and Isaac walked, the God who has been my shepherd all my life long to this day, the angel who has redeemed me from all evil, bless the boys..."	John 1:48, "Before Philip called you, when you were under the fig tree, I saw you." John 1:1, 18, "... and the Word was God ... No one has ever seen God; the only God, who is at the Father's side, he has made him known." Romans 9:5, "... the Christ, who is God over all, blessed forever. Amen."
2, 8	Word	Gen 15:1-5, "The word of the LORD came to Abram in a vision..." 1 Samuel 3:1-21, "And the word of the LORD was rare in those days; there was no frequent vision ... And the LORD appeared again at Shiloh, for the LORD revealed himself to Samuel at Shiloh by the word of the LORD." cf. 1 Kings 19:9, Jeremiah 1:4-10, etc.	John 1:1, "In the beginning was the Word, and the Word was with God, and the Word was God. Revelation 19:13, "He is clothed in a robe dipped in blood, and the name by which he is called is The Word of God." cf. John 5:38; 1 John 1:1, etc.

Ch.	Title	OT	NT
3	**Man ('ish)**	Gen 18:2, "He lifted up his eyes and looked, and behold, three men ('ish) were standing in front of him" Gen 32:24, 28, "And a man wrestled with him until the breaking of the day ... you have striven with God and with men ('ish), and have prevailed." Hos 12:3-4, "He strove with God. He strove with the angel and prevailed."	N/A
	Man ('adam)	Isa 7:14, "Therefore the Lord himself will give you a sign. Behold, the virgin shall conceive and bear a son ('adam implied) and shall call his name Immanuel."	Matt 1:23, "Behold, the virgin shall conceive and bear a son, and they shall call his name Immanuel (which means, God with us)." Luke 3:23-38, "Jesus ... being the son (as was supposed) of Joseph ... the son of Enos, the son of Seth, the son of Adam, the son of God."

Ch.	Title	OT	NT
4, 7	Name	Ex 3:13-14, "Then Moses said to God, 'If I come to the people of Israel and say to them, The God of your fathers has sent me to you, and they ask me, 'What is his name?' what shall I say to them?' God said to Moses, 'I am who I am.' And he said, 'Say this to the people of Israel: I am has sent me to you." cf. Ex 15:3; Isa 30:27; Ps 20:1,7; 54:1; etc.	John 17:6,11-12,26, "I have manifested your name to the people whom you gave me out of the world... Holy Father, keep them in your name, which you have given me... I made known to them your name, and I will continue to make it known." John 8:58, "Jesus said to them, 'Truly, truly, I say to you, before Abraham was, I am.'" Php 2:9-10, "God has highly exalted him and bestowed on him the name that is above every name, so that at the name of Jesus every knee should bow, in heaven and on earth and under the earth, and every tongue confess that Jesus Christ is Lord, to the glory of God the Father." cf. John 5:43; Acts 5:41; Rom10:9,13; Heb.1:4; Heb13:8, etc.

Ch.	Title	OT	NT
5	Face / Presence	Gen 32:30, "Jacob called the name of the place Peniel, saying, 'For I have seen God face to face, and yet my life has been delivered." Ex 33:11, "Thus the LORD used to speak to Moses face to face, as a man speaks to his friend." (compare Exodus 33:14-15,20,23) Deut 4:37, "He brought you out of Egypt with his own presence, by his great power." Isa 63:9, "In all their affliction he was afflicted, and the angel of his presence saved them; in his love and in his pity he redeemed them; he lifted them up and carried them all the days of old." cf. Ps 17:2,15, etc.	2Co 4:6, "For God, who said, 'Let light shine out of darkness,' has shone in our hearts to give the light of the knowledge of the glory of God in the face of Jesus Christ." cf. *2Th 1:9, Heb 1:3, Jude 5, etc.

Ch.	Title	OT	NT
5, 10	Form	Num 12:8, "With [Moses] I speak mouth to mouth, clearly, and not in riddles, and he beholds the form of the LORD." Ezek 1:26,28, "seated above the likeness of a throne was a likeness with a human appearance... Such was the appearance of the likeness of the glory of the Lord."	Php 2:6-7, "Though he was in the form of God, did not count equality with God a thing to be grasped, but emptied himself, by taking the form of a servant, being born in the likeness of men." Col 1:18, "He is the image of the invisible God." Heb 1:3, "He is the radiance of the glory of God and the exact imprint of his nature, and he upholds the universe by the word of his power."

Ch.	Title	OT	NT
		Josh 5:13-15, "And he said, 'No; but I am the commander of the army of the LORD. Now I have come.'"	2Th 1:7-8, "…when the Lord Jesus is revealed from heaven with his mighty angels in flaming fire, inflicting vengeance on those who do not know God and on those who do not obey the gospel of our Lord Jesus."
		Ex 15:3, "The LORD is a man of war; the LORD is his name."	Rev 17:14, "They will make war on the Lamb, and the Lamb will conquer them, for he is Lord of lords and King of kings, and those with him are called and chosen and faithful."
6	Man of War / Prince of the Host	Dan 8:11,25, "It became great, even as great as the Prince of the host… And he shall even rise up against the Prince of princes." (cf. Dan.11:36)	Rev 19:11-16, "Then I saw heaven opened, and behold, a white horse! The one sitting on it is called Faithful and True, and in righteousness he judges and makes war … And the armies of heaven, arrayed in fine linen, white and pure, were following him on white horses. From his mouth comes a sharp sword with which to strike down the nations, and he will rule them with a rod of iron. He will tread the winepress of the fury of the wrath of God the Almighty. On his robe and on his thigh he has a name written, King of kings and Lord of lords."

Ch.	Title	OT	NT
6	Right Hand / Arm	Ex 15:6, "Your right hand, O Lord, glorious in power, your right hand, O Lord, shatters the enemy." Isa 59:16, "He saw that there was no man, and wondered that there was no one to intercede; then his own arm brought him salvation, and his righteousness upheld him." Isaiah 63:11-12, "who caused his glorious arm to go at the right hand of Moses, who divided the waters before them to make for himself an everlasting name." Psalm 110:1,5-6, "The Lord says to my Lord: 'Sit at my right hand, until I make your enemies your footstool." cf. Isaiah 51:9-10, 53:1, 63:5; 1 Chron.21:13; Zech.13:7; see ch.6 for a full list of passages	Matt 22:43-44, "He said to them, 'How is it then that David, in the Spirit, calls him Lord, saying, 'The Lord said to my Lord, Sit at my right hand, until I put your enemies under your feet"? Acts 7:55-56, "But he, full of the Holy Spirit, gazed into heaven and saw the glory of God, and Jesus standing at the right hand of God. And he said, 'Behold, I see the heavens opened, and the Son of Man standing at the right hand of God." cf. Mark 12:36; Luke 20:42-43; Acts 2:34-35, etc.

Ch.	Title	OT	NT
7 (3)	**Wonderful**	Jdg13:18, "And the angel of the Lord said to him, 'Why do you ask my name, seeing it is wonderful?'" Isa 9:6, "For to us a child is born, to us a son is given; and the government shall be upon his shoulder, and his name shall be called Wonderful Counselor, Mighty God, Everlasting Father, Prince of Peace." cf. Gen 32:29, Ex 15:11-12	Luke 2:11, "For unto you is born this day in the city of David a Savior, who is Christ the Lord." (cf. Mt.4:13-16) Rev 19:12, "He has a name written that no one knows but himself." (cf. Prov.30:4)
	Prince of Peace	Isa 9:6, "And his name shall be called…Prince of peace." Jdg 6:22-24, "Alas, O Lord God! For now I have seen the angel of the Lord face to face… Then Gideon built an altar there to the Lord and called it, The Lord Is Peace." cf. Mic 5:3, Zech 6:12-13, Hag 2:9, Ps 110:4, Dan 8:11, 25	Hb 3:11, Eph.2:14, "For he himself is our peace, who has made us both one and has broken down in his flesh the dividing wall of hostility."

Ch.	Title	OT	NT
		Job 9:32-33, "For he is not a man, as I am, that I might answer him, that we should come to trial together. There is no arbiter between us, who might lay his hand on us both."	1Ti 2:5-6, "For there is one God, and there is one mediator between God and men, the man Christ Jesus, who gave himself as a ransom for all, which is the testimony given at the proper time."
8	Mediator / Intercessor	Job 33:23, "If there be for him an angel, a mediator, one of the thousand, to declare to man what is right for him, and he is merciful to him, and says, 'Deliver him from going own into the pit; I have found a ransom...'"	1Jo 2:1-2, "But if anyone does sin, we have an advocate with the Father, Jesus Christ the righteous."
		Isa 59:16, "He saw that there was no man, and wondered that there was no one to intercede; then his own arm brought him salvation, and his righteousness upheld him."	
		cf. Job 5:1, 16:19-21, 17:3, Zech 3:1-5	cf. Gal 3:20, Rev 5:1-10, Acts 4:12

Ch.	Title	OT	NT
10	**Glory**	Ex 16:10, "They looked toward the wilderness, and behold, the glory of the LORD appeared in the cloud." (compare Ex 14:19,24) Ex 24:16-17, "The glory of the LORD dwelt on Mount Sinai, and the cloud covered it six days. And on the seventh day he called to Moses out of the midst of the cloud. Now the appearance of the glory of the LORD was like a devouring fire on the top of the mountain in the sight of the people of Israel." cf. Ex 33:18,22-23; Isa 6:1 (targ.); Ezek 1:28, 9:3-4, Zech 2:5	John 1:14, "And the Word became flesh and dwelt among us, and we have seen his glory, glory as of the only Son from the Father, full of grace and truth." John 12:41, "Isaiah said these things because he saw his glory and spoke of him." Hebrews 1:3, "He is the radiance of the glory of God and the exact imprint of his nature." 2 Corinthians 4:6, "For God, who said, 'Let light shine out of darkness,' has shone in our hearts to give the light of the knowledge of the glory of God in the face of Jesus Christ." cf. John 5:44, 17:5; Acts 7:2-3, 7:55-56, etc.

Ch.	Title	OT	NT
11	Son of Man	Dan 7:13-14, "I saw in the night visions, and behold, with the clouds of heaven there came one like a son of man ('enash), and he came to the Ancient of Days and was presented before him."	Acts 7:55-56, "But he, full of the Holy Spirit, gazed into heaven and saw the glory of God, and Jesus standing at the right hand of God. And he said, 'Behold, I see the heavens opened, and the Son of Man standing at the right hand of God." Mt 26:64, "But I tell you, from now on you will see the Son of Man seated at the right hand of Power and coming on the clouds of heaven." cf. Mk 14:62; Rev 1:7, 14:14
	Son of God	Psalm 2:7, "The Lord said to me, 'You are my Son; today I have begotten you.'" Prov 30:4, "Who has ascended to heaven and come down? Who has gathered the wind in his fists? Who has wrapped up the waters in a garment? Who has established all the ends of the earth? What is his name, and what is his son's name? Surely you know!"	John 1:14,18, "And the Word became flesh and dwelt among us, and we have seen his glory, glory as of the only Son from the Father… No one has ever seen God; the only God, who is at the Father's side, he has made him known." 1 John 4:9, "In this the love of God was made manifest among us, that God sent his only Son into the world, so that we might live through him." cf. Heb.5:5; Col.1:13-20; John John 3:16, *5:18, 10:36, 17:1,5; Acts 13:33.

Ch.	Title	OT	NT
12	Shepherd	Gen 48:15-16, "The God before whom my fathers Abraham and Isaac walked, the God who has been my shepherd all my life long to this day, the angel who has redeemed me from all evil, bless the boys." Ps 23:1, "The LORD is my Shepherd." Zech 13:7, "'Awake, O sword, against my shepherd, against the man who stands next to me,' declares the LORD of hosts. 'Strike the shepherd, and the sheep will be scattered; I will turn my hand against the little ones.'"	John 10:11, 14 "I am the Good Shepherd." 1Pe 2:25, 5:4, "the Shepherd and Overseer of your souls ... the Chief Shepherd." Matt 26:31, "Then Jesus said to them, 'You will all fall away because of me this night. For it is written, 'I will strike the shepherd, and the sheep of the flock will be scattered'"" (cf. Mark 14:27).

WORKS CITED

Abelson, J. *The Immanence of God in Rabbinical Literature*. London: Macmillan and Co., 1912.

Abrams, Daniel. "The Boundaries of Divine Ontology: The Inclusion and Exclusion of Metatron in the Godhead." *Harvard Theological Review* 87:3 (July 1994): 291-321.

Ainsworth, Henry. *Annotations Upon the First Book of Moses, called Genesis*. s.l.: s.n., 1616.

Aland, Kurt et al. *Novum Testamentum Graece*, 28th Edition. Stuttgart: Deutsche Bibelgesellschaft, 2012.

Albright, William Foxwell. *Yahweh and the Gods of Canaan: A Historical Analysis of Two Contrasting Faiths*. Winona Lake, IN: Eisenbrauns, 1968.

Allix, Peter. *The Judgment of the Ancient Jewish Church Against the Unitarians*, Second Edition. Oxford: Clarendon Press, 1821.

_____. *A Dissertation Concerning the Angel Who is Called the Redeemer*. Christ in All Scripture Series Book 2. Ed. Douglas Van Dorn. Dacono, CO: Waters of Creation, 2020.

Ambrose. *Exposition of the Christian Faith*.

_____. *Three Books on the Holy Spirit*.

Andersen, Francis I. and Freedman, David Noel. *Hosea: A New Translation with Introduction and Commentary*, vol. 24. Anchor Yale Bible. New Haven; London: Yale University Press, 2008.

Aquinas, Thomas. *Summa Theologica*.

Apostolic Constitutions.

Athanasius. *Against the Arians*.

Augustine. *On the Trinity*.

_____. *Reply to Faustus* 19.

_____. *Lectures on the Gospel of John*.

Auld, A. Graeme. *I & II Samuel: A Commentary*. Ed. William P. Brown, Carol A. Newsom, and Brent A. Strawn, 1st ed. The Old Testament Library. Louisville, KY: Westminster John Knox Press, 2012.

Babington, Gervase. *The Workes of the Right Reverend Father in God Gervase Babington, late Bishop of Worcester. Containing Comfortable Notes Upon the Five Bookes of Moses*. London, George Eld, 1615.

Barbel, Joseph. *Christos Angelos: Die Anschauung von Christus als Bote und Engel in der gelehrten und volkstümlichen Literatur des christlichen Altertums*. Bottrop: 1941.

Barker, Margaret. "Isaiah." *Eerdmans Commentary on the Bible*. Ed. James D. G. Dunn and John W. Rogerson. Grand Rapids, MI: Eerdmans, 2003.

_____. *The Great Angel: A Study of Israel's Second God*. Louisville, KY: Westminster John Knox Publishers, 1992.

_____. *The Revelation of Jesus Christ*. Edinburgh: T&T Clark, 2000.

Barrett, Michael. *Beginning at Moses: A Guide to Finding Christ in the Old Testament*. Greenville, SC: Ambassador International, 2010.

Barrick, William. "Messianic Implications In Elihu's Mediator Speech: Job 33:23-28," *ETS National Meetings* (Nov 15, 2016).

Basil the Great. *Against Eumonius*.

_____. *On Proverbs* 7:22.

Bauckham, Richard. *2 Peter, Jude*, vol. 50. Word Biblical Commentary. Dallas: Word, Incorporated, 1998.

_____. *God Crucified: Monotheism & Christology in the New Testament*. Grand Rapids, MI: Eerdmans, 1998.

_____. "The Throne of God and the Worship of Jesus." *The Jewish Roots of Christological Monotheism: Papers from the St. Andrews Conference on the Historical Origins of the Worship of Jesus*. Ed. C. Newman, J. Davila, and G. Lewis. Leiden: Brill, 1999: 43-69.

Bavinck, Herman. *Reformed Dogmatics: Sin and Salvation in Christ, vol. 3*. Translated and edited John Bolt and John Vriend. Grand Rapids, MI: Baker Academic, 2006.

Beale, G. K. *Revelation: A Commentary on the Greek Text*. New International Greek Testament Commentary. Grand Rapids, MI: W.B. Eerdmans, 1999.

Becking, B. "Arm." *Dictionary of Deities and Demons in the Bible*. Ed. Karel van der Toorn and Pieter W. van der Horst. Grand Rapids, MI: Eerdmans, 1999.

Beckwith, Carl L., George, Timothy; Manetsch, Scott M. (Eds). *Ezekiel, Daniel: Old Testament, vol. 12*. Reformation Commentary on Scripture. Downers Grove, IL: IVP Academic, 2012.

Beeke, Joel R. *Revelation*. Grand Rapids, MI: Reformation Heritage Books, 2016.

Berkhof, Louis. *Systematic Theology*. Grand Rapids, MI: Eerdmans Publishing Co., 1938.

Beza, Theodore. *A Tragedie of Abrahams Sacrifice*. Trans. Arthur Golding. Toronto: University of Toronto Library, 1906.

Bird, Michael. *Evangelical Theology: A Biblical and Systematic Introduction*. Grand Rapids: Zondervan, 2013.

Block, Daniel Isaac. *Judges, Ruth*, vol. 6. The New American Commentary. Nashville, TN: Broadman & Holman Publishers, 1999.

Boettner, Loraine. *Studies in Theology*. Grand Rapids, MI: Presbyterian and Reformed Publishing Company, 1947.

Borland, James A. *Christ in the Old Testament: Old Testament Appearances of Christ in Human Form*, 2nd ed., revised and expanded. Fearn, Rossshire: Christian Focus Publications, 1999; Chicago: Moody Press, 1978.

Boyarin, Daniel. "The Gospel of the Memra: Jewish Binitarianism and the Prologue to John." *Harvard Theological Review* 94:3 (2001): 243-84.

_____. "Two Powers in Heaven; or, The Making of a Heresy." *The Idea of Biblical Interpretation: Essays in Honor of James L. Kugel*. Leiden: Brill, 2003: 331-370.

Brooks, Thomas. *A Treatise on Assurance, A New Edition Considerably Amended and Abridged*. London: J. Mathews, and J. Buckland, 1778.

Brownell, Thomas Church. *Book of Common Prayer*. New York: Sidney's Press, 1823.

Brownlee, W. H. "Gilgal." *The International Standard Bible Encyclopedia, Revised*. Grand Rapids: Eerdmans, 1979-1988.

Box, G. H. "The Idea of Intermediation in Jewish Theology. A Note on Memra and She-kinah." *The Jewish Quarterly Review* 23:2 (Oct 1932): 103-119.

Bucur, Bogdan G. "Augustine on Theophanies: An Orthodox Perspective." *St. Vladimir's Theological Quarterly* 52.1 (2008): 67-93.

_____. "Clement of Alexandria's Exegesis of Old Testament Theophanies." *Phronema* 29:1 (2014): 61-79.

_____. "Christophanic Exegesis and the Problem of Symbolization: Daniel 3 (the Fiery Furnace) as a Test Case," *Journal of Theological Interpretation* 10.2 (Fall 2016): 227-244.

_____. "Foreordained from All Eternity: The Mystery of the Incarnation According to Some Early Christian and Byzantine Writers." *Dumbarton Oaks Papers Number Sixty-Two 2008*. Washington, D.C.: Harvard University Press, 2009: 199-121.

_____. "Gregory Nazianzen's Reading of Habbakuk 3:2 and Its Reception: A Lesson from Byzantine Scripture Exegesis." *Pro Ecclesia* 20 (2011): 86-103.

_____. "Scholarship on the Old Testament Roots of Trinitarian Theology: Blind Spots and Blurred Vision." *The Bible and Early Trinitarian Theology*. Ed. Christopher A. Beely and Mark E. Weedman. Washington, D. C.: The Catholic University of America Press, 2018: 29-49.

_____. "The Early Christian Reception of Genesis 18: From Theophany to Trinitarian Symbolism." *Journal of Early Christian Studies* 23:2 (2015): 245-72.

_____. "Theophanies and Vision of God in Augustine's *De Trinitate*: An Eastern Ortho-dox Perspective." *St. Vladimir's Theological Quarterly* 52:1 (2008): 67-93.

Bünting, Heinrich. *Itinerarium totius Sacræ Scripturæ*, or, *The Travels of the Holy Patriarchs, Proph-ets, Judges, Kings, our Saviour Christ and his Apostles* … Collected Out of the Works of Henry Bünting; and done into English by R. B. London, J. Harefinch for T. Basset, 1682.

Cairns, Alan. *Dictionary of Theological Terms*. Greenville, SC: Ambassador Emerald Inter-national, 2002.

Calvin, John. *Commentaries*. Bellingham, WA: Logos Bible Software, 2010.

Cassuto, Umberto. *A Commentary on the Book of Genesis: From Noah to Abraham*. Jerusa-lem: Magnes Press, 1964.

Cathcart, Kevin, Maher, Michael, and McNamara, Martin (eds). *The Aramaic Bible A: Targum Neofiti1: Genesis*. Trans. Martin McNamara. Vol. 1. Collegeville, MN: The Liturgical Press, 1992.

Charles, Robert Henry. *Commentary on the Pseudepigrapha of the Old Testament*, vol. 2. Oxford: Clarendon Press, 1913.

Chrysostom. *Against Theater*.

_____. *Homilies on Paul's Letter to Timothy*.

Clement of Alexandria. *The Instructor*.

Clifford, Richard. *The Cosmic Mountain in Canaan and the Old Testament*. Harvard Se-mitic Autographs 4. Cambridge, MA: Harvard University Press, 1972.

Clines, David J. A. *Job 1-20*, vol. 17. Word Biblical Commentary. Dallas: Word, 1998.

Clowney, Edmund. *Preaching Christ in All of Scripture*. Wheaton, IL: Crossway, 2003.

_____. *The Unfolding Mystery: Discovering Christ in the Old Testament*. Phillipsburg, NJ: P&R, 2013.

Coblentz Bautch, Kelly. *A Study of the Geography of 1 Enoch 17-19*. Boston: Brill, 2003.

Cole, Graham A. *The God Who Became Human: A Biblical Theology of Incarnation*. New Studies in Biblical Theology, vol. 30. Ed. D. A. Carson. England; Downers Grove, IL: Apollos; InterVarsity Press, 2013.

Collins, J. J. *The Apocalyptic Imagination: An Introduction to Jewish Apocalyptic Literature*. Grand Rapids, MI: Eerdmans, 2016.

_____. "Watcher." *Dictionary of Deities and Demons in the Bible*. Ed. Karel van der Toorn, Bob Becking, and Pieter W. van der Horst. Grand Rapids, MI: Eerdmans, 1999.

Collins, J. J., Collins, Adela Yarbro. *Daniel: A Commentary on the Book of Daniel*. Ed. Frank Moore Cross. Hermeneia. Minneapolis, MN: Fortress Press, 1993.

Constitutions of the Holy Apostles. 5.20.

Cummins, Bradley J. *YHWH Preincarnate Jesus: Lost in Translation*. Enumclaw, WA: WinePress Publishing, 2010.

Currid, John D. *A Study Commentary on Genesis: Genesis 25:19–50:26*, vol. 2. Evangelical Press Study Commentary. Darlington, England; Carlisle, PA: Evangelical Press, 2003.

Cyprian. *Against the Jews*.

Cyril of Alexandria. *Commentary on the Gospel of John*.

Cyril of Jerusalem. *Catechetical Lectures*.

De Gols, Gerard. *A Vindication of the Worship of the Lord Jesus Christ as the Supreme God, in all the Dispensations, Patriarchal, Mosaic, and Christian Demonstrating that Christ was So Known and Worshiped in all Ages, from Adam to this Day*. London: J. Darby and T. Browne, 1726.

_____. *The Worship of the Lord Jesus in the Old Testament*. Christ in All Scripture Series Book 3. Ed. Douglas Van Dorn. Dacono, CO: Waters of Creation, 2020.

Doedens, Jacob J. T. "The Indecent Descent of the Sethites: The Provenance of the Sethites-Interpretation of Genesis 6:1-4." *Sárospataki Füzetek* 16:3–4 (2012): 47–57.

_____. "The Sons of God in Genesis 6:1-4." Ph.D. Dissertation Theologische Universiteit Kampen, 2013.

Drew, Charles. *The Ancient Love Song: Finding Christ in the Old Testament*. Phillipsburg, NJ: P&R, 2000.

Dulaey, Martine. "Les trois hébreux dans la fournaise (Dn 3) dans l'interprétationsymbolique de l'église ancienne." *Revue des Sciences Religieuses* 71 (1997): 33-59.

Edwards, Jonathan. *History of the Work of Redemption (with notes)*. London: T. Pitcher, 1793.

Edwards, M. J. "Justin's Logos and the Word of God." *Journal of Early Christian Studies* 3 (1995): 261-80.

Eiseman, Robert H. and Wise, Michael Owen. *The Dead Sea Scrolls Uncovered*. New York: Penguin Books, 1993.

Elwell, Walter A. and Beitzek, Barry J. *Baker Encyclopedia of the Bible*. Grand Rapids, MI: Baker Book House, 1988.

Ephrem the Syrian. *Cave of Treasures*.

Englezakis, Benedict. *New and Old in God's Revelation: Studies in Relations Between Spirit and Tradition in the Bible*. Cambridge: James Clarke & Co., 1982.

Enns, Peter. "Apostolic Hermeneutics and an Evangelical Doctrine of Scripture: Moving Beyond a Modernist Impasse." *Westminster Theological Journal* 65 (2003): 276-277.

Erskine, Ebenezer and Fisher, James. *The Assembly's Shorter Catechism Explained By Way of Question and Answer*. Edinburgh: John Gray and Gavin Alston: MDCCLXV.

Eusebius. *Ecclesiastical History*.

Evans, Craig A. "Philo, Memra, Targums, Logos." In *Word and Glory: On the Exegetical and Theological Background of John's Prologue*. Journal for the Study of the New Testament Supplement Series 89. Sheffield Academic Press, 1993: 100-145.

Evans, Paul. "Divine intermediaries in 1 Chronicles 21 an overlooked aspect of the Chronicler's theology." *Biblica* 85:4 (2004): 545-558.

Fausset, A. R. "The Revelation of St. John the Divine." In Robert Jamieson, A. R. Fausset, and David Brown, *A Commentary, Critical and Explanatory, on the Old and New Testaments*. Oak Harbor, WA: Logos Research Systems, Inc., 1997, 1877.

First Creed of Sirmium.

Fischer, Richard James. *Historical Genesis: From Adam to Abraham*. Lanham, MD: University Press of America, 2008.

Foot Moore, George. "Intermediaries in Jewish Theology: Memra, Shekinah, Metatron." *Harvard Theological Review* 15:1 (Jan 1922): 41-85.

Fossum, Jarl E. "Glory." *Dictionary of Deities and Demons in the Bible*. Ed. Karel van der Toorn, Bob Becking, and Pieter W. van der Horst. Grand Rapids, MI: Eerdmans, 1999.

_____. *The Image of the Invisible God: Essays on the Influence of Jewish Mysticism on Early Christology*. Göttingen: Vandenhoeck and Ruprecht, 1995.

_____. *The Name of the God and the Angel of the LORD: Samaritan and Jewish Concepts of Intermediation and the Origin of Gnosticism*. Tubingen: J. C. B. Mohr, 1985.

Foster, Edgar G. *Angelomorphic Christology and the Exegesis of Psalm 8:5 in Tertullians' Adversus Praxean: An Examination of Tertullian's Reluctance to Attribute Angelic Properties to the Son of God*. New York: University Press of America, Inc., 2005.

Frame, John M. *The Doctrine of God, A Theology of Lordship*. Phillipsburg, NJ: P&R Publishing, 2002.

Fulgentius. *To Monimus*.

Fürst, Alfons. "Jerome Keeping Silent: Origen and His Exegesis of Isaiah." *Jerome of Stridon: His Life, Writings and Legacy*. Ed. Andrew Cain and Joseph Lössl. University of Colorado: Routledge, 2016.

Gaffin, Richard B. "Covenantal, Christocentric and Christotelic Hermeneutics At Westminster Theological Seminary," https://d3h3guilcrzx4v.cloudfront.net/uploads/images/files/News/Christocentric/Christocentric,%20Christotelic%20Statement.pdf. Last accessed Feb 20, 2020.

_____. "The Glory of God in Paul's Epistles." In *The Glory of God*. Theology in Community Series. Ed. Christopher W. Morgan and Robert A. Peterson. Wheaton, IL: Crossway, 2010.

_____. "Observations on a Controversy," http://nbatzig.googlepages.com/Gaffin_Critique1.pdf. Accessed July 19, 2018

Garrett, Susan R. *No Ordinary Angel: Celestial Spirits and Christian Claims about Jesus*. The Anchor Yale Bible Reference Library. New Haven, CT: Yale University Press, 2008.

Gault, Brian P. "Job's Hope: Redeemer or Retribution?" *Bibliotheca Sacra* 173:690 (2016): 147-65.

Gathercole, Simon. *The Pre-Existent Son: Recovering the Christologies of Matthew, Mark, and Luke*. Grand Rapids, MI: Eerdmans, 2006.

Gavrilyuk, Paul. "Theopatheia: Nestorius's Main Charge Against Cyril of Alexandria." *Scottish Journal of Theology* 56-2 (2003): 190-207.

Genesis Rabbah.

Gieschen, Charles. *Angelomorphic Christology: Antecedents and Early Evidence*. London: Brill Academic, 1998.

_____. "The Real Presence of the Son Before Christ: Revisiting an Old Approach to Old Testament Christology." *Concordia Theological Quarterly* 68:2 (April 2004): 105-126.

Goldish, Matt. "The Battle for 'True' Jewish Christianity: Peter Allix's Polemics Against the Unitarians and Millenarians." In *Everything Connects: In Conference with Richard H. Popkin*, Brill's Studies in Intellectual History Online 91. Ed. James E. Force and David S. Katz. Boston: Brill, 1999: 143-162.

Gordon, Cyrus H. " *'elohim* in Its Reputed Meaning of Rulers, Judges." *Journal of Biblical Literature* 54 (1935): 139-44.

Greenhill, William. *An Exposition of Ezekiel*. Carlisle, PA: Banner of Truth Trust, 1994.

Gregory Nazianzen. *Oration 29*.

Gregory of Nyssa. *Against Eunomius*.

Gregory the Great. *Forty Gospel Homilies*.

Grudem, Wayne A. *Systematic Theology: An Introduction to Biblical Doctrine*. Grand Rapids, MI: InterVarsity Press, 2004.

Hamilton, Victor P. *The Book of Genesis, Chapters 18–50*. The New International Commentary on the Old Testament. Grand Rapids, MI: Wm. B. Eerdmans Publishing Co., 1995.

Hannah, Darrell D. *Michael and Christ: Michael Traditions and Angel Christology in Early Christianity*. Wissenschaftliche Untersuchungen zum Neuen Testament 109. Tubingen: Mohr-Siebeck, 1999.

Hanson, A. T. *Jesus Christ In the Old Testament*. London: SPCK, 1965.

Hanson, R. P. C. *Allegory & Event: A Study of the Sources and Significance of Origen's Interpretation of Scripture*. Louisville: Westminster John Knox Press, 2002.

Hartley, John E. *The Book of Job*. The New International Commentary on the Old Testament. Grand Rapids, MI: Eerdmans, 1988.

Hawker, Robert. *Poor Man's New Testament Commentary: Acts–Ephesians*, vol. 2. Bellingham, WA: Logos Bible Software, 2013.

Hayward, Robert. *Divine Name and Presence: The Memra*. Oxford Centre for Postgraduate Hebrew Studies. Totowa, NJ: Allanheld, Osmun, 1981.

Heiser, Michael S. "1003 BC Census: Who Authorized It—God or Satan?" In *I Dare You Not to Bore Me with the Bible*. Ed. John D. Barry and Rebecca Van Noord. Bellingham, WA: Lexham Press; Bible Study Magazine, 2014: 71-74.

_____. *Faithlife Study Bible*. Bellingham, WA: Lexham Press, 2012.

_____. "Deuteronomy 32:8 and the Sons of God." *Bibliotheca Sacra* 158:629 (Jan-Mar 2001): 52-74.

_____. "Divine Council." *Dictionary of the Old Testament: Wisdom, Poetry & Writings*. Ed. Tremper Longman III and Peter Enns. Downers Grove, IL: IVP Academic, 2008.

_____. "The Divine Council in Late Canonical and Non-Canonical Second Temple Jewish Literature." A Dissertation at the University of Wisconsin-Madison. 2004.

_____. "Does God Need a Co-Signer?" *LogosTalk* (Oct 24, 2017). https://blog.logos.com/2017/10/god-need-co-signer/.

_____. *The Unseen Realm: Rediscovering the Supernatural Worldview of the Bible*. Bellingham, WA: Lexham Press, 2015.

_____. "You've Seen One Elohim, You've Seen Them All? A Critique of Mormonism's Use of Psalm 82." *FARMS Review* 19/1 (2007): 221-66.

Hengstenberg, Ernst Wilhelm. "The Deity of the Messiah in the Old Testament," in *Christology of the Old Testament and a Commentary on the Predictions of the Messiah by the Prophets* vol. 1. Trans. Reuel Keith. Andover: William M. Morrison, 1836.

Henry, Matthew. *Matthew Henry's Commentary on the Whole Bible: Complete and Unabridged in One Volume*. Peabody: Hendrickson, 1994.

Hesiod. *Works and Days*.

Hess, Richard S. *Israelite Religions: An Archeological and Biblical Survey*. Grand Rapids, MI: Baker Academic, 2007.

Hess, Richard S. and Tsumura, David T. *I Studied Inscriptions from Before the Flood: Ancient Near Eastern, Literary, and Linguistic Approaches to Genesis 1-11*. SBTS 4. Winona Lake, IN: Eisenbrauns, 1994.

Hilary of Poitiers. *On the Trinity*.

Hippolytus. *Commentary on Daniel*.

Hodge, A. A. *Outlines of Theology: Rewritten and Enlarged*. New York: Hodder & Stoughton, 1878.

Hodge, Charles. *Systematic Theology*, vol. 1. Oak Harbor, WA: Logos Research Systems, Inc., 1997.

Hoffman, Nathan. "Were the Pyramids Built Before the Flood? (Masoretic Text vs. Original Hebrew)." *Youtube* (May 28, 2017): https://www.youtube.com/watch?v=VI1yRTC6kGE.

Homer. *Odyssey*.

Hook, Walter Farquhar. *A Church Dictionary, Seventh Edition*. London: John Murray, 1854.

Horton, Michael. *Too Good To Be True*. Grand Rapids, MI: Zondervan, 2006.

Howell, Adam Joseph. "Finding Christ in the Old Testament Through the Aramaic Memra, Shekinah, and Yeqara of the Targums." A Dissertation at the Southern Baptist Theological Seminary, 2015.

Huffstutler, Joel Ira. "He Who Dwelt in the Bush: A Biblical and Historical Theology of the Angel of the LORD." A Dissertation at Bob Jones. 2007.

Hurtado, Larry. "First-Century Jewish Monotheism." *Journal for the Study of the New Testament* 71 (1998): 3-26.

_____. *How on Earth Did Jesus Become a God?: Historical Questions about Earliest Devotion to Jesus*. Grand Rapids, MI: Eerdmans, 2005.

_____. "Jesus' Divine Sonship in Paul's Epistle to the Romans." In *Romans and the People of God*. Ed. N. T. Wright and S. Soderlund. Grand Rapids, MI: Eerdmans, 1999.

_____. *Lord Jesus Christ: Devotion to Jesus in Earliest Christianity*. Grand Rapids, MI: Eerdmans, 2003.

_____. *One God, One Lord: Early Christian Devotion and Ancient Jewish Monotheism*. Philadelphia: Fortress Press, 1988.

_____. "The Binitarian Shape of Early Christian Worship." *The Jewish Roots of Christological Monotheism*. Papers from the St. Andrews Conference on the Historical Origins of the Worship of Jesus. Ed. Carey C. Newman, James R. Davila, and Gladys S. Lewis. Supplements to the Journal for the Study of Judaism. Ed. John J. Collins. Leiden: Brill, 1999.

_____. "What Do We Mean by 'First-Century Jewish Monotheism'?" *Society of Biblical Literature 1993 Seminar Papers*. Ed. E. H. Lovering Jr. Atlanta: Scholars Press, 1993.

Irenaeus. *Against Heresies*.

_____. *Proof of Apostolic Preaching*.

Ishmael b. Yosi. b. Sanh. 38b.

Jerome. *Commentary on Daniel*.

Johnson, Ronn. "The Old Testament Background for Paul's Principalities and Powers." A Dissertation at Dallas Theological Seminary. 2004.

Justin Martyr. *Dialogue with Trypho*.

_____. *Exhortation to the Greeks*.

Keach, Benjamin. *GTropologia: A Key to Open Scripture Metaphors*. London: William Hill, 1858.

Keil, K. and Delitzch, F. *Commentary on the Old Testament: Vol. 4—Job*. Grand Rapids, MI: Eerdmans, 1980.

Kidner, Derek. *Genesis: An Introduction and Commentary, vol. 1. Tyndale Old Testament Commentaries*. Downers Grove, IL: InterVarsity Press, 1967.

Kline, Meredith G. *Glory In Our Midst: A Biblical-Theological Reading of Zechariah's Night Visions*. Eugene, OR: Wipf & Stock, 2001.

_____. *Images of the Spirit*. Eugene, OR: Wipf & Stock, 1980.

_____. *Kingdom Prologue: Genesis Foundations for a Covenantal Worldview*. Eugene, OR: Wipf & Stock Publishers, 2006.

Knauf, E. A. "Shadday." *Dictionary of Deities and Demons in the Bible*. Ed. Karel van der Toorn, Bob Becking, and Pieter W. van der Horst. Leiden; Boston; Köln; Grand Rapids, MI; Cambridge: Brill; Eerdmans, 1999.

Kohler, K. *Jewish Theology Systematically and Historically Considered*. New York: The Macmillan Company, 1918.

Kugel, James L. *Traditions of the Bible*. Cambridge, MA: Harvard University Press, 1998.

Lange, John Peter. *A Commentary on the Holy Scriptures: Acts*. Bellingham, WA: Logos Bible Software, 2008.

Lee, Aquila H. I. *From Messiah to Pre-existent Son*. Wissenschaftliche Untersuchungen zum Neuen Testament 192. Tübingen: Mohr-Seibeck, 2005.

Lete, Gregorio del Olmo. "Bashan." *Dictionary of Deities and Demons in the Bible*. Ed. Karel van der Toorn, Bob Becking, and Pieter W. van der Horst. Leiden; Boston; Köln; Grand Rapids, MI; Cambridge: Brill; Eerdmans, 1999.

Letter of Six Bishops. Translated from Mansi, *Sacrorum Conciliorum Nova et Amplissima Collectio*, Vol. I: 1033-40.

Levinthal, Israel Herbert. "The Jewish Law of Agency." *Jewish Quarterly Review* 13:2 (Oct 1922): 117-191.

Lewis, C. S. *The Horse and His Boy*. Chronicles of Narnia Vol. 5. Hong Kong, Enrich Spot Ltd., 2016.

Lind, Millard C. *Ezekiel*. Believers Church Bible Commentary. Scottdale, PA: Herald Press, 1996.

Leo the Great. *Letter 31*.

Longman, Tremper III. "Psalms 2: Ancient Near Eastern Background." *Dictionary of the Old Testament: Wisdom, Poetry & Writings*. Ed. Peter Enns. Downers Grove, IL: IVP Academic; 2018.

López, René A. "Identifying the 'Angel of the Lord' in the Book of Judges: A Model for Reconsidering the Referent in Other Old Testament Loci." *Bulletin for Biblical Research* 20 (2010): 1–18.

Lourié, Basil. "A Danielic Pseudepigraphon Paraphrased by Papias: A New Translation and Introduction." *Old Testament Pseudepigrapha: More Noncanonical Scriptures*. Ed. Richard Bauckham, James R. Davila, and Alexander Panayotov, vol. One. Grand Rapids, MI; Cambridge, U.K.: William B. Eerdmans Publishing Company, 2013: 435-41.

Luther, Martin. *Luther's Works*. Ed. Jaroslav Jan Pelikan, Hilton C. Oswald, and Helmut T. Lehmann. Saint Louis: Concordia Publishing House, 1999.

M'Causland, Dominick. *Adam and the Adamite; or The Harmony of Scripture and Ethnology*, 2nd ed. London: Richard Bentley, 1868.

Mackay, John L. *Exodus*. Mentor Commentaries. Fearn, Ross-shire, Great Britain: Mentor, 2001.

_____. *Haggai, Zechariah, Malachi: God's Restored People*. Focus on the Bible Commentary (Ross-shire, Scotland: Christian Focus Publications, 2003.

Maclaren, Alexander. *Expositions of Holy Scripture, 11 vols*. Grand Rapids, MI: Eerdmans, 1952-59.

Malone, Andrew S. "Distinguishing the Angel of the LORD." *Bulletin for Biblical Research* 21.3 (2011): 297-314.

_____. "God the Illeist: Third-Person Self-References and Trinitarian Hints in the Old Testament." *Journal of the Evangelical Theological Society* 52.3 (September 2009): 499–518.

_____. "Is the Messiah Announced in Malachi 3:1?" *Tyndale Bulletin* 57.2 (2006): 215-228.

_____. *Knowing Jesus In the Old Testament?: A Fresh Look at Christophanies*. Nottingham, England: Intervarsity Press, 2015.

_____. "The Invisibility of God: A Survey of a Misunderstood Phenomenon." *Evangelical Quarterly* 79.4 (2007): 311-329.

Martin, Ralph P. "A Hymn of Christ: Philippians 2:5-11." *Recent Interpretation & in the Setting of Early Christian Worship.* Downers Grove, IL: Intervarsity Press, 2009.

Mathews, K. A. *Genesis 11:27–50:26,* Vol. 1B. The New American Commentary. Nashville: Broadman & Holman Publishers, 2005.

Mayer, John. *A Commentary Upon All the Prophets Both Great and Small.* London: Abraham Miller and Ellen Cotes, 1652.

McDermott, Gerald R. *God's Rivals: Why Has God Allowed Different Religions? Insights from the Bible and the Early Church.* Downers Grove, IL: InterVarsity Press, 2007.

McGrath, Alister E. *Historical Theology: An Introduction to the History of Christian Thought, Second Edi*tion. Malden, MA: John Wiley & Sons, Ltd., 2013.

McNamara, Martin. *Targum and Testament Revisited: Aramaic Paraphrases of the Hebrew Bible.* Grand Rapids, MI: Eerdmans, 2010.

Meier, S. A. "Angel of Yahweh." *Dictionary of Deities and Demons in the Bible.* Ed. Karel van der Toorn, Bob Becking, and Pieter W. van der Horst. Leiden; Boston; Köln; Grand Rapids, MI; Cambridge: Brill; Eerdmans, 1999: 53-59.

Metzger, Bruce Manning and Omanson Roger L. A Textual Guide to the Greek New Testament: An Adaptation of Bruce M. Metzger's Textual Commentary for the Needs of Translators. Stuttgart: Deutsche Bibelgesellschaft, 2006.

Miller, Patrick D. "Eridu, Dunnu, and Babel: A Study in Comparative Mythology." *Hebrew Annual Review* 9 (1985): 227-51.

Moore, G. F. "Intermediaries in Jewish Theology." *Harvard Theological Review* 15 (1922): 41–85.

More, Henry. *An explanation of the grand mystery of godliness, or, A true and faithfull representation of the everlasting Gospel of our Lord and Saviour Jesus Christ, the only begotten Son of God and sovereign over men and angels.* London, J. Flesher for W. Morden, 1660.

Morris, Leon. *Galatians: Paul's Charter of Christian Freedom.* Downers Grove, IL: InterVarsity Press, 1996.

_____. *Revelation.* Tyndale New Testament Commentaries. Grand Rapids, MI: Intervarsity Press and Eerdmans, 1987.

Mosca, P. G. "Once Again the Heavenly Witness of Ps 89:38." *Journal of Biblbial Literature* 105 (1986): 27-37.

_____. Ugarit and Daniel 7: A Missing Link." *Biblica* 67 (1986): 508-517.

Mulder, M. J. "Yeshurun." *Theological Dictionary of the Old Testament.* Ed. G. Johannes Botterweck and Helmer Ringgren. Grand Rapids, MI: Eerdmans, 1990.

Mullen, E. Theodore. "Divine Assembly." *The Anchor Yale Bible Dictionary.* Ed. David Noel Freedman. New York: Doubleday, 1992.

_____. *The Divine Council in Canaanite and Early Hebrew Literature.* Harvard Semitic Monographs 24. Missoula, NT: Scholars Press, 1980.

_____. "The Divine Witness and the Davidic Royal Grant: Ps 89:37-38." *Journal of Biblical Literature* 102:2 (1983): 207-218.

Muller, Richard A. *Post-Reformation Reformed Dogmatics: The Rise and Development of Reformed Orthodoxy; Volume 4: The Triunity of God.* Grand Rapids, MI: Baker Academic, 2003.

Murray, David. *Jesus on Every Page: 10 Simple Ways to Seek and Find Christ in the Old Testament*. Nashville: Thomas Nelson, 2013.

Murray, Robert. "The Origin of Aramaic 'ir, Angel." *Orientalia* 53 (1984): 307-308.

Nevin, John W. *Mystical Presence: A Vindication of the Reformed or Calvinistic Doctrine of the Holy Eucharist*. Philadelphia: S. R. Fisher & Co., 1846.

Newman, Robert C. "The Ancient Exegesis of Genesis 6:2,4." *Grace Theological Journal* 5:1 (1984): 13–36.

Neyrey, Jerome H. *The Gospel of John in Cultural and Rhetorical Perspective*. Grand Rapids, MI: Eerdmans, 2009.

Nickelsburg, George W. E. *1 Enoch: A Commentary on the Book of 1 Enoch*. Hermeneia. Minneapolis, MN: Fortress Press, 2001.

Novatian. *On the Trinity* 18.

O'Brien, Peter T. *The Letter to the Hebrews*. The Pillar New Testament Commentary. Grand Rapids, MI; Nottingham, England: William B. Eerdmans Publishing Company, 2010.

Owen, John. *Appearances of the Son of God in the Old Testament*. Christ in All Scripture Series Book 1. Ed. Douglas Van Dorn. Dacono, CO: Waters of Creation, 2019.

_____. "Exercitation 10." In *An Exposition of the Epistle to the Hebrews*, vol. 18. Works of John Owen. Ed. W. H. Goold. Edinburgh: Johnstone and Hunter, 1854.

Owen, John; Allix, Peter; De Gols, Gerard. *The Angel of Yahweh in Jewish and Reformation History*. Christ in All Scripture Series Book 4. Ed. Douglas Van Dorn (Dacono, CO: Waters of Creation, 2020.

Ovid. *Metamorphosis* 11.250-263.

Packer, J. I. *Concise Theology: A Guide to Historic Christian Beliefs*. Wheaton, IL: Tyndale House, 1993.

_____. "God." *New Dictionary of Theology*. Ed. Sinclair B. Ferguson and J. I. Packer. Downers Grove, IL: InterVarsity Press, 2000.

Packard, Joseph. *A Commentary on the Holy Scriptures; Malachi: God's Restored People*. Focus on the Bible Commentary. Ed. John Peter Lange, Philip Schaff, and Joseph Packard. Ross-shire, Scotland: Christian Focus Publications, 2003.

Patrick, Simon. *A Commentary upon the First Book of Moses, Called Genesis*. London: Chitwell, 1689.

Pink, A. W. *Gleanings in Joshua*. Chicago: Moody, 1964.

Philo. *Confusion of Tongues*.

_____. *On the Changing of Names*.

_____. *The Works of Philo: Complete and Unabridged*. Ed. Charles Duke Yonge with Philo of Alexandria. Peabody, MA: Hendrickson, 1995.

Plato. *Critias*.

Poole, Matthew. *Annotations upon the Holy Bible*, 3 vols. New York: Robert Carter and Brothers, 1853.

Pseudo-Clementines. *Recognitions*.

Pseudo-Ignatius. *The Epistle of Ignatius to the Antiochians*.

Reeves, Michael. *Delighting in the Trinity*. Downer's Grove, IL: IVP Academic, 2012.

Richardson, John. *Choice Observations and Explanations Upon the Old Testament*. London: s.n., 1657.

Robinson, H. Wheeler. "The Council of Yahweh." *Journal of Theological Studies* 45 (1944): 151-57.

Rölling, Wolfgang. "Lebanon." *Dictionary of Deities and Demons in the Bible*. Ed. Karel van der Toorn, Bob Becking, and Pieter W. van der Horst. Leiden; Boston; Köln; Grand Rapids, MI; Cambridge: Brill; Eerdmans, 1999.

Ronning, John. *The Jewish Targums and John's Logos Theology*. Grand Rapids, MI: Baker Academic, 2010.

_____. "The Targum of Isaiah and the Johannine Literature." *Westminster Theological Journal* 69:2 (2007): 247-78;

Ross, Allen P. "Studies in the Book of Genesis - Part 2: The Table of Nations in Genesis 10 - its Structure." *Bibliotheca Sacra* 137:548 (Oct-Dec 1980): 336-50.

Rudolph, Conrad. *The Mystic Ark: Hugh of Saint Victor, Art, and Thought in the Twelfth Century*. Riverside, CA: Cambridge University Press, 2014.

Ryken, Philip. *Exodus: Saved for God's Glory*. Wheaton, IL: Crossway, 2005.

Sarna, Nahum M. *Exodus*. The JPS Torah Commentary. Philadelphia: Jewish Publication Society, 1991.

Shedd, W. G. T. In *St. Augustin: On the Holy Trinity, Doctrinal Treatises, Moral Treatises*, vol. 3. A Select Library of the Nicene and Post-Nicene Fathers of the Christian Church, First Series. Philip Schaff (ed.). (Buffalo, NY: Christian Literature Company, 1887).

_____. *Genesis*. The JPS Torah Commentary. Philadelphia: Jewish Publication Society, 1989.

Segal, Alan. *Two Powers in Heaven: Early Rabbinic Reports About Christianity and Gnosticism*. Waco, TX: Baylor University Press, 2012.

Small, James G. "I've Found a Friend." *Hymnal and Liturgies of the Moravian Church (Unitas Fratrum)*. Bethlehem, PA: Provincial Synod, 1920.

Smith, Jerome H. *The New Treasury of Scripture Knowledge: The Most Compete Listing of Cross References Available Anywhere—Every Verse, Every Theme, Every Important Word*. Nashville, TN: Thomas Nelson, 1992.

Socrates Scholasticus. *The Ecclesiastical History*.

Sozomen. *Church Histories*.

Sproul, R. C. *Tabletalk Magazine, November 2007: The English Reformation*. Lake Mary, FL: Ligonier Ministries, 2007.

Spurgeon, Charles. "Footsteps of Mercy." *Metropolitan Tabernacle Pulpit* 905.

Stead, Christopher. "Divine Simplicity as a Problem for Orthodoxy." *The Making of Orthodoxy: Essays in Honour of Henry Chadwick*. Ed. Rowan Williams. Cambridge: Cambridge University Press, 1989: 255-69.

Streeter, Burnett Hillman. *The Four Gospels: A Study of Origins Treating of the Manuscript Tradition, Sources, Authorship, & Dates*. London: Macmillan & Co., 1924.

Strong, Augustus Hopkins. *Systematic Theology*. Philadelphia: American Baptist Publication Society, 1907.

Stuckenbruck, Loren T. *Angel Veneration and Christology: A Study in Early Judaism and in the Christology of the Apocalypse of John*. Wissenschaftliche Untersuchungen zum Neuen Testament 2/70. Tübingen: J. C. B. Mohr, 1995.

Taylor, Henry. *The Apology of Benjamin Ben Mordecai To His Friends, for Embracing Christianity*. London: J. Wilkie, 1771.

Terry, Milton S. *Biblical Apocalyptics: A Study of the Most Notable Revelations of God and of Christ in the Canonical Scriptures*. New York: Eaton & Mains, 1898.

Tertullian. *Against Praxeas*.

_____. *An Answer to the Jews*.

"The Letter of Six Bishops." *Sacrorum Conciliorum Nova et Amplissima Collectio*. Vol. 1. 1033-40.

Theodoret. *Questions on the Ocatateuch*.

Theophilus of Antioch. *To Autolycus*.

Tigay, Jeffrey H. *Deuteronomy*. JPS Torah Commentary. Philadelphia Jewish Publication Society, 1996.

Trigg, Joseph W. "The Angel of Great Counsel: Christ and the Angelic Hierarchy in Origen's Theology." *Journal of Theological Studies* 42:1 (April 1991): 35-51.

Van Dorn, Douglas. *Giants: Sons of the Gods*. Erie, CO: Waters of Creation Publishing, 2012.

_____ (ed.). *The Angel of the LORD in Early Jewish, Christian, and Reformation History: Three Previously Published Pieces by Peter Allix and John Owen with Quotes from the Church Fathers*. Erie, CO: Waters of Creation Publishing, 2018.

von Heijne, Camilla Hélena. *The Messenger of the Lord in Early Jewish Interpretations of Genesis*. New York: De Gruyter, 2010.

Vos, Geerhardus. *Biblical Theology: Old and New Testaments*. Eugene, OR: Wipf & Stock Publishers, 2003.

Waltke, Bruce K. *Genesis*. Grand Rapids: Zondervan, 2001.

Warfield, Benjamin B. *The Works of Benjamin B. Warfield: Biblical Doctrines*. Bellingham, WA: Logos Bible Software, 2008.

Way, R. J. "God, Names of," in *The International Standard Bible Encyclopedia*, Revised. Ed. G. W. Bromiley. Grand Rapids, MI: Eerdmans, 1982.

Wilson, J. M. *The International Standard Bible Encyclopedia*, revised. Ed. Geoffrey W. Bromiley. Grand Rapids: Eerdmans, 1979-1988.

Walton, John. *The Lost World of Genesis One: Ancient Cosmology and the Origins Debate*. Downers Grove, IL: InterVarsity Press, 2009.

_____. *Genesis*. The NIV Application Commentary. Grand Rapids, MI: Zondervan, 2001.

_____. *Zondervan Illustrated Bible Backgrounds Commentary (Old Testament): The Minor Prophets, Job, Psalms, Proverbs, Ecclesiastes, Song of Songs*, vol. 5. Grand Rapids, MI: Zondervan, 2009.

Watson, Thomas. *The Select Works of the Rev. Thomas Watson, Comprising His Celebrated Body of Divinity, in a Series of Lectures on the Shorter Catechism, and Various Sermons and Treatises*. New York: Robert Carter & Brothers, 1855.

Watts, Isaac. *The Works of the Rev. Isaac Watts*, vol. 6. Leeds; London: Edward Baines; William Baynes; Thomas Williams and Son; Thomas Hamilton; Josiah Conder, 1813.

Webb, Barry G. *The Book of Judges*. Ed. R. K. Harrison and Robert L. Hubbard Jr. The New International Commentary on the Old Testament. Grand Rapids, MI: Eerdmans Publishing Company, 2012.

Wenham, Gordon J. *Genesis 16–50*, vol. 2. Word Biblical Commentary. Dallas: Word, Incorporated, 1998.

Willet, Andrew. *Hexapla in Genesin*. Cambridge, 1605; second ed., enlarged, 1608.

Wolff, Hans Walter. *Hosea: A Commentary on the Book of the Prophet Hosea*. Hermeneia—a Critical and Historical Commentary on the Bible. Philadelphia: Fortress Press, 1974.

Young, E. J. *The Book of Isaiah*, vol. 1. Grand Rapids, MI: Eerdmans Publishing Company, 1965.

Zanchi, *de creat* 1.I.c.i.§12.

Zimmerli, Walther. *Ezekiel 2: A Commentary on the Book of Ezekiel, Chapters 25-48*. Hermeneia. Philadelphia: Fortress Press, 1983.

Zinner, Samuel. *The Gospel of Thomas: In the Light of Early Jewish, Christian and Islamic Esoteric Trajectories*. London: The Matheson Trust, 2011.

AUTHOR INDEX

SCRIPTURE INDEX

Books in the Christ In All Scripture Series

(the supplement series to this book)

John Owen's treatment is perfect for those wanting to ground their theology of the Angel in the high orthodoxy of the Reformation. The quotations from the Fathers bolster his thesis.

Peter Allix's work is comprehensive and is especially helpful for those familiar with modern scholarship wishing to root their theology in conservative Protestant/Reformed orthodoxy.

Gerard De Gols' study, especially the second half, is imminently practical and would help anyone wanting to learn more about why it matters that Christ is present in the Old Testament.

Owen, Allix, & De Gols. The full texts together in one volume, minus quotations from the Fathers and Reformers.

The Second Edition of *From the Shadows to the Savior*, it explores even more of the titles given to Christ in the OT than Allix goes into.

Practical sermons are for the further exploration of the fullness of Christ, especially as he is found in the New Testament.

ABOUT MATT FOREMAN

Matt Foreman has been the pastor of Faith Reformed Baptist Church since 2003. A native of Atlanta, he was brought to Christ in college at Furman University through a Reformed Baptist ministry, and later completed studies at Westminster Theological Seminary in Philadelphia.

He served as the organizing and founding Chairman of the Reformed Baptist Network, is the secretary for the RBN Missions Committee, and is a lecturer in Practical Theology at Reformed Baptist Seminary. In addition to his pastoral calling, Pastor Matt also writes music for worship.

Matt and his wife, MaryScott, have four children. In his free time, Matt loves reading, writing and playing music, playing basketball, and spending time with his wife and kids. While he is a converted Philadelphia Eagles fan, he has held firm and fast to the Atlanta Braves.

Ekklesia Hymns Vol. 1

Ekklesia Hymns is the music ministry of Matt Foreman, pastor of Faith Church in Media, PA. His goal is to serve the church by writing, arranging, and recording music for worship – specifically, new tunes to old hymns, bringing the ancient truths of the Gospel to a new generation.

Matt was raised in suburban Atlanta. From an early age, he studied piano and began writing music. He became a Christian in college in 1994 and was very influenced by the new hymn movement happening on college campuses that grew into Indelible Grace Music. Matt graduated with a degree in Music from Furman University and later completed a Master's degree in theological studies from Westminster Theological Seminary. He became pastor of Faith Reformed Baptist Church in 2003. He is also a lecturer in Practical Theology at Reformed Baptist Seminary, teaching on Worship and Music. He has written over 40 songs for worship, many of which can be accessed at http://ekklesiahymns.org/.

In 2015, after many years of planning, Matt finally completed his first studio album. Ekklesia Hymns, Vol.1 – is a collection of 14 retuned hymns intended for corporate worship.

The album is available to listen and download from **Bandcamp.**
It is also available on **Amazon** and iTunes.

ABOUT DOUG VAN DORN

Doug Van Dorn has pastored the Reformed Baptist Church of Northern Colorado since 2001. He graduated from Bethel College in 1992, majoring in Marketing and minoring in Bible. He was a youth pastor for four years in Denver. He holds the Master of Divinity degree from Denver Seminary (2001).

Doug has served on councils and boards for two Baptist Associations, the current one which he helped found in 2016. The Reformed Baptist Network seeks to glorify God through fellowship and cooperation in fulfilling the Great Commission to the ends of the earth. There are currently 42 churches in this international association of churches.

Doug has co-hosted the radio show Journey's End, the Peeranormal podcast, started the Waters of Creation Publishing Company, owned two small business in Minneapolis, and has appeared on numerous podcasts and radio shows.

Married since 1994, he and Janelle are the proud parents of four beautiful young girls. Born and raised in Colorado, he has climbed all 54 of Colorado's 14,000 ft. mountains and also Mt. Rainier (WA) and Mt. Shasta (CA).

To find out more about any of these things go to:
https://www.dougvandorn.com/

The Church website is
https://rbcnc.com

Other Books by Doug Van Dorn

Giants: Sons of the Gods (2013)

The bestselling non-fiction book on
Genesis 6 and the Nephilim.
150 reviews. 4.5+++ stars on Amazon.

Goliath. You know the story. But why is it in the Bible? Is it just to give us a little moral pick-me-up as we seek to emulate a small shepherd boy who defeated a giant? Have you ever wondered where Goliath came from? Did you know he had brothers, one with 24 fingers and toes? Did you know their ancestry is steeped in unimaginable horror? Genesis 6. The Nephilim. The first few verses of this chapter have long been the speculation of supernatural events that produced demigods and a flood that God used to destroy the whole world. The whole world remembers them. Once upon a time, all Christians knew them. But for many centuries this view was mocked, though it was the only known view at the time of the writing of the New Testament. Today, it is making a resurgence among Bible-believing scholars, and for good reason. The Nephilim were on the earth in those days, and also afterward...

This book delves deep into the dark and ancient recesses of our past to bring you rich treasures long buried. It is a carefully researched, heavily footnoted, and selectively illustrated story of the giants of the Bible. There is more here than meets the eye, much more. Here you will learn the invisible, supernatural storyline of the Bible that is always just beneath the surface, lurking like the spawn of the ancient leviathan. It is a storyline no person can afford to ignore any longer. Unlike other more sensational books on the topic, there is no undue speculation to be found here. The author is a Bible-believing Christian who refuses to use such ideas to tell you the end of the world is drawing nigh. Once you discover the truth about these fantastic creatures, you will come to see the ministry and work of Jesus Christ in a very new and exalting light. Come. Learn the fascinating, sobering, yet true story of real giants who played a significant role in the bible ... and still do so today.

Available in Paperback or Kindle at Amazon.com

The Unseen Realm: Q & A Companion (2016)

Edited by Michael Heiser.
Published by Lexham Press.

In *The Unseen Realm*, Dr. Michael S. Heiser unpacked 15 years of research while exploring what the Bible really says about the supernatural world. That book has nearly 900 reviews and a five-star rating. It is a game-changer.

Doug helps you further explore *The Unseen Realm* with a fresh perspective and an easy-to-follow format. The book summarizes key concepts and themes from Heiser's book and includes questions aimed at helping you gain a deeper understanding of the biblical author's supernatural worldview.

The format is that of a catechism: A Question followed by the Answer. There are 95 Questions (nod to Martin Luther) divided into 12 Parts:

Chapters:
Part I—God
Part II—The Lesser Gods
Part III—The Sons of God
Part IV—Divine Council
Part V—Sin, Rebellion, and the Fall
Part VI—Rebellion before the flood
Part VII—Rebellion after the flood
Part VIII—The Promise Anticipated
Part IX—The Promise Fulfilled
Part X—The Good News

Available in Paperback or Kindle at Amazon.com
or on the Bible-software platform Logos at Logos.com

From the Shadows to the Savior:
Christ in the Old Testament
(2015)

Few subjects are as important—yet ignored or misapplied--as the one addressed in this book. Jesus Christ is the absolute center and focus of the totality of God's word. Many people confess this belief, since Jesus himself taught it (Luke 24:27; John 5:39). Christians have done well to see this on one or two levels, yet truly understanding just how primary he is as an actor—even in the Old Testament—is something few have considered.

In this book (the first edition of *Patterned, Promised, Present* in the Christ in All Scripture Series), adapted from a series of blog posts for the Decablog, Doug helps us see the light of Christ that emerges from the dark hallways of Scriptures that so many find outdated, unintelligible, and irrelevant for today's Church.

Learn how Christ is found in such things as prophecy, typology, and the law. Then, come in for a deeper study of how the Person himself is actually present, walking, speaking, and acting, beginning in the very first book of the Bible. Learn how words such as "Word," "Name," "Glory," and "Wisdom" are all ideas that the Scripture itself attaches to Christ who in the OT is called The Angel of the LORD. Then see if such ideas don't radically change the way you think about all of God's word in this truly life-changing summary of Christ in the Old Testament.

Chapters:
NT Passages and Reflections
Christ in Prophecy
Christ in Typology
Christ and the Law
Christ: The Angel of the LORD
Christ: The Word of God
Christ: The Name of the LORD
Christ: The Wisdom of God
Christ: The Son of God
Christ: The Glory of God
Christ: The Right Arm of God

Available in Paperback or Kindle at Amazon.com

Waters of Creation:
A Biblical-Theological Study of Baptism
(2009)

This is the one book on baptism that you must read. It was seven years in the making. Doug believes that until a new approach is taken, separations over the meaning, mode, and recipients of baptism will never be bridged.

This new approach traces the roots of baptism deep into the OT Scriptures. When understood properly, we discover that baptism is always the sign that God has used to initiate his people into a new creation. Baptism in the NT is not "new." Rather, it derives its origin from OT predecessors. It has a direct, sacramental counterpart, and it isn't circumcision. It is baptism. When we understand that baptism comes from baptism, especially in its sacramental expression in the priestly covenant, reasons for the NT practice begin to make perfect sense.

Now Baptists have an argument that infant Baptists can finally understand, because we are beginning our argument in the same place. This is an Old Testament covenantal approach to the Baptist position with baptistic conclusions as to the mode and recipients of baptism. That's what happens when we root baptism in baptism rather than circumcision.

Chapters:
The Baptism of Jesus
Baptism and the Sanctuary
Baptism and the Priesthood
Baptism and the Covenant
Implications for Christian Baptism

Available in Paperback or Kindle at Amazon.com

Douglas Van Dorn

Covenant Theology:
A Reformed Baptist Primer
(2014)

Covenant theology is often said to be the domain of infant Baptists alone. But there really are such things as Reformed Baptists who believe in covenant theology as a basic system for approaching Scripture.

This primer sets out to give the basics of a Reformed Baptist covenant theology and to do so in a way that is understandable to the uninitiated. It was originally a series we did on Sunday nights at our church. It agrees with classical formulations of covenant theology in that there is a Covenant of Redemption, a Covenant of Works, and a Covenant of Grace in the Bible.

The book takes a multi-perspective approach to the Covenant of Redemption in that this covenant is the basis for the classic formula that Christ's death is sufficient for all, but efficient for the elect. It sees the Covenant of Works for Adam in a broader context of a covenant made with all of creation, a covenant where laws establish the parameters for creation's existence.

It differs from Paedobaptist covenant theology in that it sees the Covenant of Grace as only properly coming through Jesus Christ. OT gracious covenants are typological of the Covenant of Grace but save people on the basis of the coming work of Christ through faith alone. This is the traditional way Reformed Baptists have articulated the Covenant of Grace.

Finally, it sees an entire covenant in the Old Testament as often (but not always) missing from formulations of covenant theology. In the opinion of the author, this "priestly covenant" is vital to a proper understanding of 1. The continuity of the practice of baptism from OT to NT, 2. The answer to why we never find infants being baptized in the NT, and 3. A more precise way to parse the legal aspects of the OT economy, thereby helping us understand why the moral law continues today. This volume works from the basic presupposition that continuity in God's word is more basic than discontinuity. In this, it differs from dispensationalism and new covenant theology. The book suggests that this is the greatest strength of covenant theology, which does also recognize discontinuity.

Available in Paperback or Kindle at Amazon.com

Galatians:
A Supernatural Justification
(2012)

A play on words, the subtitle of this book gives you the two main points it tries to get across. Galatians central message teaches how a person is *justified* before a holy God. This once precious and central teaching of Protestant theology is often misunderstood or relegated the pile of irrelevant, stale doctrine.

Perhaps that is why the Apostle Paul supercharges his teaching with an oft-overlooked side of this letter - the *supernatural* beings who tempt us and teach us to give up the only truth that will save us. Galatian Christians would have been familiar with these supernatural beings; their culture was steeped in it. Thus, they mistake Paul for the messenger-healer god Hermes, and Barnabas for Zeus. Paul's warning: "Even if we or an angel from heaven should preach to you a gospel contrary to the one we preached to you, let him be accursed." This is Paul's fatherly way of showing his children in the faith that the gospel is paramount; it alone is able to save. Such a warning like this can have new power, as people are returning with reckless abandon to the worship of the old gods.

This book is from a series of sermons preached at the Reformed Baptist Church of Northern Colorado in 2011.

Available in Paperback or Kindle at Amazon.com

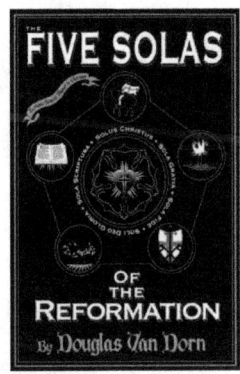

The Five Solas
of the Reformation
(2019)

The 500th anniversary of the Reformation occurred in 2017. It was October 31, 1517 that Martin Luther nailed his 95 Thesis to the door of the great cathedral at Wittenberg, Germany. He had no idea what that simple act would do. His bold proclamation and challenge to for Rome to reform her ways and beliefs was met with hostility from some and great sympathy from others. Out of this sympathy arose Protestantism, a movement deeply concerned with grounding all things on Holy Scripture, giving glory to God alone, and recovering for that generation the biblical gospel of Jesus Christ. In five chapters, Doug Van Dorn takes us back to these ancient catchphrases that once moved a continent. Scripture Alone, Grace Alone, Faith Alone, Christ Alone, and To God Be the Glory Alone became the rallying cry of all who longed to see men and women, boys and girls saved and set free from sin, death, and the devil. The end of the book contains four helpful Appendices on songs, Church Fathers on the solas, a bibliography for further research, and a letter from Martin Luther.

Available in Paperback or Kindle at Amazon.com

Conspiracy Theory
A Christian Evaluation of a Taboo Subject
(2020)

These days, when you throw "conspiracy theory" at someone, it is for one purpose—to be a thought-stopper and a discussion killer. But having this discussion grows more important by the day. People are engaging in "conspiracy theories" whether some want to admit it or not. Frankly, it is a discussion that needs to happen. This book is not about specific conspiracies, but rather is a serious look at the phrase from a definitional, historical, biblical, and Christian point of view. The main goal is to come to some helpful conclusions on how a Christian can remain sane in a world of conspiracy theories. And, we'll have some fun along the way.

Chapters
Origin of this Book
The Origin of a Phrase
A Brief History of Conspiracies
A Brief Biblical Theology of Conspiracies
A Textual conspiracy
Evaluating Conspiracy Theories
Remaining Sane in a World of Conspiracies

Available in Paperback or Kindle at Amazon.com

CPSIA information can be obtained
at www.ICGtesting.com
Printed in the USA
LVHW021525030521
686348LV00009B/751